DiDA

DIPLOMA IN DIGITAL APPLICATIONS

Molly Wischhusen
Janet Snell
Jenny Johnson

Heinemann

Inspiring generations

Heinemann Educational Publishers
Halley Court, Jordan Hill, Oxford OX2 8EJ
Part of Harcourt Education

Heinemann is a registered trademark of
Harcourt Education Limited

Text © Molly Wischhusen, Janet Snell and Jenny Johnson, 2006

First published 2006

10 09 08 07 06
10 9 8 7 6 5 4 3 2 1

British Library Cataloguing in Publication Data is available
from the British Library on request.

10-digit ISBN 0 435 45006 9
13-digit ISBN 978 0 435450 06 9

Designed by Lorraine Inglis
Typeset by 𝍏 Tek-Art, Croydon, Surrey
Original illustrations © Harcourt Education Limited, 2006
Printed by Bath Colourbooks Ltd
Cover photo: © Stock Image/Pixland/Alamy

Acknowledgements
Every effort has been made to contact copyright holders of material reproduced in
this book. Any omissions will be rectified in subsequent printings if notice is given
to the publishers.

Post-it® is a registered trademark of 3M.

Travelbug and *travelbug.co.uk* are fictitious names and have no connection with
any company with such names at the time of printing, or in the future.

Websites
Please note that the examples of websites suggested in this book were up to date at
the time of writing. It is essential for tutors to preview each site before using it to
ensure that the URL is still accurate and the content is appropriate. We suggest
tutors bookmark useful sites and consider enabling students to access them through
the school or college intranet.

Screen shots reprinted with permission from Microsoft Corporation.

Contents

Acknowledgements

A very special thank you to Samantha Moss and Jeanette Theaker students at Croydon College, who assisted in the preparation of the Graphics Unit by producing designs for the CD Player, the MP3 Player and the lollipops and patterns used as examples of cloning. We are full of admiration for their attitude to their work and wish them all the best for the future.

The publisher would like to thank Matthew Strawbridge for his meticulous editing.

BAA plc
BBC
Department of Transport
Gameplay GB Ltd
Google
Haywards Heath College (now Central Sussex College)
Jade Teo
Lloyds TSB
London Borough of Merton
Long Tall Sally
Meningitis Research Foundation
Norwich Union Direct
Post Office
Royal Institute of Chartered Surveyors
Starfish Design and Print, Heathfield, East Sussex
Steve Holmes of Signet Construction Ltd, Eastbourne
Thomson Holidays
VL Systems Ltd

Photo acknowledgements

The authors and publisher would like to thank the following for permission to reproduce photographs:

Alamy Images – page 386
Alamy Images/Photodisc – page 67
Canon Images – pages 385, 387
Corbis – page 110
ePop – page 403
Getty Images/Photodisc – page 289

Getty Images/Stone – page 89
Getty News and Sport – page 64
Harcourt Education/Gareth Boden – page 65
Logoart – pages 110, 114
Rex Features – page 174
Sandisk – page 223

Dedications

I could not wish for better co-authors and friends to work with than Janet and Jenny. My very sincere appreciation to Janet for holding the fort for Jenny and me when we needed it. My thanks also to Elaine Tuffery and her colleagues for their understanding and support. As always the encouragement from my family and friends is invaluable and the arrival of Sophie Grace hardly delayed me at all!

Molly Wischhusen

My thanks to the team at Heinemann for their support and especially to my special friends Molly and Jenny, my husband Bob and all my family.

Janet Snell

I dedicate this book to my beloved husband Ray who died suddenly before it was completed.

My sincere thanks go to Molly and Janet and my sons Ian and Colin and my daughter-in-law Helen, without whose support I would not have been able to finish my contribution. Thanks also to the Heinemann team for their encouragement during what has been an extremely difficult time for me.

Jenny Johnson

Introduction

Welcome to the programme of study in digital applications. You may be studying for the Award, the Certificate or the Diploma in Digital Applications. These qualifications are designed to create confident users of digital applications, who are able to apply their skills purposefully and effectively.

Which units do you need to take?

- For the **Award** in Digital Applications (AiDA) you will achieve Unit 1.
- For the **Certificate** in Digital Applications (CiDA) you will achieve Unit 1 plus one other unit of your choosing.
- For the **Diploma** in Digital Applications (DiDA) you will achieve all four units.

Each unit is the equivalent of one GCSE. The assessment for each of the units is a summative project that is set by Edexcel, the awarding body.

This book provides you with the necessary knowledge and skills to complete all four units.

What do you have to do to succeed?

To enable you to complete the projects, you will need to use ICT efficiently, legally and safely. You will learn all about this in Part 2, Section 1 on standard ways of working.

You will also need to develop ICT skills in a wide variety of software applications, which you then apply to complete the projects. ICT skills that are applicable to each unit are identified in each unit chapter and detailed in Part 2 of this book.

✓ **TiP**

In preparing for your project it is essential for you to build up expertise in each of the software packages that you will be using. The project will consist of a number of tasks, each of which will require careful planning and thoughtful implementation. Therefore it is vital that you work steadily, allowing plenty of time for each task. You will find some tasks cannot be completed unless you have finished others.

In addition, you must

- learn how to plan, review and evaluate your projects
- learn what is meant by an e-portfolio and create one
- understand the topics specific to this unit.

The aim of this course is to produce a range of materials that are aimed at a specific audience. Each final product must be fit for its intended purpose. Each of the separate activities will be given a range of possible marks. The quality and complexity of your work will determine the mark you receive for each activity.

The completed project will **not** be printed out in the traditional way. Instead you will create an **e-portfolio** that displays your work in electronic form. An e-portfolio is rather like a website where links lead the user to the different activities you have been asked to complete. The e-portfolio will be assessed by an internal assessor and an external moderator.

Features of the book

Many of the illustrations and activities in the book are centred around a fictitious company called Travelbug. Throughout the book you will find hints, tips and tasks to help you develop the skills, knowledge and understanding you need to successfully achieve your qualification.

Skills evidence – a general signpost to advise you when to save results in activities undertaken in the skills chapters, for possible inclusion in your e-portfolio

Go out and try! – practice tasks to help you develop the skills that have been described in that section of the book

Jargon buster – explanations of some of the technical language which may be unfamiliar

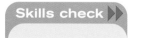

Skills check – cross-references to related information in other parts of the book

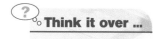

Think it over – activities to get you thinking about how you will go about or prepare for the practical tasks

Tip – guidance, notes and hints to help you

Skills builder task – practice closely linked to the skills you will need to complete your summative projects (not as demanding as the full project required by Edexcel, but it will be good preparation for learning how to develop an e-portfolio)

Assessment hint – hints to guide you on what would make the difference to achieving a merit, credit or distinction compared to a pass grade

We wish you good luck and hope you enjoy your course.

Molly Wischhusen
Janet Snell
Jenny Johnson

PART 1

Unit 1 — Using ICT

Introduction

Information is all around us. We find things out by watching and listening to television and radio; we talk to other people; we read books, newspapers and magazines; we search for information on the Internet, on CDs, etc. What do we do with this information?

- We gather it together.
- We reflect on what we have found out.
- We pass the information on, use or present it in various ways.

LEARNING OUTCOMES

After working through this chapter you should be in a position to

- ✓ search for reliable, up-to-date information from a wide variety of sources
- ✓ extract relevant information
- ✓ analyse and present the information in meaningful and effective ways.

How will I be assessed?

You will be given a project brief for this unit and you will be required to carry out research on a particular topic. The project brief will specify exactly what you will be required to produce, how you will present your findings, and to whom you will present them. You can expect to spend about 30 hours working on your project.

You will be assessed on **six** separate activities as follows:

1. Plan and manage the project
2. Select and capture information from a variety of sources
3. Collate and analyse data to produce information
4. Present and communicate information
5. Present evidence in an e-portfolio
6. Review the project.

The marks you will be awarded will depend on the quality and complexity of your work. Your teacher or tutor will be able to show you how the marks are allocated against each activity.

The project brief will give you hints and tips on successfully completing the assessment. The skills chapters provide help on the various software applications you will be using. In addition you will find detailed guidance throughout this chapter, and we strongly suggest you also read the following chapters, which contain specific help on completing the assessments:

- Project planning
- Review and evaluation
- Creating an e-portfolio.

Skills file

The table below lists all the skills required to complete this unit successfully. The pages where you will find these skills explained are identified in the Page column.

WORD-PROCESSING SOFTWARE

	Page
enter, cut, copy, paste and move text	248
use page formatting features:	
headers and footers	267
margins	264
page breaks	266
page numbering	268
alignment	265
line spacing	269
tables	272
text boxes	279
columns	271
use paragraph formatting features:	
alignment	255
bullets and numbering	257
tabs	260
indents	262

SPREADSHEET SOFTWARE

DATABASE SOFTWARE

	Page
○ create simple flat-file database structures	333
○ set and modify field characteristics including name, data type, size and format	334
○ create validation rules	345
○ enter, edit and delete records	
● import data sets	348, 358
○ design and create data entry forms that facilitate data entry	340
○ sort on one field with a secondary sort on another field	351
○ create and use searches to extract relevant information:	
● single criterion	350
● multiple criteria	352
● relational operators	351
● logical operators	352
○ produce customised reports	354
○ export information from a database into other applications	357

PRESENTATION SOFTWARE

	Page
○ use colour schemes	363
○ use master slides	363
○ use slide formatting features:	
● frames	366
● alignment	367
● line spacing	367
● bullets	367
○ create, select and insert components:	
● text	367
● images	368
● sound	375
● lines and simple shapes	370
● hyperlinks	375
○ use images/objects	
● position	287
● crop	289
● resize	289

Using information sources

In order to complete your project you will need to undertake *research*, which means gathering *information*. Before you begin this, it is essential to decide on the purpose of your research – *what you need to find out*. The purpose may be to

- increase knowledge
- help with decision-making
- make recommendations.

Once you have established the aim of your research, you need to identify the *most suitable sources of information*. This is the key to successful research. To complete this unit you will use a wide variety of sources, both primary and secondary.

Jargon buster

*A **primary source** is where the evidence is something you find out directly yourself.*

*A **secondary source** is where the evidence has been produced by someone else and therefore you find out indirectly.*

Primary and secondary sources

A primary source might be

- conducting an interview (Figure 1.1)
- carrying out a survey, possibly face-to-face or by email
- taking photographs
- recording sound clips.

Figure 1.1 An interview is a primary source

A secondary source might be

- paper-based – books, newspapers, magazines/journals, directories, maps
- ICT-based – Internet, CDs, DVDs, databases
- broadcast via the media – radio, TV.

Figure 1.2 A book is a secondary source

How can you decide what is a suitable source?

If you were asked to write a report explaining what software is, and to identify the various types of software available, the purpose of your research would be to increase your knowledge in that area. Undoubtedly you would already have *some* knowledge of software, but you would almost certainly need more detailed information to complete the report. In that particular case you would be able to find lots of information through paper-based sources and the Internet.

In contrast, if the head of a school were considering introducing this Edexcel qualification for the first time – perhaps as an alternative

Skills check ▶▶

- Refer to page 239 in the chapter on standard ways of working to find out why you should check your research.

- The Internet is an invaluable tool but can be overwhelming because of the amount of information available. Look at page 430 in the chapter on the Internet and intranets to find out how to search the Internet effectively.

- Textbooks are not usually read from the beginning to the end like a novel, so use the index.

option to a GCSE in ICT – and you were asked to present a report about the programme, the purpose of your research would be to help with decision-making and to make recommendations. In that case you would probably use both primary *and* secondary sources. The primary sources might include interviews, or a survey with current pupils to establish how many would be interested in choosing this as an option. Secondary sources might include information from the Edexcel website, and reports in the educational press to establish whether the content of the course looked appropriate. As a result of your research you would be able to make recommendations and the head of school would be able to decide whether to run the programme.

Selecting appropriate sources and using suitable techniques

When using secondary sources you need to be confident that the information is

- reliable/trustworthy
- up-to-date
- unbiased.

It would be pointless relying on a ten-year-old textbook on software, as ICT changes so quickly. A very recent textbook would be useful to explain the general definitions – such as the basic *role* of the operating system – but a computer magazine or the Internet is more likely to have the very latest information on current operating systems. The Microsoft and Apple websites, too, would provide useful information – but they will be biased somewhat towards their own products and therefore might not present the advantages and disadvantages compared with their competitors' products.

Sometimes secondary sources are enough, as with the earlier example of researching software. On other occasions you will need additional information obtained through primary sources. The report relating to the possibility of the school head offering a new Edexcel programme of study is a good example. Secondary sources would be ideal to find out the content of the programme, but you would need primary sources through face-to-face interviews or an email survey to find out the interest level of students in the school.

Recording information and acknowledging sources

Go out and try!

Figure 1.3 Do you know what korfball is?

Look at Figure 1.3. Do *you* know what korfball is? Use a variety of secondary sources (such as your library and the Internet) to see what information you can find. Word-process approximately 200 words (about half an A4 page) about korfball and remember to record and acknowledge the sources you use.

Skills check ▶▶

You will need to acknowledge all your sources, and you must respect legislation relating to copyright. Refer to the section starting on page 240 to remind yourself of the requirements.

During the course of your research you will gather information from a number of different types of source – information that will be useful for different sections of your e-portfolio. It is important to keep track of all this information, so that it is easily available when you are ready to use it. You may record it by

- *making notes* – listing key points can be more useful than writing long paragraphs
- *copying it into another document* – don't forget to put inverted commas around the text and to acknowledge who originally wrote it if you copy word-for-word

- *digitising and storing* – scan a map or a picture, or download a digital photograph
- *storing the URL* – keep a record of web addresses you have used, in order to acknowledge them
- *using bookmarks* – include any useful websites in your list of favourites to make it easy to find them again later.

Go out and try!

You will find it impossible to simply remember all your sources when your project is complete, so *immediately* create a new file where you will be able to list all the textbooks, magazines, journals, newspapers, URLs etc. you have used. Save the file as 'Sources'.

Skills check

If you are set this project as a mini project, you should think about *how to plan and manage the project*. Refer to page 490.

Skills Builder Task 1

At this stage you should be able to tackle this first task of a small project that will run throughout this chapter. The project scenario is set out below. Study the scenario carefully so you are clear about the project's objective.

The scenario

Your school Head or college Principal has received the following letter from a new mobile phone company.

Prelude is a new, innovative mobile telephone company. We are looking for partners in all parts of the country to host our up-to-the-minute service.

We are dedicated to providing a fair deal for young people. We ensure they receive a service that protects them from unscrupulous scams whilst enabling them to indulge their favourite pastime.

We are prepared to pay a substantial rent for a suitable site upon which to erect a new telecommunication mast in your area and believe your school has large grounds which might offer an appropriate location. We are sure the additional income your school would receive for hosting the mast would be most useful.

Our local representative would very much like to meet you to discuss this proposal and will contact you shortly to arrange an appointment.

The Head/Principal is aware that there is considerable controversy over health issues relating to both telecommunication masts and the use of mobile phones by young people. He is anxious to study the facts before coming to any decision, so he has asked you to carry out some research on his behalf so that he can give guidance to the governors and parents.

Your first task is to use *secondary* sources to investigate the health issues surrounding the location of telecommunication masts and the use of mobile phones by young people. Produce a report of your findings.

Using surveys

Have you ever been stopped in the street by a researcher and asked whether you can spare a few minutes to answer some questions (Figure 1.4)? The researcher will be conducting a survey on behalf of an organisation, so he or she will record your answers to a series of questions on a questionnaire, and in some cases on audio tape.

Figure 1.4 A market researcher in action

Millions of pounds is spent every year on this *market research* by organisations that want to know the public's views on a variety of topics. A large proportion of this money will be spent on surveys. These are used by all sorts of organisations to gather information.

Figure 1.5 Topics of market research

Opinions

Market research is frequently carried out by manufacturing companies. For example, if a company is considering updating the brand image of an established product, the company will want to know the public's opinion of the proposed new image before investing considerable sums of money on promoting it.

Television companies sometimes produce *pilot* shows of work by new writers to find out viewers' opinions before commissioning a whole series. An invited audience will be asked to watch the show and complete a questionnaire recording what they thought of it.

Likes and dislikes

If a school headteacher was considering a change in the school uniform, a survey might be used to find out what pupils and parents would like or dislike when choosing a new uniform. For example, how many people like having a school uniform? How many people like the idea of girls wearing trousers rather than skirts? Would a new summer uniform prove popular? Is there a preference for a particular colour?

Purchasing patterns

Suppose a major high street clothing retailer is considering opening a new branch. A survey carried out in that town's shopping centre would reveal information about the shopping patterns of the local community.

The results of the survey could ultimately affect the decision on whether to open a store. If the results of the survey showed that local people generally went out of town to buy their clothes, the retailer may decide not to open a branch in that particular town.

Lifestyles

Some organisations conduct surveys on a national scale. These surveys gather information about our age, social class, marital status, housing, working life, income, leisure time, etc. Once analysed, the data provides valuable information on the lifestyles of groups with different jobs and incomes, and people living in different parts of the country. This data is then often sold on to other organisations that use it to target specific social groups with mailshots on products that would appear to fit in with their lifestyles.

Planning your survey

Your first step is to think about exactly what you need to find out and who the best people are to give you this information. Every survey should start with well defined objectives that state the reasons for carrying out the survey. When the objectives are clear, the questions can be drawn up and the questionnaire designed.

Questionnaires

Questionnaires fulfil several purposes:

- Most importantly they should enable you to gather accurate data.
- They ensure that each person is asked exactly the same question.
- They provide the easiest way of obtaining and analysing data by providing a structure from which the answers can be counted easily.

There is a skill in designing a questionnaire that will meet all of these requirements.

Question design

There are basically three types of question used in surveys: open questions, closed questions and scaled questions.

An *open question* allows the *respondent* to give any answer. For example, if 30 people were asked the question 'What is your age?' you could end up with 30 different answers. It is almost impossible to analyse the responses to questions of this nature.

A *closed question* will usually have anticipated replies.

? Think it over ...

A publishing company is thinking of producing two new weekly magazines. One would be aimed at teenage boys and the other at teenage girls. How could the company research the potential markets? What information would the company be trying to find?

Jargon buster

A **respondent** *is the person answering a question.*

For example, the following question provides a set of answers that can be counted easily and then analysed.

Please indicate your age group	Under 18	☐
	18 – 29	☐
	30 – 39	☐
	40 – 49	☐
	50 – 59	☐
	60 or over	☐

If you use questions of this nature, make sure there is no overlap in the possible answers. For example, if you include two age response boxes '20–30' and '30–40', which box would a 30-year-old be expected to tick?

A *scaled question* is sometimes used to find out how much a person likes or dislikes the idea of something.

How likely are you to consider a weekend shopping trip to France by coach?

On a scale of 1 to 10 [where 1 represents very unlikely and 10 represents highly likely], please circle the number that reflects your thoughts

Very unlikely									*Highly likely*
1	2	3	4	5	6	7	8	9	10

This question will show you the scale of possible interest, *but be careful if you use questions of this type*. The secret is to include an *even number* of possible responses, such as 6, 8 or 10, so that respondents have to make a decision one way or the other. If you had a scale of 1 to 9 it is possible for all your respondents to choose number 5 – which is right in the middle of the scale and does not show any preference.

Once you have decided what types of questions to use, there are some other points to consider.

- Your questions should not be too long or complicated. Use simple language – you will not score points for using difficult words that people may not understand.
- Your questions should relate to the specific objective of the survey and should not be included just because you like the sound of them.

TiP

As you design each question, think about the likely answers you will get. Make sure the question and anticipated replies meet the objective and can be analysed.

- Your questions should definitely not influence the responses given. They should be unbiased and not lead the respondent to a particular answer.
- Consider the order of the questions. They should flow easily from one to another, and questions on the same topic should ideally be grouped together.
- Finally, be prepared to rewrite your questions. Your questionnaire will need to be thoroughly tested before it is used. Sometimes a question will not be understood in the way you intended. Don't rely on the comments of just one tester – ask several people to test the survey for you. Testing of this nature will also help you to find out whether you can collate the data easily, ready for analysis.

Go out and try!

You have already considered the sort of information a magazine would need before deciding whether to produce two new magazines (one for boys and one for girls) for the teenage market.

1 Write a series of questions that a researcher might use in a survey on behalf of the publisher.
   - Think carefully about the survey's objective. What exactly are you trying to find out?
   - What types of questions will help you to achieve this objective?
   - Try to write clear questions that will encourage an honest response.
2 Try out your questions on a friend.
   - Do the questions produce the types of response you expected?
   - Are there any questions missing that would help you to meet the survey's objective or to better analyse the responses?
3 Rewrite your questions if necessary and repeat the trial with another person.

Designing a questionnaire

The visual appearance of a questionnaire is important, and you should make use of plenty of white space so that it is easy to read. Use a standard (i.e. not fancy) font style and size so that the questions are clear, and make sure the spaces for answers line up with the questions. If you are including tick boxes or a scale – as in the previous examples on page 17 – make sure you give a clear instruction to tick a box or circle a number. Make it clear whether your respondents should tick just one box per question, or as many as they wish.

TiP

You will find the tick box through *Insert*, *Symbol*, *Wingdings*.

Use the features in your word-processing software to help you present your questionnaire. For example, use the **Tab** key to line up answers and boxes.

Consider using a table to produce a questionnaire. You could replace the standard borders with other borders of your choice. Figure 1.6 shows an example.

Please tick one box		✓
Please indicate your age group	Under 18	
	18–29	
	30–39	
	40–49	
	50–59	
	60 or over	
Please indicate your gender	Male	
	Female	

Please tick one box		✓
Please indicate your age group	Under 18	
	18–29	
	30–39	
	40–49	
	50–59	
	60 or over	
Please indicate your gender	Male	
	Female	

Figure 1.6 Part of a questionnaire produced using a table, and the same questionnaire printed with selected borders

Finally, think about producing a sheet on which to record the answers to the questions. When you count the answers, a useful way of recording them is to group them in fives. Use one vertical stroke for each of the first four answers and record the fifth answer horizontally, like this: 卌. You can then total them easily by adding up in fives. Figure 1.7 illustrates this.

	Please tick one box	✓	Total
Please indicate your age group	Under 18	|||	3
	18–29	卌 |||	8
	30–39	卌 ||||	9
	40–49	卌	5
	50–59	||||	4
	60 or over			1

Please indicate your gender	Male	卌 卌 卌 ||	17
	Female	卌 卌 |||	13

Figure 1.7 One method of collating data before it is entered into a spreadsheet

Go out and try!

The questionnaire in Figure 1.8 was produced by a student studying for a qualification in health and social care. It was designed to provide information on underage drinking. Study the questionnaire carefully and think about any improvements you could make to the design. Share your ideas with your class, and then collaborate on the design of an improved questionnaire.

Questionnaire on underage drinking

- Please tick only one for each question that applies to you.

1. Male □
   Female □

2. age: 12–13 □
        13–15 □
        15–17 □

3. Do you drink alcohol?
   Yes □
   No □

4. How often do you drink alcohol?
   ....
   ....

5. Can u purchase your own alcohol?
   Yes □
   No □   Sometimes □

6. How do you usually get alcohol? □
   Parents □   Off licence □   Pub/bar □

   Friends □   People off the street □

   Other..

7. Why do you drink alcohol?
   Peer pressure □   Nothing else to do □
   To feel older □

   Other..

8. Do you think if there were more activities for younger people, you would drink less alcohol?
   Yes □
   No □
   Maybe □

   Please explain your answer, why? ....
   ....

9. If yes or maybe, what activities do you think should be provided for younger people?
   ....
   ....

10. What are your opinions on underage drinking in general? ....
    ....
    ....

Figure 1.8 A questionnaire produced by a student – some improvements are necessary

Go out and try!

There is concern amongst teachers that some students are not spending enough time on their homework or coursework. Your Headteacher/Principal would like to invite parents and guardians into school one evening to discuss the problem, but first of all she needs to investigate how the situation affects students in your school/college.

You have been asked to find out how students in your peer group spend their leisure time. For example, how much time do they spend in paid employment, doing homework, playing sports, watching television, and so on? You won't need the wide age range indicated in Figure 1.7, but choose a range that is most suitable for the students in your school or college.

Carry out a survey to gather together data that the Headteacher/Principal will be able to use as evidence when talking to parents and guardians.

Assessment Hint

To achieve top marks you must

- identify and use **at least three** secondary sources, also checking that the data is valid and reliable

- identify and use **one** primary source, thinking carefully about how to ensure you gather the information you need

- if you use a questionnaire, test it, and revise it if necessary before conducting your full survey

- acknowledge your sources fully and accurately.

Skills Builder Task 2

At this stage you should be able to tackle the next task of the mini project introduced in Skills Builder Task 1 on page 13. Again, don't forget to study the scenario carefully so that you are clear about the project's objective.

Conduct a survey amongst your peer group to find information on

- current service providers
- pay-as-you-go and monthly billing
- how frequently handsets are updated
- the average number of text messages sent and received each day
- the average number of phone calls made and received each day
- the average monthly cost of text and phone messages
- who pays the bill
- any other relevant information you can think of.

Collating and analysing data to produce information

Using a spreadsheet

Once you have finished your survey you need to collate the data in a spreadsheet. If the questionnaire has been prepared well, the design of your spreadsheet will follow closely the format of the questions.

You can then include formulas and functions to make calculations, from which you can analyse and interpret the results. You will then be able to produce meaningful information – some or all of which will probably be in the form of bar charts or graphs.

Figure 1.9 shows how a spreadsheet can be used to analyse the data shown in Figure 1.7 on page 19.

From the analysis of the data you can then produce useful graphs or charts to illustrate the information more clearly. For example, the bar charts in Figure 1.10 show that the majority of respondents in this particular survey are aged 19 to 39, and there are 14 per cent more males than females.

	A	B	C	D	E	F
1	Age Range of Respondents	No in each category	% of Total in Each Category	Breakdown by Gender	No in each category	% of Total in Each Category
2	Under 18	3	10%	Male	17	57%
3	19 - 29	8	27%	Female	13	43%
4	30 - 39	9	30%			
5	40 - 49	5	17%			
6	50 - 59	4	13%			
7	60 or over	1	3%			
8	Total respondents	30				

	A	B	C	D	E	F
1	Age Range of Respondents	No in each category	% of Total in Each Category	Breakdown by Gender	No in each category	% of Total in Each Category
2	Under 18	3	=B2/$B$8	Male	17	=E2/$B$8
3	19 - 29	8	=B3/$B$8	Femal	13	=E3/$B$8
4	30 - 39	9	=B4/$B$8			
5	40 - 49	5	=B5/$B$8			
6	50 - 59	4	=B6/$B$8			
7	60 or over	1	=B7/$B$8			
8	Total responden	=SUM(E2:E3)				

Figure 1.9 The spreadsheet data from Figure 1.7 and the formulas to analyse it

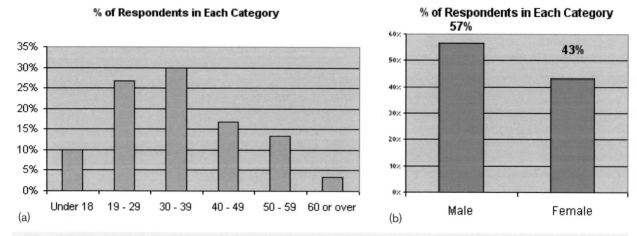

(a)

(b)

Figure 1.10 Graphs illustrating (a) the percentages of respondents in each category, and (b) the percentages of male and female respondents, for the data in Figure 1.7

Go out and try!

Create a spreadsheet based on the questions you have asked in your survey. Try to make the row or column headings much briefer than the actual questions. For example, the questions in your survey might all start with 'How many hours ...?' Instead of writing out every question in full as row or column headings, think about other options as shown in Figure 1.11. The heading 'No of Hours Spent On' has been centred across the columns relating to the questions asked.

No of Hours Spent On:		
Paid Employment	Homework	Watching TV

Figure 1.11 Possible heading styles to analyse the survey results

If the respondents have been asked to indicate their age in categories, as suggested earlier, then you can design the spreadsheet to establish (a) the total number of respondents, (b) how many are in each age group, and (c) the percentage of the total that are in each group. When you analyse the responses to the questions in your survey, you will be able to identify whether there is any significant difference in the replies depending on the age of the respondent.

Skills check ▶▶

As explained on page 331, databases are used to store large quantities of structured data covering a huge variety of topics – from stock control, to travel or theatre bookings, to medical records and much more. Make sure you read this information on databases.

✓ TiP

*Remember that it is very important to consider the nature of the data to be stored and what information you hope to obtain from it **before** you start to design your database.*

Information handling

In order to complete your project for this unit you may be able to extract information from databases that have been created by someone else. Alternatively you might need to create your own database to store and analyse the results of your research.

When creating your database you will need to

- use validation rules when designing the fields – see page 345
- import given data sets – see page 358
- enter, edit and delete records – see page 348
- design data entry forms – see page 340
- use queries to extract valid and meaningful information for a specified purpose – see page 350
- use reports to present information clearly – see page 354
- export data for use in other applications, such as mail merge – see page 357.

Importing data

If you already have a set of data stored elsewhere, it may not be necessary to copy the data into the database records. Instead the data can be imported directly into the database. For example, if you have entered data into a spreadsheet file, you can import that data directly into your database.

Exporting data

If you are sending the same letter to a large number of people, you can use the names and addresses already stored in your database by *exporting* the data to use in a mail merge file.

Sometimes you may need to analyse data using both a spreadsheet and a database file, because these software applications provide different facilities for representing the data.

- The spreadsheet is the most suitable way to analyse numerical data and produce graphs and charts to visually represent that data.

- Whilst the *filter facility* of a spreadsheet enables you to extract particular information just as you would by creating a query in a database, the advantage of the database is that you can present that information more clearly by producing a report from the results of the query.

Therefore it may be appropriate and beneficial to import the data from your spreadsheet into a database file.

Skills check ▶▶

See page 358 for step-by-step instructions for importing data into a database.

Go out and try!

1   Having set up a spreadsheet to record the results of your survey of homework and coursework, design a database into which you can import the data from your spreadsheet. The fields in your database must follow the relevant column headings in your spreadsheet. For example, the small snapshot shown in Figure 1.11 (page 23) showed three relevant headings: Paid Employment, Homework and Watching TV. The field names in your database would match these and you would choose a suitable field type – in this case *number*. You need to consider whether it should be an *integer* (whole number) or *two decimal places* to allow for quarter or half hours.

2   💾 Save the table and then import the data from the spreadsheet.

Skills Builder Task 3

At this stage you should be able to tackle the next task of the mini project introduced on page 13. Again, don't forget to study the scenario carefully so that you are clear about the project's objective.

① Analyse your results using a spreadsheet and create relevant graphs or charts to illustrate your findings.

② Record your results in a database and produce suitable reports for the Principal.

Working with information

Identifying the purpose

When you have completed your research and gathered the data together the summative project brief will identify the information you must obtain from it.

○ Sometimes this might simply be a case of extracting relevant items and passing the information on in a straightforward way.

○ At other times you might have to study a wide range of information and present it in your own words. You could be asked to draw conclusions or make recommendations.

You must learn to present your information in a way that will be immediately helpful to the readers, by providing answers to the questions that they are most likely to have. The information you provide may ultimately influence their decision-making in some way. If you are

○ *presenting your own views*, remember that whatever you write or say should be justified or explained.

○ *passing on information*, make sure you have the facts right and that what you are saying is accurate.

○ *quoting from somewhere or someone*, you should put the quote in quotation marks and acknowledge the source of the information.

While you are writing, think about the purpose of your document and make sure that every word you write contributes to that purpose. The purpose helps to determine the writing and presentation style that is most appropriate, and you will learn to approach different purposes in different ways.

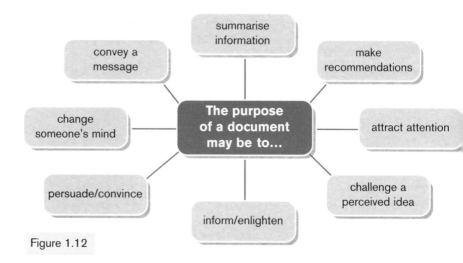

Figure 1.12

Let's look at each of these possible purposes in turn.

Conveying a message

Figure 1.13 shows how easy it is for a simple message to be conveyed incorrectly! It is essential that you learn to pass information on to other people in an accurate way without altering the facts or imposing any ideas of your own (unless your opinion is asked for).

The message you are passing on might be very straightforward, such as confirming the arrangements for a meeting. It might be more complex, such as the description of a technical problem with machinery. The consequences of passing on an inaccurate message could be disastrous. For example, a letter to clients advising them of

Figure 1.13 It is important to convey messages accurately!

a change in the arrangements for ordering goods must be accurate or the company could be liable to lose business worth thousands of pounds. One thing always remains the same: you must make sure that what you are writing is accurate.

Think it over...

This is something the whole class can do together or in two groups. Ask your teacher or tutor to write down in secret a message that contains several key points. He or she will speak softly and pass the message to one person in the group. That person will pass the message on to the next person and so on until everyone has been given the message. You are not allowed to hear the message repeated. The last person to receive the message will state it out loud.

- Did the final message match the original message?
- If the original message was different from the final message, why do you think it changed?
- What steps can you take to ensure a message is passed on accurately?

Summarising information

Learning to summarise information is a bit trickier than just being accurate. You have to read through all the information you have gathered and then pull out the relevant facts from the various sources. You must then *reassemble* the facts in your own words without altering the facts or changing the meaning.

Look at the page from a holiday brochure in Figure 1.14 (page 28). It provides a summary of the holiday resort together with some local information on currency, local food specialities, etc. Relatively few words have been used, and information on the weather has been summarised in graphical form to make it much easier to understand.

Think it over...

Earlier in this chapter you used secondary sources of information to find out about korfball and wrote about half a page on the subject. At that time you were summarising information. Now compare your work with that of a friend.
- Do the two summaries contain very similar information?
- What differences can you find?
- Is any of the wording exactly the same? That is, have any sentences or phrases just been copied from the original text?
- Do you agree that both passages contain all the important facts about the topic? Refer back to your source material and see what relevant information has been left out.

Costa del Sol

"From the fine sands of exuberant Torremolinos to the chic allure of exclusive Marbella, the Costa del Sol is a vibrant mix of sun, sea and spectacular sights."

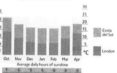

Andalucia embodies all that is typically Spanish...sun-soaked beaches, passionate flamenco dancers, Moorish castles, orange groves, proud matadors and sleepy whitewashed towns perched on dramatic hillsides. The Costa del Sol is the perfect gateway to this quintessential picture of Spain and offers so much more besides.

From the cosmopolitan marinas of Marbella to the top class golf courses of Fuengirola, from the glittering sands of Torremolinos to the lively tapas bars of Nerja, the resorts that make up Spain's 'sunshine coast' offer all ages a fascinating spectrum of sights and activities by day and night.

Averaging 300 days' sunshine a year, it's little wonder that the Costa del Sol is widely acknowledged as the playground of Europe. The coastline is famed for its miles of wide, sandy beaches lapped by the sparkling waters of the Mediterranean. Most offer a wide range of watersports if you're feeling energetic and sunbeds and parasols if you prefer to while away your days in the sun. Torremolinos has a 7km stretch of unbroken sandy shoreline while Nerja is known for its pretty coves tucked under cliffs - perfect if you're looking for a little more seclusion.

If you like to relax by day and party by night, you'll love the cheerful exuberance of Torremolinos, Benalmadena and Fuengirola. The streets are lined with an abundance of lively bars, discos and clubs where you can dance the night away. In contrast, evenings in Estepona, Nerja and Marbella are more low key. Visitors often prefer to enjoy the buzz of local tapas bars, romantic waterfront restaurants or the flamenco shows where you can experience the compelling rhythm of a Spanish guitarist and flashing moves of a dancer.

From small souvenir shops to smart boutiques, the Costa del Sol overflows with shops of all shapes and sizes. Marbella is the place to head if you're after classy designer wear while Malaga is home to a large shopping mall and a number of department stores. Fuengirola stages a weekly street market every Tuesday. Leather goods are particularly good value, as is Andalucian blue and white coloured pottery.

factfile Ask your travel agent for further information on accommodation in this resort. See A-Z guide.

Your Local Expert "Some local knowledge to make you make the most of your holiday."

Money There are 1.41 euros to the £1.00 as at 31st August 2004. Banking hours are Monday-Friday 08.30-14.00. Major credit cards are accepted at most shops, hotels and restaurants.

Meals Southern Spain is the birthplace of tapas bars. Sometimes called 'pinchos', tapas are small bar snacks that are usually served as an accompaniment to a glass of sherry, wine or beer. Even the smallest of villages in Andalucia play host to at least one tapas bar where locals head in the evenings to enjoy a drink, a bite to eat and of course a chat with friends.

Whet your appetite with 'jamon serrano', salt-cured ham that's dried out in the mountain air, or 'tortilla espanola', Spanish omelette made from potato and onions bound with eggs. Other tempting dishes include 'calamares fritos', deep fried squid rings drizzled with lemon juice, 'albondigas', meatballs served in a rich tomato sauce, and 'queso manchego', a mature sheep's cheese. Tapas are normally eaten standing rather than sitting down which adds to the vibrant atmosphere experienced in the bar.

Dress Code In most hotels and apartments gentlemen are required to wear long trousers.

Thomson 175

Figure 1.14 A typical page from a holiday brochure will include a summary of information about the resort. It may also include a graph or chart to illustrate the annual temperature and rainfall

Making recommendations

A recommendation usually follows a detailed investigation into a particular subject. For example, the decision to introduce the theory element to the car driving test was the result of a recommendation made following a study of driving standards in the UK and in Europe.

An idea to change the school/college year from three terms to four terms is quite topical. In fact some areas have already adopted the new proposals. If the Head Teacher of your school or the Principal of your college wanted to make the change, he or she could not just wake up one morning and announce the change. Any decision would have to follow an investigation that would take into account the views of parents and guardians, the local education authority, local employers, teachers, trade unions and students. The investigation would make a recommendation to the Head Teacher or Principal, who would then make the recommendation to the governors.

In business, recommendations are usually made in writing, such as a letter recommending a particular course of action, or a detailed report with recommendations in the conclusion. Sometimes a multimedia presentation will be used to support a recommendation. Whichever method is chosen, the facts will be presented and arguments offered for and against the proposal in order to support the final recommendation.

Go out and try!

You now know the facts about korfball. The Head of Sports in your school or college has asked you to make a recommendation on whether the sport should be adopted there. Make your own decision based on the information you have obtained, and then write about 150 words in support of your recommendation.

TiP

Sometimes graphs and charts are used to attract attention. They can demonstrate the highs and lows with far more impact than a paragraph of words and numbers. The tip is to make the image relevant and the words notable.

Attracting attention

If you are trying to attract someone's attention, the message needs to be 'short, sharp and to the point'. Posters and advertisements provide fine examples of publications that are designed to attract attention. Compare any selection of advertisements in magazines or on hoardings and try to analyse which advertisements are eye-catching and why. The chances are that the eye-catching ones will contain a relevant graphical image and few words – little enough to be taken in with a quick glance but sufficient to make you want to find out more.

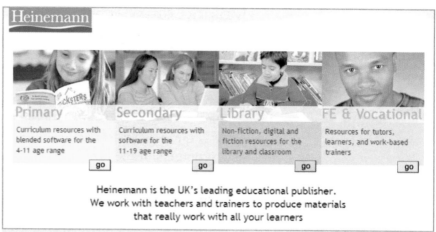

Figure 1.15 The front page of Heinemann's website is designed to attract attention

Skills check ▶▶

Refer to pages 480 and 496–497 for information on mind mapping.

? ○○Think it over...

Whether this goes along with your recommendation or not, the Head of Sport has decided to introduce korfball on a trial basis and wants to arrange a meeting with students who may be interested in trying the new sport.

Get together with a group of your friends and brainstorm ideas for a 'catchy' phrase that will attract the attention of students and make them want to find out more. Use a *mind map* to organise your ideas.

Challenging a fixed idea

From time to time we come across people who have very fixed ideas about certain topics, but these ideas do not always agree with the widely accepted view on the same subject.

If you read a daily newspaper you will know that stories are often printed that cause a public outcry. When this happens, the story is followed by a series of articles and television and radio interviews where people have the opportunity to offer varying views on the topic. These people are challenging the original idea and presenting arguments based on evidence they have collected.

We are all free to express our opinions and to challenge the ideas of others, but we must support our point of view with true and relevant facts.

- Some radio stations raise issues of topical interest and invite viewers to phone, email or text their opinions on the matter being discussed.
- Many websites invite users to contact them with suggestions or complaints. The BBC website invites feedback from the public

Figure 1.16 Ideas are regularly contested in debates

not only on suggestions or complaints but also regarding factual errors. This allows someone to point out a mistake, but the validity of these comments must be backed up by evidence. The BBC is, of course, free to accept or reject these opinions.

? Think it over...

'Most people think that teenagers eat too much junk food and this is having an adverse effect on their behaviour.'

Do you agree with this statement? Discuss your ideas with a group of your friends and agree a list of arguments that you could put forward to challenge the statement.

Informing/enlightening

Many of the things we buy today come with a set of instructions, written to explain to the new user how the item works, how it is put together or how to care for it. Look in the information rack in your local library or post office and you will see leaflets that cover all sorts of subjects. The purpose of these is to make things clear to us or to let us know about something. They are written and presented in an unbiased, easy-to-understand style that passes information to the reader – but they do not represent anybody's personal views.

Go out and try!

What do you like doing in your spare time? Do you have a hobby? Do you have an interest in something unusual? Do you have a part-time job? Do you take part in any sporting activities? Does a member of your family do anything unusual in his/her spare time?

Prepare a two-minute presentation to explain how you like to spend your spare time. Deliver your presentation to an audience made up of students in your class.

Persuading/convincing

Many businesses – both manufacturing and commercial – employ advertising agencies, whose job it is to persuade us to buy those businesses' products or services. Judging by the amount of money spent on advertising each year, it would seem that they are successful. Constant advertising ensures that products and services become household names. Before you know it, you have fallen into the advertiser's trap and parted with your money!

In order to persuade us to buy their products, companies tell us the benefits their products will bring to our lives and how much better these products are than the competition's.

Government agencies try to convince us that healthy eating is a good thing and recommend that we should eat five servings of fruit and vegetables each day. Similarly they try to convince us that smoking or excessive drinking is not good. To persuade us to change our habits, they must also tell us why! In order to be persuaded or convinced, we need to be provided with reliable facts and arguments that inform us of the advantages and disadvantages. Then we are in a position to make an informed decision.

Go out and try!

The Head of Sport is taking a team of korfball players from your school/college to Holland and Belgium for an international tournament during the Easter holiday. Write about 150 words to persuade or convince him/her that you should be included in the team.

Changing someone's mind

How often do you change your mind? Probably quite often! What makes you change your mind? What wins you over? Sometimes you will change your mind because of something you are shown or something you are told. If you are trying to make someone change his or her mind, your line of reasoning must be clear, concise and relevant to the purpose.

The target audience

When you are clear about the purpose of a document you intend to produce, you must ask yourself who is going to read it. In other words, who is the *target audience*? This might be the general public, colleagues at work who have some knowledge of day-to-day business operations, or specialists who are experts in a particular field. It could be a group of adults, young people or perhaps visitors from another country. You need to be able to produce documents that are directed towards different target groups in a way that will be helpful to them.

? Think it over...

Look at Figure 1.17, which shows pages taken from two different student books. Who would you consider to be the target audience for each book? Why did you reach that conclusion?

Figure 1.17 Pages from two different student books

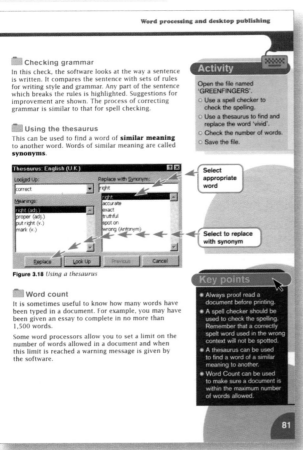

Word processing and desktop publishing

Checking grammar

In this check, the software looks at the way a sentence is written. It compares the sentence with sets of rules for writing style and grammar. Any part of the sentence which breaks the rules is highlighted. Suggestions for improvement are shown. The process of correcting grammar is similar to that for spell checking.

Using the thesaurus

This can be used to find a word of **similar meaning** to another word. Words of similar meaning are called **synonyms**.

Thesaurus: English (U.K.)

Looked Up:
correct

Replace with Synonym:
right

Meanings:
right (adj.)
proper (adj.)
put right (v.)
mark (v.)

right
accurate
exact
truthful
spot on
wrong (Antonym)

Replace | Look Up | Previous | Cancel

Figure 3.18 *Using a thesaurus*

Word count

It is sometimes useful to know how many words have been typed in a document. For example, you may have been given an essay to complete in no more than 1,500 words.

Some word processors allow you to set a limit on the number of words allowed in a document and when this limit is reached a warning message is given by the software.

Activity

Open the file named 'GREENFINGERS'.
○ Use a spell checker to check the spelling.
○ Use a thesaurus to find and replace the word 'vivid'.
○ Check the number of words.
○ Save the file.

Select appropriate word

Select to replace with synonym

Key points

● Always proof read a document before printing.
● A spell checker should be used to check the spelling. Remember that a correctly spelt word used in the wrong context will not be spotted.
● A thesaurus can be used to find a word of a similar meaning to another.
● Word Count can be used to make sure a document is within the maximum number of words allowed.

81

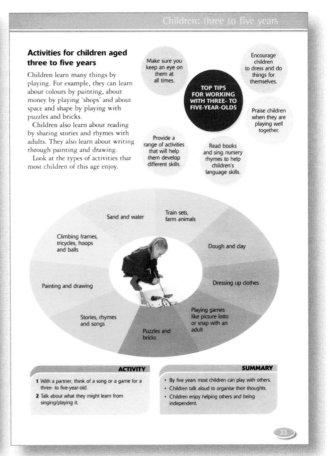

Children: three to five years

Activities for children aged three to five years

Children learn many things by playing. For example, they can learn about colours by painting, about money by playing 'shops' and about space and shape by playing with puzzles and bricks.

Children also learn about reading by sharing stories and rhymes with adults. They also learn about writing through painting and drawing.

Look at the types of activities that most children of this age enjoy.

Make sure you keep an eye on them at all times.

Encourage children to dress and do things for themselves.

TOP TIPS FOR WORKING WITH THREE- TO FIVE-YEAR-OLDS

Praise children when they are playing well together.

Provide a range of activities that will help them develop different skills.

Read books and sing nursery rhymes to help children's language skills.

Sand and water

Train sets, farm animals

Climbing frames, tricycles, hoops and balls

Dough and clay

Painting and drawing

Dressing up clothes

Stories, rhymes and songs

Playing games like picture lotto or snap with an adult

Puzzles and bricks

ACTIVITY

1 With a partner, think of a song or a game for a three- to five-year-old.
2 Talk about what they might learn from singing/playing it.

SUMMARY

• By five years most children can play with others.
• Children talk aloud to organise their thoughts.
• Children enjoy helping others and being independent.

33

As you plan each project, always keep these questions about your readers in mind.

Figure 1.18 Thinking about your target audience

Go out and try!

Imagine you have been given the task of promoting an international junior korfball tournament in your home town. You have a variety of target audiences:

- ○ VIPs – perhaps the mayor, whose presence at the event will add credibility to it
- ○ the general public – who you must attract in order to sell tickets to help cover the costs of the tournament
- ○ young people – who might be persuaded to take up the sport if they come along and watch some games
- ○ potential sponsors
- ○ travel and tour operators – who might wish to bring visitors from the other countries who have teams participating in the event.

Would you target each of these groups in different ways? How might your approach differ for each group? Work in small groups and brainstorm ideas. Compare your ideas with those of the other groups.

Presenting information

Most people with very basic skills can sit at a computer and produce pages and pages of text. The essential skill for you to develop is to be able to make full use of the ICT features available within the software to increase your document's *readability and effectiveness*.

The work you produce will give your readers an image of you or the organisation you work for, so it is essential that there are no mistakes and that it looks good. The initial impression of any document or on-screen publication is very powerful in swaying or influencing people. You must therefore make sure that on first glance your readers want to find out more.

A document's content and structure

If your document is going to be made up of more than just a few paragraphs of text, it is a good idea to sketch some designs on paper before you even turn the computer on. This can help you to visualise the finished document and will enable you to compare one possible design against another.

Figure 1.19 Sloppy presentation style

Before you begin to draft any text to be included in your document you should consider the overall composition.

- *What components are to be included?* Will there be text, charts, diagrams or graphics? If it's a slide presentation, will there be animation, video or sound? How can the message be conveyed to the audience in the most effective way? Will you rely on one component or combine two or three? Your final decision will obviously depend on whether your document will be published on paper or electronically, on the purpose, and on the audience.

- *How will the key items be positioned on the page?* Think about headings or headlines, graphics, and buttons or other links. Remember that you want to maximise the impact of these elements in order to grab the reader's attention. It makes sense to think carefully about these features during the initial stages of planning. For example, from the reader's point of view it is useful if you position similar features in the same place on every page. This presents a consistent appearance and shows that you have given thought and care to the design.

- *What is the relative importance of the various components?* The proportion of text to visual/audio information will probably depend on the target audience and their subject knowledge. It is often easier to learn about a topic by looking at pictures and listening to information rather than having to plough through pages of text. Make sure that any images you include are clearly labelled and positioned close to any text relating to them.

Writing style

Once you know the purpose of a document, who is likely to be reading it and the components you wish to include, you should be able to decide on a suitable writing style without too much difficulty. Good writing mostly depends on choosing the best style for the type of document you are producing so that you can get your message across in the most effective way.

Formal or informal?

Language can be *formal* or *informal*. Business correspondence is generally written in a formal style. Your aim then is to create the right impression to encourage the reader to read what you have to say.

TiP

Look at a wide selection of documents to get an overview of different writing styles. If you base your document on something similar, you should get the style about right.

A letter that begins

'Dear Sir, I refer to your recent advertisement in the Whychton Gazette for a travel consultant' is definitely more formal and more appropriate than 'Hey Mister Travelbug, I hear you've been looking for someone to do all your bookings and stuff and I'm just who you need.'

At other times a more informal language style might be appropriate or acceptable. A sentence that reads 'Travelbug are here to help you sort out your travel needs' is far more suitable and more likely to catch the reader's attention than 'The staff of Travelbug cordially invite you to attend their premises to discuss your travel requirements.'

Exactly where to pitch the level of language between formal and informal is not always easy to decide. As a rough guide, somewhere in the middle is pretty safe. Just remember to keep in mind the *reason* for the document and the *type of readers* and you should not find it difficult to produce a document that is entirely appropriate.

Simple or complex language?

If what you are writing is to appeal to a broad range of ordinary people, you should choose a straightforward and uncomplicated language style – one that can be understood by everyone.

If you are writing for a young audience, don't use words that they are unlikely to have heard before and so will not readily understand. On the other hand, if you are writing something of a more technical or specialist nature then it is quite likely that your language style will need to be more complicated. Even so, don't try to use complex language if you do not understand the subject well enough yourself, because you are quite likely to end up writing nonsense. If in doubt, stay on the cautious side!

TiP

If you find it difficult to get the right words down on paper, try speaking them out loud first. More often than not you will find the sentences start to flow.

? **Think it over...**

Think about the writing styles you would use for the following:
- a letter to thank a relative for a birthday present
- a letter to the supplier of a faulty computer game
- a web page giving details of an art exhibition of work produced by students
- a letter applying for part-time work in a bookshop
- a leaflet advising students of various facilities available in a library
- a presentation to school or college governors designed to get their agreement to a group of students taking part in an international sporting event in France.

The tone

The tone you use can affect the way that people interpret your document. For example, if you feel angry about a subject, that anger may be reflected in the tone of your document and may prevent your readers from reaching an open-minded decision. In contrast, too much humour introduced into an important topic could give the impression that you are not treating the subject seriously – although a little humour might make a difficult or boring subject more interesting. You must learn to match the tone against both the purpose and the audience.

Presentation features

Remember that any document or publication that you produce is going to present an image of you. For this reason it is important to make good use of the presentation features in the software applications available to you. You will then feel good about the document you have produced.

Headings and sub-headings

Use headings and sub-headings to break a document down into sections, particularly if the document is long. This will help your readers (and you!) to navigate around the document and make it easier to read.

Layout and use of white space

Make full use of the available page or screen size to ensure that your documents are laid out clearly. It isn't always necessary to place text on every line of the page or screen. In fact, sometimes it is more effective to leave some areas clear – this is usually referred to as *white space*, although of course it might not be white! These clear areas can be a useful way of highlighting certain information.

Font type and size

It is usually accepted that most 'standard' documents – and particularly letters and reports – are produced in certain font types and sizes. The most common fonts are Arial and Times New Roman, simply because they are available on all modern computers. Arial is an example of a *sans serif* font, while Times New Roman is a *serif* font.

TiP

The rule-of-thumb to remember is: 'An uncluttered document is a clear document!'

Jargon buster

A **serif** is a small cross-stroke at the end of a main stroke in a letter.

Skills check ▶▶

There is more information on font type and size on page 251.

Times New Roman – Size 10	Times New Roman – Size 12	Times New Roman – Size 14
Arial – Size 10	Arial – Size 12	Arial – Size 14
Daves Hand – Size 10	Daves Hand – Size 12	Daves Hand – Size 14
Comic Sans - Size 10	Comic Sans - Size 12	Comic Sans - Size 14
Garamond – Size 10	Garamond – Size 12	Garamond – Size 14
Tahoma – Size 10	Tahoma – Size 12	Tahoma – Size 14

Figure 1.20 Different fonts and font sizes – which are serif and which are sans serif?

For printed documents the most common sizes are 11 and 12 point, but a slightly larger font size is helpful to very young or older readers because it makes the text clearer. Posters and flyers are easier to read from a distance if a much larger size of font is used.

As a general rule, do not mix several different font styles on the same document, or use too much decoration, such as WordArt. This can distract the reader from the purpose of the document.

Similar guidelines apply to screen-based publications, which also need to be clear and easy to read.

Line spacing

Skills check ▶▶

There is more information on line spacing on page 269.

Text presented in single line spacing is the generally accepted standard for documents such as letters and reports. One-and-a-half or double line spacing can make text more prominent, especially if viewed on a screen or from a distance. Always keep the purpose of the document and the target audience in mind when considering which style of line spacing to use.

Alignment

Skills check ▶▶

There is more information on alignment on page 255.

When we talk of alignment we are usually referring to the way paragraphs line up on the page. The default paragraph setting on most computers is left alignment, and this is used for most paper-based documents.

Full justification spreads the text between the margins and looks good for things like columns, newsletters and leaflets because the left and right margins remain straight and equal.

Centring of headings, text and whole paragraphs can successfully be applied to posters and flyers. In fact you might consider combining centred headings with fully justified paragraphs in documents such as flyers, to keep the margins even and present a unified appearance.

Skills check ▶▶

There is more information on bullets on page 257.

Skills check ▶▶

There is more information on text wrapping on page 288.

Bullets

It is sensible to use the standard bullet point for most text-based documents. This is represented by the character symbol •. You can be more imaginative with on-screen publications, advertisements, etc., but don't get carried away, and always keep the purpose of the document in mind.

Text wrapping

Various layout styles are available to wrap text around images and objects. Use these to avoid leaving unnecessary white space, but also remember the advice given earlier about the usefulness of some white space for clarity.

Figure 1.21 An example of wrapping text around a graphic

Colour

Posters, flyers and screen-based presentations provide the best opportunities for using colour. However, if your viewers are likely to print out pages from a website you should make sure the font is dark so that it can be read when printed on white paper. Remember also that light text colours need to be presented on dark screens or dark paper.

Dark colours should be used on printed white paper.

Light text colours need to be presented against a dark background to make them easier to read.

Paper-based documents are clearer to read and can be photocopied successfully if the text is in black ink.

Tables

Skills check ▶▶

There is more information on using tables on page 272.

Numerical data is often easier to understand if it is presented in a table, and lists of information can also be displayed in a table format as an alternative to using tabs. Tables can provide a very adaptable structure to help you present a wide variety of information. For example, the questionnaire illustrated in Figure 1.6 on page 19 used a table structure. Folded leaflets can also be produced in two- or three-column tables. Remember too that you can remove lines from a table and even include another table within a table cell.

Borders and shading

Skills check ▶▶

There is more information on using borders and shading on page 274.

A border and/or shading added to a paragraph of text will make it stand out from the rest of the document.

You may choose to use borders in a table, or to remove them completely. Use whichever style makes the table easiest to read.

You can be imaginative and apply different styles of lines to different sections of a table, but don't get too carried away and detract from its purpose. It is a good idea to check your document in Print Layout view before printing to make sure the borders and lines are where you expected them to be.

Use shading with care, especially if you are using a black and white printer. Sometimes the shading can be so dark that the text becomes unreadable. It can, however, be very effective to apply dark shading to a selection of cells in a table and then to change the font colour to white.

Jargon buster

Single-sided means that print appears on one side of the paper only. **Double-sided** means that both sides of the paper are used.

Skills check

There is more information on setting margins on page 264.

Skills check

There is more information on using tabs on page 260.

Margins

If you are producing a paper-based document that is to be printed single-sided, the left and right default margin setting of 3.17 centimetres (about $1\frac{1}{4}$ inches) in Word is quite suitable. If you are printing double-sided you might consider setting mirror margins (*inside* and *outside* instead of *left* and *right*) or, if the work is to be bound, you should set a gutter margin to ensure the binding doesn't cut through the text.

Tabs

Tabs provide a very useful way of lining up text across the page. Don't rely on the space bar because you will end up with an uneven line of text down the page. If you want to use tabs within a table, hold down the **Ctrl** key whilst using the **Tab** key.

Indents

A paragraph indent can be used to make a section of text stand apart from the rest of a document. There are three styles of indent that you might consider using, as shown in Figure 1.22.

This style of indent is called a **first line indent** because the first line of every paragraph is set in from the margin.

It can be used effectively to separate paragraphs of text if you don't wish to leave a clear line space in between.

This style of indent is known as a **hanging indent**.
It is often used in a document which has "side headings".
Each new heading starts alongside the margin making it clearer to read.

Sometimes a paragraph of text is indented within a document.

This paragraph has been indented from both margins.

It makes the paragraph stand out within the document.

Figure 1.22 Three styles of indent

Skills check

There is more information on using columns on page 271.

Columns

Columns are generally applied to newsletters and leaflets, especially if the finished document is going to be folded. Work presented in columns usually looks more professional if you use fully justified margins.

To place text at the beginning of a new column, do not use the **Enter** key repeatedly to move it across! Instead, insert a column break by clicking on the **Insert** menu and selecting **Break**, **Column break**. Similarly, insert a column break if you wish to leave one column empty – do not rely on the **Enter** key.

NEWTOWN PRIMARY SCHOOL PTA NEWSLETTER

The PTA

All parents of Newtown Primary School are members of the PTA. The committee, elected by members, consists of 8 parents and 1 teacher representative. Committee members can serve for a maximum of 4 years. Meetings are held every 4 weeks and all members are welcome. The details of these meetings are displayed on the PTA noticeboard in the main school corridor.

The committee's officers comprise a chairperson, vice chairperson, treasurer and secretary. These posts are for a 2-year period. The officers must be serving on the committee and are elected by the committee members.

The main function of the PTA is to raise funds for the school. These monies help provide the more luxurious items such as IT equipment, musical instruments, library books and play equipment. It also subsidises school trips which means that trips are affordable by all. Funds are raised by 3 or 4 main events each year. These usually include a Christmas Bazaar, Summer Fete and Sponsored Spell. The children are actively involved in these events which prove to be educational and enjoyable.

As well as fund-raising the PTA also organises social events. Discos, barn dances, barbecues and quiz nights are a few of the events that have been held in the last few years. These are well supported and great fun.

If you would like to be involved in the PTA but haven't the time to join the committee don't worry! We are always looking for willing helpers to man stalls, make refreshments and, of course, wash up.

During the coming year we will need to replace 3 committee members as their children will be leaving the school. If you are interested in joining please contact Marge Lovell, the committee secretary.

Auction of Promises

Our next main fund-raising event should prove to be a great night out for parents and supporters of the school. We are holding an Auction of Promises on 23 March at 7.30 pm in the school hall.

The auction lots will consist of 'promises' made or donated by parents and local businesses. A promise can be anything from a pair of theatre tickets to receiving a freshly baked cake for a birthday party.

We have been given a number of promises but we could do with lots more. You can promise almost anything. Ideas include doing the ironing, walking the dog, looking after a pet hamster for a week, digging the garden, an evening's babysitting – whatever you can do. If you can persuade your company to give as well, so much the better.

We need to have your promise by the end of February as catalogues need to be collated. Please contact Jenny Riseman as soon as possible.

If you can't help, please attend the meeting as it should be lots of fun. Philip Malcolm, a local auctioneer, has kindly agreed to run the proceedings, giving his services free of charge. Refreshments will be available and there will also be a raffle.

Tickets will be available at the end of next week and will cost £1.50 per person.

School Clothing

We have been asked by the Headteacher to remind parents that we sell school clothing on Tuesdays in the dining hall.

From 3.30 pm to 4.15 pm you can purchase any of the school garments including sweatshirts, gym kit and polo shirts. These items are all embroidered with the school logo.

The garments are made from 100% cotton and we feel they represent excellent value for money. They are machine washable and can be tumble dried. These garments do not shrink and are very hard wearing.

We usually have all sizes in stock. Given below are examples of the low cost of these garments.

Item	Price
Sweatshirt	£9.50
Polo shirt	£5.00
Gym shirt	£4.50
Gym shorts	£4.00

Dates for your Diary

As well as the Auction of Promises we have some more events lined up for this term. On March 17 we will be helping with the annual Sponsored Spell. About a week beforehand your child will be given 20 words to learn and a test will be given on the day. Prizes are given for children who get all 20 words correct. Please help your child by sponsoring them per word. Last year we raised over £700.

A cake sale will be held on Friday 3 April. This is to tie in with the children's charity day. As you are aware, children are encouraged to raise money for a local charity and can help to do this by paying a fee to wear 'civilian' clothes on Charity Day. The proceeds from the cake sale will go to our local charity, the Homeless Shelter. Please send in cakes on Friday morning and come and buy after school at 3.30 pm.

Book week is another important event in our school calendar. This will be held the week beginning March 10. The PTA will be holding a book sale each day after school in the main hall. Please support this event by coming along and buying a book. The proceeds from the sale will enable us to purchase more books for the school library.

Figure 1.23 A multi-column newsletter – notice that each section starts with a dropped capital

Skills check ▶▶

There is more information on styles on page 284.

Styles

If you look for the word 'style' in a thesaurus you will find a variety of alternative words such as *technique, elegance, flair, smartness, good taste,* and *design*. The Style feature therefore makes it simple to apply formatting styles to make your documents more interesting and stylish. You can apply paragraph styles, character styles, list styles and table styles to ensure that the style of presentation is consistent throughout a document.

TiP

You can apply a dropped capital to the first letter in a paragraph through **Format, Drop Cap**.

Skills check ▶▶

There is more information on text boxes on page 279.

Text boxes

You can use a text box to position text anywhere on a page and can apply various effects from the *Drawing* toolbar. The use of these features can make a publication more interesting and professional. For example, you can use text boxes to label diagrams or add prominence to headings. In Figure 1.24 we have used three text boxes, changed the fill and font colours and applied a 3-D style.

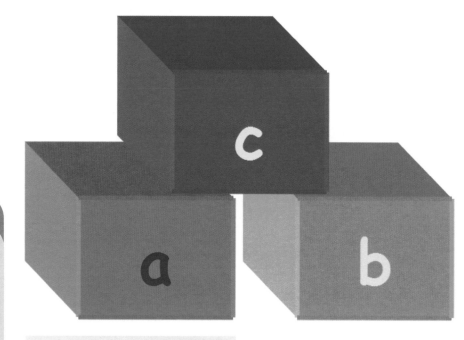

Figure 1.24 Styles applied to text boxes

✔ TiP

If you wish to apply a water-mark as a background to a document, copy it into the header and then reposition and resize the image on the page. In that way you will be able to work on top of the image and it will appear on every page.

Skills check ▶▶

There is more information on headers and footers on page 267.

Skills check ▶▶

There is more information on page numbering on page 268.

Headers and footers

Remember that anything inserted in a header or footer will appear on every page of the document. It is very useful to record the filename and date in the footer area of documents you are still working on.

Page numbering

You should apply page numbers to multi-page documents. The bottom right-hand corner is a good place to put the number. Remember too that you can hide the number on the first page – this is especially useful when the first page is also the cover or title page.

Skills check

There is more information on page breaks on page 266.

✓ **TiP**

A quick way to start a new page is to use the **Ctrl** and **Enter** keys together.

Skills check

There is more information on image resolution on page 394.

Page breaks

Do *not* use the **Enter** key repeatedly to move text on to a new page. Instead insert a page break by using **Insert, Break, Page break**. Make sure headings remain with the following text, and try not to end up with just one or two lines of a paragraph on the following page.

Using images

It is very likely that you will include images in your final documents, so their *quality* is an important consideration. The skills section on artwork and imaging software introduces bitmap and vector images (page 394) and shows you why enlarging an image may impair its quality.

This section also compares the *file sizes* of various image formats and looks at the most appropriate format for print and screen-based publications.

Whatever you intend to do with graphic images, you must remember to keep in mind the overall purpose of the document.

Transferring information to different types of software

After carrying out research into a topic, it is highly likely that you will want to include the results in a document or presentation. Earlier in this unit you will have used a spreadsheet to help you analyse results, and may well have produced a series of charts or graphs. These can be copied and pasted into the new document or presentation.

Think carefully about any headings you want. For example, do you need to insert them in the spreadsheet software, or will you type them in under the chart or graph. If you paste spreadsheets, charts or graphs using the **Edit, Paste Special** function in Word and select the **Paste link** option, any subsequent amendments to the data in the spreadsheet will automatically be reflected in the pasted chart or graph.

Paper publications

Types of paper publications

Organisations use a range of styles of documents. These include

- letters
- reports
- leaflets
- newsletters
- posters and flyers.

We will look at each of these in turn.

Writing letters

A business letter is a formal, written communication from one organisation or individual to another organisation or individual. The first impression of an organisation is often established as a result of the letter sent out. In much the same way, organisations form an impression of you based on the letters you send them. Clearly then, a letter should be written in an appropriate style and be well presented.

Letter format

Most organisations adopt what is called a *house style* to ensure that all their documents have a similar appearance. Many of these organisations have templates set up in their house style that employees are expected to use if they are writing letters. Nevertheless, each organisation has to rely on their employees' knowledge of how to compose a business letter.

Figure 1.26 (page 48) is a closer detailed look at one of the letters in Figure 1.25. This illustrates the most widespread style of layout and presentation. These are the main points to remember:

- Every line starts at the left margin – this is called *blocked style*.

- The only punctuation you will see is within the body or content of the letter. Notice that there are no commas or full stops in the reference or addressee details, nor after the opening or close. This style is called *open punctuation*.

- The postal town in the recipient's address is shown in capital letters with the postcode underneath (or on the same line if space on the page is tight).

Today, people with visual impairment can receive cassettes and CDs containing audio letters via the Internet. L-mail enables Internet users to submit typed text to its website, which is then recorded as an audio file and saved on the recipient's choice of media. There is a fee for using the service. Audio letters are posted from the UK to addresses worldwide. Braille letters can also be sent.

?○○ Think it over...

Figure 1.25 illustrates two letters produced in different writing styles.
○ Can you identify the common features in each letter?
○ What do you think is the purpose of each letter?
○ Do you think the styles of the letters suit the target audiences?

Figure 1.25 Two letters produced in different writing styles

○ Clear lines are left throughout the letter to separate the different sections or paragraphs. In most cases one clear line is sufficient. In order to leave enough space for the signature, five clear lines should be left. If a letter is short, you should leave bigger spaces so that more of the page is used – the spaces between the reference, date, addressee and greeting may be increased as long as the spacing is consistent. Within the letter itself you must keep to one clear line.

○ The close must match the opening. Did you notice that the two examples in Figure 1.25 are different in this respect?

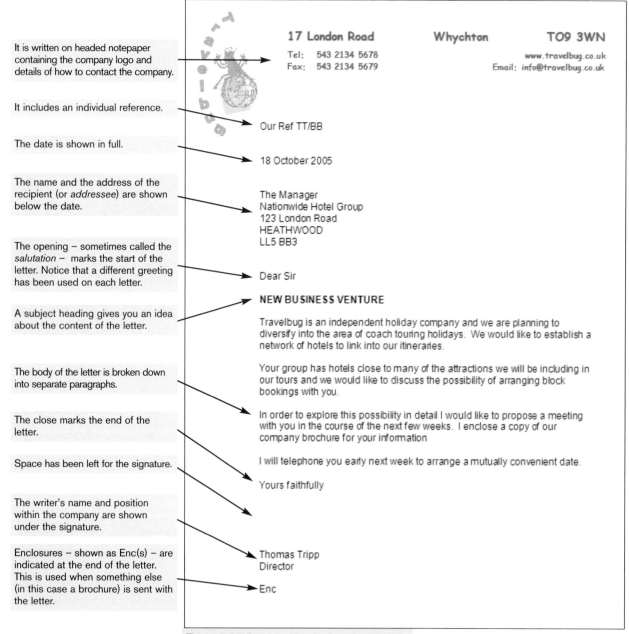

It is written on headed notepaper containing the company logo and details of how to contact the company.

It includes an individual reference.

The date is shown in full.

The name and the address of the recipient (or *addressee*) are shown below the date.

The opening – sometimes called the *salutation* – marks the start of the letter. Notice that a different greeting has been used on each letter.

A subject heading gives you an idea about the content of the letter.

The body of the letter is broken down into separate paragraphs.

The close marks the end of the letter.

Space has been left for the signature.

The writer's name and position within the company are shown under the signature.

Enclosures – shown as Enc(s) – are indicated at the end of the letter. This is used when something else (in this case a brochure) is sent with the letter.

17 London Road   Whychton   TO9 3WN

Tel: 543 2134 5678
Fax: 543 2134 5679

www.travelbug.co.uk
Email: info@travelbug.co.uk

Our Ref TT/BB

18 October 2005

The Manager
Nationwide Hotel Group
123 London Road
HEATHWOOD
LL5 BB3

Dear Sir

NEW BUSINESS VENTURE

Travelbug is an independent holiday company and we are planning to diversify into the area of coach touring holidays. We would like to establish a network of hotels to link into our itineraries.

Your group has hotels close to many of the attractions we will be including in our tours and we would like to discuss the possibility of arranging block bookings with you.

In order to explore this possibility in detail I would like to propose a meeting with you in the course of the next few weeks. I enclose a copy of our company brochure for your information

I will telephone you early next week to arrange a mutually convenient date.

Yours faithfully

Thomas Tripp
Director

Enc

Figure 1.26 An example of a business letter

Letter content

The first paragraph of a letter introduces the topic. You may be referring to a telephone conversation, a letter you have received or an advertisement you have seen. You are likely to start a letter with an opening sentence that begins like one of these:

> 'Thank you for your letter dated ...'
> 'I refer to our recent telephone conversation ...'
> 'I am writing to enquire ...'
> 'With reference to ...'

The next paragraph or paragraphs expand on the reason for writing. The final paragraph concludes the letter and often starts with a sentence like one of these:

> 'Please contact me if you would like further information.'
> 'I/We look forward to hearing from you.'
> 'Thank you for ...'
> 'I/We will contact you again in due course.'

Style of language

Business letters are written in a formal language style. Some organisations expect their employees to use the *plural* – 'we' and 'us' – if a letter is sent on behalf of the organisation. If you were writing a business letter as a private individual, you would use the *singular* – 'I' and 'me'. If you look at a selection of the business letters that come into your home you will soon get a good idea of the writing style to use.

Go out and try!

1 Write a letter to the marketing department of a car or bike manufacturer asking for information on their production processes to help you with a school or college project.

2 Write a letter to Tommy Tripp at Travelbug asking whether you can interview him at his office for information on a school or college travel project.

Skills Builder Task 4

At this stage you should be able to tackle the next task of the mini project introduced on page 13. Again, don't forget to study the scenario carefully so that you are clear about the project's objective.

Write a letter to parents and local residents to make them aware of the proposition from Prelude, also inviting them to attend a special meeting to discuss the proposal.

Assessment Hint

To achieve top marks you must do the following:

○ *Produce a range of suitable print and digital publications. The range will be specified in the summative project brief – make sure you cover the whole range!*

○ *Use appropriate structures and styles to ensure that the publication is suitable for the target audience and is the most appropriate way of presenting the information you are trying to get across.*
  – Should the writing style and tone be formal or informal?
  – Should you be using simple or complex language?
  – How can the information be best presented (text, charts, diagrams, etc.)?
  – Did you check the spelling and proofread thoroughly?
  – Did you take account of feedback?

○ *Respect copyright. If you quote someone's work, acknowledge it by using quotation marks and identifying the source.*

○ *Avoid plagiarism. Don't download material from the Internet or copy from a textbook and pretend you have written it. Finding a suitable source and identifying relevant information from that source does not make it your own work.*

Writing reports

A report is usually prepared following an investigation into something. The investigation might be necessary to find a way to put right a problem, to look at the possibility of introducing new working practices, or to pass on information following a study.

Report format

Reports are usually divided into four sections:

  ○ *Introduction.* This briefly explains the purpose of the report.

- *Methodology*. This provides details on how the investigation was undertaken.
- *Findings*. This records what the investigation revealed; that is, what the author found out about existing systems and practices. This section is often broken down under headings or divided into sub-sections.
- *Conclusions/recommendations*. The final section considers everything that has been found out. Where appropriate, the report will recommend suitable action to improve the situation that was investigated.

Unless it is very brief and simple, a formal report usually adopts a system known as *decimalised numbering*, as shown in Figure 1.27.

Skills check ▶▶

You can apply this style of heading numbering through **Format**, **Bullets and Numbering**, **Outline Numbered**. Refer to the exercise starting on page 258 in the word processing chapter to see how to do this.

Think it over ...

Find out what report templates are available on your computer.

```
1 xxxxxxxxx
2 xxxxxxxxx
        2.1 xxxxxxxxx
        2.2 xxxxxxxxx
3 xxxxxxxxx
        3.1 xxxxxxxxx
                3.1.1 xxxxxxxxx
                3.1.2 xxxxxxxxx
        3.2 xxxxxxxxx
                3.2.1 xxxxxxxxx
                3.2.2 xxxxxxxxx
4 xxxxxxxxx
```

Figure 1.27 Decimalised numbering system used in reports

Creating leaflets

Leaflets are frequently used to provide general information. The leaflets illustrated here serve a variety of purposes.

For example, the leaflets in Figure 1.28(a) and (b) were issued on behalf of government departments, and are intended only to provide facts. Their purpose is to bring the public up to date on certain matters. The leaflet in Figure 1.28(c) was produced by the publisher of this book to advertise the range of products available and to persuade potential customers to purchase their books. Each of the leaflets in this series follows a similar design. Notice that different font sizes have been used on the inside pages for the headings.

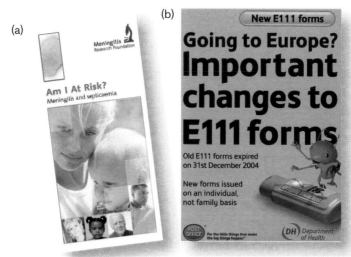

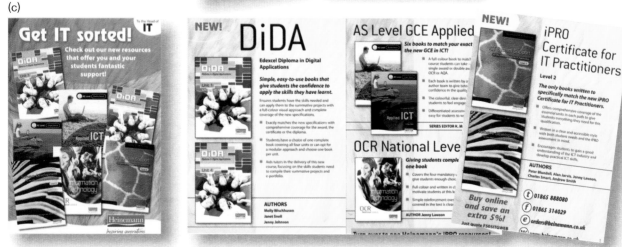

Figure 1.28 Leaflets issued (a) on behalf of a charity, (b) by The Post Office Ltd., and (c) by Harcourt Education Ltd.

Although these leaflets serve different purposes, there are some common features:

- They provide information on a product or service.
- They are colourful and include relevant images.
- The front page contains a short 'snappy' message.
- Leaflets from the same organisation adopt a distinctive house style.
- They include a contact telephone number or web address for further information.

Most such leaflets fold down to A5 size and open up to present more detailed information.

Front of sheet   **Back of sheet**

(a)

Back cover of Page 4	Front cover of Page 1

Page 2	Page 3

(b)

The page on view when opened	Back	Front

Inside 1	Inside 2	Inside 3

Figure 1.29 You must be careful to assemble the pages in the right order: (a) a single fold, and (b) a double fold

If you produce a leaflet it will probably be printed double-sided, and you must be careful to assemble the pages in the right order! Figures 1.29(a) and (b) show the principles of getting this right.

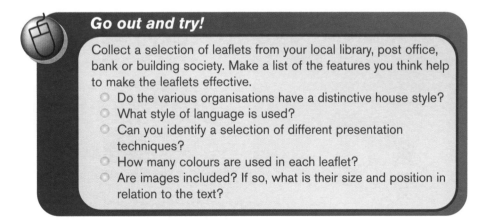

Go out and try!

Collect a selection of leaflets from your local library, post office, bank or building society. Make a list of the features you think help to make the leaflets effective.

- Do the various organisations have a distinctive house style?
- What style of language is used?
- Can you identify a selection of different presentation techniques?
- How many colours are used in each leaflet?
- Are images included? If so, what is their size and position in relation to the text?

Skills Builder Task 5

At this stage you should be able to tackle the next task of the mini project introduced on page 13. Again, don't forget to study the scenario carefully so that you are clear about the project's objective.

Prepare an informative leaflet for other students, to present the facts that you have discovered.

Creating newsletters

Newsletters are a popular way of keeping people up to date with what is happening in an organisation. Sometimes they are used within an organisation as a way of informing staff, and sometimes they are used externally to keep in touch with customers. They may be sent to customers in the post or by email.

A newsletter usually has a banner heading that stretches across the top of the page. The newsletter will have several headings and short paragraphs written on a variety of subjects, and will usually include relevant images. Newsletters are usually presented in columns.

Figure 1.30 A selection of newsletters

Posters and flyers

Posters and flyers are used to attract our attention. The message might be saying 'buy me', 'watch me' or 'visit me'. The poster or flyer will usually be short, to the point, eye-catching, colourful and designed to persuade the reader. They will almost certainly include a significant amount of white space and sometimes a border to help draw the eye towards the message.

Flyers frequently find their way on to our doormats or inside the local newspaper because they are a relatively inexpensive way for local companies to advertise their products or services. Occasionally new businesses opening in your area may hand flyers out to passers-by in an attempt to entice them into the shop.

Go out and try!

1 Collect some examples of flyers, possibly including those that are delivered to your own home. Compare the information they contain.
2 Look at posters on the noticeboard in your school or college, your library and other public places. What do you think makes some more effective than others?

TiP

Flyers are usually printed on A5 paper. There is a very simple way to produce an A5 flyer if you do not have A5 paper. First produce the flyer to A4 size using your computer's word processor and then copy the contents onto page 2 of the document. Then select to print two pages per sheet, as shown in Figure 1.31. Each flyer will then be equivalent to A5 size after cutting.

Select this to print two pages per sheet.

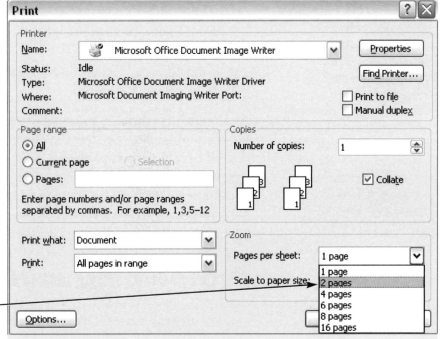

Figure 1.31 The dialogue box that allows printing of two pages per sheet

Skills Builder Task 6

At this stage you should be able to tackle the next task of the mini project introduced on page 13. Again, don't forget to study the scenario carefully so that you are clear about the project's objective.

Produce a poster to be displayed in local public places to invite the public to attend the special meeting.

On-screen publications

Nowadays more and more documents are being prepared electronically for viewing on a computer screen. These can be in many different formats, such as websites, slide presentations and information points.

The National Health Service (NHS) is introducing information points in a variety of public places including libraries, supermarkets and chemists, as well as hospitals. These are in the form of touch-screen computers and give a guide to common health problems.

Many on-screen publications use features that you will learn about if you study for the multimedia unit. These include

- creating and linking web pages or slides using hyperlinks
- using frames to position text and objects in a slide presentation
- using different backgrounds and transitions to enhance a multimedia production.

As always it is crucial to thoroughly test and check your work by proofreading it and checking the layout. It is essential that you ensure that all hyperlinks and pathways in a website or slide show work. It is very easy to edit your work and forget to ensure that the change has not interfered with the links. Remember also that not everyone uses the same computer system or browser. You must therefore check that your end product will work on a variety of systems.

Prototyping and testing

Quality assurance is explained in the chapter on standard ways of working (page 76), and you should be familiar with the many tools

TiP

Just because you can include video clips and blinking text, it does not mean that you should. Having too many features will detract from the information you want to put across, so use these effects only if they enhance your message. It is no use having too many gimmicks but little information.

that are available to help you present documents that are accurate and clearly understood.

However, these tools alone will not guarantee that you produce professional-looking documents. The final check must come from you – by carefully proofreading every document you produce to ensure that it is accurate, easy to understand, and says what you intended it to say.

You must remember to check everything you produce for

- accuracy
- clarity
- readability
- consistency
- layout
- overall fitness for its purpose.

In addition to the checks listed above, your on-screen publications will require additional testing to make sure that all the features (such as buttons and links) actually work, enhance the publication and do not detract by being too fancy or gimmicky.

When you are happy with your publications, remember to ask other people to review them for you. Listen carefully to any comments and feedback offered, and be prepared to modify your publications if necessary.

Skills Builder Task 7

At this stage you should be able to tackle these tasks of the mini project introduced on page 13. Again, don't forget to study the scenario carefully so that you are clear about the project's objective.

(1) Prepare a short presentation to be given at a special meeting of parents and governors to support the findings of your research.

(2) Design a single web page to present the same information you used for the poster and leaflet.

(3) When you have finished your project, review your work. Produce a short evaluation outlining how well it met the requirements explained in the scenario and any aspects you feel could be improved. Justify your comments. For example, if you say the poster is effective, explain what makes it effective. If something needs changing, explain why and how. You should attach to your evaluation the records of the feedback you received and the actions you took in response.

(4) Finally, present your work in an e-portfolio using suitable file formats. Your e-portfolio should show the following:
- Home page
- Table of contents
- Report outlining the results of your investigation using secondary sources
- Database reports
- Letter to parents and local residents
- Presentation to be given at the special meeting
- Poster informing the general public of the special meeting
- Leaflet for your peers.

You should also include some supporting evidence:
- Project plan
- References to secondary sources and links if appropriate
- Evidence of data collection using a survey
- Questionnaire used for the survey, including evidence of testing
- Evidence of the design and implementation of the database
- Spreadsheet showing the survey results and the formulas you used
- Storyboard for your presentation
- Review and evaluation of the project, including feedback from others.

Skills check

For more information on preparing your e-portfolio, including suitable file formats for saving your work, refer to page 509.

★ Assessment Hint

You will find that the requirements for the e-portfolio, project planning, and review and evaluation are almost identical for each of the units.

Unit 2 · Multimedia

Introduction

Since the early days of the Internet and personal computing there have been rapid advances in technology. Nowadays, information communicated using ICT is not limited to text, but may also include a variety of other components such as graphics, sound, animations and video, together with interactive features such as buttons. When information is presented using a combination of these components it is known as *multimedia*. Examples are websites, computer games, presentations, e-learning CD-ROMs and DVDs.

LEARNING OUTCOMES

After working through this chapter you should be able to

- ✓ investigate a range of multimedia products and assess their appropriateness

- ✓ design new multimedia products, using existing components together with new components, such as a video or sound recording, created by yourself

- ✓ implement the end product, ensuring that it is tested and amended as necessary.

How will I be assessed?

You will be given a project brief for this unit and you will be required to create multimedia products for a specified audience and purpose. The project brief will specify exactly what you will be required to produce, how you will present your findings, and to whom you will present them. You can expect to spend about 30 hours working on the assessment for this unit.

You will be assessed on **six** separate activities as follows:

1 Plan and manage the project
2 Design multimedia products
3 Collect, edit and create multimedia components
4 Develop multimedia products
5 Present multimedia products in an e-portfolio
6 Review the project.

Read the project brief carefully, as it will give you hints and tips on how to complete the assessment successfully. The skills chapters provide help on the various software applications you can choose to use. In addition you will find detailed guidance throughout this chapter and we advise that you also refer to the following chapters, which contain specific help on completing the assessment:

- Project planning
- Review and evaluation
- Creating an e-portfolio.

Skills file

As explained in the introduction to this book, many of the skills are relevant to all units, but in some cases extra skills are required for a particular unit. The table below lists all the skills required to complete this unit successfully. The pages where you will find these skills explained are identified in the Page column. The skills shown in **bold** you will not have studied in Unit 1.

WORD-PROCESSING SOFTWARE	Page
enter, cut, copy, paste and move text	248
use paragraph formatting features:	
alignment	255
bullets and numbering	257
tabs	260
indents	262
format text:	
font type and font size	251
bold, underline, italic	253
colour	253

PRESENTATION SOFTWARE

ARTWORK AND IMAGING SOFTWARE

MULTIMEDIA AUTHORING SOFTWARE

	Page
○ create simple web pages	450
○ **use colour options:**	
● **contrast**	**459**
● **pattern**	**457**
● **background**	**457**
○ create and select components:	
● text	461
● images	465
● sound	475
● **video**	**476**
● **animation**	**477**
○ create and modify tables	463
○ edit text:	
● fonts	454, 460
● alignment	462
● bullets	462
● line spacing	462
○ edit images:	
● align, rotate and flip	391
● crop and resize	289, 389
● colour	398
○ **optimise resolution and file size**	**394, 466**
○ add lines and simple shapes	467
○ **use hyperlinks to link pages**	**470**
○ **create interactive components:**	
● **buttons**	**473**
● **text links**	**470**
● **hotspots**	**474**
● **rollovers**	**469**
○ **implement animations, moving images and sound**	**399, 402, 409, 475, 476**

? Think it over ...

Have you used an interactive CD-ROM? If so, think about these questions:

- How easy did you find it to use use?
- What features did you find helpful?
- Was there anything that you found annoying?

If you have never used an interactive CD-ROM, go to your school, college or public library and choose one to look at and test.

? Think it over ...

Conduct a survey within your class to find out:

- What system do they use to play games?
- Which is their favourite game?
- What multimedia features do they like?
- Which features do they find annoying?

Investigating multimedia products

It is essential that you investigate how multimedia is used in various contexts before you plan a multimedia production for your own project. You will learn how different components, such as sound or graphics, are used to convey a message. By doing this, you will acquire a good understanding of the possibilities offered by a range of multimedia products.

Multimedia in context

Multimedia in education

You may have used computer-based e-learning packages or other training materials at your school or college. Your teachers might have given a PowerPoint presentation to explain a topic, or shown a DVD or video on a particular subject. You may also be familiar with interactive CD-ROMs, which assist learning about different topics and make the subjects come alive.

Multimedia in entertainment

You may be one of the many people who enjoy playing games – either on your computer or on a games console such as X-box or Playstation – and watching the latest films on DVD or video.

Figure 2.1 Selection of video games

Multimedia in marketing and advertising

Successful businesses make full use of multimedia to promote their products and services. A website is an essential tool for most businesses today. They may also give out CD-ROMs that include a presentation on their company or their latest brochure. Companies may use trade fairs or exhibitions to demonstrate their goods and services. Here they can utilise a range of multimedia products, such as multimedia presentations, videos or access to their website. Customers can subscribe to a company's mailing list to receive emails updating them on new products (Figure 2.2).

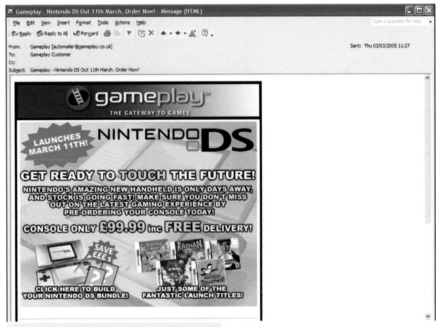

Figure 2.2 Example of marketing by email

Figure 2.3 A Pocket PC

Multimedia in publishing

Publishing has changed dramatically since the development of multimedia. Although many people still prefer to see 'hard copy' (publications printed on paper) more and more companies are using 'soft copy' (electronic format). Via the Internet it is possible to purchase books in electronic format that can be read on a PC or handheld device.

Some people subscribe to receive up-to-date news from a company by email. Newsletters such as this are also known as *e-zines*, an example of which is shown in Figure 2.4.

Figure 2.4 Example of an e-zine

Another fairly new phenomenon is the web log, or *blog* for short. Blogs are online diaries where people write about all sorts of things, from their daily lives to views of politics, music or other subjects that are of interest to them.

Multimedia in virtual reality

Virtual reality is experienced using, for example, 3D goggles so that the user feels that he or she is within a virtual world. Virtual reality can simulate a real environment, such as the interior of a building, or an imaginary environment, such as in a game or educational adventure. Virtual tours are being used increasingly on websites to promote a service or product. For example, estate agents may include a tour of a property for sale in order to increase interest in it.

Virtual prototyping (sometimes referred to as *digital prototyping*) is being used more and more by businesses for the development of new products. Virtual prototyping tests models of products created using special 3D modelling software. This stops companies having to build a physical prototype, and so has the advantage of reducing development time and cost.

Think it over ...

Try to find an example of a virtual reality tour. You may be able to find something on the Internet, or while you are out shopping. Alternatively, find out whether someone in your family has experienced a virtual reality tour and ask him or her to describe the experience.

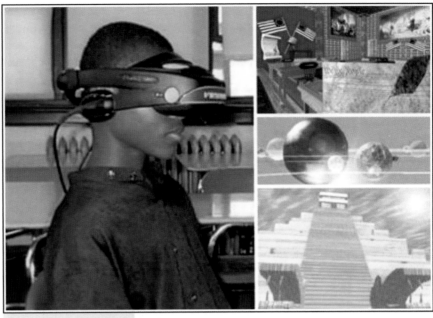

Figure 2.5 Virtual reality

Think it over ...

You have almost certainly used touch-screen technology yourself. Next time you are out and about, make a list of all the examples of touch-screen technology you come across. Wherever possible, try it out and assess how easy it is to use. Compare your experiences with those of others in your class.

Multimedia in public access

Many public services and businesses – councils, libraries, museums, building societies, and so on – have introduced touch-screen public access points. These enable people to access information without needing to speak to a member of staff.

Many shops offer a wedding-present service. Some of these shops use touch-screen technology for people in the shop to search the wedding list and choose their gifts.

Figure 2.6 A public access point

Evaluating multimedia products

It is important that you evaluate the techniques and technology used in each type of multimedia product you investigate. You can use the prompts in Figure 2.7 to help you do this.

- *Ease of access*. How accessible was the product? What accessibility features have been used? Did you need special software and equipment? If you had a disability, such as being partially sighted, would the product be accessible?

- *Ease of navigation*. How easy was it to navigate around the product? Did you get lost? Was it easy to return to the home page of a website? Did the product have a clear structure?

- *Appropriateness of the content*. Was the content of the product what you expected? For example, if the title of a CD-ROM is 'Learn Basic French' and the content is an advanced course in French, the content would not be appropriate.

- *Impact*. Was the product interesting and memorable, or did you find it dull and boring?

- *User interface*. Was the user interface easy to use? Was there a help feature to assist new users?

- *Interactivity*. Were there interactive features that allowed you to control your progress? Did you get a different response according to the options you chose? Were text boxes used for you to enter information?

- *Use of colour*. Has colour been used effectively? For example, an online clothing catalogue would be very unattractive to customers if all the clothes were shown in black and white – the catalogue would be little better if the colours of the clothes were not shown accurately.

- *Mix of different types of components such as text, graphics, sound and video*. Has an appropriate mix of components been used? Sometimes, simple is best. For example, a web page with too many components on one page can put visitors off rather than being appealing. Did the components work together?

- *Use of presentation techniques*. Was the text readable, or were the font sizes too small? Did the presentation move from one subject to another in a logical sequence? Were the timings right, or were they too fast or too slow? If it was a product produced by a company for marketing purposes, did it reflect the corporate image?

- *Fitness for the intended audience*. For example, was the product aimed at the correct age group? A CD-ROM with an interactive brochure for clothes aimed at the 50+ age group would not be very effective if the images used were of young people modelling the clothes!

Figure 2.7 Evaluation criteria for multimedia products

Think it over...

Working in pairs, choose one multimedia product to evaluate against the headings in the list above. Try to choose a different product from the rest of your class. When everyone has finished, compare the results.

Designing multimedia products

Every multimedia product will have a different purpose. How effective it is will depend on how well it has been designed and whether it meets its objectives.

For your project, you will be designing several multimedia products in a *multimedia showcase*. Before you start the design stage of each product you should consider the following:

- Is the product meant to entertain, educate, inform or sell? The overall purpose will influence the design.
- Who is it for? In other words, who is the intended audience? You need to take into account aspects such as age group, gender, location, special interests and language.
- Where will it be used? For example, will it be viewed on a computer or as a presentation in a large hall?
- What content must it have? Think about everything you should include to ensure that the product meets its intended purpose. How will you choose to represent the information? Should you include text, images, animation, video, audio, and so on?

Your main aim will always be to produce multimedia products that are fit for purpose and meet the needs of the intended end-users.

Having considered the above points, you will need to make detailed decisions about the product's content and components, and its structure.

Deciding on content and components

You will need to choose the most appropriate methods for representing the information. This will depend on your product's intended purpose.

There will be a limit to the overall size of the e-portfolio for final assessment of Unit 2. The summative project brief (SPB) will specify exactly what the limit will be. You must ensure that you do not exceed the limit.

Text

What information, if any, should be represented by text? Think about whether the text should be in long paragraphs, or in short snappy sentences. Do you need text on every page of a presentation or

TiP

*Remember that you do **not** have to use every method available for representing the information. Multimedia products that try to include too many components can end up being very off-putting for the end-user. Remember the rule: if it doesn't add to the content, leave it out!*

website? Will you write the text yourself, or do you need to ask permission from the source to use it?

Images

Images might be photographs, pictures, or clip art. Where will you get the images from? What information is best represented by images? Which images are appropriate for your target audience?

Tables

Do you need to include tables to represent data? Will you use data imported from a spreadsheet or a database? Are you going to use tables to present text?

Animations

Are animations *relevant* to the content?

Sound

Should you use sound – music or commentary – to accompany your production? Think about your target audience when you choose music or sound effects for a production. Ensure that any music used is in context and suitable for the likely end-users.

> ### ✔ TiP
>
> *If you are using speech to accompany a production, you must make sure that the person talking speaks loudly enough for the audience to hear. You should make sure that the speech is delivered using natural speech patterns, with highs and lows, and different pace at times. For example, important points should be spoken at a slower pace.*

> **? Think it over...**
>
> When looking at television programmes or films, listen to the accompanying music. Think about the following:
> - Was the music popular at the time depicted in the programme?
> - Was a variety of music used?
> - Did the sound effects enhance the mood of the storyline?

> ### ✔ TiP
>
> *You must take into account copyright issues if you are using a video produced by someone else. The same is true of all components of a multimedia production.*

Video

You have probably heard the expression 'a picture is worth a thousand words'. On that basis, a well-presented video clip, used wisely, is worth a small book!

Do, however, bear in mind always that the files of video clips, even when compressed, tend to be very large. An hour-long video, for example, can take as much as 800 MB of storage space!

Links

No doubt you will want to include hyperlinks within your multimedia production. You have learned about absolute and relative cell references in spreadsheets during Unit 1. It is also possible to include absolute and relative hyperlinks in a multimedia production.

An *absolute hyperlink* will always give the full address (URL) of the destination document. Figure 2.8 shows an example of the absolute hyperlink used by Thomas Tripp in the Travelbug website. This links to a website giving the current weather in Paris.

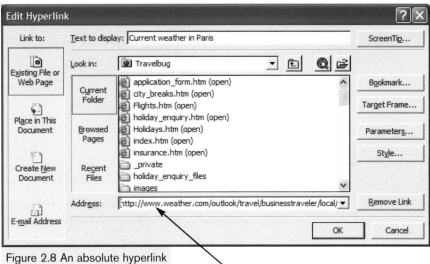

Figure 2.8 An absolute hyperlink

An absolute hyperlink

In contrast, a *relative hyperlink* will not include the full address, only the address relative to the current document. To understand this better, look at Figure 2.9. This shows the hyperlink Thomas Tripp used to add a link from Travelbug's *Our Holidays* page to the *City Breaks* page in the same website.

TiP

*When you are creating a hyperlink to a **different** website, you must use an absolute link. When you are creating a link within **your own** website, either type of hyperlink will work. If you use relative links, you will be able to move the whole website without breaking its internal navigation links. This allows you to test a website on your PC before uploading it to the Web.*

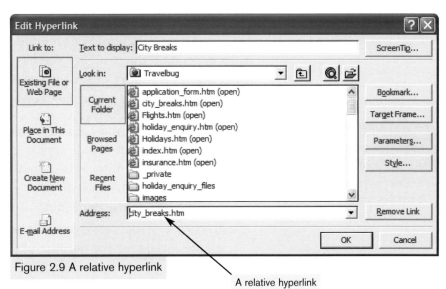

Figure 2.9 A relative hyperlink

A relative hyperlink

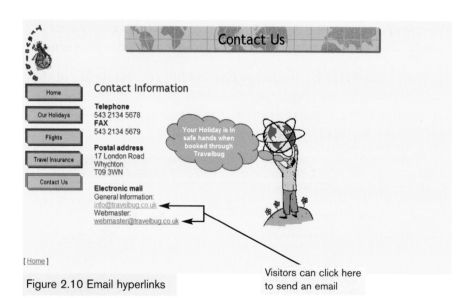

Figure 2.10 Email hyperlinks

Visitors can click here
to send an email

You may also wish to include an *email hyperlink* for visitors to click on. The link launches the visitor's email program (if necessary), opens a new email and automatically includes the correct email address in the 'To:' box. Thomas Tripp used this type of hyperlink on Travelbug's *Contact Us* page (Figure 2.10).

Deciding on structure

Once you have considered the content and components of your multimedia product, you must decide on the structure. The two alternative approaches you should consider are

- sequential
- hierarchical.

Detailed descriptions of these are given later in this chapter (page 86). First we will look at how visitors can be guided around your product.

Navigation

The *navigation system* of your multimedia production will very much depend on the structure you have chosen, as it will affect how the end-user will move around it and access the information.

A good navigation system

- is easily learned and consistent throughout the product (for example, navigation aids appear in the same position throughout)
- appears in context and offers alternatives (so that users do not have to rely on the **Back** buttons of their browsers)
- gives clear visual messages with understandable labels
- is appropriate for the purpose of the product.

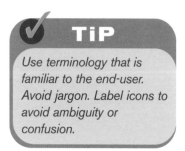

TiP

Use terminology that is familiar to the end-user. Avoid jargon. Label icons to avoid ambiguity or confusion.

Navigation aids include

- internal links
- backtracking
- an overview, site map or table of contents (index)
- a guided tour.

Links and buttons

Users will need to have clear prompts that tell them where they are and where to go next. Thomas Tripp has used both links and buttons on the Travelbug home page to allow visitors to navigate around the website (Figure 2.11).

Backtracking

Figure 2.12 shows an example of backtracking in a web directory. Even though you are looking at search results in a specific category, you can easily return to any of the higher-level (more general) categories.

Figure 2.11 Navigation aids

Buttons   Hyperlinks

Jargon buster

Backtracking allows a user to return to a certain set point earlier in his or her visit.

Figure 2.12 A web directory with backtracking

Backtracking link to more general category

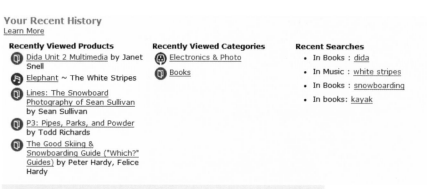

Figure 2.13 Amazon's 'Recent History' – a form of backtracking

When a website's purpose is to sell things, it is important that users can find their way around easily. Amazon uses backtracking (as shown in Figure 2.13) to allow shoppers to quickly return to items that they have recently viewed; perhaps, after browsing some products, they have decided what they want to buy.

A useful feature of hyperlinks, which aids navigation, is that a link will (by default) change colour once it has been visited. An unvisited link is usually blue, changing to purple after being visited. The colours and styling can be changed by the designer.

Overview, site map or index

Many multimedia productions provide an overview, a site map or a table of contents (index) to familiarise users with the product before they start to browse. Figure 2.14 shows the site map of a very useful website for multimedia students: macromedia – see www.heinemann.co.uk/hotlinks (express code 0069P) for more.

? Think it over ...

If you were designing a quiz, which backtracking features might you include? Think about the different paths a user might take through the quiz.

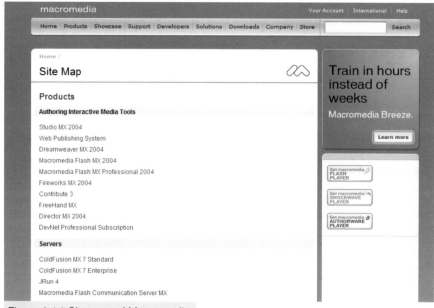

Figure 2.14 Site map of Macromedia

Large websites, such as the BBC's – see www.heinemann.co.uk/hotlinks (express code 0069P), have indexes to help visitors access information easily (Figure 2.15).

Figure 2.15 Index of the BBC's website

Figure 2.16 shows the index for a Learn Spanish CD–ROM. When the user points at a button with the mouse, the image in the centre changes to provide an overview of the topic.

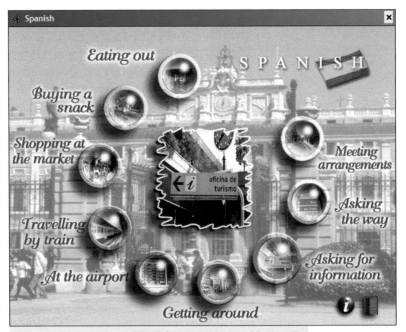

Figure 2.16 Index for a CD–ROM from Vecktor Multimedia

Guided tour

Many multimedia products include a guided tour that a user can work through (at his or her own pace) as an introduction to the product. These tours go over all the main features so that the end-user can become fully familiar with the product before beginning to use it.

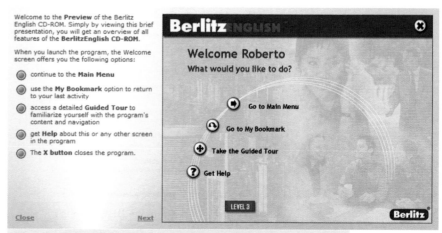

Figure 2.17 A guided tour for a CD-ROM from Berlitz International

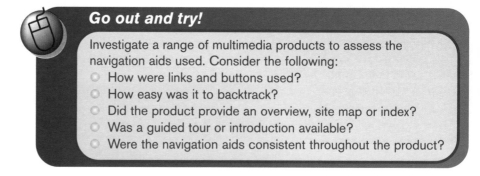

Go out and try!

Investigate a range of multimedia products to assess the navigation aids used. Consider the following:

○ How were links and buttons used?
○ How easy was it to backtrack?
○ Did the product provide an overview, site map or index?
○ Was a guided tour or introduction available?
○ Were the navigation aids consistent throughout the product?

Interactivity

Menus

A *menu system* is an easy way to give the end-users choices and control over how they use the product. A menu system will usually have a series of sub-menus – just as in application software such as Microsoft Word – from which the user can make choices.

Good menus should

○ have no more than 12 options presented on any one list
○ be carefully structured (for example by being in alphabetical order, or with the most commonly used options first, or in the logical order in which the options will be selected)

- be consistent throughout the system (**Exit** is always the last option in the **File** menu of Microsoft software)
- avoid abbreviations and jargon.

Text boxes

Text input boxes allow specific information from the user to be collected. They are often used on forms on websites. For example, Thomas Tripp used text boxes on Travelbug's Cruise Club application form (Figure 2.18).

Text boxes used on an application form

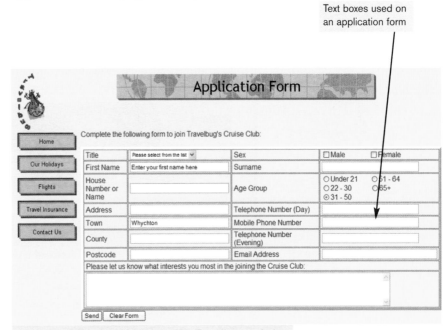

Figure 2.18 Text boxes used on the Travelbug website

Good layout

It is very important to achieve the best layout for each screen of a multimedia product. The following aspects should be taken into account in order to achieve a screen that is appealing and that minimises the time required to find information:

- balance
- sequence
- displayed size
- emphasis
- unity.

We will look at each of these in turn.

Balance

You need to ensure that each element of a screen is correctly *proportioned* so that you achieve a sense of evenness. You can use *symmetrical balance* by arranging the components on a screen as horizontal or vertical mirrored images on both sides of a centre line. The design of the home page of www.heinemann.co.uk is an example of this (Figure 2.19).

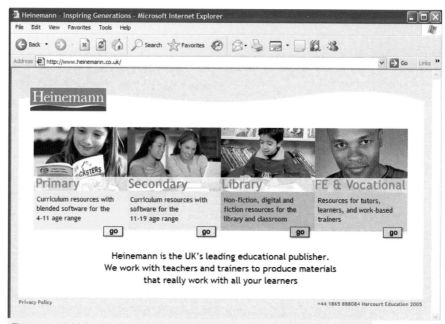

Figure 2.19 Heinemann's home page – a symmetrical balanced screen

Alternatively, *asymmetrical balance* is achieved by arranging non-identical components on both sides of the centre line (Figure 2.20).

Sequence

The sequence in which the information is presented should be logical. It should follow the processes involved and correspond to other information sources used in the product.

Displayed size

You need to ensure that the proportions of your product are correct for the hardware on which it will be viewed.

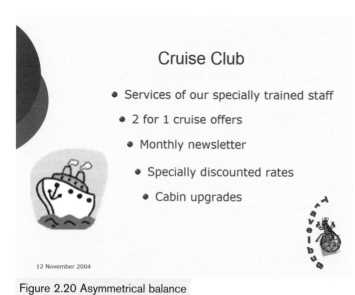

Figure 2.20 Asymmetrical balance

Pages should not look too small on modern high-resolution monitors, but should still look acceptable on lower-specification equipment. The proportions of graphics and other components used should be appropriate for the end product.

Emphasis

You need to ensure that the layout puts emphasis on the most important aspects of a screen. If you want the user to see one aspect first, this should be given the greatest emphasis.

Unity

Unity can be achieved by maintaining consistency in shapes, colours, text styles and themes. Using consistent borders around information on a screen will help you to achieve unity. Common items on different displays and screens should appear in roughly the same positions on the display. Also, you can help to improve the readability of a screen by *grouping* items in a display rather than scattering the components. Grouping also highlights the structure of information being presented and helps the user to locate specific information.

Good use of fonts

No doubt you will use text in most of the multimedia products you produce. If you use fonts wisely, they can be a major asset for conveying a message, but incorrectly used fonts can detract from the message.

You will need to consider the style of text, and what typefaces and sizes to use.

Guidelines for using text

- Do not use too many fonts in one document: two in a one-page document and no more than four in a longer publication.
- Use *complementary* fonts together – usually a sans serif font (without the little tails on the ends of a character) for headings and titles and a serif font (with tails) for the body text (see Figure 2.21).

> Arial is an example of a sans serif font.
>
> Times New Roman is a complementary font to Arial and is an example of a serif font.

Figure 2.21 Two popular complementary fonts

Jargon buster

Unity means that all the parts of a product *look right for the part*, and hang together comfortably.

 TiP

In recent years the number of fonts available has increased dramatically, and there are more and more exotic fonts. Be warned! When designing a multi-media product for use on a computer, not all fonts are available on every machine. If the font you chose is not available on the user's machine, the user's software will convert it to another font – such as Courier, which is now considered very old-fashioned.

- Use upper-case and lower-case text for presentations – it is quicker and easier to read.
- Words in all upper-case can be used if you need to attract attention, such as in a warning (Figure 2.22).
  - Restrict the length of text lines to about 60 characters.
  - Limit the text on a page to one-third of the area.
  - A font size of 12 points should be regarded as the minimum for PC screens. You should use 14 points or higher for screens with poorer resolution than a normal desktop monitor. Where a screen is to be used in a public place, 16 points should be used to make the text readable by people with visual impairments.
- Keep sentences short and concise. Never split sentences over pages.
- Avoid technical jargon and abbreviations unless the product is for users who will be familiar with them in their daily routine. Ensure that abbreviations are used in a consistent way throughout the production. Give an explanation of abbreviations, either through an online help facility or in accompanying documentation.

WARNING
DO NOT PRESS THE BIG RED BUTTON

Figure 2.22 A warning sign with upper-case (capital) letters

> ✔ **TiP**
>
> If you are designing a product that will be used in a public place, you need to take into account the varying eyesight of users. A clear, fairly large font should be used. Long blocks of text are difficult to read, and should be broken up into shorter paragraphs.

Good use of colour

Colour plays an extremely important role in a multimedia product because it can be used to enhance and emphasise information. It makes the screen display more attractive, can reduce errors in interpretation, and can be very good at directing an end-user to a part of the screen that you want to highlight. Colours can be used for contrasting items, in patterns and for the background and borders.

You need to choose colours to suit the purpose of your product. For instance, if you are producing a multimedia product that uses cartoons and is designed for children, bright colours will be appropriate. On the other hand, for a production aimed at adults on the history of World War II you will probably want to use more subdued colours, or even consider using just black and white in places.

Here are some guidelines for using colours:

- Don't use too many different colours. By limiting colours, you can avoid difficulties in maintaining balance in your production.

○ Make sure that the product can be used effectively without colour, so that you are not making access difficult for someone with an eyesight impairment.

Figure 2.23 Two BBC web pages: bright CBBC home page and subdued history of World War II – see www.heinemann.co.uk/hotlinks (express code 0069P)

Figure 2.24 Use of colour for text – the good and the bad

Figure 2.25 Slide with an inappropriate background pattern

- If you are using a contrasting colour for text against a coloured background, make sure that you do not use a colour that makes it difficult to read. Look at Figure 2.24 – which slide is easier to read?
- Choose the background pattern of a screen very carefully. You should avoid using strong non-random patterns in colours that contrast, or patterns that overpower the screen. You will see that in Figure 2.25 the text on the screen is very difficult to read.

Go out and try!

Look at a range of websites. Identify one site where you consider the use of font styles, sizes and overall use of colour to be effective, and another where it is ineffective. In both cases write down your reasons.

Ensuring maximum accessibility

Access to your product is an extremely important issue. Some potential users might be hard of hearing or have an eyesight impairment. Others might not be able to read very easily, or understand what they read. Others may not be able to use a keyboard or mouse.

Here are some guidelines on accessibility:

- When using images that contain essential information, provide a text alternative.
- Provide text captions and transcripts of audio content.
- Provide text descriptions of video content.
- Ensure that text hyperlinks make sense when read out of context. For example, avoid 'Click here'.
- Use headings, lists and a consistent structure when designing a screen layout.

TiP

Site maps and indexes help all end-users to navigate around a product, and they aid accessibility.

Businesses today need to ensure that their websites comply with the Disability Discrimination Act 2004, and failure to do so could result in prosecution. Also, there is a Web Accessibility Initiative (WAI) associated with the World Wide Web Consortium (W3C), which works with organisations throughout the world to increase the accessibility of the Web. Guidelines have been produced that web developers follow to ensure that their sites conform to one of three levels – from **A**, the most basic standard, to **AAA** which denotes a high standard of accessibility. You can find more information about this via www.heinemann.co.uk/hotlinks (express code 0069P).

Go out and try!

Use a search engine to find the website for the Royal National Institute for the Blind. Make a list of the features they have used to make their site accessible.

Flow charts and storyboards

As you have learned, it is important to plan carefully all the individual aspects of your production *before* you start creating it. Flow charts and storyboards can help you to do this.

Flow charts

A flow chart can be used as a graphical representation of the paths a user can take through a multimedia product. It will indicate the sequences and decision points, as well as starting and stopping points.

Flow charts are an important tool when designing a multimedia product as they help you to avoid leaving out essential steps in a process. Flow charts are not 'set in stone' – they can be modified as the development of the product progresses.

Figure 2.26 shows common symbols that are used in flow charts, and Figure 2.27 shows an example of their use.

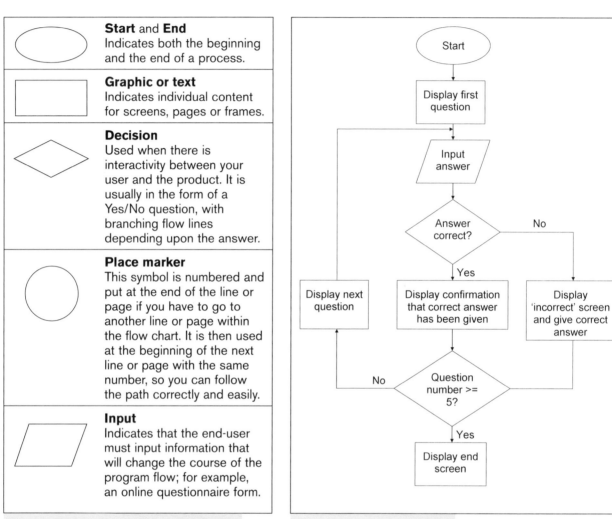

Start and End	Indicates both the beginning and the end of a process.
Graphic or text	Indicates individual content for screens, pages or frames.
Decision	Used when there is interactivity between your user and the product. It is usually in the form of a Yes/No question, with branching flow lines depending upon the answer.
Place marker	This symbol is numbered and put at the end of the line or page if you have to go to another line or page within the flow chart. It is then used at the beginning of the next line or page with the same number, so you can follow the path correctly and easily.
Input	Indicates that the end-user must input information that will change the course of the program flow; for example, an online questionnaire form.

Figure 2.26 Flow chart symbols and their uses

Figure 2.27 A simple flow chart

Use the following checklist when producing a flow chart:

- Are all the major elements of the production indicated?
- Are all the elements clearly labelled?
- Is the sequence of the elements clear, with no gaps or dead-ends?
- Is the sequence of events logical from the end-user's point of view?
- Have the flow-charting symbols been used correctly?

Storyboards

Whereas a flow chart will focus on the user's progress through a system, a storyboard allows far more detailed illustration of the

TiP

*Take time to create a detailed storyboard for each screen. If a storyboard **looks** wrong, the end product will probably be wrong too. It is easier to spot omissions at the design stage if you produce a storyboard.*

contents of each element. Storyboards are used to map out the layout and content of each screen. You will use a storyboard to consider where the different components will be used on each screen, as well as aspects such as what images will be seen and for how long, and what audio and text will accompany the images.

A good storyboard should

- include a brief statement of what the end product will be
- state the aim of the product
- state any knowledge that the end-users are assumed to have (for example, if your product is about chart music, it might be acceptable to assume that the end-users will be familiar with the latest bands)
- give a visual representation of the screen layout
- define any other data or information that you may need
- list any resources, such as images, audio or video, to be included
- define links between each screen
- define navigation to and from each screen.

You will find Figure 2.28 useful as a template for each screen in a storyboard.

Figure 2.28 A storyboard template

Screen description	*Give a brief description of the screen*
Screen layout	*Draw your intended layout*
Text attributes	*Fonts used, sizes and attributes for each text element*
Still images	*List details if used*
Moving images – Animation – Video	*List details if used*
Audio – Speech – Music – Sound effects	*List details if used*
Interactivity	*Details of links and any other interactive components such as text boxes*
Navigation – From screens – To screens	
Project	Screen ⟶ of
Date	

Structure charts

A *structure chart* provides a graphical representation of the overall structure of a multimedia product. There are two types of structure you should consider: sequential and hierarchical.

Sequential structure

A PowerPoint presentation that goes through from one slide to another in sequence is an example of a multimedia production with a sequential structure (Figure 2.29). This type of structure is best for information that needs to be read in a specific order.

Jargon buster

A **sequential structure** (or **linear structure**) is one in which there is a single defined path that will take the end-user through all of the elements.

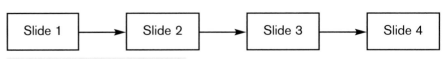

Figure 2.29 A sequential structure

Hierarchical structure

A hierarchical structure is the traditional top-down approach, rather like a family tree. It is often used in websites. It uses high-level categories and then arranges pages underneath in logical subcategories. Thomas Tripp has used a hierarchical structure for the Travelbug website (Figure 2.30).

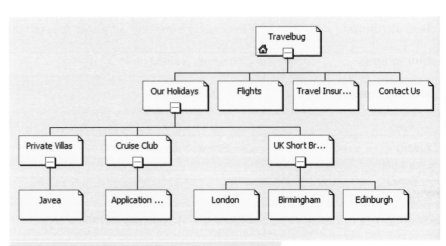

Figure 2.30 The more common hierarchical structure

Most end-users of a multimedia product are very familiar with the hierarchical type of structure. It helps them create a mental map of the structure, which in turn helps them navigate it easily without getting lost.

If a hierarchical structure is created in a narrow and deep fashion, as shown in Figure 2.31, there are only a few categories at the top. This type of structure forces the end-user to move down through the levels to access the information he or she requires.

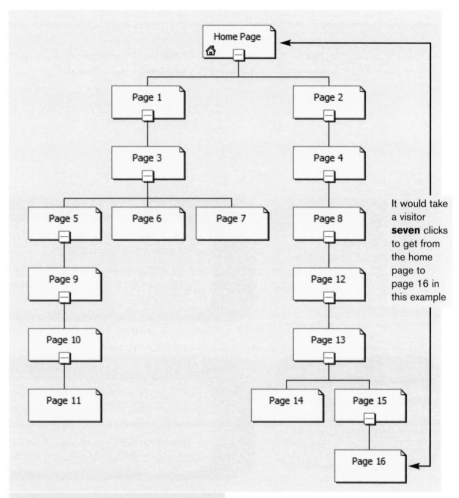

It would take a visitor **seven** clicks to get from the home page to page 16 in this example

Figure 2.31 A narrow and deep hierarchy

TIP

A good rule of thumb is to structure a multimedia application so that users can access the information they want in a maximum of three or four levels. After this they may quickly get lost within the structure and become frustrated.

On the other hand, if the hierarchical structure is broad and shallow – so that the categories at the top level outnumber the levels underneath, as shown in Figure 2.32 – this can result in the end-user having too many choices to remember.

When using a broad structure, you should take into account that human short-term memory is limited to around seven items. When users get to the eighth or ninth category they will start forgetting the earlier ones. If the subject is complex, the ability to remember categories decreases.

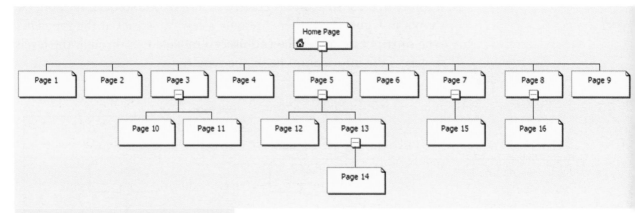

Figure 2.32 A broad and shallow hierarchy

TiP

Keep the number of categories down to five if the subject is complex, or to a maximum of nine for more simple subjects.

Go out and try!

Look at the website for your own school or college. Identify the structure used in its design.
- Is it sequential (linear) or hierarchical?
- Do you think the most appropriate structure has been used? State your reasons.

Skills check ▶▶

We will be looking at prototyping and testing your product later on in this chapter (page 97).

Go out and try!

Having made decisions on your initial designs for your multimedia product, obtain feedback to ensure that the final product will meet the needs of the target audience. It may be necessary to make modifications to your flow chart, storyboard and structure as a result of the feedback you have received.

Skills Builder Task 1

At this stage you should be able to tackle tasks M1, M2, P1, P2, Q1 and Q2 of the skills builder mini project on page 99. Don't forget to study the scenario carefully so you are clear about the project objective.

Collecting, editing and creating multimedia components

When you start collecting the content for your multimedia showcase, you need to bear in mind the purpose and the target audience. Think carefully about the end-user and always remember the four basic points you learned about on page 69:

- Is the product meant to entertain, educate, inform or sell?
- Who is it for?
- Where will it be used?
- What content must it have?

You can use a combination of both components created by yourself and ready-made ones. These components can include text, images, video clips and audio clips. You may be able to use the same component in more than one product if it is suitable.

Using ready-made components

You will be able to use a range of secondary sources to collect components. Examples are

- text from books, newspapers, magazines, brochures, handbooks and websites
- images from a variety of sources such as picture galleries, clip art collections and websites, books and magazines
- video and audio recordings from archives, film libraries, video clip collections and news websites.

Figure 2.33
A selection of magazines

Editing and logging permissions for ready-made components

Editing

It is highly likely that you will need to edit some of the components you collect from secondary sources. Therefore you will find it useful to refer to the appropriate chapters in the skills sections.

You may need to

- crop an image to use only a selected portion of it
- resize the image to ensure that it is the correct size for the production
- adjust the colour or shading
- make adjustments to the style formatting – for example, changing the font and size of text to ensure that it is appropriate for your production
- trim audio and video clips so that only selected parts are used – for example, trimming an audio clip to remove a long introduction from a piece of music
- alter the time dimension – for example, altering the speed at which an audio clip is played.

Logging permissions

Some components that you find may be copyright-free, but for others you must obtain permission before you can use them. For example, some of the images in this book have been obtained from secondary sources, so we had to approach the sources to obtain permission to use them before publishing the book.

It is very easy to forget where components come from when you are busy collecting materials. Therefore it is extremely important to keep a record (log) of the following:

- Where was the component found?
- Who produced it?
- How much of the material has been used?
- Where in your product did you use copyright material?
- Who gave you permission?

You should create a table similar to that shown in Figure 2.34 to record these details.

Skills check ▶▶

Refer to page 240 for more guidance about acknowledging sources and respecting copyright.

Component	Where found	Produced by	What has been used	Where	Permission given by
Sample e-zine	Email received by JJ	Norwich Union	Screen shot showing e-zine	Page 8 of Multimedia unit	Marketing Manager
Index page	Learn Spanish CD-ROM	Vecktor Multimedia	Screen shot showing index	Page 11 of Multimedia unit	Quality Manager

Figure 2.34 Recording the sources of your components

Never be tempted to include a component before you have received written permission – there may be a very good reason why a company does not want it used.

Creating your own components

When you produce your own original components for a multimedia production, you will be using a wide range of techniques and skills. It is likely that you will want to include

- text written using word-processing software
- drawings and animations you have created using website authoring and drawing software
- images you have captured using a scanner or digital camera
- sounds captured from a musical keyboard or microphone
- video clips you have shot using a digital camera or mobile phone.

Saving files

It is important that you use the appropriate compression techniques when learning to use the ICT tools.

- When creating a movie using Microsoft Movie Maker, you can enter the maximum disk space that you want the video to take up (Figure 2.35).
- You can choose to save a Word document as a PDF file in order to reduce its size. The seven-paragraph document (with images) shown in Figure 2.36 has been saved as a PDF file, reducing the file size from 3509 KB in Word to 594 KB as a PDF.

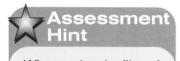

Assessment Hint

When saving the files of components you create, ensure that you choose appropriate filenames and formats. Bear in mind that the overall file size of your completed showcase must not exceed the limit stated in the project brief.

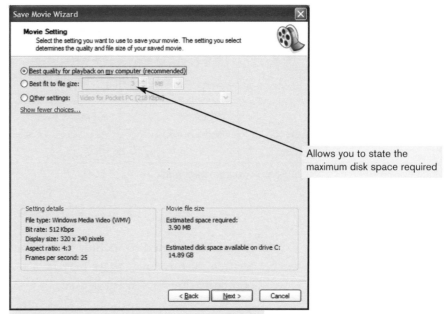

Allows you to state the
maximum disk space required

Figure 2.35 Compressing a video in Movie Maker

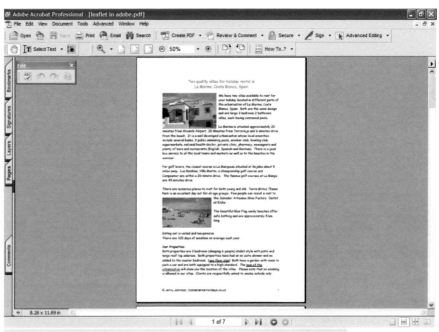

Figure 2.36 A Word file converted to PDF format in Adobe Acrobat

- You might decide to save a sound file in MP3 format in order to compress it.
- FrontPage will automatically convert images for a photo gallery to thumbnails, thus reducing file sizes. However, the thumbnails will link to the full size images, so the overall file size will increase.

○ PowerPoint will allow you to compress images and remove unnecessary data, for example by deleting cropped areas of pictures from the file.

These are a few examples of how you can use the techniques you have learnt to reduce the overall size of your showcase.

Developing your multimedia product

There are a large number of multimedia authoring packages you can use to develop a multimedia product for your showcase. Each piece of software will require you to learn a different approach to creating your final multimedia production. For this book, we have used PowerPoint to create presentations and FrontPage to create websites. However, your school or college may use different authoring software, such as Dreamweaver or Flash.

Selecting and using appropriate software tools

Using frames and tables for layout

Frames can be used in many multimedia products. The term *frame* might have a slightly different meaning according to the product you are using.

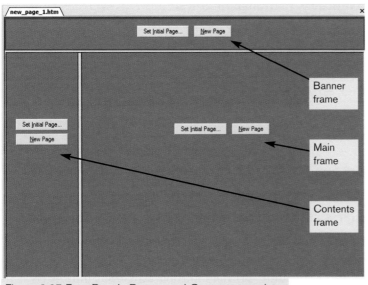

Figure 2.37 FrontPage's Banner and Contents template

○ In PowerPoint, each slide can be considered a frame, or the boxes in which objects are held are sometimes referred to as frames.

○ In Movie Maker, a frame is one of many sequential frames that make up a video.

○ In website design, frames can be used to organise a web page by combining several pages into one, each in a frame. FrontPage comes with a number of framed templates, a popular one being the *Banner and Contents* template shown in Figure 2.37.

Most software packages will allow you to create tables. In FrontPage, for example, tables can be used either as a means of presenting text in rows and columns or as a way to structure the page. You may not even realise that a table has been used in the design if its gridlines have been turned off (Figure 2.38 and Figure 299, page 464).

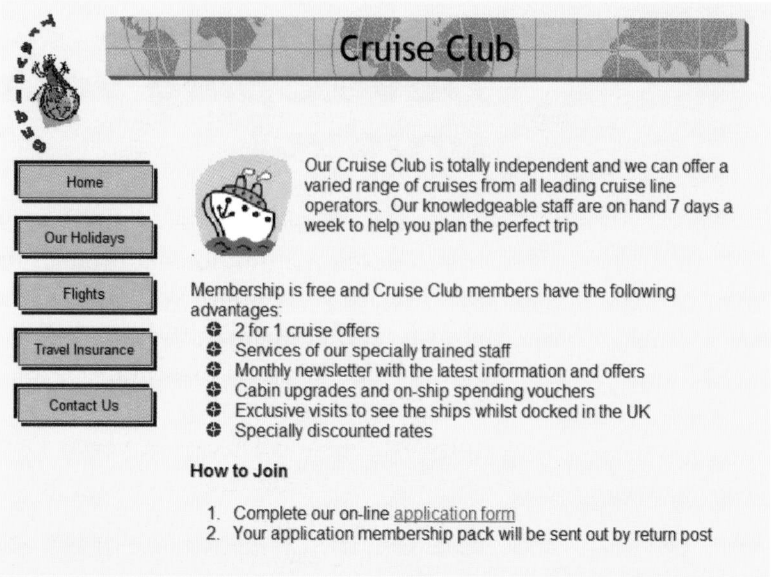

Figure 2.38 Travelbug's website with a table used to design the page

Skills check

Information on changing the style of templates in FrontPage is given on page 457. Information on changing fonts and styles in FrontPage is given on page 461.

Skills check

Information on applying colour schemes when using PowerPoint is given on page 363. If you are using different software, familiarise yourself with how to apply different schemes.

TiP

Take care when using background images, because they are often the last to load on a web page. If you use a very light colour for text over a dark background image, nothing will be readable until the background has loaded!

Cascading style sheets

Cascading style sheets (CSS) allow you to define styles and then apply them consistently throughout a website. This will save you time and allow you to change the look of the entire site by simply changing the style sheet. In modern professional web design, almost all formatting is controlled by CSS.

Fonts and styles

You must learn how to change the fonts and styles available within the particular software package you are using. For example, you will learn how to edit and use text when creating a website using FrontPage and how to change the style of fonts used throughout a theme.

Colour schemes, borders and backgrounds

You must consider the use of colour when you are at the design stage of your multimedia product, so you might find it helpful to refer back to page 80 of this unit. Borders and backgrounds add interest to multimedia products.

TiP

Many people print out useful web pages, but light fonts can be hard to read when printed. Bear this in mind.

Skills check ▶▶

Refer to pages 470–475 to learn how to incorporate interactive elements into a website.

Interactive elements

Familiarise yourself with how to use interactive elements when designing your multimedia production. Interactive elements include buttons, text links, hotspots and rollovers.

Hyperlinks

You can create hyperlinks within a product, or link to an external file or website. You can also create an email hyperlink. You need to be able to use hyperlinks effectively so that the end-user can successfully navigate through your product according to your chosen structure.

Pop-ups

You may decide to include one or more small windows that pop up over the main window. They can be initiated by a single or double mouse click or a rollover, or simply timed to occur. A pop-up window will always be smaller than the background window.

Figure 2.39 A pop-up window that allows the user to select a date (mattkruse.com)

TiP

Many users consider pop-ups extremely irritating and use the pop-up blocker available on Internet Explorer versions 5.5 and above (Figure 2.40). Your clever work may never be seen!

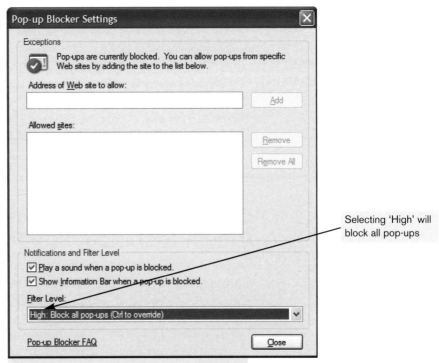

Figure 2.40 Internet Explorer's pop-up blocker

Editing HTML code

The website authoring software skills section (page 449) teaches you how to use simple HTML, the code used to write pages for the Web. When you use FrontPage, the software automatically converts what you have written to HTML. However, FrontPage still gives you access to the code, so that you can use your knowledge of HTML to edit it (Figure 2.41).

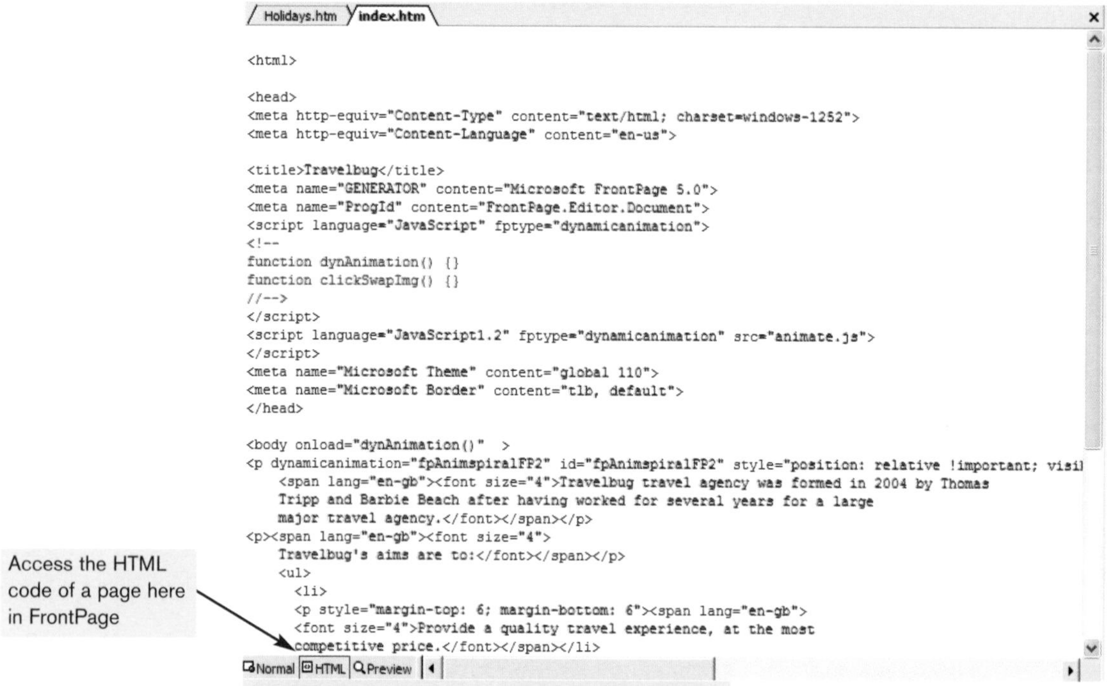

Access the HTML code of a page here in FrontPage

Figure 2.41 FrontPage's HTML viewing facility

Ensuring your multimedia product meets technical specifications

You should ensure that you meet the technical specifications of the multimedia showcase you need to produce for your summative project. Therefore you will need to take the following into account:

- *File size*. The overall size of your showcase and supporting evidence must be as specified in the project brief.

- *Download time.* Remember that the larger the graphics included in your product, the longer they will take to download. Download times must be acceptable for all products you produce.
- *Compression.* To ensure that your showcase does not exceed the limit specified, you will need to use the compression features you have discovered.
- *Fitness for purpose.* As has been stressed throughout this chapter, you must ensure that your end products are fit for purpose. Always have the four keys points outlined on page 69 in mind.

Skills Builder Task 2

At this stage you should be able to tackle tasks M3, P3 and Q3 of the Skills Builder mini project on page 99. Don't forget to study the scenario carefully so you are clear about the project objective.

Prototyping and testing

Having learned new and exciting skills, it is very easy to get carried away when designing a multimedia product and be tempted to use all the features available. However, no amount of flashy interactive features or graphics are going to encourage someone to use your product if it does not do what they want it to, or if it does not work as they expected it to. You should never use technology for technology's sake, and you must always ensure that your product is fit for purpose.

You can ensure that the end product meets all its objectives by thoroughly prototyping and testing it throughout its design and production. You should prototype a product by producing working versions of it at various stages during its development. You should then test these working versions with potential users to identify and iron out any problems as you go along.

It is recommended that you get feedback from a range of potential users: complete novices as well as people with a good knowledge of multimedia products.

Since it is so important that you test every detail of your product, you might find the checklist in Figure 2.42 helpful.

TiP

The people you choose to test your products should be broadly representative of the end-users. For example, if you are designing a quiz aimed at young people it would not be sensible to test it with a group of senior citizens just because they happened to be available!

Is the content correct and engaging, and does it convey the right meaning?	If you are designing a fun quiz, for example, is it fun to do or is it boring? Are all the questions and answers correct? It would look very silly if it gave an incorrect answer to a question! You need to ensure that each possible response receives the correct feedback. If you have to design a quiz with at least five questions, it is no good creating one with only four questions, however engaging they are.
Does every link go where it should with no dead-ends?	You should check every link, both to and from each screen, to ensure that they all work.
Do all the interactive features work as you intend them to?	Check that all buttons, hotspots, rollovers and links work. If you have included a form for gathering information, check that it works. If you have set a text box to a maximum length of 10 characters, is this going to be sufficient?
Is the product robust (cannot be made to fail)?	Deliberately try to make the product fail. For example, if you are allowing two attempts to get the correct answer to a question, ask someone to give two incorrect answers and then to try for a third time.
Does the product work with different browsers?	Ensure that you test the product in different browsers. It is also a good idea to test your product on both PC and Apple Macintosh machines, if possible.
Can people use the product without help?	Arrange to test the product with appropriate users, without giving them any guidance beforehand.
Does the product meet all your objectives?	Carefully check the criteria for the product. If you are required to produce a movie that (1) does not need any user interaction, (2) starts automatically, (3) lasts for 40–50 seconds and (4) makes use of a variety of components, does your end product meet these four objectives? Have you produced a product with reasonable download times?

Figure 2.42 Checklist to test a product

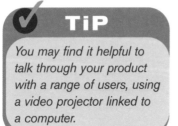

TiP

You may find it helpful to talk through your product with a range of users, using a video projector linked to a computer.

After each stage of testing, you should note any potential problems and decide how you are going to put them right. You may need to modify the structure charts, flow charts and storyboards you have produced. By thoroughly prototyping and testing your product, you should be able to ensure that it does what it is meant to do and conforms to the assessment brief.

TiP

You must check that any changes you make do not impact on other parts of the product. For example, it is very easy to change the structure of a website and delete or rename a page, but doing so might make a hyperlink unusable.

Distribution

It is important to recognise that the specialised software you use to produce a multimedia product for your showcase might not be available on the computers of all your target users. To ensure that your products are available to as many people as possible, you will need to create *run-time versions* of them.

For example, PowerPoint's 'Pack And Go' feature enables a presentation to be run on a computer even if it does not have PowerPoint installed (see page 382).

Skills Builder Task 3

At this stage you should be able to tackle tasks M4, M5, P4, P5, Q4 and Q5 of the Skills Builder mini project below. Don't forget to study the scenario carefully so you are clear about the project objective.

Skills builder mini project

Imagine that your school or college will soon be holding an open day. The Principal has announced a competition to produce a multimedia showcase highlighting the opportunities available for prospective students.

The Principal would like to include information about the different kinds of courses on offer and the facilities available. The showcase should show examples of students and staff in their day-to-day environment, including short oral commentaries where appropriate. The best productions will be used at the actual event. The showcase must be of interest to both prospective students and their parents or guardians.

The total showcase should be a maximum of 15 MB, use appropriate file formats and run in all common browsers. It will consist of three multimedia products: a movie, a presentation and a questionnaire.

Product overviews

The movie

Your short movie should give a brief flavour of the school or college. It should

- start automatically
- run for up to a minute

○ include a variety of components such as images, sound, animation and video.

The images might be of the entrance, library and other key areas, and the video might be existing footage of a school event. These are merely suggestions – you should use your imagination.

The presentation

Your presentation should give a more detailed overview of the school or college. It should

- ○ include a minimum of eight slides and a maximum of fifteen slides
- ○ be a hierarchical structure rather than linear
- ○ include a variety of components such as images, sound, animation and video.

You could include information about the courses and facilities, photographs of staff and students, and short oral commentaries. Again, these are merely suggestions.

The questionnaire

You need an interactive questionnaire to collect information from visitors at the open day. The Principal wishes to find out

- ○ contact details
- ○ how people heard about the open event
- ○ their impressions of the event
- ○ whether they are interested in Science, Arts or Vocational courses
- ○ within those three categories, which specific course or courses they are interested in studying.

Your movie

Task M1

Think about the design of your movie. What components will you include? Will these be available from secondary sources or will you need to create them yourself?

- ○ Will you include a voiceover, accompanying music or other sounds?
- ○ Which picture shots of the school or college should you include?
- ○ Is there any existing movie footage that could be included, such as drama productions, prize-giving or sports day?
- ○ Do you want to include any text and graphics, such as titles?
- ○ Are all of the above available now or do you have to produce them?

Task M2

Having identified the components you wish to include, create a storyboard to plan the content.

Task M3

Assemble the components you have identified and create the first prototype of your movie.

Task M4

Test your prototype with three reviewers who represent a cross-section of the target audience.

Task M5

Taking into account the reviewers' feedback, modify both your storyboard and prototype as necessary. Test your product again to ensure that it is now fit for purpose.

Your presentation

Task P1

Think about the design of your presentation. What components will you include? Will these be available from secondary sources or will you need to create them yourself?

- Will you include a voiceover, accompanying music or other sounds?
- Which images of the school or college should you include? Will these be still or animated?
- Are there any existing components that could be included, such as photographs or a logo? If not, what components will you need to create?

Task P2

Having identified the components you wish to include, create a structure chart and storyboard to plan the content.

Task P3

Assemble the components you have identified and create the first prototype of your presentation.

Task P4

Test your presentation with three reviewers who represent a cross-section of the target audience.

Task P5

Taking into account the reviewers' feedback, modify your structure chart, storyboard and presentation as necessary. Test your product again to ensure that it is now fit for purpose.

Your questionnaire

Task Q1

Think about the design of your questionnaire. You should include the following components:

- text boxes
- drop-down boxes
- check boxes
- option buttons
- navigation tools (such as buttons)
- anything else you feel will *enhance* the presentation of the questionnaire.

Task Q2

Having identified the components you wish to include, create a flow chart and structure chart to plan the content.

Task Q3

Create the first prototype of your questionnaire.

Task Q4

Test your questionnaire with three reviewers who represent a cross-section of the target audience.

Task Q5

Taking into account the reviewers' feedback, modify your flow chart, structure chart and questionnaire as necessary. Test your product again to ensure that it is now fit for purpose.

Your review, evaluation and presentation

Assessment Hint

You should attach to your evaluation the records of the feedback you received and the actions you took in response.

Task 6

When you have finished your project, review your work and produce a short evaluation outlining how well it met the requirements explained in the scenario and any aspects you feel could be improved.

Justify your comments. For example, if you say the movie is effective, explain what makes it effective. If something needs changing, explain why and how.

Task 7

Finally, present your work in an e-portfolio using suitable file formats. Your e-portfolio should be designed to present the following:

- Home page
- Table of contents
- Movie
- Presentation
- Questionnaire.

You should also include some supporting evidence:

- your project plan
- the folder structure you used to store the components
- preparation of *at least three* ready-made components
- development of *at least two* different types of original components
- components table

TiP

Throughout your project, in order to achieve top marks you must
- *create appropriate folder structures*
- *use suitable filenames and file formats*
- *carry out regular backup procedures.*

- storyboard for the movie
- storyboard and structure chart for the presentation
- flow chart and structure chart for the questionnaire
- some evidence of prototyping and feedback
- review and evaluation of the project process and outcomes, including feedback from others and suggestions for improvement.

Assessment Hint

Your showcase should
- *be no more than 15 MB*
- *run in all common browsers*
- *contain only acceptable file formats:*

.html (or *.htm*)	*.jpg*	*.avi*	*.wav*
.pdf	*.gif*	*.png*	*.mp3*
.swf	*.wmv*	*.mov*	*.ppt*

Assessment Hint

You should consider the following:
- *Respect copyright – if you quote someone's work, acknowledge it by using quotation marks and identifying the source.*
- *Avoid plagiarism – don't download material from the Internet or copy from a text book and pretend you have written it. Finding a suitable source and identifying relevant information from that does **not** make it your own work.*

Unit 3 Graphics

Introduction

Close your eyes for a short time. When you open them what is the first thing that you see? It will almost certainly be an image of something – the room you are sitting in, a view from your window, a picture in a book. We register images continuously and we rely on images to help us understand many of the things that we come into contact with every day of our lives. Can you even begin to imagine how dull life would be without the stimulation provided by images?

It is only in recent years that ordinary, everyday computer users have had the opportunity to discover the versatility of graphics software. It is no longer confined to the world of the designer or the computer expert. Today we can all be designers and use the technology of ICT to capture, create and develop images and to use them as highly effective methods of communication.

LEARNING OUTCOMES

After working through this chapter you should be in a position to

✓ use graphics software to create and edit artwork and images that communicate effectively in print and on screen.

How will I be assessed?

You will be given a project brief for this unit and you will be required to produce images and artwork for a specified audience and purpose. The project brief will specify exactly what you will be required to produce. You can expect to spend about 30 hours working on the assessment for this unit.

You will be assessed on **six** separate activities as follows:

1 Plan and manage the project
2 Select and capture digital materials from a variety of sources
3 Develop design ideas using vector-based tools
4 Develop design ideas using bitmap-based tools
5 Exhibit work in an e-portfolio
6 Review the project.

Read the project brief carefully, as it will give you hints and tips on how to complete the assessment successfully. The skills chapters provide help on the various software applications you can choose to use. In addition, you will find detailed guidance throughout this chapter, and we advise that you also refer to the following chapters, which contain specific help on completing the assessment:

- Standard ways of working
- Project planning
- Review and evaluation
- Creating an e-portfolio.

Skills file

The table below lists all the skills required to complete this unit successfully. The pages where you will find these skills explained are identified in the Page column. The skills in **bold** you will not have studied in Unit 1.

WORD-PROCESSING SOFTWARE	
	Page
⊙ enter, cut, copy, paste and move text	248
⊙ use paragraph formatting features:	
• alignment	255
• bullets and numbering	257
• tabs	260
• indents	262
⊙ format text:	
• font type and font size	251
• bold, underline, italic	253
• colour	253

PRESENTATION SOFTWARE

	Page
○ design and create structure and navigation routes of presentations	361
○ select and create colour schemes	363
○ create and select components:	
● text	367
● graphics	368
○ use frames	366
○ edit text:	
● fonts	367
● alignment	367
● bullets	367
● line spacing	367
○ edit graphics:	
● align, rotate and flip	391
● crop and resize	289, 389
● colour	225, 398
● resolution	394
● optimise file size	370, 396

ARTWORK AND IMAGING SOFTWARE

	Page
○ select, create and modify images	383
○ **scan images or use other capture devices such as digital microscopes**	**386**
○ download pictures from a digital camera	386
○ **choose appropriate image resolutions for print and screen**	**394**
○ **choose appropriate file formats and sizes for print and screen:**	
● **native file formats (e.g. PSD, PNG)**	**151, 225**
● **common file formats (e.g. PDF, WMF)**	**151, 225**
● **formats for print (e.g. TIFF) and web (e.g. BMP, GIF, JPEG, PNG)**	**151, 398**
○ **prepare images for screen, considering:**	
● **image resolution**	**144, 394**
● **file size**	**152, 396**

About graphic products

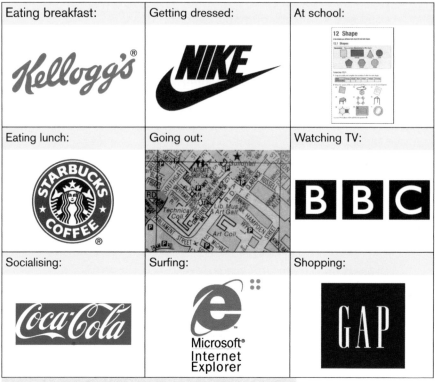

Figure 3.1 Graphical associations with common activities

It is said that 'pictures speak louder than words'. We tend to remember something more easily if there is an image associated with it. The images we are familiar with nowadays may have been produced in one of a number of ways:

- traditionally (e.g. a sketch, diagram, painting or photograph)
- digitally (e.g. captured with a digital camera or created in graphics software)
- by a combination of both (e.g. a sketch or photograph scanned and then edited in graphics software).

You see and use these images every day, for example as

- illustrations in books, magazines, newspapers and posters
- symbols and signs in public places
- symbols and icons on websites
- digital fine art on screen and paper
- brands and logos on labels and packaging
- plans, diagrams and models.

Think it over ...

What do you think of this textbook? Do you find it easy to use? What is your impression of the selection of graphics (icons, etc.) that have been used in the design? Do you think the front cover is effective? Do you think the screen shots, diagrams and other illustrations serve a specific purpose? Do you think the size and positioning of the graphics is appropriate? Crucially, would you find the book interesting if it didn't include any graphic images, or had only black and white images?

Illustrations in books, magazines, newspapers and posters

Graphics play an important part in helping to make any text more interesting and engaging, but they should be chosen with great care and thought. They should be relevant to the topic and included to serve a specific purpose, and should have been selected to suit the readers of that publication.

Consider the size of the image. An image in a poster tends to be more predominant than the text because the first thing that a passer-by will register is the image. However, the image will not detract from the written words that accompany it. Images in books and magazines are not uniform in size and they are not necessarily placed in the same position on every page. A great deal of discussion goes into the design of a publication even before the text is written, to ensure that any images used are going to enhance the overall design of the book.

Go out and try!

Your local library will have a vast range of books, magazines, newspapers and posters, all together under one roof. Visit the library to browse through a selection of books, magazines and other illustrated materials to familiarise yourself with the types of illustrations used.

1 In the children's section, look at the images in both fiction and non-fiction books and note the similarities or differences.

2 Choose a general topic that interests you, and look at books on this topic written for adults. What do you notice about the styles of images used?

3 Look at magazines written for different groups of readers – for example, car magazines directed mainly at the male market and fashion and beauty magazines for female readers. Are there any significant differences in the images used?

4 Look at the posters. There will probably be a mixture: some that have been produced professionally by national organisations and others that have been produced in-house. Look at the size of the images used and consider whether they support the message? Do the in-house posters display a particular house style?

Symbols and signs in public places

The use of signs and symbols enables a message to be simplified and presented in a familiar form. Many signs and symbols are universally recognised – which is of great benefit in an age when people travel far and wide. Look at the two examples in Figure 3.2. The designs are quite simple and uncluttered, making them easily recognisable.

Figure 3.2 Two familiar public signs that inform

? Think it over ...

Think of two designs for new signs to be displayed in public places to indicate that mobile phones can or cannot be used.

The triangular design of the road sign tells us that it is a warning sign. The simple black line and the arrowhead indicate that the road bends. It doesn't take any time to understand the implications of the sign, which is vital if you have only a split second to register and react to the image.

A very simple line drawing has been used to symbolise the concept of disability. It is used the world over to identify reserved parking bays, access and exit routes in buildings, designated spaces for wheelchairs on public transport, and so on.

Symbols and icons on websites

Just as symbols in public places are standardised for ease of recognition, so are the symbols on many websites. Examples are the padlock symbol that indicates you are using a secure website, and the shopping basket icon that is used increasingly on many websites that sell products or services online (Figure 3.3). Both of these images leave the user in no doubt about their purpose because relevant symbols have been chosen.

Figure 3.3 Two website symbols

You will find a wide selection of buttons and icons available on the Internet that you are free to copy and use without charge and without infringing copyright laws. Examples are shown in Figure 3.4, which came from CoolArchive – see www.heinemann.co.uk/hotlinks (express code 0069P) for more.

Figure 3.4 Examples of free website icons

Navigation links are a vital element of good website design and there are many innovative buttons in use. There are many websites that also let you download buttons for free. Figure 3.5 shows a selection of buttons that can be downloaded free of charge – see www.heinemann.co.uk/hotlinks (express code 0069P) for more.

Figure 3.5 Examples of free website buttons

Digital fine art on screen and paper

Digital art is a relatively new art form; it began in the mid-1950s when computer programmers started experimenting with visual images. The widespread introduction in the 1980s of graphics software, such as Microsoft Paint, which didn't require programming skills, encouraged artists and designers to put down their paint brushes and experiment with computer art – and it has gradually evolved to the high-tech artwork we see today.

You will see on your television screen a lot of digital art, such as backgrounds to music videos on the music channels, introductions to programmes, advertisements and cartoons. Creators of digital fine art find it more difficult to display exhibitions of their work than do artists who still use brushes and canvas. However, you will find some excellent examples of digital art on the Internet, and in particular on the website of the Digital Art Museum. This is an online resource for the history and practice of digital art, exhibiting the work of many artists. The website can be accessed via www.heinemann.co.uk/hotlinks (express code 0069P).

If you look carefully at items such as posters, CD and book covers, and greetings cards you will find many examples of digital art in print. As its popularity develops, more and more books are published about this art form.

Brands and logos on labels and packaging

Companies spend hundreds of thousands of pounds on their brand images and logos (Figure 3.6). The brand is the 'trademark' of the company. For example, Pepsi and Pizza Hut are household names that are easily identified by their logos and product brands. The logo provides the key to establishing a corporate identify and raising its profile.

Figure 3.6 Examples of brands and logos

A logo is often produced in corporate colours, and the same colours will be reflected on company documentation, merchandise and the company's website. Companies want something that is clear, simple and easily recognised. Simple shapes or line drawings are often used to symbolise the product.

For example, a logo representing a food or drink company might simply include a 'whiff of steam' emerging from one of the letters in the company name. A company offering a wedding service might incorporate a heart as part of the letter W in Wedding.

A logo is used to promote the company and will appear on everything the company produces. If you walk through any supermarket you will recognise many products by their packaging and brand image. Think of some well-known breakfast cereals and chocolate bars for example. Companies spend millions of pounds on package design to make sure that their products stand out from the rest.

Clothing designers will market their products through their brand name, and will hang labels from the garments to promote their image as well as sewing labels inside. Some garments even have the label on the outside as a design statement! Most designers will also have their own distinct carrier bags that also carry the logo or brand name.

Airlines incorporate their logo on the tail fins of their fleet, travel tickets, luggage labels, brochures, merchandise, uniforms, and so on.

The website LogoLounge – see www.heinemann.co.uk/hotlinks (express code 0069P) – is a showcase of the work of many top designers throughout the world and is an interesting site to browse for ideas.

Some brand images are considered to be a status symbol. Burberry is a brand that is instantly recognisable by its distinctive check pattern, and handbags carrying the Louis Vuitton logo are very exclusive fashion accessories.

Go out and try!

Sapheena is going to open a hairdressing salon. She is thinking of calling it something like 'Shape'. She would like a logo designed that she can put up above the new shop. Work with a group of your friends and brainstorm ideas. Can you come up with a more appropriate shop name? Produce a *simple* sketch design for a new logo based on the name you choose.

Plans, diagrams and models

An architect prepares detailed plans that guide the builder through the construction stages of a building project. The plans show the size and shape of the building, the position of doors and windows, and construction details such as sizes of roof supports and colours of bricks and roof tiles. Site diagrams show the position of the building relative to surrounding landmarks (Figure 3.7).

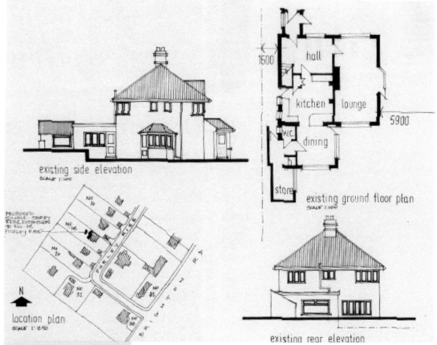

Figure 3.7 A house plan

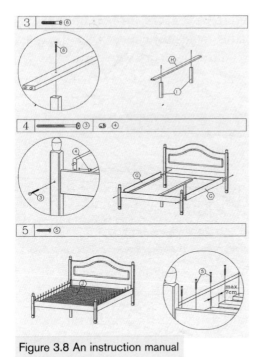

Figure 3.8 An instruction manual

Diagrams are often used to simplify detailed descriptions of complex processes. Textbooks contain diagrams illustrating topics such as the human digestive system, or flow charts illustrating the navigation routes through websites. Most flat-pack furniture requiring self-assembly will come with diagrams showing how the furniture is to be assembled (Figure 3.8).

Models are often produced to help people to visualise a finished product. This may be the prototype of a new product, or a model of a proposed town centre development scheme put on display in the town hall. However, the time and cost involved in producing models is enormous, so many designers now use computer-aided design (CAD) software to transform a two-dimensional image into a three-dimensional (3D) visual model of the product. They can then work with the digital model and try out different colours and effects before putting the product into production.

Go out and try!

Collect examples of a variety of graphics, logos, brand images, interesting font styles and other design features, from packets and magazines that you have at home. Look for interesting graphics on leaflets in high street shops. Ask at home if you can look at examples of logos on business letters. Keep a record (notes or sketches) of any interesting graphics you see on advertising hoardings.

Evaluating the effectiveness of images

To be able to design your own successful graphic images in the future, you must learn how to evaluate the effectiveness of images in relation to

- purpose
- composition
- use of colour
- impact/visual effect
- size and position
- message.

Purpose

Published images are usually created for a specific purpose:

- to express an idea
- to give directions
- to tell a story
- to convey a message
- to sell a product.

Some images will be designed to stand alone and some will be supported by text.

We look at illustrations in magazines to get ideas for fashion or interior design trends. We use maps and diagrams to find and give directions. If the purpose of the image is to tell a story, it may be necessary to create more than one image or even a whole cartoon strip. Images whose purpose is to convey a message or sell a product must make a visual impact that will hold the attention of the intended audience.

Whatever the purpose, an image is a powerful communications tool and the right choice of image is therefore very important.

Composition

Whether you are drawing a sketch, taking a photograph or creating an image in graphics software, you must give some thought to the composition of the graphic, both in terms of overall appearance and how the image will be put together.

Consider the position of the main elements in relation to each other and how the graphic will be built up. For example, if you were taking a digital photograph you would not normally position a person in front of a tree if it would appear that the tree was growing out of the person's head!

If the purpose of your image were to illustrate a recipe, you would have to consider many things when planning the overall composition of the image:

- Will the image be in black and white or colour?
- Will the image of the food be in the foreground?
- What would make an appropriate background?
- What background colour would enhance the food rather than overwhelming it?

- What size is the image intended to be?
- Might the overall image be enhanced by using accessories (such as a vase of flowers, a jug or a glass of wine)?
- Will text be layered over the image? If so, would your choice of background lend itself to the addition of text, or does the background image contain too many contrasting colours and textures?
- How will the image appear in relation to other images on the page or screen?
- Does the image have to fit in with an overall colour scheme?

The image in Figure 3.9 is a digital photograph, taken by an amateur photographer late on an autumn day to capture the effect of the clouds and sun against a church standing on a clifftop. The bright sky appears to outline the church. It is a simple photograph but the contrast of the dark church to the bright sky adds some interest. Imagine this image with a text overlay. It would work well because the intensity of the sky is fairly even and text in a dark colour would stand out. Similarly, text at the foot of the picture could be presented in a light colour to contrast with the dark shade of the fields.

Figure 3.9 A digital photograph

Use of colour

You must consider an image's purpose and where it will be published before you can decide whether or not to use colour.

TiP

*When considering the effectiveness of colour, you should be guided by the **purpose** of the image, the **audience** who will view the **image**, the **medium** on which it will be published, and the **resources** available.*

Skills check ▶▶

Check out the sections about colour systems (page 147), colours and fonts suitable for web pages (page 148), and converting files to different formats (page 152).

Black and white can create a strong visual identity and can be more economical to reproduce on paper than colour. Sometimes an image on a white background can be far more effective than an image on a coloured background.

When you investigate logos, you will probably notice that their designs rely on very few colours, whereas other art forms use many more colours. Background colours applied to screen-based publications can increase their effectiveness and provide you with an opportunity to use contrasting colours for the text. Dark backgrounds on screen, in particular, can be very effective.

You should also consider whether paper-based documents could be printed on coloured or textured paper, or even on acetate.

Impact/visual effect

If the purpose of an image is to sell a product or convey a message, it must make a visual impact to persuade the audience to stop and take notice. To attract the public to buy something, an image must depict the product in a very positive way. Happiness, laughter, sunshine, fun and bright colours are all positive elements.

Charities often use simple images to create impact. For example, during the Comic Relief appeal we see faces of children, often with sad, tear-filled eyes. Quite often the images are in black and white to add to the overall sombre effect. The images presented are designed to stir our emotions, and require little or no text to support them.

Graphics software can be used to achieve visual effects such as blurring, rippling, texture and crayon. You will learn how to apply these as you begin to develop your own images. Using a background or theme is another successful way of adding impact to an on-screen publication.

Figure 3.10 This poster was used by the London Borough of Merton in a recent anti-graffiti campaign to achieve the maximum impact

Size and position

The size of an image must reflect its purpose. A diagram or map, for example, must be large enough for the details to be read without a magnifying glass. If an image doesn't include fine detail then the size may not be so critical, although the position on the screen or page may influence the final size. Images on posters must be visible from a distance, and images used on company notepaper, business cards, labels and other stationery should not be overwhelming. Sometimes an image used as a watermark can also be an effective solution.

The message

Sometimes a picture alone can be enough to make a statement. At the time of the Tsunami disaster at the end of 2004, one picture in particular seemed to sum up the whole tragedy. It was of a father carrying the body of his child. No words were necessary to understand the suffering that he and the thousands of other survivors were having to face.

Your skill will be to ensure that the images you use either support the message you are trying to get across or stand alone in their own right without the need for words.

Go out and try!

1 Look through images you have collected and choose one that you think is particularly effective. Look at the images your friends have collected. Compare and evaluate the images in terms of purpose, composition, colour, impact, size and message.
2 Choose two or three images that you all agree to be the most effective. As a class, produce a list of the elements that made the images successful.
3 Make a copy of the list so that you can refer to it when designing your own graphics.

Selecting and capturing digital materials

Inspiration and ideas

Most people need something to inspire them with ideas, and one source of inspiration comes from looking at work created by other

people. The wider the range of graphic styles you experience, the more ideas you will have to apply to your own designs. It is essential that you start collecting examples of a wide range of graphic images as soon as possible so that you build a library of ideas. You are likely to draw your ideas from

- photographs or parts of photographs
- sketches, drawings or paintings of people, places or objects
- diagrams, maps and plans
- background images or textures
- text of a particular font
- unusual colours, patterns or effects you would like to recreate.

Look *critically* at graphics you see around you. If you come across a graphic or an idea that you like, add it to your collection. In fact, look at your own computer screen, which is full of graphic images designed to represent features or actions.

- Material from *primary sources* is likely to come from your own drawings, sketches or photographs and from images you have taken using a digital camera.
- *Secondary sources* will include photographs taken by other people, books, newspapers, magazines, collections of images on CD–ROM or material found on the Internet.

Some of this material will be in the form of paper-based publications, and you will have to scan these images to include them in your collection.

It is always wise to check that the images you collect and save in your catalogue appear on screen as you intend.

- Occasionally an image file is corrupted. When you open the file, part of the image may be damaged or even missing.
- If you are scanning an image, diagram or map, check to make sure you have scanned the whole image and that the map or diagram is complete. It is very easy for a document to slip or move slightly when the scanner cover is closed.
- When you are using a digital camera, don't just rely on the LCD panel on the camera to check the detail. It will be more reliable to view the larger image on the computer screen.

We have already suggested one or two websites that will provide some excellent source materials, but you must remember the laws of copyright. *Do not* use any materials or images that are protected by copyright without first obtaining the permission of the person who

Skills check ▶▶

To add items to your collection you will need to be able to
- scan images
- import files
- copy and save images
- upload images from a digital camera.

These skills are covered in the artwork and imaging chapter on page 383.

TiP

*You might choose to use an **image database**, such as Adobe Album or Picasa, to organise your image files. Image databases give you a thumbnail view of your images, and make searching easier. You may even be able to store information as notes or comments against an image.*

Skills check ▶▶

Look at the artwork and imaging skills chapter (page 383) for information on vector and bitmap images. On the following pages you will discover more detailed information about these graphic types.

owns the copyright (usually, but not always, the person or organisation who produced the work).

Examples of work in the Digital Art Museum are protected by copyright. However, the copyright notice states that you may print, store or download information from the site *for your personal non-commercial use*. This means that you can store copies of work as reference materials. It is important to check all copyright notices carefully, because this right may not apply to other sites.

Organising and storing your graphics

You will need to devise a system for storing graphic files in a logical order so that you can find them easily at any time. It is sensible to do this as soon as you start to save the first few images. If you leave it, your files will get into such a muddle that you won't be able to find anything without wasting a lot of time. Devise a structure with one folder for each of the different types of graphics that you intend to collect.

You must be able to acknowledge the sources of all the materials you use. Keep a word-processed catalogue which records the following:

- graphic title or description
- artist/creator
- graphic type (font style, clip art, logo, diagram, digital photo, texture, web button, etc.)
- source
- date acquired
- file saved as ...
- file location (folder/sub-folder)
- file type (JPEG, bitmap, vector, etc.)
- copyright details.

If you record this information in a table, you will be able to sort the data to find what you are looking for. This will be especially useful when you have built up a large collection in your graphics library.

Developing images

To prepare for your assessment, you will spend a considerable time investigating the various images you will read about in this chapter. The software packages you will use have a variety of tools and techniques. You will be able to recreate (i.e. copy) some of the designs of other artists by experimenting with these tools and techniques in both vector and bitmap software, and with the aid of a digital camera. You will be able to look at alternative ways of achieving the same effect, and you will gradually develop a style of your own. At the same time, you will explore a variety of ways in which you can deliver your message.

As you create and save your images, it is essential to store each one in an appropriate *digital format*, taking into account whether the image is intended for print or screen. The summative project brief will identify the file types you must choose for the project, but as you prepare your practice material you must also give this some consideration. Here are some questions you should ask yourself:

- What size and quality is required?
- Is colour needed?
- What resolution should be used?
- What file format should it be saved in?

We have already looked at the basics that combine to produce an effective image:

- purpose
- composition
- use of colour
- impact/visual effect
- size and position
- message.

You must remember to keep these attributes in mind as you develop your own ideas, in order to ensure that each image meets its specific objective.

Skills Builder Tasks 1 and 2

At this stage you should be able to tackle Tasks 1 and 2 of the Skills Builder mini project on page 158. Don't forget to study the scenario carefully so that you are clear about the project objective.

Assessment Hint

As you develop your project, you will no doubt discard some ideas in favour of others. You will also ask other people for their opinions of your graphics. As a result of this, you will need to refine your images many times before arriving at a satisfactory product. Throughout this process, it is important that you keep a record of all your ideas, and the stages in their development, because you must present this supporting evidence in your e-portfolio along with your final products. In addition, you should ensure that you record the comments and suggestions from the people who review your images.

Your assessment project

When your teacher or tutor feels that you have developed your skills sufficiently, you will carry out the summative project for Unit 3.

The assessment project will be presented as a short scenario. After studying the scenario, you will be able to identify the specific project objectives and produce a list of the tasks to be completed.

The task list will include a series of effective graphic images that you must produce in order to meet the objectives of the project brief. Some of these images will be selected from secondary sources, such as books or the Internet, while others will be from primary sources, created by you using vector and bitmap software or captured with a digital camera or scanner.

Your project will be looked at by an assessor and a moderator. They will be looking to see how effectively each of your images meets its objectives and suits its purpose (what each image is meant to do), which might be to

- express an idea
- give directions
- tell a story
- convey a message
- sell a product.

In addition they will be looking to see whether your images effectively address the following questions:

- Who is the target audience?
- What medium is your image for?
- Where will it be displayed?

Developing design ideas using vector-based tools

A vector image is made up of a collection of independent objects – lines, circles and squares – each of which can be individually selected, moved, resized, filled with colour and edited. As a result, they are easier to edit than bitmap graphics. You can draw a circle 2 cm in diameter and then resize it to 4 cm in diameter (Figure 3.11), or even 100 cm – the quality of the image will be retained.

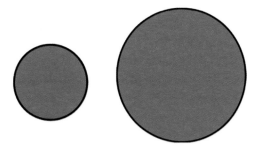

Figure 3.11 Vector-based images can be enlarged without losing quality

Vector images are ideal for maps and technical drawings, where precise line detail is required, or images that do not require the full photographic colour range (such as clip art, lettering and logos).

There are many specialist graphic software programs available: some examples are CorelDraw, Corel Photo-Paint, Printshop Pro, Adobe Photoshop and Photoshop Elements (which is a cut-down, cheaper version of Adobe Photoshop). If you do not have access to one of them, you can still create very imaginative artwork using the drawing tools in Microsoft Word.

Drawing lines and curves

The drawing tools in Word provide an extensive selection of lines and shapes. Using the **Line Style** tool ▤ or **Arrow Style** tool ⬍, you can draw lines in a variety of thicknesses and formats, with or without arrows (Figure 3.12). In addition to straight lines, there are freehand

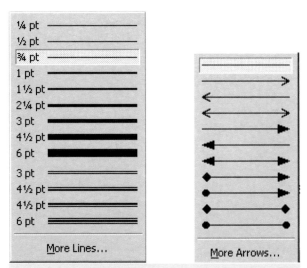

Figure 3.12 A choice of line thicknesses and arrow styles

TiP

It can be difficult to control the freehand tools. It is easier if you set your mouse speed to 'slow'.

TiP

Lines and borders can be drawn in a variety of line thicknesses, styles, colours and patterns (Figure 3.14). Sometimes the pattern will not be effective unless the line thickness is increased.

lines available through the *AutoShapes* menu: the **Curve** ⌐, **Freeform** ⌐ and **Scribble** ⌐ tools (Figure 3.13).

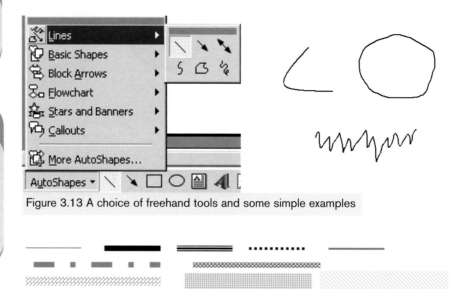

Figure 3.13 A choice of freehand tools and some simple examples

Figure 3.14 Styles of lines and borders

To draw the line or shape you require, select its icon from the menu, click on the drawing area and drag with the mouse to the size you need. If you wish to be more precise, you can give exact measurements through a dialogue box (select **Format**, **Format AutoShape** and then click the **Size** tab), as shown in Figure 3.15.

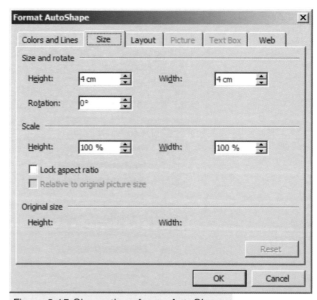

Figure 3.15 Size options for an AutoShape

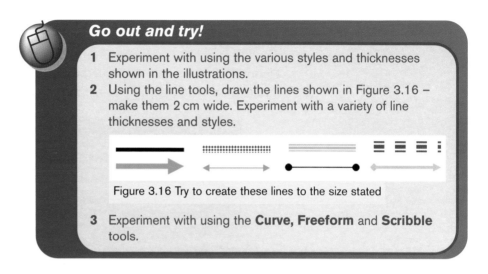

Go out and try!

1 Experiment with using the various styles and thicknesses shown in the illustrations.

2 Using the line tools, draw the lines shown in Figure 3.16 – make them 2 cm wide. Experiment with a variety of line thicknesses and styles.

Figure 3.16 Try to create these lines to the size stated

3 Experiment with using the **Curve, Freeform** and **Scribble** tools.

Start a file called 'Unit 3'. Create a new bold heading called '**Drawing lines**' and write a paragraph describing the skills you have learned. 💾 Save the file in your 'Artwork and imaging software' sub-folder.

Drawing basic shapes

As well as the rectangle and oval available on the *Drawing* toolbar, AutoShapes provide a wide range of basic shapes: block arrows, flow chart symbols, stars, banners and callouts (Figure 3.17).

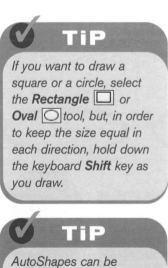

TiP

*If you want to draw a square or a circle, select the **Rectangle** ☐ or **Oval** ◯ tool, but, in order to keep the size equal in each direction, hold down the keyboard **Shift** key as you draw.*

TiP

AutoShapes can be enhanced with colours, line styles and patterns.

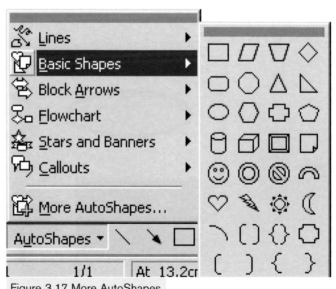

Figure 3.17 More AutoShapes

Using colour, line styles and patterns

The **Fill** tool ⬨ ▾ provides numerous options for filling objects. Figure 3.18 shows the dialogue box in which you can choose a fill type (gradient, texture, pattern or picture) and the colour or colours to use.

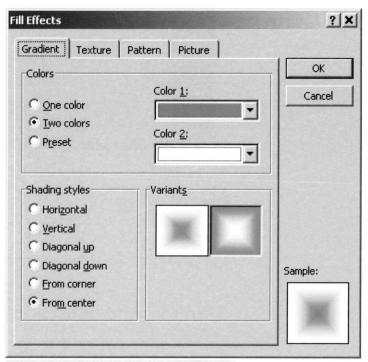

Figure 3.18 The dialogue box for Fill Effects

In Figure 3.19 the three ovals were drawn with a black outline, 4.5 points thick. One is filled with a solid yellow, the second with a pattern and the third with texture. Figure 3.19 shows also how pictures can be used to fill shapes.

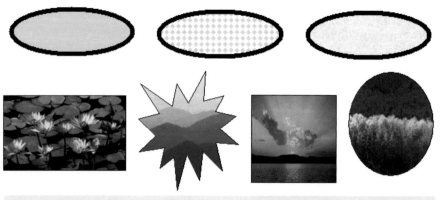

Figure 3.19 Shapes filled with colours, patterns and pictures

Go out and try!

Recreate the various shapes used to illustrate the fill effects of colour, pattern, texture and picture in Figure 3.19. You can use any pictures.

Open your file 'Unit 3'. Create a new bold heading '**Fill effects**' and write a paragraph describing the skills you have learned. Save the file.

Applying flat and three-dimensional effects

Objects can be further enhanced by using flat effects such as shadow ▣ or three-dimensional ▣ effects. Figure 3.20 shows some examples – an arrow enhanced using shadow, and a sun and heart filled with colour and shadowed.

Figure 3.20 An arrow enhanced using shadow, and a sun and heart filled with colour and shadowed

Figure 3.21 shows three shapes to which different 3D options and fills have been applied.

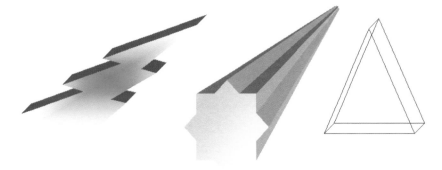

Figure 3.21 Three shapes with 3D effects applied

TiP

*If you want the same shape again, highlight the shape and press **Ctrl+D**. You will then have a duplicate that you can move or change. Try this when creating the 3D images of the rectangle, square and oval.*

TiP

*You can move a shape or image by left-clicking on it and dragging it to a new position, or by using the arrow keys to move it up, down, left or right. Sometimes you want to move the shape or image very slightly. If you click on the image and hold the **Ctrl** key while you use the arrow keys, the image will move by tiny amounts. This can be really useful if you need to position an image precisely.*

Go out and try!

1 Copy the various shapes used to illustrate flat and 3D effects.
2 Using the AutoShape tools, draw the shapes in Figure 3.22 to the exact sizes shown, and experiment with fill colours and the line thicknesses or styles.
3 Draw at least three other shapes of your own choosing. Experiment with using different fill, flat and 3D effects.

Figure 3.22 Try to create these shapes to the sizes stated: a 2D and 3D rectangle 1.5 cm by 3 cm; a 2D and 3D square 2 cm by 2 cm; an oval 2 cm in height by 3.5 cm in width; a circle 3 cm in diameter. Copy the oval and change to a 3D effect. Copy the circle and change the outline and fill effect. Draw the smiley face at any size.

 Open your file 'Unit 3'. Create a new bold heading '**Flat and 3D effects**' and write a paragraph describing the skills you have learned. Save the file.

Inserting, formatting and editing text in vector images

Using a drawing package such as CorelDRAW, text can be added to a vector image as *artistic text* or *paragraph text*.

- Use artistic text to include short lines of text to your document, especially if you want to use special effects.
- Use paragraph text where you need to include large amounts of text, for example when producing newsletters, brochures or flyers.

Artistic text

To add artistic text, select the **Text** tool  and click anywhere in the document where you want the text to appear. The text becomes an object in the file and can be moved around on the page. Figure 3.23 shows an example.

Figure 3.23 An example of artistic text, and sizing handles

Drag a handle to resize the text

The text can be formatted just as you would in a normal text document: you can change the font and apply effects such as bold, italics and underline. The font size can be changed by dragging the handles of the text object, as shown in Figure 3.23.

Paragraph text

To add paragraph text, select the **Text** tool, click anywhere in the drawing window and draw a frame. Write the text in the frame (Figure 3.24).

Figure 3.24 Paragraph text added in a frame

TiP

In Word, you can add text using WordArt or a text box.

If the frame is too small then you can increase its size by dragging on the handles. In a drawing package such as CorelDRAW, you can also allow the size of the frame to expand and shrink to fit the text, by selecting this through **Tools, Options** and ticking the box (Figure 3.25).

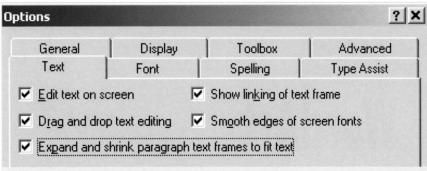

Figure 3.25 Select the option to expand and shrink the paragraph text frame to fit the text

Applying shadows and special effects

The formatting of text can be enhanced in numerous ways: shadow, outline, rotate and perspective. On selecting **Format, Font** and the **Text Effects** tab, Word even enables you to create movement or shimmer in text (Figure 3.26).

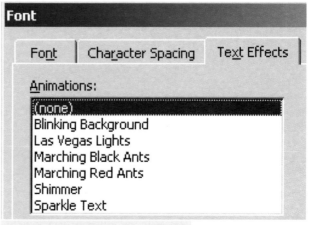

Figure 3.26 Text effects (animations)

Figure 3.27 shows some of the many possibilities for creating attractive text-based graphics. For example, the 'Perspective' image was obtained by selecting **Add Perspective** and then dragging on one of the corner nodes to stretch the text. The 'Rotate' image was obtained by double-clicking on the text to get the rotation handles, which were then dragged clockwise.

Figure 3.27 Examples of text effects

Fitting text to a path

You can position text along the path of a graphical object. This is illustrated in Figure 3.28 by the images of two globes promoting Travelbug, which could become an effective part of a flyer or other promotional material.

Figure 3.28 Wrapped text to fit a shape

The text can be placed exactly on the line or, as in this case, slightly away from the line. The line for the path was created by drawing a circle exactly matching the size of the globe, but hidden by selecting 'No colour' once the text was in place.

Go out and try!

1   Experiment with creating text using the following effects: shadow, outline, perspective, rotate, shimmer, sparkle and any other effects of your own choice. In each case, write the word and then add the effect.
2   Draw a circle and, using **Fit to Path**, add the words 'Around the World'. Add a suitable image of the world to the circle.

Open your file 'Unit 3'. Create a new bold heading **'Text effects'** and write a paragraph describing the skills you have learned. 💾 Save the file.

Combining basic shapes and freehand drawing

By combining various lines and shapes it is possible to create some interesting drawings in Word, even though the drawing tools are simple compared to the facilities provided by specialist graphics software.

Computer-aided design (CAD) software is used by companies to plan layouts for new kitchens, bathrooms or bedrooms, and at a touch of a button they can give you a 3D image of the room. If you did not have this software available, and you wanted to plan a new bedroom for yourself, you could prepare a basic plan in Word.

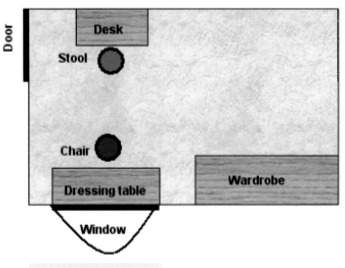

Figure 3.29 A room plan

Editing and arranging vector graphics

The plan in Figure 3.29 was created using lines and shapes which were grouped and ungrouped several times. At one stage the bed (see Figure 3.30) was very slightly outside the edge of the room, and the desk was so close to the doorway that it would not have been possible to open the door! The ungroup facility made it very easy to correct these errors, so that the bed could be moved and the desk reduced in size, after which the various sections of the plan were regrouped.

Order

When using the drawing tools, sometimes you find that one object hides another and the order in which they are *layered* may need to be changed. For example, when grouping a large number of objects, it is very easy to miss one or two. After the other objects are grouped, the ones omitted will be hidden. This is exactly what happened when the various objects in the bedroom plan were grouped – the rectangle for the bed was missed from the group and disappeared from view as shown in Figure 3.29. This was easily corrected by selecting the plan layout and choosing **Send to Back** from the **Draw, Order** menu; then the bed became visible again (Figure 3.30).

Skills check ▶▶

The skills section on artwork and imaging (page 383) includes many techniques that can be applied in the same way to edit and manipulate vector graphics: cut, paste, crop, resize and align. You can cut and join lines and shapes, as illustrated in the plan of the bedroom (Figure 3.29), and group or ungroup objects.

Think it over ...

Study the plan shown in Figure 3.30 and list all the shapes, lines and fill effects that have been used. Check your list against the answers given on page 138.

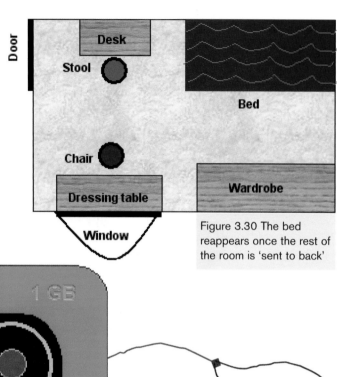

Figure 3.30 The bed reappears once the rest of the room is 'sent to back'

Figure 3.31 A graphic of a Sony MP3 player

Go out and try!

1 List all the tools you think you will need to recreate the graphic of a Sony MP3 player shown in Figure 3.31.
2 Recreate the drawing.

Open your file 'Unit 3'. Create a new bold heading **'Vector drawing of an MP3 player'** and write a paragraph describing the skills you have learned. Save the file.

Copying and cloning

Cloning is an alternative way of copying an image. The difference between copying and cloning is that any changes made to the original will be updated in the cloned image.

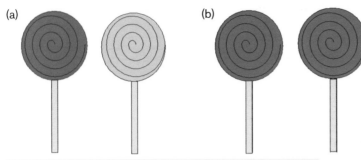

(a)   (b)

Figure 3.32 (a) A copied lollipop. (b) The same image cloned

Look at Figure 3.32(a), a design of lollipops. The original colour was yellow. When the colour was changed to red, the copied image remained as yellow but the cloned image automatically changed to red, as in Figure 3.32(b). This technique can be very useful if you are designing fabric or wallpaper with a repeating pattern.

Go out and try!

1 Study the pentagons (five-sided shapes) in Figure 3.33 and decide which pentagon was copied and which was cloned.

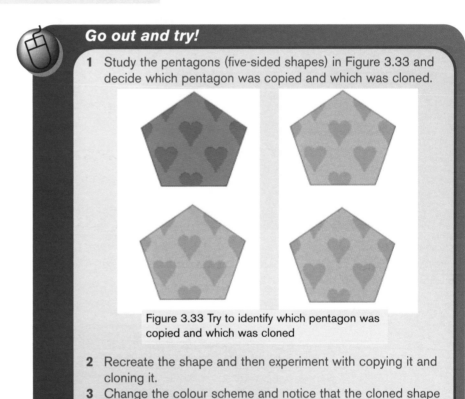

Figure 3.33 Try to identify which pentagon was copied and which was cloned

2 Recreate the shape and then experiment with copying it and cloning it.
3 Change the colour scheme and notice that the cloned shape automatically changes, but the copied shape stays the same.

 Open your file 'Unit 3'. Create a new bold heading '**Cloning images**' and write a paragraph describing the difference between copying and cloning an image. Save the file.

Combining and breaking apart objects

Objects can be merged with each other or with the background. The difference between combining objects that make up an image, rather than grouping them, is that once you have combined the objects they become one object, rather than separate objects that have been simply connected together. Once you are satisfied that the image is exactly as you want it, combining the objects has the considerable advantage of reducing the file size and so increasing the speed at which the objects can be downloaded.

Skills Builder Task 3

At this stage you should be able to tackle Task 3 of the Skills Builder mini project on page 158. Don't forget to study the scenario carefully so that you are clear about the project objective.

Save vector images in appropriate formats

Formats for print and web

To use a vector image on a website, it must be converted to bitmap format.

To convert the file's format, select **File, Export** and choose **Windows bitmap** format. You can retain the original size. However, if you then decide the image is too small, you will need to open the *original file* and repeat the conversion process, using a higher ratio of pixels or increased resolution.

 TiP

Before converting a vector file's format, it is wise to make a copy that retains the original format. Once it has been converted it loses the benefits of vector graphics – primarily that the image can be enlarged without reducing the quality.

Skills check ▶▶

Look at page 398 in the skills section on artwork and imaging, which explains more about file formats for different purposes.

Go out and try!

1 List the vector-based software applications that are available to you at school/college or at home. Identify their native file formats, and which allow you to save files in common file formats that can be opened by different software applications.
2 Copy one of the vector files you have created and export it to bitmap format using a resolution of 75 dpi (dots per inch). 💾 Save it as 'Export 1.bmp'.
3 Open the file in Paint and, using the zoom facility (**View, Zoom**), increase the size to 200 per cent or larger. Notice how the image becomes less sharp.
4 Copy the same file again. This time, when you export the file to bitmap format, increase the resolution to 150 dpi. 💾 Save it as 'Export 2.bmp'. Notice that the second image takes up much more disk space than the first.

Open your file 'Unit 3'. Create a new bold heading '**Exporting vector files to bitmap format**' and write a paragraph describing the skills you have learned. 🖫 Save the file.

? Answer to **Think it over ...** on page 135

Figure 3.34 shows the shapes and fill effects that were used to create the plan of the room.

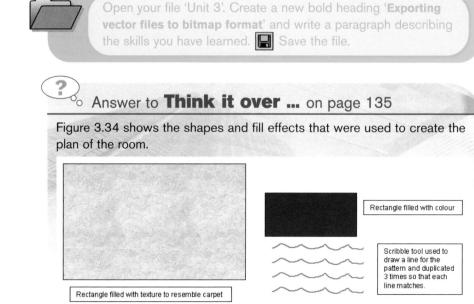

Figure 3.34 The answer to the question about Figure 3.30 on page 135

Developing design ideas using bitmap-based tools

Skills check ▶▶

Look at page 394 in the skills section on artwork and imaging for more information on bitmap graphics.

Bitmap graphics are best suited to photographs or images that require a very large colour palette, such as those carrying intricate shading detail.

Bitmap graphics are made up of individual pixels, each of which can be coloured separately. If a bitmap image is resized, the quality of the image is lost and sharp lines become fuzzy and blurred. Bitmap file sizes are generally larger than those of vector images.

Bitmap images can be developed in a similar way to vector images – that is, in stages, building up to a completed picture. Basic shapes are available, and you can also use freehand tools.

TiP

*Windows comes with a simple application for editing bitmaps: **Paint**.*

Drawing and painting bitmap images

This section shows how a simple drawing of a CD player can be created using draw, paint and freehand tools.

Figure 3.35(a) shows the oval outline of the player and one of the buttons. Both are filled with colour and effects using the **Color Fill** tool ![]. The track window was created using the **Basic Shapes** tools, filled with colour and effects, as shown in Figure 3.35(b). The **Text** tool **A** was used to write the wording over the top. The earphones were drawn using the **Pencil** tool ![] and then filled with colour as shown in Figure 3.35(c). The design was gradually built up until the CD player was complete, as shown in Figure 3.35(d).

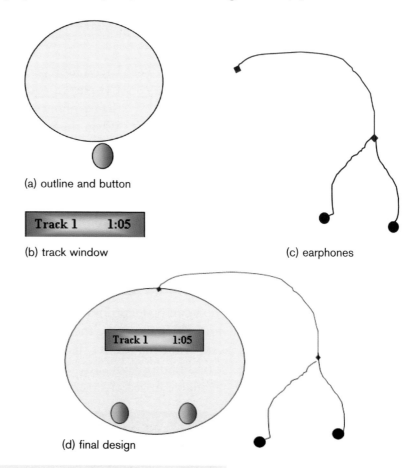

(a) outline and button

(b) track window

(c) earphones

(d) final design

Figure 3.35 The CD player created as a bitmap

Editing bitmap images

Bitmap images can be edited in a similar way to vector images. Use the **Select** tool ⬚ and then cut, crop or move the selected area. Bitmaps can also be edited more precisely at individual pixel level. The individual pixels become clearly visible by zooming to 800 per cent using the **Custom** option and displaying the gridlines (Figure 3.36).

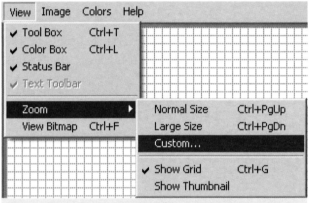

Figure 3.36 Using the zoom facility and displaying gridlines

(a)   (b)

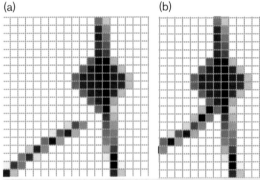

Figure 3.37 (a) There is a piece of wire missing.
(b) The missing pixels have been added

If you look carefully at the completed image of the CD player, you will see a slight gap in the wire for the earphones just where the two wires join together. When the image is zoomed, this gap becomes very clear, as shown in Figure 3.37(a). Using the pencil and selecting the black or grey colour, the missing pixels can be filled in to complete the wire, as shown in Figure 3.37(b). If you need to delete a small section of the bitmap, the **Eraser** tool ⬚ provides very fine control with its four different sizes.

Adding text to bitmap images

Text can be incorporated into a document by clicking on the **Text** tool **A** and placing the cursor where you want to enter the text. The text will be an object that can be moved around. Applications such as Corel Photo-Paint provide a variety of text effects similar to those available in vector formats: 2D, 3D, shadow, etc.

Go out and try!

Recreate the design for the CD player as illustrated in Figure 3.35(c).

Open your file 'Unit 3'. Create a new bold heading '**Bitmap images**' and write a paragraph describing the skills used to design the CD player. Save the file.

Combining bitmap images

Once several objects are exactly the way you want them, they can be combined into one object. After doing this, there is no risk of accidentally moving part of the image you have created, and the combined image can be resized as a whole.

Skills Builder Task 4

At this stage you should be able to tackle Task 4 of the Skills Builder mini project on page 158. Don't forget to study the scenario carefully so that you are clear about the project objective.

Applying special effects to bitmap images

There is a wide range of special effects that may be applied to bitmap images, including sharpen, soften, negative, emboss, watercolour, stained glass, chalk and charcoal. Some are illustrated in Figure 3.38.

original picture of roses

stained glass effect

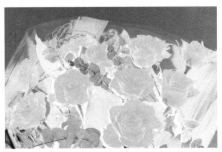

negative effect

chalk and charcoal effect

Figure 3.38 Special effects added to an image of roses

> **TiP**
>
> Before combining bitmap images it is important to make sure the combination is exactly right, as you may not be able to undo the combine command (depending on the application you are using).

Sometimes, applying one of these effects is not successful; at other times, it can make a definite impact. You just have to try out an effect to decide whether it achieves your aim. For example, the stained glass effect on the roses could possibly be used if you wanted to illustrate it as if it were a jigsaw puzzle.

Go out and try!

1 Select a suitable photograph from a clip art library and apply effects such as stained glass, negative, chalk and charcoal, or any others of your own choice.
2 Working in groups of two or three, compare the images and discuss which effects you think are the most effective and in what circumstances they might be useful.

Open your file 'Unit 3'. Create a new bold heading '**Special effects in bitmap images**' and write a paragraph describing the skills you have learned. Save the file.

Skills Builder Task 5

At this stage you should be able to tackle Task 5 of the Skills Builder mini project on page 158. Don't forget to study the scenario carefully so that you are clear about the project objective.

Using layers in bitmap and vector images

Graphic images typically consist of two or more individual items that together have made the completed image. Frequently these individual items are placed one on top of the other and then grouped together. If you need to edit a design that has been grouped, you then have to ungroup it in order to make the changes to the relevant object.

However, if you use *layers*, each layer is a separate image that can be edited on its own. Think of a layer as an image on a sheet of clear material. Together, all the layers form a stack of images, but the order can be changed as necessary.

The picture of the dogs playing in the snow (Figure 3.39) was built up in stages (there are many image manipulation programs that will provide these facilities). Some graphics software allows you to combine vector and bitmap images into the one document. In this case the photographs are bitmap images, but the text is a vector image. Edits were made to the various layers, and layers were moved up and down the stack.

- In stage 1, the photograph of the garden was opened.
- In stage 2, a suitable photograph including a dog was found on the Internet.
- In stage 3, the outline of the dog was cropped, copied, flipped horizontally and positioned in the garden scene.
- In stage 4, the text was written. It was later changed to 'What's this stuff?'

  Figure 3.40 shows the final layers for the completed graphic.

Figure 3.39 Layers as they appear at the side of the screen

Figure 3.40 Final layers for a completed graphic

Go out and try!

1 Choose a magazine that interests you and study the front cover.
2 Working in pairs or small groups, make a list of the layers that are probably included to complete the front cover.
3 Try to recreate the front cover using layers.

Open your file 'Unit 3'. Create a new bold heading '**Layers**' and write a paragraph describing the skills you have learned. Save the file.

Skills Builder Task 6

At this stage you should be able to tackle Task 6 of the Skills Builder mini project on page 158. Don't forget to study the scenario carefully so that you are clear about the project objective.

Preparing images for screen publication

In preparing images for screen or web publication you will need to consider

- the qualities of the graphic
- colours and text (fonts) suitable for on-screen viewing
- the file format
- the size of the file.

Considering the qualities of the graphic

Image resolution

The typical computer monitor has 72 or 96 pixels per inch (ppi). In other words, there are 72 or 96 dots of colour in each one inch (2.54 cm) horizontally and vertically.

Suppose you have an image that is 400 pixels wide and 400 pixels tall. If you need to display this in a two-inch-square box on the screen, the drawn image will have an effective resolution of 200 ppi

Jargon buster

The **resolution** of an image is the density of the pixels contained in the image. This is usually measured in **dots per inch (dpi)**. An equivalent term is **pixels per inch (ppi)**.

Skills check ▶▶

Look at page 394 in the skills section on artwork and imaging for more information on image resolution.

(200 pixels spread across each inch). Since the monitor's resolution is only 96 ppi, not all of the pixels can be drawn. To compensate the computer is effectively displaying approximately alternate pixels, which means that some detail will be lost.

As some detail will be lost anyway, you could resize the image using graphic software to make the file smaller. The image will then load more quickly and take up less memory.

large image

both images look identical when fitted to a small box on screen

resized image

Figure 3.41 An image for on-screen viewing does not need a high resolution

Display monitor characteristics

The maximum resolution available to display images on a screen depends also on the type and screen size of the monitor. There are many types of monitors available today. Monitors based on cathode-ray tube (CRT) technology now range from 15 inches to 21 inches in size – measured diagonally across the tube face (not all of which is viewable). Most monitors have an aspect ratio of 4:3, which means that the width is larger than the height. A 19-inch (48-cm) CRT monitor actually has a viewable area of approximately 14 inches width and 11 inches height. (Despite the fact that the UK started to adopt the metric system of measurement in 1965, monitor screen sizes are still stated in inches.) The size of a liquid-crystal display (LCD) monitor is measured along the diagonal of the actual viewable area, so an 18-inch LCD monitor will provide a similar viewable area to that of a 19-inch CRT monitor.

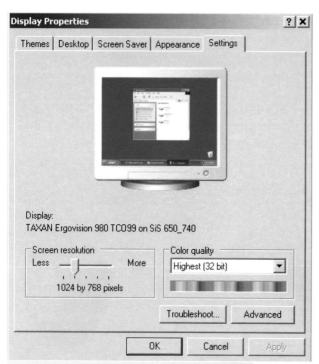

Figure 3.42 Dialogue box for Display Properties

The resolution of a monitor is the number of pixels that can be displayed on the screen, usually given as the number of columns followed by the number of rows. Currently 800×600, 1024×768 and 1280×1024 are the most common display resolutions. Since about the year 2000, 1024×768 has been the standard resolution. Many web sites and multimedia products are designed for this resolution.

Figure 3.42 was produced on a 19-inch CRT monitor with a resolution set at 1024×768 pixels. You will notice that this is approximately a third of the way along the scale for the screen resolution; on a 14-inch monitor, this would probably be at the maximum. The resolution of the 19-inch monitor used can be increased to 1600×1200 pixels. The advantage of the higher resolution is that you can display large pictures without having to zoom in to see the detail.

Many people tend to think that the picture on the screen is static. This is true for an LCD monitor, but on a CRT monitor the picture is continually 'redrawn'.

A refresh rate of 60 Hz (hertz) allows the screen to refresh itself 60 times per second. If the refresh rate is too slow then the picture will no longer appear static but will flicker and be uncomfortable for the viewer, possibly producing eyestrain.

Jargon buster

The **refresh rate** is the speed at which a CRT monitor screen image refreshes or 'redraws' itself.

 TiP

The ideal refresh rate is set for the monitor and should not be adjusted.

Go out and try!

1 Right-click with your mouse on the desktop area on the screen. The *Display Properties* dialogue box will appear (Figure 3.42).
2 Select the *Settings* tab and look at the resolution of the monitor you are using.
3 Make a note of the pixel setting now in case you need to revert to it after changing it.
4 Change the resolution to the maximum allowed by the scale (drag the pointer to the right), and click **Apply** to find out the effect this change has on the desktop icons.
5 You will be given the option to retain the settings – select **No**. If you do lose the settings, you can repeat the process to revert back.

Open your file 'Unit 3'. Create a new bold heading '**Screen resolution**' and write a paragraph describing the skills you have learned. 💾 Save the file.

Choosing colours and text suitable for on-screen viewing

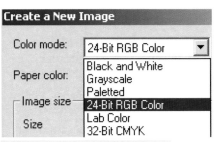

Create a New Image

Color mode: 24-Bit RGB Color ▼

Paper color:
- Black and White
- Grayscale
- Paletted
- 24-Bit RGB Color
- Lab Color
- 32-Bit CMYK

Image size

Size

Figure 3.43 Color mode options

When creating images, you have a choice of colour systems to use, as shown in the *Color mode* text box (Figure 3.43). The option you choose will depend on how you want the finished graphic to look, and considerations of file size.

What traditionally was called 'black and white' is in graphics terminology known as *greyscale*. The 'black and white' option means exactly that – there are no shades of grey – and it is used for cartoons or any other line drawing that does not involve colour or tints. Figure 3.44 shows the difference.

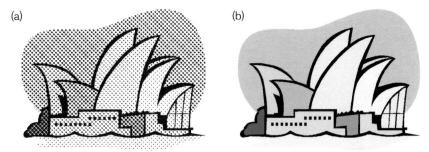

(a)   (b)

Figure 3.44 (a) Sydney Opera House in black and white. (b) The same image in greyscale

Go out and try!

1 Find a clip art image of your choice and save it in full colour.
2 Convert the image to greyscale. To do this in Corel Photo-Paint, select **Image, Convert To** and then **Grayscale**. 💾 Save the file as 'Greyscale'.
3 Convert the image to black and white. 💾 Save it as 'Black and white'.
4 Compare the original and the two new images. Which one do you prefer? Which one do you think is the most effective?
5 What are the three file sizes?

Open your file 'Unit 3'. Create a new bold heading '**Using different colour systems**' and write a paragraph describing the skills you have learned. 💾 Save the file.

Skills check ▶▶

Look at page 251 in the section on word-processing skills for more information on fonts.

TiP

One in twelve men have problems viewing certain colours or colour combinations. This may cause them difficulty when navigating web pages or using software, and in some cases makes the text and images totally illegible. So it is worth considering which colours are most likely to cause confusion, and avoiding them.

Colours suitable for the web

The use of so-called 'web-safe' standard colours may not be so crucial now that more and more computers are able to display millions of different colours. When you design a website, it can be very tempting to use a wide range of colours, but it is essential that you consider your audience, rather than just your personal preferences.

We do not all see colours the same, and some people are *colour blind*. That does not necessarily mean that they don't see *any* colours, but a typical problem can be that very dark colours all appear black, or orange on a red background may not be visible.

Fonts suitable for the web

The fonts you use for on-screen viewing should not be too small or too fancy. Of course you will use interesting styles for your text, rather than plain styles that are appropriate for reports and business documents, but make sure the text is clear and easy to read.

Go out and try!

1 Visit the websites W3 Schools and BT Age & Disability Action – via www.heinemann.co.uk/hotlinks (express code 0069P) to see the range of 'web-safe colours' available and to learn more about colour-deficient vision.

2 Study the two rectangular blocks in Figure 3.45. How many colours can you see in each?

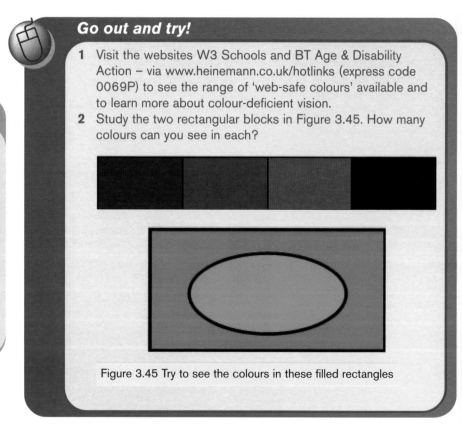

Figure 3.45 Try to see the colours in these filled rectangles

Open your file 'Unit 3'. Create a new bold heading '**Colours and fonts for the web**' and write a paragraph describing what you have learned. 💾 Save the file.

Colour balance

If the colour of an image is not effective, you can use the **Colour Balance** tool to adjust it. For example, the photograph of a windmill shown in Figure 3.46(a) has a very dull sky. By adjusting the 'red' colour balance from 0 to –23, we made the sky more blue and the whole picture noticeably brighter.

Figure 3.46 Windmill photo before and after improving the colour balance

Levels and curves

If you wish to change the brightness or contrast of an image in software such as Microsoft Photo Editor, there is a simple control to make these adjustments. However, any changes will affect the whole image. For example, if a photograph is too dark in just one area, adjusting the contrast will over-expose the areas that are correctly exposed, making these sections too light: You will have corrected one problem, but created another one.

More sophisticated software, such as Adobe Photoshop, provides tools that enable you to make more controlled changes.

1. The **Levels** tool enables you to adjust individually three aspects of an image: the shadows, midtones and highlights. These three aspects can be adjusted for part of the image or for the whole image.

2. The **Curves** tool provides even more versatile control for making changes to an image. You can adjust up to 14 different points throughout an image's tonal range, from shadows to highlights.

The use of the levels and curves tools is very complicated, and requires a great deal of skill and experience to obtain effective results. Likely users would be professional photographers, magazine editors and serious photographic enthusiasts.

Rendering text as an image

Normal text is entered into a document and may be edited by highlighting it, increasing the font size or style, or perhaps changing it to bold or italics. The text cannot be 'lifted' and moved around the page in the same way as an image.

However, when you create text in WordArt, for example, the text is an 'object' which can be edited just by dragging its handles, and it can be 'lifted' and moved around the page.

Sometimes you may need to change standard text into an object. Programs such as Flash enable you to do this. Let's imagine you wish to create a link to a spreadsheet file and you have created a text box with the words 'Link to spreadsheet'. Although you can create a link to the text, there is a disadvantage to the user in that it can be tricky pointing to the right spot to activate the link. However, if you select the box and, from the **Image** menu (Figure 3.47) select **Convert to Symbol** and then **Button**, the text will look the same but will become an object. The object can be positioned more flexibly on the web page and the user can click anywhere in the object to activate the link.

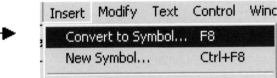

Figure 3.47 Converting text to be an object that can be manipulated

Skills check

Look at pages 225 and 398 for more information on file formats.

Considering the file format of an image

There are numerous file formats for graphic images. The file sizes vary considerably, but one thing is constant – the larger the file size, the slower it will download for viewing on a user's system. The table in Figure 3.48 highlights the key points for file formats.

File format	Features	Advantages	Disadvantages
BMP	Traditionally used for Windows Colour quality as good as TIFF		Cannot be compressed Files very large
GIF	Supports only 256 colours Excellent quality where there are only a few distinct colours or sharp contrasts Popular for storing stand-alone animated files	Files can be compressed even more than JPEG Ideal for fast electronic transfer of data Excellent choice for online publishing of photographic images	May be subject to royalties
JPEG or JPG	Most suitable for photographs or scanned images Full colour or greyscale	Files can be considerably reduced or compressed Excellent choice for online publishing of photographic images	Not so effective for text, cartoons or black and white drawings May lose clarity if the file is compressed to a very low quality
PDF	Entire content and layout of documents are retained when transferred into PDF format	Can be viewed on any computer system using Adobe Acrobat Reader software, which is free Ideal for sending files via the Internet	If you want to edit the files, not simply to look at the page, then you will have to pay for the software.
PNG	Supports millions of colours	Better compression than GIF Not liable to royalties	Not ideal for printed graphics Does not support animations
PSD	Native file format for Adobe PhotoShop	Facilitates advanced editing	File size tends to be large
SWF	File format for Flash Vector-based format for animations on the web	Very fast download times Images can be resized without affecting quality	Will need Flash player to play back the files – comes as a stand-alone program or a plug-in that 'snaps' into your browser
TIFF	Supports 16.7 million colours Can be any resolution and greyscale or full colour	Flexible Files can be compressed Produces excellent printing results	
WMF	Used to store most Microsoft clip art files and for transfer via the clipboard Suitable for vector and bitmap graphics	Windows-based file format	Some other operating systems can support this format, but not all

Figure 3.48 Features, advantages and disadvantages of file formats

Compression and compressibility

Ideally you want the images you use on a website to look just as they did on your screen in the original file format, but you also want the file sizes to be small so that download time is short. The standard compressed format is JPEG, which reduces the file size by removing data. Some of the image quality will be lost, but as long as the compression factor is not too great this will not be noticeable to the human eye.

The compressibility of a file has reached its maximum level when the reduction in file size has removed too much data, so that the deterioration in the quality of the image is clearly visible. Look at the three photographs of the chair in Figure 217 on page 397. There is a noticeable difference in the quality of the picture for the third chair because the file was compressed almost to the maximum level.

Converting files to different formats

To convert an image to GIF format, the colour mode of the image must be 8-bit (256 colours) or less. To check the colour mode, select **Image, Image Info** and a dialogue box will give the file details (Figure 3.49).

If necessary, convert the colour mode by selecting **Image, Convert To** and choose **Paletted (8-bit)**, as in Figure 3.50. To convert an image to JPEG format, the colour mode should be 24-bit RGB.

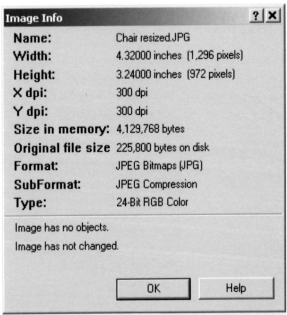

Figure 3.49
You can check the colour mode through Image Info

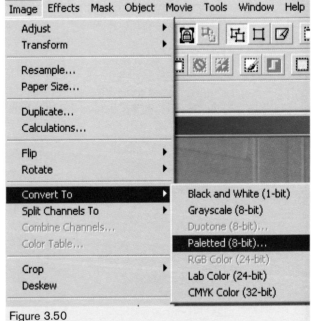

Figure 3.50
Converting the colour mode to 8-bit format

TiP

Websites such as GifCruncher (see www. heinemann.co.uk/hotlinks (express code 0069P) for more) will automatically reduce your GIF pictures without sacrificing quality.

Considering further effects of an image file's size

The impact of file sizes has been mentioned numerous times in this book – the larger the file size, the slower it is to appear on the user's screen. We have looked at ways of reducing the file size and considered the impact of

- combining objects
- colour systems
- file formats
- resizing photographs
- compression.

Sometimes, how images are seen on a user's system is out of the designer's absolute control.

Download speed

The speed at which images can be downloaded depends on the Internet service the user has and the quality of his or her connection. The Internet connection may be dial-up or broadband.

Jargon buster

Transmission speeds are measured in **kbps** (kilobits (1000 bits) per second) or **Mbps** (megabits (1 000 000 bits) per second).

The speed of a broadband connection varies depending on the speed of the *modem* used. A 512-kbps modem is up to ten times faster than dial-up, but a 2-Mbps modem is up to 40 times faster than dial-up. With dial-up you pay for the cost of the phone call while you are online, but you cannot then receive or make telephone calls at the same time. With broadband you pay a monthly charge and it does not interfere with your phone calls.

We have become so used to systems with fast reaction times that we can become frustrated if the download speed is unduly slow. If, for example, someone is researching to buy a new car and has to wait more than about 30 seconds for an image to download, he or she is likely to switch to a different website.

TiP

While it can be tempting to put every possible feature into a web page, it is better to be sparing in your use of special effects, animations, scrolling text and images; this will optimise the site for fast download.

Browser characteristics

The two most commonly used Internet browsers are Microsoft Internet Explorer and Netscape Navigator. Both have retained the core HTML coding, but have added their own personal touches – their own HTML tags. They also use different methods to render websites on screen.

TiP

To make sure your website will be available to all users, keep to the original HTML specification issued by the W3C (World Wide Web Consortium) and you won't have a problem.

If a website was created for a different browser technology from the one on your system, you may not be able to view that site or use all of its features.

Skills Builder Task 7

At this stage you should be able to tackle Task 7 of the Skills Builder mini project on page 158. Don't forget to study the scenario carefully so that you are clear about the project objective.

Preparing images for print publication

When you prepare images for the screen, you can see what they will look like, but when you prepare images for other mediums – paper, acetate or fabric – you can't guarantee that the colours will look the same. For example, you may have bought clothes by mail order that turned out to have different colours from those you had been expecting, because of the way the photos appeared in the printed advert.

You also need to take into account other factors, such as

- printer characteristics
- the medium
- layout considerations
- viewing distance
- colour management.

Printer characteristics

Types of printer

There are two main types of printer that you are likely to encounter at home or in school or college – *laser* and *inkjet* (also known as *bubblejet*).

- Laser printers may print in black and white or in colour. They are quiet and are used for high-quality low- or high-volume work.
- Inkjet printers have one or more heads carrying coloured inks, with the best ones providing a wide range of colours. They are rather slow but generally cheaper than laser printers and are suitable for all types of high-quality low-volume work.

Laser printers produce better definition for text and graphics, but inkjets produce superior results for printing photos. The speed and quality of print will depend on the specification of the printer, which is often related to the cost of purchase.

Resolution and other preferences

When you are printing primarily text documents, it is not usually necessary to change the default settings for the printer. However, for the printing of graphics, printers provide 'printing preferences' – different resolution options – to improve the quality of the image.

Figure 3.51 shows the graphics options for a black and white laser printer. Notice that the 'Best' resolution is 1200 dpi (dots per inch), double that of the 'Normal' setting. The advanced options also allow you to change the 'Darkness' of the printout.

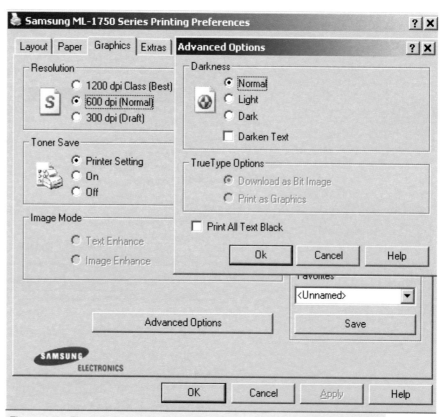

Figure 3.51 The graphic options of a black and white (monochrome) printer

✔ **TiP**

Printers often have a 'draft' option which produces a lower-quality output. This is satisfactory if you wish to save ink and are not printing the finished version of your work.

A colour printer will generally provide a wider range of printing preferences for the user to choose from. Figure 3.52 indicates that the default setting for this inkjet printer is 'Text'. Notice that in addition to draft, you can also select from 'Text & Image', 'Photo' and 'Best Photo'. The latter will be the highest resolution and best quality. In addition there is a wide variety of paper options, depending on whether you are printing on paper, photo paper or transparencies (acetate). For this inkjet machine, selecting the 'Advanced' option produces a warning not to make changes unless you are an experienced user.

Figure 3.52 Printing preferences of an inkjet colour printer

The medium

As already mentioned, when preparing images for print, the medium on which you are printing may be plain paper, photographic paper, card, acetate or fabric. You are unlikely to print on fabric yourself, but remember to check the printer settings for the right medium, as explained above.

Layout considerations

Paper size and orientation

Study Figure 3.53 for a moment. It shows the standard sizes of paper used in many countries (not the USA).

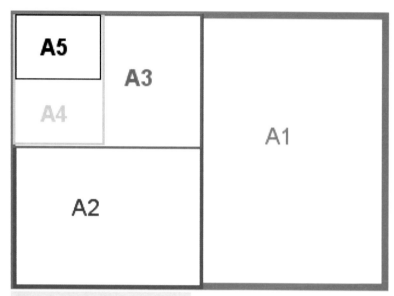

Figure 3.53 Standard paper sizes

A0 is the largest of the standard sizes for paper and has an area of exactly one square metre. Then

- A1 is half of A0
- A2 is half of A1
- A3 is half of A2
- A4 is half of A3
- A5 is half of A4.

A0 and A1 are very large and are used for technical drawings and posters. A1 and A2 are the common sizes for flip charts. A3 is used for drawings and smaller posters. A4 (210 mm by 297 mm) is the paper size that you will be most familiar with, and you will almost certainly use it for printing your work. Sometimes you may use A4 paper folded in half to make an A5 leaflet, or folded in three to make a leaflet with three columns on the inside of the fold. Postcards are half the size of A5 and – yes! – they are known as A6.

Every size of paper can be used in portrait or landscape *orientation*.

Margins, gutters and bleeds

You will need to consider whether to change the default settings for the margins. The term 'gutter' refers to a margin setting that adds extra space to the side or top margin of a document that will be bound (such as a book) to prevent the binding obscuring the text. 'Bleed' allows printing right to the edge of the paper. It is ideal for posters and photos, provided you have a printer with this capability.

TiP

You may not have access to printing on paper larger than A4, but you may be able to have A4 work enlarged to A3 using a photocopier.

Viewing distance

When you are looking at your work on the monitor, you are obviously seeing it at close quarters. If the size of the text and images is clear on screen, your document will probably be fine for a leaflet. However, if you are designing a poster that will generally be viewed from a distance, it is important to ensure that the words and images are much larger.

Colour management

If you send a colour image from the computer to two different printers, even if they are exactly the same model, it is quite likely that the results will be different. This is not a problem for personal use, as long as the results are satisfactory. However, for commercial use this is a potential problem. If a manufacturer of wallpaper or fabrics sends out samples to customers, it is crucial that the colours be accurate. Printer calibration tools will ensure that each digital device – monitor, scanner, printer – is standardised to produce consistent results. You are not likely to be able to implement calibration procedures, but it is important to be aware of when it would be necessary.

Skills Builder Tasks 8, 9 and 10

At this stage you should be able to tackle Tasks 8, 9 and 10 of the Skills Builder mini project that follows. Don't forget to study the scenario carefully so that you are clear about the project objective.

Skills builder mini project

Skills Builder project introduction

This activity provides an opportunity to develop the skills you will need in order to complete a summative project for Unit 3. Your teacher or tutor may decide to use the tasks in this mini project as further practice as you work through the unit, or may alternatively set it as a mini project all at once. If it is set as a mini project then, before you begin, you should think about how to plan and manage the project – refer to page 490.

The scenario

Your school/college has recently completed a major rebuilding programme and, to complete the transformation, needs an updated corporate identity. In this respect the governors have decided that initially they would like a new logo, updated stationery and a new brochure. With particular regard to the brochure, you have been asked to produce a design for the front and back cover, together with a double-page spread that will illustrate specific design features of the brochure, such as

- *a background design/style layout for the page*
- *graphic styles for main headings and sub-headings*
- *icons to represent specific course types.*

In addition, there is to be a design feature on every page to include passport-style photographs of students and short comments from them about their courses – similar to the features identifying tips, jargon busters and so on in this book.

The Principal knows that you have developed a wide range of graphic skills and has asked you to help with this project.

Task 1

Use secondary sources to put together a collection of relevant stimulus materials by investigating a range of

- corporate logos
- brochures
- icons and other design features.

Make sure that each item in your collection is catalogued and acknowledged appropriately.

Task 2

Use primary sources to capture a range of images that will be appropriate for inclusion in your brochure. Ensure that each item in your collection is catalogued and acknowledged appropriately.

Task 3

Use vector-based software to produce *three* logo designs for your school/college, exploring a wide range of styles and techniques. Test your designs by showing them to at least three of your friends and three adults. Record their comments and, taking these comments into account, produce one final product.

Task 4

Use bitmap-based software to produce icons designed to represent the different courses on offer, exploring a wide range of styles and techniques. Test your designs by showing them to at least three people. Record their comments and, taking these comments into account, produce your final products.

Task 5

Design a double-page spread of the inside pages of the brochure, incorporating examples of the design features outlined in this project.

Task 6

Think about the front and back covers, and include a digital photograph of your school/college for the front and a map on the back cover. You could practise layering techniques to add in the logo, suitable text and any other relevant topics to enhance your design.

Show your design to at least three people and record their comments. Edit the cover, taking into account these comments, and produce the final product.

Task 7

Design a single web page to advertise your college. Include the college logo, a photograph or video clip, map and some supporting text.

Task 8

Design a poster, incorporating the logo and a photograph plus any other suitable material, to advertise an open event for prospective new students, identifying the factors to be considered when printing a poster compared to printing on a typical A4 sheet.

Task 9

Assessment Hint

You should attach to your evaluation the records of the feedback you received and the actions you took in response.

When you have finished your project, review your work and produce a short evaluation outlining how well it met the requirements explained in the scenario and any aspects you feel could be improved. Justify your comments. For example, if you say the design layout is effective, explain what makes it effective. If something still needs changing, explain why and how.

Task 10

Finally, present your work in an e-portfolio using suitable file formats. Your e-portfolio should be designed to present the following:

- home page
- table of contents
- the finished logo
- a selection of icons representing college courses
- the design of your college brochure, including front and back covers and the double-page spread
- a new web page.

You should also include some supporting evidence:

- your project plan
- the stimulus material you collected, showing full acknowledgement of the sources
- evidence of the development of the design of your logo, including details of feedback from other people
- evidence of the development of the design of the icons, including details of feedback from other people
- evidence of the development of the design of the front and back covers and the double-page spread
- evidence of the development of your web page
- review and evaluation of the project, including feedback from others.

TiP

Throughout your project, in order to achieve top marks you must
- *create appropriate folder structures*
- *use suitable filenames and file formats*
- *carry out regular backup procedures.*

You will find that the requirements for the e-portfolio, project planning and review and evaluation are almost identical for each of the units. If you follow the guidelines given in the relevant chapters in the book it will help you to achieve top marks.

ICT in Enterprise

Introduction

Every year, hundreds of people start a new business. Their ideas stem from new inventions, turning hobbies into a business, providing a service, and so on. If you had a brilliant idea for a new business, people would think you were very enterprising. They would admire you for taking the risk of setting up a new business enterprise and developing a business opportunity.

Because any such venture carries a risk, it essential that you carry out careful planning and preparation to make sure the idea is viable. For example, you would need to

- carry out market research to make sure there is sufficient interest
- produce financial forecasts
- develop a business plan
- develop a corporate identity
- present your plans to people whose support you need – the bank manager, for example
- promote your business.

LEARNING OUTCOMES

After working through this chapter you should be able to

✓ use ICT effectively to help you research and plan for the launch of a new business enterprise.

How will I be assessed?

You will be given a project brief for this unit and you will be required to use ICT to explore and plan for a business activity. The project brief will specify exactly what you will be required to produce. You can expect to spend about 30 hours working on the assessment for this unit. You will be assessed on **six** separate activities as follows:

1 Plan and manage the project
2 Investigate an enterprise opportunity

3 Create a corporate image

4 Promote a product or service

5 Use an e-portfolio to present an enterprise proposal

6 Carry out an end-of-project review.

The marks you will be awarded will depend on the quality and complexity of your work and your teacher will be able to show you how the marks are allocated against each activity.

The project brief will give you hints and tips on successfully completing the assessment. The skills chapters provide help on the various software applications you can choose to use. In addition, you will find detailed guidance throughout this chapter, and we strongly suggest you also read the following chapters, which contain specific help on completing the assessments:

- Standard ways of working
- Project planning
- Review and evaluation
- Creating an e-portfolio.

Skills file

The table below lists all the skills required to complete this unit successfully. The pages where you will find these skills explained are identified in the Page column. The skills in **bold** you will not have studied in Unit 1.

ARTWORK AND IMAGING SOFTWARE	
	Page
select and capture images:	
• use a digital camera	386
• use a scanner	385
• download images from the Internet	433
• use clip art and library images	383
modify images:	
• group and ungroup	387
• cut, paste, crop, trim, resize	289, 389
• align, rotate	391
choose appropriate image resolutions and file formats for	
• print publications	394
• digital publications	394

COLLABORATIVE SOFTWARE

EMAIL

INTERNET AND INTRANETS

SPREADSHEET SOFTWARE

	Page
○ enter, cut, copy, paste and move data	298
○ format cells to match data types	298
○ insert/delete rows and columns	307
○ enter formulas:	
● use operators	301
● replicate formulas	303
● use simple functions	310
● use absolute and relative cell references	303, 304
○ sort data	315
○ produce fully customised charts/graphs:	
● titles	323
● axis and data labels	323
● legend	323
○ use headers and footers	327
○ print selected areas	328
○ **insert comments**	**317**
○ **filter data**	**318**
○ **link sheets**	**320**

WEBSITE AUTHORING SOFTWARE

	Page
○ use colour schemes	457
○ use page formatting features:	
● tables	463
● fonts	454, 460
● alignment	462
● colour	457
● line spacing	462
● bullets	462
○ produce content:	
● text	461
● images	465

WORD-PROCESSING SOFTWARE

Identifying a business opportunity

If identifying a business opportunity were an easy process, we would all be running our own successful businesses! Unfortunately, it is not easy and requires a lot of careful planning, quite apart from having the idea in the first place. Businesses that are successful have usually discovered a gap in the market and stepped in to fill that niche before anyone else. The growth of the Internet in recent years has provided new avenues for existing business such as banking and retail, and opened up new business ventures such as eBay and lastminute.com. The owners of these businesses were fortunate to have had the ideas and to have discovered the gap in the market.

A business idea might be

- ○ developing a new product or service that you feel would be useful
- ○ marketing a new invention
- ○ expanding an existing business into a new line of work
- ○ turning a hobby into a business
- ○ developing an idea that you have seen somewhere else.

Developing an idea for a business is a creative process, and one that can't be rushed. Brainstorming is one way to generate ideas, and you have probably been doing this throughout the planning of your other projects. You will have drawn up mind maps to help you record and organise your ideas. In the Project Planning Software chapter (page 480) we look at specialist mind-mapping software that you can use to help you plan and organise your ideas. You will be using software such as this to develop your project.

Skills Builder

At this stage you should be able to tackle Tasks 1 and 2 of the Skills Builder mini project on page 213. Don't forget to study the scenario carefully so that you are clear about the project objective.

Once an idea has taken shape, you must look at the viability of your new business venture and carry out some detailed market research. Market research is a fact-finding exercise carried out by a business to identify product development opportunities. In carrying out this research, businesses will gather information about the goods and services their customers want, to enable them to supply those products. When contemplating the launch of a new product or service, a business would want to find answers to the following questions:

- Is there a demand for the product/service?
- What is the customer profile?
- What area will the customers be from?
- How much are they prepared to pay?
- What level of quality/service do they require?
- What competition is there?
- When and how can you sell your product/service?
- how will the business be affected by changing trends and fashions?
- What materials and supplies will you need and where can you find them?

Let's look at each of these in turn.

Demand

If you are starting on a new venture, you will be very excited about your business idea and could easily get carried away with it. However, it is essential you ensure that there is a demand for your product or service and that prospective customers are as enthusiastic as you are. You must make sure that your product or service is different from anything else in the local market and that customers will be prepared to pay for it. If you are offering a product similar to that of another local business, you must be sure that the market is big enough for both of you. If you are producing something new,

Jargon buster

People who buy **products** from a business are called **customers**; those who pay for **services** are called **clients**.

you might consider 'testing' the market to find out how people react to the product or service before you spend too much time pursuing your idea. If you are thinking of turning an interest or hobby into a business, make sure that there are potential customers who might want to share your interest.

Customer profile

Customers are the key to any successful business. The more you know about your potential customers, the better the chances of success. Customers don't just appear when you open your doors for the first time; you must make sure your business attracts them in. If you are thinking of opening a business in a shopping area, one way to find out who your potential customers are likely to be is to observe and count them. There would be little point in opening a shop selling trendy fashion items if the local market comprised mainly senior citizens. If you have a new service in mind, you must make sure that there are enough people in the area who would use the service. For example, in a community where a large proportion of families are on low incomes, a cleaning or ironing service would probably not be within their means.

Customer location

You will need to consider if your product or service can rely on the local market alone or whether it must attract customers from a wider area. For example, a corner shop would generally expect to attract customers from the surrounding roads, and would probably serve a large number of regular customers. A clothes shop in the high street of a larger town would expect their customers to come from a wider area, and the shop would probably pick up a considerable amount of passing trade. If you were pursuing the cleaning or ironing service, would you have to spend time travelling to your clients? If this was the case, you might waste a lot of time earning nothing because you were travelling and not cleaning.

Price

Your customers will generally be looking for value for money, but the price you can charge will depend on several factors. If customers have a perception that your business is rather special and 'up-market' they are more likely to be prepared to pay a higher price. If you are competing with other similar local businesses, your prices must be in line with your competitors. Changes in income can also have an effect. For example, if taxes or interest rates were to be raised then customers would have less money in their pockets. They would be less inclined to spend money and you might have to lower your prices to encourage them to spend.

Level of quality/service

Your customers might be attracted to your business because it offers a high-quality service with regular and frequent deliveries. Are you going to be able to maintain the service if you are sick and unable to work? If you are offering an after-sales service, what days and times would your customers need the service? Would you have to be prepared to work evenings and weekends in order to visit customers who were at work during the day?

How often are your customers likely to want to buy from you? If you are selling a product that has a long lifespan, your customers will not normally be buying the product regularly. Therefore you will need to attract customers from a wide area. On the other hand, if you are selling fresh produce then your customers are more likely to come back regularly; in this case a business relying on the local market might be profitable.

Figure 4.1 For your business to be successful, you need to get the right balance between quality and price

Competition

You should identify other businesses that sell similar products or services, and compare your offerings with theirs. If they sell similar products to you, but to a different market, they may not be competitors as they will not be trying to attract the same customers.

For example, if you had a sandwich business in the town centre another sandwich business operating from a delivery van selling direct to out of town offices would not be a competitor. However, if they opened a shop in the town centre, selling products that could be substituted for yours, then they would be a competitor. Is there room in the market for the two businesses?

Selling

A business must sell its products or services to make an income. That income must exceed all the costs in order for the business to make a profit. There are several ways that you can consider selling your product:

- *In a shop where customers would come to you*. You and your team of sales assistants would help customers to make their choices. You would have to consider the cost of renting the shop and paying staff.
- *By mail order*. You might consider selling your products solely via the Internet, where customers can shop when it suits them. You might also advertise in a magazine or newspaper, particularly if you are trying to make contact with a specific group of readers. These methods would be more successful if you were selling a product that was easy to pack and post. You may be able to rent storage space more cheaply than you could rent shop space.
- *Hand delivery*. If you deliver your goods to customers' homes and businesses (for example, if you had a sandwich round or were selling goods from a catalogue) you would have to consider the transport costs.
- *Service at clients' homes*. If you were offering a service such as cleaning, decorating or building, you might drop leaflets in an area, leaving a telephone number for potential customers to contact you. You might also consider placing advertisements or posters in places such as supermarkets or libraries.

Changing trends and fashions

If your shop stocks fashion items such as clothes, you know that fashion is constantly changing and you must shift your stock quickly to make room for new lines. If you sell food, drink, sweets, and other foods, you have to deal with the shelf life of products and turn the stock over before products reach their sell-by

Figure 4.2 A 'puff ball' skirt – how long will it stay in fashion?

dates. Is your potential market likely to be influenced by issues such as these?

For example, at the time of writing, the latest fashion shows have featured numerous variations on the theme of the 'puff ball' skirt. It is likely that such a distinctive style will be short-lived, so it would be unwise to buy too much stock.

Materials and supplies

If you are **selling** a product, you will have to buy in your stock from another business such as the local cash and carry warehouse. A sales representative may call on you, on behalf of a supplier, to persuade you to order more stock and to try new lines. If you are **making** a product, you will need to obtain raw materials and possibly machinery and equipment. If you are offering a service, you will generally not carry much stock – possibly spare parts, stationery, cleaning materials, office equipment and other items you need for your work.

Successful businesses operate on a 'just in time' policy. This means they purchase just enough stock to meet demand, so that they don't have to pay out large sums of money before the goods are sold.

Technology plays a vital role in the modern world to identify the minimum stock levels to achieve the maximum return, without having to turn away dissatisfied customers.

Carrying out market research

In order to find the answers to these questions, a business will carry out **market research**. Successful market research will draw on primary and secondary sources of information.

Primary research will stem from observations you may have made, and from interviews or questionnaires. You should aim to gather information from a sample of people who represent the groups you are hoping to sell to. The larger the sample you interview, the more accurate your research is likely to be, although you must always remember that no survey is perfect and there will always be a margin of error. It would be helpful to look back at the section entitled 'Using surveys' in Unit 1 before you start to design any questionnaire for market research purposes.

Secondary research material can be sourced from published reports that reveal the results of surveys carried out by the Government and other organisations. This material may be available in the form of Government publications, retail audits or reports by key operators in the market, such as retailers, wholesalers and suppliers. In addition, established businesses will have their own sales and customer records. Published research may not have been carried out for exactly the same purpose as you require and you should bear in mind that it may be less useful and reliable than your own research findings.

You must remember to record and acknowledge all sources of information.

Think it over ...

When Thomas Tripp and Barbie Beach first had the idea of opening Travelbug, it was necessary for them to carry out research as to the viability of their venture.
- How do you think they went about this?
- Give examples of the questions they may have included in a questionnaire?

Skills Builder

At this stage you should be able to tackle Task 3 of the Skills Builder mini project on page 213. Don't forget to study the scenario carefully so that you are clear about the project objective.

Financial planning

Spreadsheet models

Financial planning is crucial to business success. A successful enterprise needs to identify the flow of income and expenditure, to ensure that costs can be covered. This analysis can then be used to calculate the break-even point and to predict profits. Spreadsheet software is an invaluable tool for creating a computer model of the financial side of a business. The model may be a simple forecast, such as a budget plan for planning an 18th birthday party, or something extremely complicated, such as a model of a school's income and expenditure.

A spreadsheet model to identify the potential break-even and profit points is based on

- different values of input data
- formulas which define the rules of the model
- output data, which will vary according to the values of the input data.

An effective model will consider alternatives and the effect of various actions, such as

- increasing the price of an item to establish how much more income would be generated and how much profit might be made
- the importance of timing to ensure that costs can be met without encountering cash flow problems, and to identify which points in the year have the most expenditure or the lowest income
- varying the source of supplies or the type or quantity of raw materials used, to establish whether expenditure can be reduced.

Using spreadsheet software to design and build models enables you to make decisions such as

- *how much to charge for a product/service* – the more that is charged, the greater the profit may be, but if the product/service becomes too expensive then sales may drop and profit is reduced.
- *how much stock to purchase* – it is important to have enough stock available so that customers are not turned away, but not to be over-stocked so that business capital (money) is tied up. The capital would be better left earning interest in the bank or used to finance new opportunities that arise.
- *how much you need to sell to break even*
- *whether to expand or reduce existing activities*:
  - If an item is selling really well, do you place another large order from the supplier, or is there a risk that the market is saturated and you will be unable to sell the items?
  - If an item that was popular and profitable is no longer selling well, you have to make a decision to continue or to withdraw the line. For example, cold air fans are popular during a heat wave, but do not sell well in cold weather. You may decide not to re-order in October, but still continue the line. On the

Jargon buster

In stock terms a **line** is one particular product for sale.

Skills check ▶▶

As with all the work you prepare for your projects, you must make effective use of the presentation and formatting facilities offered by the software. Refer to the Spreadsheet Software skills section (page 297) for information about using

- font style and size, colours, borders and shading to enhance the layout
- formulas and formatting techniques – such as conditional formatting, linking worksheets, limit data input to acceptable values only, hiding or protecting cells – to ensure the accuracy of the data and the information obtained from it
- charts and graphs to present the results of the model.

other hand, if a new version of a games console is due to be launched within the next month or two then it is good business sense to discontinue the previous model and to wait until the new model is available before placing your next order.

Before you can develop a useful spreadsheet model, you need to decide what

- information you want from the model
- data should be entered
- calculations must be performed
- output is required.

Let's consider a simple spreadsheet model. Travelbug are thinking of offering day trips to France via Eurotunnel, with a meal included. Thomas Tripp wants to know the costs for

- a coach and driver
- fuel
- crossing to France using Eurotunnel
- a meal in France.

He can use this information to decide how much they should charge their customers.

Barbie Beach has established that the fixed costs are

- 55 seater coach – £300
- driver's wages – £100
- Fuel – £120
- Eurotunnel – £300
- Food/drink – £500 regardless of the number of people. (This is a good price for the meal provided they sell enough tickets.)

Barbie is considering charging £40 per person. She has created a spreadsheet model to establish the costs, the income and how many customers they will need in order to break even. Figure 4.3 shows the spreadsheet model, giving the total of fixed costs and the variable income depending on the number of tickets sold. You can see that if they charge £40 per person then they must sell 33 seats to break even. If they sell all the seats then they will make a profit of £880.

Notice that the use of suitable font style and size, bold and colour makes the spreadsheet much clearer. The 'If' function was used in row 15 so that the words 'Loss', 'Break Even' or 'Profit' would appear automatically, depending on the values in row 14.

Conditional formatting was used in rows 14 and 15 so that the result would be illustrated in red, blue or green, depending on the values of the data.

Having established the layout of the spreadsheet model, it is a simple matter to try out different values. For example, what if they increase the charge for the day trip to £44 each? Figure 4.4 shows the model after the fare has been increased. This time they need to sell only 30 seats to break even, and if they fill the coach then the profit will increase from £880 to £1100.

Barbie Beach has decided that it is worth trying out the new service, and feels that she can make an introductory offer of £40, but will increase it to £44 for future day trips.

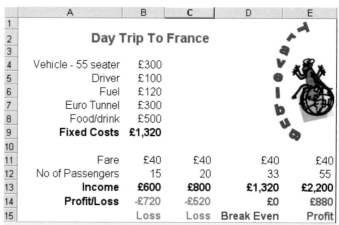

Figure 4.3 A spreadsheet model of the costs and income to run a day trip to France

Figure 4.4 A spreadsheet model of the costs and income to run a day trip to France, showing an alternative fare price

The data can also be illustrated as a line graph. This style of graph is most suitable to illustrate a break-even point. This is the point where the fixed costs and the income meet, and is clearly visible in Figure 4.5.

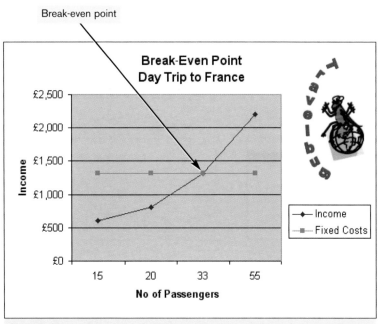

Figure 4.5 Line graph showing the break-even point for a day trip to France

Testing

There is a great danger of assuming that results produced using a computer must be right. It is essential to check that your spreadsheet model is accurate. There may be an error in one of the formulas, or the data type may be unsuitable. For example, should a numerical value be set to *integer* (whole number) or *decimal*? When the model is first designed, enter test data and then check the results using a calculator. For example, in the model shown in Figure 4.3, you could multiply the number of passengers by the cost of the fare, and confirm that the total income is correct.

The use of validation rules helps to ensure the accuracy of a model. There is a range of validation criteria available (Figure 4.6). For example, the cells containing the number of passengers were each set to be a whole number with a maximum of 55, as there are only 55 seats in the coach. If you then enter a number higher than 55, an error message appears warning you that the value you entered is not valid. Obviously it is still possible to make data entry errors, but setting a data validation rule reduces the risk of mistakes.

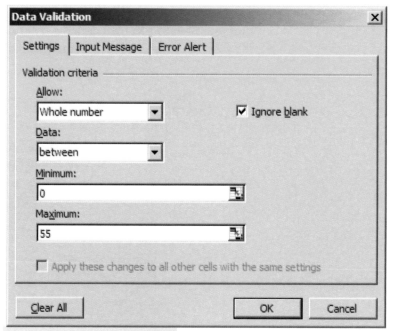

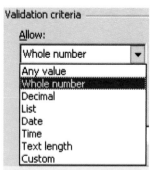

Figure 4.6 Validation criteria

Figure 4.7 Setting data validation

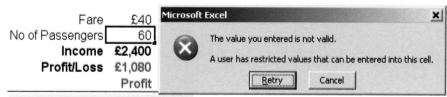

Figure 4.8 Validation error message

Go out and try!

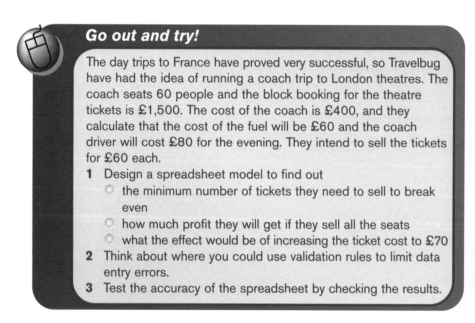

The day trips to France have proved very successful, so Travelbug have had the idea of running a coach trip to London theatres. The coach seats 60 people and the block booking for the theatre tickets is £1,500. The cost of the coach is £400, and they calculate that the cost of the fuel will be £60 and the coach driver will cost £80 for the evening. They intend to sell the tickets for £60 each.

1 Design a spreadsheet model to find out
   ○ the minimum number of tickets they need to sell to break even
   ○ how much profit they will get if they sell all the seats
   ○ what the effect would be of increasing the ticket cost to £70
2 Think about where you could use validation rules to limit data entry errors.
3 Test the accuracy of the spreadsheet by checking the results.

Start a file called 'ICT and Enterprise'. Create a new bold heading called '**Spreadsheet models**' and describe the skills you have learnt.

Skills Builder

At this stage you should be able to tackle Tasks 4 and 5 of the Skills Builder mini project on page 54. Don't forget to study the scenario carefully so that you are clear about the project objective.

Creating a marketing plan

You should prepare a marketing or business plan to show that you have thought about the way you are going to develop your business. The information you have researched will form the basis of your marketing plan. Marketing plans may vary depending on the type of organisation and the reason they are being prepared. However, all marketing plans will include the '**4Ps**' of marketing:

- Product – a description of the products and/or services
- Place – where they are sold and how they will be distributed
- Price – how much is to be charged
- Promotion – how they will be promoted.

Your marketing plan may follow the structure in the table below:

Enterprise aim	Short-term and long-term aims of the enterprise.
Current position	Analysis of the market and the potential customers: • Identify any competitors • Is there a unique selling point? • Which resources are available and which do you need to obtain?
Marketing targets	For example, how many products do you expect to sell in the first year?
Marketing mix	Give details here of the 4Ps of marketing referred to above.
Marketing strategy	How do you intend to market (inform the public about) your product?
Summary and conclusions	Summarise the main features of the whole marketing plan.

Presenting business proposals

If you are to be successful with a new enterprise, it is imperative that you are able to communicate your ideas effectively. You will need to learn to use presentation software, such as PowerPoint, to convey information in a professional way.

Have you ever attended a presentation where the speaker merely reads his notes or the text on slides word for word? If you have, you will know that this is not an effective way of communicating information, as the presentation will be very dull and boring. You will need, therefore, to think about the best way of presenting information; for example, you might use the text on each slide to jog your memory so that you can elaborate and give further details on each point.

Skills check ▶▶

You will learn how to create presentations using PowerPoint in the skills chapter on page 360.

The presenter of a successful business presentation will have taken the time to design slides that convey the main points clearly.

Content and Structure

In the same way as when you are creating a website or other multimedia product, you will need to plan the content and structure. Creating a storyboard and structure chart is essential before you start building the slides.

You will need to make decisions about the multimedia components you want to include; for example text, graphics, sounds, video, animation, charts or diagrams. Remember that having too many different components can take the focus off the overall aim of a presentation – don't use a component such as animation just to show off your new skills; use it only if it adds to the overall content and message you want to convey. The position on the page of key items is also very important – if you do not give much thought to this, the overall impression can be messy.

Finally, you should pay attention to the proportion of text to any visual or audio information. Often it is easier to convey a message using images rather than blocks of text.

Think it over ...

Compare the two slides in Figure 4.9. The content is exactly the same, but the positioning of the components is different. Which do you think has the most effective layout and why?

Figure 4.9 Position of components on a slide

Presentation techniques

Layout, font type and size

In the presentation skills section you will learn how to lay out each slide either using the PowerPoint design templates or by building a slide from scratch. When choosing the font and size, remember that you will need to ensure that people at the back of the audience can read the slides, so do not use too small a font – 24 point or above is a good size.

> You also need to consider the **x-height** of a font: the height of the lower-case x, and of many other lower-case letters such as a, c and e. Two fonts may both be the same point size but have different x-heights.
>
> Look at the following two lines of text, both of which are in 16-point fonts:
>
> ## This text is in 16-point Arial
>
> ## This text is in 16-point Verdana

Line spacing and alignment

You can use the same skills that you use in word processing to change the line spacing of text (for example from single to double) and its alignment (centred, justified and so on).

Bullets

You can easily create bulleted lists with PowerPoint. Bullet points are helpful when used as prompts and to summarize points.

Text wrapping

PowerPoint allows you to word wrap text in an AutoShape. To do this you need to ensure that the **Word wrap text in AutoShape** checkbox is selected in the *Format AutoShape* dialogue box, as shown in Figure 4.10.

Thomas Tripp selected this option for the final slide of his PowerPoint presentation (Figure 4.11).

Ensure this option is selected to word wrap text

The text in the AutoShape has been word wrapped

Figure 4.10 Format AutoShape dialogue box

Figure 4.11 Word wrapping text in an AutoShape

Colour and backgrounds

You will need to consider the colour scheme for your presentation. The Presentation Software skills chapter (page 360) covers how to change such things as the colours used for text and lines, shadows, title text, fills, accents, hyperlinks and backgrounds.

TiP

Use colours carefully; remember that if you change the colour scheme from slide to slide, it will take the audience time to adjust. It is acceptable to change the colour on one slide in order to draw special attention to the slide, or to break a long presentation into appropriate chunks with a different colour scheme for each chunk, but never change the colour scheme without a specific purpose.

Take the following design considerations into account when creating a presentation.

- You should choose text and background colour combinations carefully, and go for high contrast. If you choose a subtle difference, the text may be difficult to read. Also, if the data projector cannot handle these slight differences, both the text and background colours may default to the same colour!
- You need to consider the environment where you will be giving the presentation. A dark background with light text is best for dark rooms, whereas a light background with dark text is best for light rooms.
- You will see from Figure 4.12 that you should avoid patterned backgrounds behind text – the text is almost impossible to read!

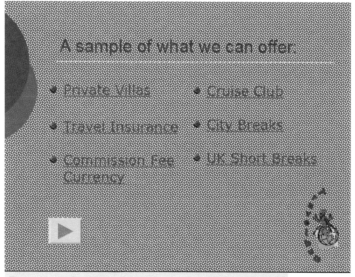

Figure 4.12 Example slide with a patterned background

Transitions

When you show a PowerPoint presentation, you can apply different slide transitions when you move from one slide to the next. When you design a PowerPoint presentation, each slide has a transition associated with it. PowerPoint offers a large number of different transition styles to choose from – for example *box in*, *box out*, *blinds horizontal* and *blinds vertical*. If you prefer, you can set the slide transition to *no transition*. Any special effects should be used with care – they should be used to enhance your presentation, so take care that they do not distract or irritate.

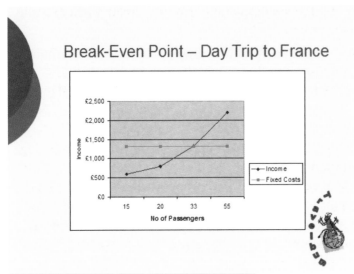

Figure 4.13 Inserting a graph into a presentation

Transferring information

One useful feature of PowerPoint is that you can include information in a slide from another software application. For example, you can insert a table produced in a word processor into a slide. When Thomas Tripp and Barbie Beach were forming Travelbug, they created a presentation to show their bank manager. As you can see in Figure 4.13, they were able to copy a graph produced in Excel and paste it into a slide.

Delivering the presentation

You should prepare for a presentation by doing the following things.

- *Rehearsing what you are going to say.* PowerPoint allows you to record the narration so that you can check what the presentation will sound like to an audience. You can do this by choosing the **Record Narration** option from the **Slide Show** menu (Figure 4.14). Having recorded what you want to say, you can run the presentation and sit back and listen. You will find that you get an entirely different point of view when you pretend to be the audience. You will find it easier to pick up any unclear passages, boring aspects or any awkward moments.

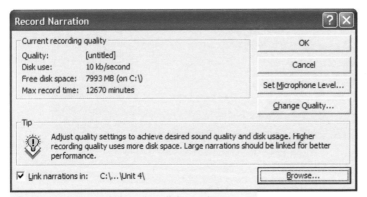

Figure 4.14 Record Narration dialogue box

Having made any changes, you can simply turn off the narration by choosing **Set Up Show** from the **Slide Show** menu and selecting the **Show without narration** option.

- *Checking timings, transitions and content.* As well as rehearsing what you are going to say, you should check any timings carefully. You need to estimate how long it will take you to present a slide, or how long you need between animations on a slide. By choosing **Rehearse Timings** from the **Slide Show** menu you can ensure that you do not have to speak too rapidly or too slowly when doing your final presentation.

○ *Checking your content carefully.* There is nothing worse than realising halfway through a presentation that you have spelt a word incorrectly, and it will not create a very good impression!

Producing speaker notes and handouts

You will learn in the Presentation skills section (see page 380) how to create speaker notes; this feature allows you to include notes with a slide. You can add anything you want in these notes, and the slides can be printed out with the notes. Thomas Tripp can use this facility to give extra details on the different cities shown on the City Break slide of his presentation. He can print out the slide, together with the notes, to give to prospective customers.

No one in the audience will realise that you have included speaker notes, unless you print them out as handouts, so you can use them for reminders about what you want to say. When you are running the presentation, if you right-click on the slide with speaker notes and select **Speaker Notes** from the menu, the *Speaker Notes* dialogue box will appear, but will not be seen by the audience (Figure 4.15). You can even edit the notes during a show!

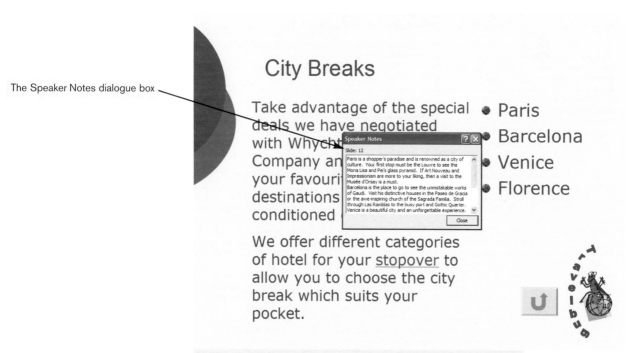

The Speaker Notes dialogue box

Figure 4.15 Presentation being run with Speaker Notes revealed

Finally, it is useful to be able to give your audience handouts either at the beginning or the end of the presentation. You can choose to print three slides on each page, with a space on the right-hand side for notes (Figure 4.16); it is useful for an audience to receive these handouts at the outset so that they can write their own notes whilst you are presenting.

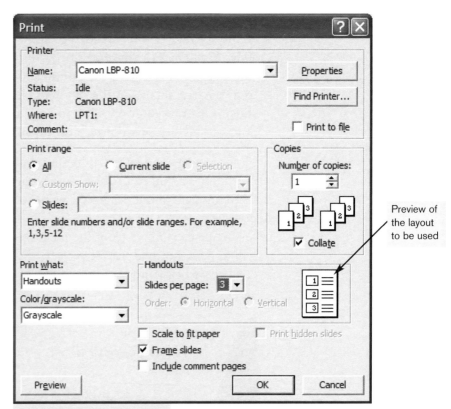

Preview of the layout to be used

Figure 4.16 Printing handouts

If you are trying to sell a new idea for an enterprise, you need to ensure that you hold your audience's attention rather than distract them. You could be tempted to spend time using all the features available, such as creating a fancy animation, whilst forgetting the basic rules of presenting:

- tell to the audience what you are going to tell them
- tell them
- tell what you have told them.

A first-class presentation will be of little use if, when you come to deliver it, you are ill-prepared or a poor presenter.

Skills Builder

At this stage you should be able to tackle Tasks 6 and 7 of the Skills Builder mini project on page 213. Don't forget to study the scenario carefully so that you are clear about the project objective.

Creating a corporate identity

The first thing most people conjure up in their mind when talking about well-known companies or products is a vision of the brand image. For this reason, it is of the utmost importance that a business establishes a recognisable corporate image or identity. The corporate identity encompasses all aspects of the business: packaging, stationery, websites, fleets of delivery vehicles, publications and even the uniform worn by employees. Millions of pounds are spent every year by businesses promoting their brand image or corporate identity.

A brand image may be based on a name, a logo or a particular colour. Football clubs are big business and they are instantly recognised from their name, logo and team colours. For example the colour we associate with Chelsea is blue, whereas with Manchester United it is red. If you think of easyJet, the budget airline, the colour orange will spring to mind; Virgin products and services are associated with red.

You will develop a corporate identity or brand image for your business enterprise. You must decide on the type of image you want your business to have, such as trendy, efficient, high-tech, stylish, environmentally friendly or customer focussed. When designing your brand image you will need to think about a logo and strap-line, a colour scheme, and the format and style you want to use.

Logo

Your logo should make your business easily recognisable. It may be formed from the initials of the business name, or you may choose a simple image to represent the business. The logo should be clear and uncomplicated. If you have already studied Unit 3, you will be familiar with the website LogoLounge – available via http://www.heinemann.co.uk/hotlinks (express code 0069P) which showcases the work of many top graphic designers. If not, it would be a good idea to browse the website for ideas before you embark on your logo design.

Strap-line

A *strap-line* is a snappy little phrase that businesses use to let people know what their business is about. For example, Travelbug use the strap-line 'Your holiday is in safe hands'. You will need to think of a suitable strap-line to represent your business enterprise, and you might use a strap-line to emphasise an aspect of your business that you are trying to promote, such as the environment, value for money or personal service.

Figure 4.17 The Royal Institute of Chartered Surveyors incorporate a strapline that describes the principles they represent

Colour scheme

The colours in your logo will usually be reused throughout the business. When considering colour, you should bear in mind that whatever you choose will probably be used for both printed and on-screen publications. For example, the logo will be used on letterheads, business cards, brochures and web pages. You may decide to select one colour from the logo to be used for text and another colour for the background. You must make sure there is sufficient contrast between the background and foreground colours so that any text can be read easily either on a screen or in print.

Black and white can be very effective, a combination of grey and white can look stylish and modern, and green is associated with the environment.

You will probably experiment with a variety of colour combinations as you develop your ideas; you must remember to keep your early design work as evidence for your e-portfolio.

Format and style

Your choice of font style and size is also an important consideration. A consistent approach gives the impression of a well-organised business. You may decide to adopt a particular font style and colour for the business name and a different style for other details. You

Think it over ...

Look at a range of company websites and consider the following:
- Does the overall image reflect the nature of the business?
- Is the logo easily identifiable?
- Is a strap-line used to communicate what the company does?
- Does the house style reflect the colours used in the logo?

should make sure that the font style you choose is suitable for both print and screen, and that it is accepted by different browsers. Don't choose something too flamboyant unless you are promoting a showy, colourful business image. A more modest approach will generally be taken more seriously.

Business Communication

Templates

An initial impression of any business is usually formed from the way that it communicates. For example, an unhelpful employee at the end of a telephone does little to promote the image of the business.

Figure 4.18 What sort of impression does this give to customers?

In the same way, poorly presented documentation does nothing to enhance the image of the business. To ensure that all correspondence sent from any department in the organisation looks the same, businesses use templates that reflect their house style. Templates are frequently used for letters, faxes, invoices, receipts, business cards, and other customer documents.

One advantage of using a template is that every time you open it, the layout and style of the document is ready for you to use straight away. You do not have to spend time changing font styles, margins, text alignment, and so on.

For your project, you will create a series of templates for standard business documents. You will need to consider the purpose of each template when creating its content and structure. Your templates should all reflect your chosen corporate identity. For example, each template should include the logo and use the same font style and colour, although the size of font will probably vary between templates. Wherever possible, common components, such as the business address, should be displayed in a similar position to give an overall impression of consistency in layout.

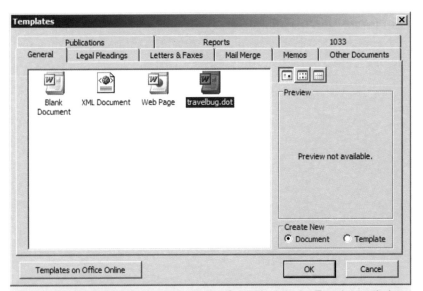

Figure 4.19 Templates are stored under the General tab in the Templates window

When you are satisfied with the design of each template, you should test it in two ways. First, use it to prepare a document for which it was designed. Make sure you are able to complete it in the way you intended – that all the information fits in the right place. Second, show your design to other people for their comments and, if necessary, modify your design to take account of their feedback. When you are sure your design is complete, you must save it as a template file. Templates created in Word take the file extension **.dot** and templates created in Excel become **.xlt**. They will automatically be saved in the *General* template folder and can be identified as templates by the yellow band on the icon.

A document created from a template will be saved with a normal extension (**.doc** or **.xls**). Adding content to the new document will not change the template, which will be ready next time you need it.

Business letterhead

A business letterhead is used for written communications that are sent outside the business. Because the letterhead will be sent to customers and suppliers, and may even be their first form of contact with the business, it must be designed to reflect the business's corporate identity.

TiP

To ensure that the positions of text and images on your letterhead are not affected when you use the template to prepare letters, it is a good idea to create the letterhead in Header and Footer view. On screen the colours will appear to be dull when you write a letter based on the template, but when you print it the colours will be as you created them.

A letterhead will usually include

- a logo
- the name of the business
- the full address, including the post code
- the telephone number
- a fax number, where applicable
- an email address
- the website URL.

When you design the letterhead for your business enterprise, you must think about where you will place the logo, company name and address, and other components on the page. Since the purpose of a letterhead is to provide space for a letter to be written, you should aim to make as much white space available as possible. Therefore, to maximise usable space, make full use of the top and bottom margin areas for the business information. In addition, think about margin size, your corporate colours and the font style and size you will use to make your letterhead effective.

17 London Road   Whychton   **TO9 3WN**

Tel: 543 2134 5678
Fax: 543 2134 5679

www.travelbug.co.uk
Email: info@travelbug.co.uk

17 London Road   Whychton   **TO9 3WN**

Tel: 543 2134 5678
Fax: 543 2134 5679

www.travelbug.co.uk
Email: info@travelbug.co.uk

Our Ref TT/BB

18 October 2005

The Manager
Nationwide Hotel Group
123 London Road
HEATHWOOD
LL5 BB3

Dear Sir

NEW BUSINESS VENTURE

Travelbug is an independent holiday company and we are planning to diversify into the area of coach touring holidays. We would like to establish a network of hotels to link into our itineraries.

Your group has hotels close to many of the attractions we will be including in our tours and we would like to discuss the possibility of arranging block bookings with you.

In order to explore this possibility in detail I would like to propose a meeting with you in the course of the next few weeks. I enclose a copy of our company brochure for your information

I will telephone you early next week to arrange a mutually convenient date.

Yours faithfully

Thomas Tripp
Director

Enc

Figure 4.20 The Travelbug letterhead maximises the use of white space

Figure 4.21 A letter presented on Travelbug's letterhead

In Unit 1 we looked at the style of presentation used for business letters. We found that most businesses adopt a fully blocked style of presentation, where all text starts at the left-hand margin and the only punctuation used is included for grammatical purposes. When you prepare business letters on your new letterhead, make sure you refer back to Unit 1 to remind yourself of the information that you should include in your letter. You must also make sure that the writing style and tone are suitable for the purpose of the letter.

Fax cover sheet

A *facsimile message* – or *fax* – is used to send a copy of a document over a telephone line. The document is converted into electronic signals, which are transmitted through the telephone system. The signals are converted back into a copy of the original document and printed on the receiving fax machine.

Think it over ...

Look at the various fax template styles that are available in your word processing software. Which do you prefer? What changes would you need to make to a standard template if you wanted to use it for your business?

Some computer systems have fax software, which overrides the need for a fax machine. The fax is sent from the computer to a fax machine or computer at the other end. Faxes received are displayed on the computer screen.

A document sent by fax may have any number of pages, and can contain text and images. However, so that the person receiving the fax knows what is being sent, from whom and how many pages have been sent, a fax cover sheet is usually sent first.

A fax cover sheet will include

- a logo and strap-line
- the name and full details of the company sending the fax
- the name, fax and telephone numbers of the person to receive the fax
- the name, fax and telephone numbers of the person sending the fax
- today's date
- the number of pages being sent (including the cover sheet)
- the subject heading
- space for a short message.

The telephone numbers are included so that the person receiving the fax can be contacted to say the message has been sent. If there is a problem and only part of the message is received, the person sending the fax can also be contacted and asked to resend it. Any message included on the fax cover sheet is usually quite brief and informal, whereas the document that is being attached may be written in a more formal style and tone.

The fax cover sheet that you design for your business should reflect the corporate identity in the same way as your letterhead. It can be helpful to use a table to display the information that you wish to include. Borders and shading can be used effectively to improve the appearance of the table.

Figure 4.22 Travelbug's Fax Cover Sheet clearly reflects the corporate identity

Invoice

An invoice is sent to a customer requesting payment for goods or services supplied. It will list the individual items that have been sent to the customer and will show the cost of each item and the overall value of the invoice. Each invoice is given a unique reference number.

The appearance of the invoice will reflect the corporate identity in the same way as a letterhead or fax. It will include the following details:

- the logo and strap-line
- full details of the company, including name, address and telephone number
- space for customer's name, address and account number
- the invoice number
- the date
- the supplier's VAT number, if they have one
- details of goods supplied – typically *quantity*, *reference*, *description* and *unit price*
- the total cost of the invoice, including goods and services, VAT, postage and packing charges, and anything else the customer is being charged for
- terms and conditions for settling the invoice.

Skills check ▶▶

Refer to the skills section on Spreadsheet software (page 297) for information about using the formatting tools.

You will prepare your invoice in spreadsheet software so that you can build in formulas to calculate the cost of each item and the total cost of the invoice. You can remove the gridlines from the spreadsheet and include borders and shading where you think they are necessary. In this way your invoice will be clear to read and the totals will stand out.

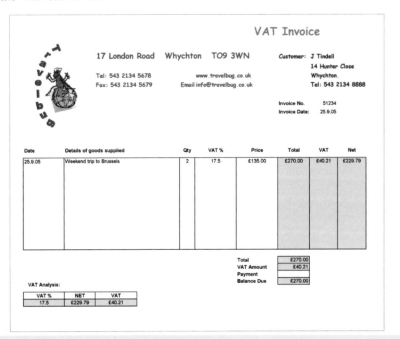

VAT Invoice

17 London Road   Whychton   TO9 3WN

Tel: 543 2134 5678   www.travelbug.co.uk
Fax: 543 2134 5679   Email info@travelbug.co.uk

Customer: J Tindell
14 Hunter Close
Whychton.
Tel: 543 2134 8888

Invoice No.   51234
Invoice Date: 25.9.05

Date	Details of goods supplied	Qty	VAT %	Price	Total	VAT	Net
25.9.05	Weekend trip to Brussels	2	17.5	£135.00	£270.00	£40.21	£229.79

Total	£270.00
VAT Amount	£40.21
Payment	
Balance Due	£270.00

VAT Analysis:

VAT %	NET	VAT
17.5	£229.79	£40.21

Figure 4.23 This is the invoice Travelbug use to confirm holiday bookings. It has been designed to suit the purpose of the business. In this case the details of goods supplied refers to holiday bookings and the quantity indicates the number of people

Receipt

If you were running a business that took in customers' personal belongings to repair them, you may give the customer a receipt to confirm that the goods are in your possession.

For example, a jeweller repairing some earrings will give the customer a receipt with a receipt number. The item of jewellery will also be allocated the same number, so the jeweller can match the item with the receipt when the customer calls to collect it. The customer must produce the receipt in order to collect the goods. Without the receipt, the jeweller has no way of knowing for certain that the item actually belongs to the person claiming it.

The receipt is usually in two sections – one for the business and one for the customer. It may be perforated to allow the two sections to be separated easily.

Another use for a receipt is to confirm that a payment has been received. If you buy something in a supermarket, you are given a receipt printed from the till. This lists the items you have bought and how much you paid for them. If you buy expensive products from other types of shops, you will also be given a receipt to confirm that you have paid for the goods; this receipt may be handwritten or printed from a computer document. Sometimes the receipt confirms that you have paid a deposit at the time of ordering goods, and that there is still an outstanding balance to be paid before the goods are delivered. The exact details on a receipt will vary depending on the purpose of the receipt, but typically will include

- the logo and strap-line
- a receipt number
- the date
- the name and full details of the business
- the name and full details of the customer, including telephone number
- a brief description of the goods for repair and an indication of the problem, or a description of the product or service paid for
- an indication of the cost of repair or the amount of money paid
- the name or initials of the person accepting the repair.

Go out and try!

Design two receipts:
- one that can be given to customers when they take electrical goods in for repair
- one that can be given to customers when they pay for the repair.

Open your file called 'ICT and Enterprise'. Create a new bold heading called '**Designing receipts**' and describe the skills you have learnt.

Business cards

If you are browsing round a retail store and you stop to ask a sales assistant for some advice, it is likely that the sales assistant will offer you his or her business card before you leave the store. When people look at new cars in a showroom, or arrange for a salesperson to call at home to discuss a new kitchen or replacement windows, they will also be offered a business card by the salesperson.

The sales staff have realised that there is a potential sale, and they are anxious to ensure that the customer doesn't forget which salesperson was helping them. Many sales staff rely on commission from the goods they sell to boost their salaries, so it is important to them that customers feel they have received a personal service and want to come back to the same assistant.

Most businesses ensure that all staff who come into contact with the public have a supply of business cards to give away. The purpose of a business card is therefore to make sure a business or salesperson is not forgotten and to make it easy for potential customers to get in touch again.

> If I put it with the others, I won't lose it!

Figure 4.24 A business card should be memorable

A business card measures approximately 8.5 cm × 5.5 cm – just large enough to contain essential information but small enough to fit into a customer's wallet. The details on a business card will usually include

- the logo and strap-line
- the name and address of the business
- the name and job title of the person giving the card together with his/her office and mobile telephone numbers and e-mail address.

Figure 4.25
Travelbug business card

The business card will reflect the corporate identity of the business and will usually make use of white space to make it easy for the customer or client to find specific information.

Using your templates

Once your templates are saved in their final versions, you will be able to use them to prepare a variety of letters, invoices, faxes and other business documents. The overall appearance of the documents you produce is very important in order to create a good impression of the business. You should remember to use the various presentation techniques you learnt about in Unit 1 to make your documents readable and professional.

- Use headings and sub-headings to highlight different sections within the document.
- Lay your documents out so that they are clear to read, use paragraphs to break the text up into readable chunks and use white space to help your presentation. You do not have to use every single line that is available on a page.
- Ensure that the font style and size remain the same throughout the document.
- Vary the line spacing to make sections of text stand out, for example in long lists of descriptions and prices. It can be easy to read the wrong price alongside an item if the text is spaced too closely together.
- Use bullet points to identify items in a list.
- Use tables, borders and shading to present information more clearly.
- Choose an appropriate writing style and tone to suit the purpose of the document.
- Proofread every document and don't forget to use the spellchecker too!

Skills Builder

At this stage you should be able to tackle Task 8 of the Skills Builder mini project on page 213. Don't forget to study the scenario carefully so that you are clear about the project objective.

Using email effectively

You will learn in the advertising and promotion section of this chapter (page 204) that modern businesses are making extensive use of email to market their goods and services. Furthermore, email has replaced the internal memo and is now the principal method of communication within organisations.

Anyone that uses email (and fax, telephone, text and picture messaging) to send direct marketing messages must comply with the Privacy and Electronic Communications (EC Directive) regulations 2003. This law was introduced in order to reduce the problem of spam (unsolicited commercial email). Recommended best practice when using email for marketing includes the following:

- Ensure at the point of collection (often on an order form) that it is clearly stated that the email address will be used for marketing.
- Give the person the opportunity to refuse permission for this to be done.
- If the email is to be sent to existing customers, the content of the email should be in respect of similar products and services.
- If the email address is to be shared with a third party, this should be clearly stated.
- Email addresses should not be 'harvested', for example copied from lots of websites.
- If you have received a marketing email, you should be able to refuse permission for further emails to be sent to you. Therefore there should be a clear and simple way of opting out from receiving future emails (see Figure 4.26).

TiP

Think carefully before clicking any links, even 'unsubscribe' ones, sent by businesses you have not had any dealings with. These links might not be legitimate – you might start to get more, not less, spam if you click them!

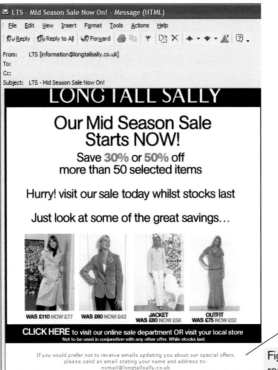

Instructions explaining how to opt out of receiving further emails

Figure 4.26 Opting out from receiving further emails

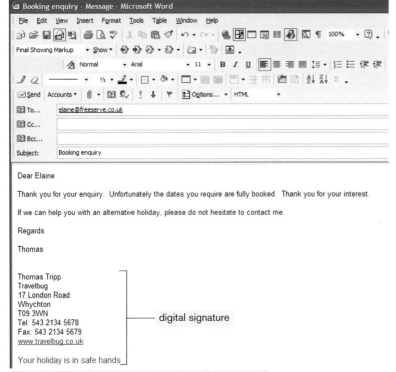

Figure 4.27 Example of a formal digital signature

Digital Signatures

When using an email for communication, whether internally or externally, it is good practice to add a digital signature to your message. Most email software will allow you to set up more than one, which has the advantage that you can use a more formal digital signature for external emails, a less formal signature for internal emails and an informal signature for emails to friends and family. Thomas Tripp has used the full contact details, including the Travelbug strap-line 'your holiday is in safe hands', as his external contact digital signature (Figure 4.27).

Automated responses

Most businesses provide an email option for contact because it is quicker for customers to type a few lines via email than to make a phone call to a call centre and be put in a queue. One negative aspect of this is that a business may be swamped with large numbers of emails and, as a result, it may take several days for them to respond to a request, which can lead to customer dissatisfaction.

To respond more quickly, many companies are using the features of email software to set up automated responses to email enquiries. Automatic responses can be used for such things as requests for additional information, requests to have a forgotten password sent and acknowledgement of orders. Companies find that they can handle a large proportion of their emails using automated email responses (see Figure 4.28).

TiP

It is not advisable to set up an automatic response saying that you are going to be away on holiday for your personal email account. This is because it can advertise the fact that your home may be empty and therefore open to burglars.

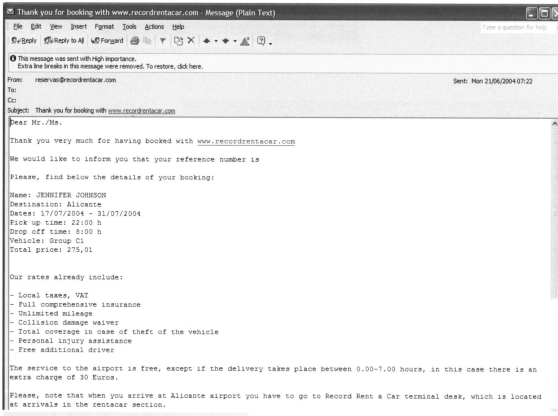

Figure 4.28 Example automated response email

Automatic responses are also useful for individual employees to set up when they are going to be out of the office, for example when they are going on holiday.

Distribution lists

A *distribution list* (sometimes referred to as a *group*) allows you to send an email to a number of email contacts simultaneously, without having to type all the email addresses in the To: box. Businesses find this a useful tool, as they can set up distribution lists for specific purposes; this can save a considerable amount of staff time. For example, as you can see in Figure 4.29, Travelbug use a distribution list to send electronic newsletters to all customers on a monthly basis.

Figure 4.29 Sending an email to a distribution list

Attachments

You can easily attach one or more files to an email. The email can be sent to one email contact or to a large number of people. You can attach any file, although you need to be aware that emails with large attachments may be blocked by the receiving mail server. It may be necessary to use compression techniques, such as creating a zip file, to send large files. Organisations find emails with attachments to be a quick and economic way to send such things as newsletters, leaflets and brochures. Not only do businesses save time, but they do not have to pay for the printing or postage costs. In Figure 4.29 above, you will see that Thomas Tripp attached the March newsletter to the email sent to the Newsletter distribution group.

Skills check ▶▶

Refer to page 439 for detailed information about sending emails with attachments.

Advertising and promotion

Figure 4.30 An example of a poster displayed outside a shop in order to entice customers into the shop!

Businesses must promote the goods or services they supply, both to inform existing customers and to persuade potential customers that this is a product or service they need. Sometimes, special offers are used to entice new customers. For example, you will often see supermarkets with posters saying 'buy one get one free' or 'three for the price of two'. These offers are often heavily advertised in order to get customers in the shop. Once in the shop, customers are likely to buy more than they originally came in for.

Advertisements in magazines, newspapers and on hoardings are a favourite way of catching the attention of customers. Passers-by can also easily see posters in shop windows. Some large companies use sponsorship as a means of advertising, and many sporting teams, both amateur and professional, are willing to display a company logo on their kit in return for sponsorship money.

You will produce a variety of promotional material for your business, including

- advertisements
- leaflets
- posters/flyers
- mail shots
- websites.

When designing these items, you must also consider

- *Structure* – for example, if you are producing a leaflet, will you have one or two folds? What size will you choose for a poster compared to a flyer? Will you opt for portrait or landscape page orientation?
- *Composition* – what components will you include: photographs, images, text?
- *Balance* – how much of the available space will be taken up with text, images or white space? Will the size of one overpower the others?

Skills check ▶▶

Before you design any paper-based advertising and promotional material, it would be a good idea to refer to the Word processing software chapter (page 247) to remind yourself of the tools that will help you in the presentation of your promotional material. In addition, look at the section on leaflets and posters in Unit 1 and read about images in Unit 3 (if you are studying that unit).

○ *Colour* – this will depend very much on where you will be publishing the material. Posters are generally more eye-catching in colour, but advertisements in newspapers can be very effective in black and white. Flyers might be more economical to produce in just two or three different colours. Will the use of colour enhance the product or service you are promoting?

○ *Message* – what is the message you are trying to get across? Make sure you choose an appropriate style and tone. Keep your words to a minimum so they grab the attention of passers-by. Think of promotional words and phrases that catch your attention, such as 'Free', 'Special Offer' and '3 for the price of 2'.

○ *Corporate image* – follow the design principles you applied to the templates you produced for business communications. Be proud of your company name and logo. The more often people see them, the more familiar they will become. Finally, remember to include details of how and where customers can contact you?

SPECIAL OFFER

£75 per person

Valentine's Day in Paris

Romantic dinner for two
Guided tour of the city
including
Cruise on the River Seine

Luxury coach leaves Whychton on 14 February
at 0715, returning 0145.

Please contact us using the details below or return the form.

17 London Road	Whychton	TO9 3WN
Tel: 543 2134 5678		www.travelbug.co.uk
Fax: 543 2134 5679		Email: info@travelbug.co.uk

Your holiday is in safe hands

Please return to Travelbug, 17 London Road, Whychton. TO9 3N

Name ....

Address ....

....

Telephone .... Email ....

Please send me full details of the Valentine's Day coach trip to France.

Travelbug would like to contact you again in the future regarding special offers and travel deals. If you are happy for us to do so please tick the box. ☐

Figure 4.31 This is a flyer Travelbug delivered to homes in the local area. They used an image of a red rose as a watermark because red roses are associated with Valentine's Day

Skills Builder

At this stage you should be able to tackle Task 9 of the Skills Builder mini project on page 213. Don't forget to study the scenario carefully so that you are clear about the project objective.

Mail shots

Skills check ▶▶

Remember that such marketing information must only be used in accordance with the Data Protection Act (see the Standard Ways of Working section, page 242).

Nowadays, personal details are often obtained when someone has to complete a form, whether on paper or online, which says something like 'if you do not wish to receive further information about products or services please tick here'. Quite often, this box goes unnoticed and your details are added to a database, which can then be used or sold on to other businesses to use for marketing.

> Travelbug would like to contact you again in the future regarding special offers and travel deals. If you are happy for us to do so, please tick the box. ☐

Figure 4.32 These are the words Travelbug used at the foot of the flyer in Figure 4.31

These details are used for mail shots to inform the public about a product or special offer. This is where mail merge is so useful, because a company can easily reach a huge number of potential customers. Many organisations purchase mailing lists in order to reach their potential market.

Skills check ▶▶

See page 292 for more information about using mail merge.

You will use mail merge to produce a sales letter to customers whose personal details are stored in a database. Think carefully about the most appropriate writing style for your letter and ask someone to look at it and give you their comments. Be prepared to modify your letter as a result of their comments.

Technology is increasingly used to market new products and services. Many companies will ask you for an email address as well as a home address. They are then able to use the email address to email promotional material to you automatically. Web technology is also used as a means of advertising and no doubt you have come across 'pop-ups' advertising goods or services, often totally unconnected to the website you are viewing.

Think it over ...

Working in small groups, gather together a range of promotional material, such as advertisements from newspapers or magazines, leaflets, posters/flyers and screen prints from websites. Consider the following:

○ Does the advertisement grab your attention?
○ Is it well structured?
○ Is the balance of the components effective?
○ Is there a clear message?
○ Does it include promotional words such as 'special offer'?
○ Does it convey the corporate image, including colour schemes?

Skills Builder

At this stage you should be able to tackle Task 10 of the Skills Builder mini project on page 213. Don't forget to study the scenario carefully so that you are clear about the project objective

Promotional website

Since 1998 the number of households in the UK who could access the Internet from home has risen from 9 per cent (2.3 million) in 1998 to 52 per cent (12.9 million) by the end of 2004 (see Figure 4.33).

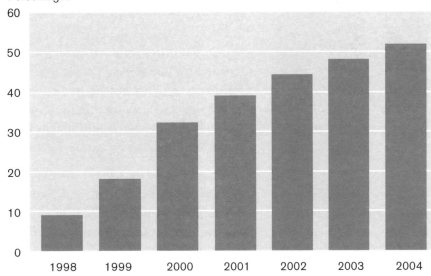

Figure 4.33 UK Households with home access to the Internet

Of these people, 61 per cent had used the Internet in the previous three months, and over half of these had bought or ordered goods, tickets or services. (Source: National Statistics website Crown copyright material is reproduced with the permission of the Controller of HMSO.) It is hardly surprising therefore that it is increasingly important for businesses to have a website to promote their products and services. The unique advantages of a website over other forms of marketing include the following:

○ Websites are almost always available (except, of course, when the web server on which the website is hosted is unavailable for possible maintenance or there are problems on the Internet itself).

○ Websites are easily updated. A brochure that needs to be updated would have to be sent to the printers for a reprint, which is costly and time-consuming.

○ There are low distribution costs. For example, the cost of distributing a brochure includes not only the postage and stationery, but also the staff costs involved in these activities. On the other hand, the cost of ensuring that a website is found easily through Internet searches, and the cost of hosting a website, are far less.

When building and designing a website to promote goods and services, you will need to make decisions on the following aspects.

Number of pages

This will very much depend on the overall content of the website and how you design its structure. You will need to gather the data and then sort it into groups of similar information, discarding any information you decide is not appropriate to the purpose of your website. If your website is for a company promoting travel, such as Travelbug, information regarding the history of travel agencies, although interesting, would not meet the requirements of the overall purpose of the site.

Once you have grouped all the subject matter together, break the information down into manageable chunks. Unlike readers of books, website visitors will scan web pages for the information they require. Keeping the chunks of information relatively small will allow visitors to scan the page easily.

By doing these preliminary tasks you are working towards the organisation and structure of the website.

Content of each page

You will probably decide to structure your website so that each page has a different subject, remembering at all times to keep the data in manageable chunks of bite-sized information. You will also need to consider what graphics, videos or animations will enhance the information.

Also bear in mind download times. If a visitor has to wait a minute for a page to load, they will probably give up. You will therefore need to ensure that any images or videos are compressed in order to enhance download times.

Skills check

Refer to the Website Authoring Software chapter (page 449) for information about how to design and build a website.

TiP

Always ask yourself whether the multimedia elements you are going to use actually add value to the website. If they do not contribute to the website content, leave them out.

The visual design

As well as the content of the website, you need to consider the corporate image and to ensure that there is uniformity between pages. You can use templates and styles to help you achieve this. You will also need to consider colour schemes, fonts styles and sizes, and accessibility issues.

Navigation around the site

A good navigation scheme is extremely important if you want visitors to find the information that they want easily. If they can't navigate their way round a website, they will give up and leave.

You should keep your navigation system the same across the whole website. This means keeping colours, styles and the location of links consistent. It is important to make sure that the Home and Contact links are on every page. Thomas Tripp designed the Travelbug website to ensure that visitors can easily navigate to the home and contact pages (Figure 4.34).

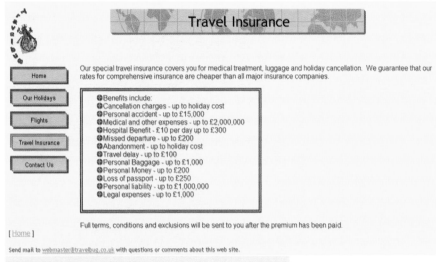

Figure 4.34 Navigation links used by Travelbug website

Contact details

Be aware that some visitors will be very cautious when buying goods or services over the Internet, and will want to check that the company actually exists. There have been many tales of people being taken in by bogus companies advertising on the Internet. Most people will therefore want to know the full telephone number and postal address of the organisation, and could be wary if they can only contact it by email.

For this reason, the Travelbug website includes full contact details (Figure 4.35).

Figure 4.35 Travelbug Contact Us web page

Storyboards and structure charts

Storyboarding is an extremely handy tool for designing the layout and features of multimedia products such as websites. Navigation is one of the most important aspects of website design, for if a visitor cannot find the information they require easily then they may quickly become lost and give up. It is essential to design the navigation of a website and to decide what structure it will take by creating a structure chart.

When designing a website, you will need to produce storyboards and structure charts that show

- the layout and components of each page
- how each page links with the others
- the navigation and structure of the website.

In business, a website developer will always show the initial designs to their client so that they can ensure that the website will be fit for purpose. It is essential that, after you have designed your storyboard and structure chart, you obtain feedback to check that your design meets the requirements of the overall purpose of the website.

Having obtained feedback about the initial designs, and made any necessary adjustments, the website developer will go on to create a working prototype. This will be shown to the customer and once again changes made to ensure that the finished product will meet the customer's needs. Because of the importance of having a suitable website to promote an organisation, any mistakes may be very costly. The testing of the finished website will include ensuring that its functionality is tested in full. This will include testing that

- each page has the correct layout and presentation and the entire site conforms to the corporate style
- all the hyperlinks, both internal and external, work correctly and there are no dead-ends or 'page not founds' (see Figure 4.36)
- all the information is accurate and up to date – for example, it may be a very costly mistake for a company if the website 'contact us' page had an incorrect email address or telephone number
- contact details are available and easy to find
- the site can be viewed in different browsers, and with different types of computer.

The page cannot be found

The page you are looking for might have been removed, had its name changed, or is temporarily unavailable.

Please try the following:

- If you typed the page address in the Address bar, make sure that it is spelled correctly.
- Open the www.costablanca-holidays.co.uk home page, and then look for links to the information you want.
- Click the ⇐ Back button to try another link.
- Click 🔍 Search to look for information on the Internet.

HTTP 404 - File not found
Internet Explorer

Figure 4.36 Example of a 'page not found' page

A web developer will always ask a range of users to test the final prototype to evaluate its usability. The developer will then make any necessary modifications as a result of feedback before the website is finally published on the Internet. A website that is not fully functional and is poorly presented can be very damaging to a business. It is important when you are developing a website that you test it thoroughly.

There are millions of websites on the Internet and every business is keen that their website will be the one that people visit. Publishing a website on the Internet is not sufficient to draw attention to it. Businesses will want to ensure that their websites are listed on search engines; even when a business's website is listed, it will probably be competing against many other websites offering the same goods and services. Often a search will result in thousands of results, and if your site is not listed on the first few pages then it is unlikely that it will be found.

Here are some steps you can take to ensure that a site has a high profile:

- use keywords carefully, so that your pages contain terms that people are likely to search for
- build reciprocal links between external websites – you link to a website and they place a link back to your website
- make sure you have a site map – many search engines like these, as they can visit the whole site from one place
- include 'meta tags' in the html
- ensure that you continuously update your website – some search engines note when a site was last updated.

Meta tags

Meta tags are html code inserted into the beginning (or *head*) of a webpage to describe the website and provide a list of keywords. Some search engines will use meta tags to collect data and list a website. The search engines that do search for meta tags also scan the content of the whole webpage to see if the keywords are repeated.

For example, Thomas Tripp has included the following code in the Travelbug website:

```
<meta name="description" content="Travelbug -
Independent Travel Agency in Whychton">

<meta name="keywords" content="holidays, holiday,
travel agency, independent travel, villas,
cruises, coach trips, holiday insurance">
```

Jargon buster

Keywords refer to the words and phrases most commonly associated with the product or services described in a website. In order to help search engines know what a web page is about, you should use your top keywords six to eight times on a page. If a company sells a number of different services and products, they will need to build individual pages for each set of keywords.

TiP

You can find keyword tools on the Internet which will help you decide the best keywords to use for the product or service you are promoting in your website. For examples, go to www.heinemann.co.uk/ hotlinks (express code 0069P).

For a website to be successful, it must attract visitors and then entice them to return time and time again.

Think it over ...

Investigate a number of well known corporate websites to assess their effectiveness as a marketing tool. Consider the following:

- Does the website reflect the corporate style?
- Is the information accurate and up to date?
- Can you navigate easily round it without getting lost?
- Do all the links work?
- Are full contact details provided?

Skills Builder

At this stage you should be able to tackle Task 11 of the Skills Builder mini project below. Don't forget to study the scenario carefully so that you are clear about the project objective.

Skills Builder mini task

Skills Builder mini task

This activity provides an opportunity to develop the skills you will need in order to complete a summative project for Unit 4. Your teacher may decide to use the tasks in this mini project as further practice as you work through the unit or may set it as a mini project all at once. If it is set as a mini project then, before you begin, you should think about how to plan and manage the project by referring to the Project Planning section (page 490).

Introduction

You have had an idea to organise a leavers' ball. The Principal has suggested that you investigate and make a presentation to her; she will consider agreeing to it if you can show there is enough interest to make your idea viable so that it makes a profit of at least £50, which can be donated to charity. The Principal has indicated that the hall would be made available free of charge.

Your idea was to investigate the possibility of a formal dinner dance with live music or a less formal buffet and disco.

Task 1

Brainstorm ideas with your friends and use mind-mapping software (see page 480) to organise your ideas. Think about the timescales for all the aspects of preparing for the event.

Assessment Hint

Throughout your project, in order to achieve top marks you must

- *create appropriate folder structures*
- *use suitable filenames and file formats*
- *carry out regular back-up procedures.*

Task 2

Prepare a project plan using project planning software (see page 481) and, from this, produce a Gantt chart. You must remember whilst working through this mini-project to modify this plan to take account of any delays that may occur.

Task 3

Design a questionnaire to conduct a survey amongst the top year students to establish
- how much interest there would be
- how much they would be prepared to pay
- what type of music they would like – live band or disco
- what type of food they would like – sit down dinner or buffet
- what dress style they would prefer – formal, informal, fancy dress.

Task 4

Analyse the results of your survey using spreadsheet software.

Task 5

Investigate a selection of menus, prices of discos or bands, printing costs for invitations, and other information you might find useful. Prepare a spreadsheet model to illustrate the break-even point.

Task 6

Having considered these various issues, you are now ready to prepare your formal marketing plan. Follow the structure suggested in the text (see page 181).

Task 7

You should now have available all the information you need to prepare your presentation to the Principal. Think about including the following in your presentation:
- the Gantt chart
- the financial model

- any charts or graphs produced after analysing your data
- a summary of the marketing plan
- any other relevant information.

Prepare a storyboard and structure chart for your presentation. You should also produce speaker notes and handouts to accompany it.

Task 8

The Principal was very impressed with your presentation and has agreed that the dance can go ahead. You now need to decide on a corporate identity for the event and should design

- a logo
- letterhead and fax templates, including an appropriate strap-line
- the tickets.

Use your fax template to confirm the booking for the band or disco and caterers.

Task 9

Design a poster and flyer to promote the event.

The Principal asked you to make sure that key staff involved in the event are kept informed about it. You have decided that the easiest way to do this is by email. Create a distribution list of five names and send an email to the names on the list, attaching the flyer to check that they are satisfied with the design. You should remember to use a digital signature which includes the strap-line.

Task 10

It has occurred to you that, since the profits are going to charity, you might be able to attract sponsorship from local businesses. Create a database containing the names and addresses of six local businesses who might be willing to sponsor the event. Prepare a mail merge letter on your letterhead to these local businesses describing the event, identifying the charity and asking if they would be willing to sponsor it.

Task 11

Create a website with a minimum of five linked pages to promote the event. You will need to prepare a storyboard and structure chart before implementing your design. Make sure you maintain the corporate design.

Assessment Hint
Tasks 6, 7, 8, 9, 10 and 11

To achieve top marks you must use appropriate structures and styles to ensure that all products are suitable for the target audience, and are the most appropriate way of presenting the information you are trying to get across.

- *Choose an appropriate writing style and tone – formal or informal – and stick to it.*
- *Decide whether to use simple or complex language.*
- *Think about how the information can be most clearly presented – use text, charts and diagrams where appropriate.*
- *Check the products to ensure accuracy – remember to spell check and proofread.*
- *Take account of feedback when modifying the products.*
- *Ensure that evidence of clear planning and appropriate use of components are illustrated in the storyboards and structure charts for the presentation and the website.*
- *Use appropriate speaker notes and handouts to support the presentation.*
- *Make certain that the website's links are effective and the end product is fit for purpose.*

Task 12

When you have finished your project, review your work and produce a short evaluation outlining how well it met the requirements explained in the scenario. Record any aspects you feel could be improved. Justify all of your comments; for example, if you say the corporate design is effective, explain what makes it effective – if something needs changing, explain why and how. You should attach to your evaluation the records of the feedback you received and the actions you took in response.

Task 13

Finally, present your work in an e-portfolio using suitable file formats. Your e-portfolio should be designed to present the following:

- home page
- table of contents
- presentation to be given to the Principal
- poster
- flyer
- mail merge letter produced on the letterhead template
- fax confirming booking
- website.

You should also include some supporting evidence:

- mind map
- project plan
- evidence of data collection using a survey
- questionnaire used for the survey
- spreadsheet showing the survey results including formulas
- references to secondary sources, such as menu prices
- spreadsheet model including formulas
- full marketing plan
- storyboard and structure chart for presentation
- example email and screen print of distribution list
- storyboard and structure chart for the website
- review and evaluation of the project, including feedback from others.

Assessment Hint

You will find that the requirements for the e-portfolio, project planning and review and evaluation are almost identical for each of the units. If you follow the guidelines given in the relevant chapters in the book it will help you achieve top marks.

PART 2

Section 1
Standard ways of working

While working on your projects you will be expected to use information communication technology (ICT) efficiently, legally and safely. So it is important to understand the need for good practice both in your studies and your future work. The guidelines in this section will ensure that you work with ICT in the correct manner and avoid problems that may cause you to lose your coursework at a crucial stage.

LEARNING OUTCOMES

You need to learn about

✓ file management

✓ personal effectiveness

✓ quality assurance

✓ legislation and codes of practice

✓ working safely.

File management

You may be absolutely brilliant at creating spreadsheets, designing complex databases and producing imaginative websites, but is your file management system just as brilliant? If it becomes so disorganised that you cannot remember what a file was called, waste time trying to find the right file, or have no backups, you may not achieve your qualification simply because you were unable to hand in the assignment!

In a work environment, your employer would become frustrated with you if, despite being very capable, you never met your deadlines because of poor file management skills.

So what do you need to do?

- Save work regularly and make backups.
- Use sensible filenames that indicate their contents.
- Use appropriate file formats.
- Set up folder structures.
- Limit access to confidential and sensitive files.
- Use effective protection against viruses.
- Use 'Readme' files where appropriate.

Saving work regularly and making backups

Probably the most obvious and simplest rule to remember is to *save* your work regularly. It is so easy to do, but just as easy to ignore!

You might be so busy designing a superb poster or flyer, thoroughly enjoying working with the graphics and using your imagination, that you forget to save the document. Then, when it is almost finished, you lose *all* the work because there is a power failure or you accidentally delete everything. If you are lucky, when you reopen the application software the file will be 'recovered' by the computer, but you can't guarantee this.

As well as saving your work regularly, it is important to keep backups. Information stored on a computer can be corrupted or lost through a power surge or failure, or by damage to or failure of the hardware. If 'disaster' strikes then you can use the backup copy. It might be slightly out of date, but at least it can be updated.

In business, backups are usually made at the end of every day. At the end of the week another backup is made, and stored separately from the daily backups. To avoid the damage done by viruses or other system-wide disasters, it is not enough to back up files into a different folder on the same computer – files should be regularly backed up onto external storage media. Here are some examples.

- *Floppy disks* are used for fairly small amounts of data – up to 1.4 megabytes (MB). However, files containing graphics quickly become too large to save on a floppy disk.
- *Pen drives*, *flash drives*, *keychain drives* and *memory sticks* (Figure 1) are portable devices that connect to a USB (*universal*

TiP

*As soon as you start a new file, save it with a sensible name. After that you can just keep clicking the **Save** icon* *to update the saved version.*

TiP

It is a good idea to keep separate copies of your files each time you make major changes. This way you can record your progress in your e-portfolio. Also, sometimes you decide that an earlier version was better after all, so you can easily go back to it.

Figure 1 Memory stick

serial bus) port of a computer. They can store between 32 MB and 2 GB (gigabytes) of data. These removable drives are the latest method of data storage and are automatically detected by the computer. You can use them to store or move files that won't fit on a floppy disk. These drives are extremely small so they are ideal for transferring files between work or college and home.

○ A second hard drive can be installed, either within the same computer or externally. The disadvantage of a second internal drive is that it cannot be stored off-site or in a fireproof safe.

○ *Zip drives* are another magnetic disk medium, with storage capacities of up to 250 MB. These are also suitable for domestic or small business use.

○ *CD–R* (recordable) and *CD–RW* (re-writable) compact discs can store up to 700 MB. Most modern home PCs are now fitted with built-in CD–RW drives, making this a convenient and inexpensive method of backing up large amounts of data (such as the text and illustrations for this book).

○ *DVDs* look the same as CDs, but can store up to 9 GB of data. Several different types of recordable DVD are available.

○ A *tape streamer* is a magnetic tape generally used by large businesses. Cartridges that can store up to 300 GB of data are currently available. This method is the most affordable method of backing up the extremely large amounts of data required by large businesses. It also has the benefit that the tapes are small and, as they are removable, they can be stored off-site or in a fireproof safe. The disadvantage of making backup copies on magnetic tapes is that to recover a particular file you must search through the tape starting from the beginning until you reach the file you want – just like with a tape for music.

Go out and try!

By the time you read this book, the storage capacity of pen or flash drives, Zip drives and DVDs will probably have increased. Research the Internet (see Internet and intranets, page 420) to check out whether the storage capacities given above are still correct. Are there any new methods of backing up data?

Create a new word-processed document. Enter a bold heading called '**SW Activity 1**' and write a short paragraph describing the information you have found from the research in the task above.

Save the file as 'Standard ways of working'.

Using sensible filenames

 TiP

However clearly you name a file, it can still be difficult to find the right one later. So, for your coursework, it is excellent practice to include in the footer not only your name, the date and page number, but also the filename and path, like this: **F:\Digital Applications\Standard Ways\Standard ways of working.doc.** *Information on inserting footers appears on page 267.*

When working on any project, *as soon as you have written just a few words on the page*, save the file – naming it in such a way that it is easy to identify later. By having a sensible system for all your filenames, it is easy to find the right one without having to search through (and possibly open) several files.

Older operating systems limited filenames to eight standard characters, but modern operating systems allow more than enough space to identify each file clearly. That is why you were able to name your first file in this chapter 'Standard ways of working'.

With Microsoft operating systems, files usually have more characters, called *extensions*, added to the filename. Filenames are followed by a stop (.) and then an extension of up to three characters. When you save a file, the file extension is usually added automatically to the name you have given the file.

Why is an extension necessary? The extension tells the computer which program to start so that the file can be opened. For example, a Microsoft Word (word processor) document will be followed by '.doc', an Excel (spreadsheet) file by '.xls', and a bitmap graphic by '.bmp'. Another important extension is '.exe', which means an *executable program* – an application. Figure 2 is a list of the most common file extensions.

Extension	Application or type of file
.bmp	Microsoft Paint bitmap image
.doc	Microsoft Word document
.dot	Microsoft Word template
.exe	Executable program
.gif	Graphics interchange format image
.html	Hypertext markup language (web page)
.jpg	Joint Photographic Experts Group (JPEG) image
.mdb	Microsoft Access database
.pdf	Adobe portable document format
.ppt	Microsoft PowerPoint presentation
.pub	Microsoft Publisher publication
.swf	Macromedia Flash vector graphics
.tiff	Tagged image file format image
.tmp	Temporary file
.xls	Microsoft Excel spreadsheet
.xlt	Microsoft Excel template

Figure 2 The most common file extensions

Choosing appropriate file formats

Assessment Hint

Your e-portfolio must be saved by using the formats **.html**, **.pdf** *or* **.swf**, *so that they are suitable for use on any computer.*

TiP

Sometimes you may wish to rename a file – if you do, be sure to add the appropriate file extension to the new name, otherwise Windows might have trouble in opening it.

In most cases the file format is automatically selected by the software application. For example, Excel will always use the extension **.xls** for spreadsheets and **.xlt** for templates.

When saving images you often have a choice about which format to use. The screen shots for this book were saved in Corel PhotoPaint and the *TIFF Bitmap* format was chosen (Figure 3) as it allows 16.7 million colours. TIFF graphics are very flexible: they can be any resolution, and can be black and white, greyscale, or full colour. It is the preferred format for desktop publishing as it produces excellent printing results.

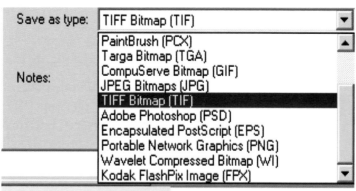

Figure 3 File formats

JPEG format is the most suitable format for full-colour photographs or greyscale images, such as scanned photographs, with large variations in the colour. It is not so effective for text, cartoons or black and white line drawings.

The maximum number of colours a *GIF format* image supports is 256, much less than the TIFF and JPEG formats. However, GIF format is significantly better for images with a just a few distinct colours, where the image has sharp contrasts – such as black next to white, as in cartoons.

PNG (Portable Network Graphics) is an alternative format for a variety of applications. PNG offers many of the advantages of both TIFF and GIF file formats, but the file size is smaller. This may be an important consideration, as your complete e-portfolio will be limited to a maximum file size.

Each project brief for your e-portfolio will specify acceptable file formats. These are likely to be PDF for paper-based publications, JPG or PNG for images, HTML for on-screen publications and SWF (Flash movie) for presentations, although may change depending on future developments. To convert files such as Word to PDF format you will require software such as Adobe Acrobat. Files that have not been created in HTML (or web format), can be converted from Word, Excel and PowerPoint by selecting **File**, **Save As** and choosing the **Web Page** format from the *Save as type* box. You can choose other alternative formats through this method and may need to experiment to find the most suitable one.

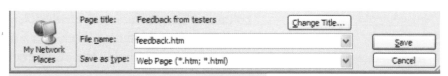

Figure 4 Saving a Word document as a web page

Setting up folders to organise files

If you save all your files in one place on a hard drive, it can be quite difficult to find the one you want. The solution is to create a main folder for a particular project, and then sub-folders to contain particular elements of the project. Figure 5 shows a main folder called 'Digital Applications', which contains a sub-folder called 'Standard Ways'. All the work for this book was saved in the main folder, and the material for this chapter was saved in the first-level sub-folder. As more and more chapters were written, more sub-folders were created to contain them. One sub-sub-folder is called 'Screen dumps', where all the screen shots were saved in TIFF format.

If you need to copy or delete files or folders, open Explorer as explained below, right-click on the relevant file or folder and select **Copy** or **Delete**. If you are copying the file or folder, move your mouse pointer to where you wish to place the copy, right-click the mouse and select **Paste**.

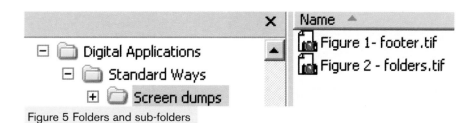

Figure 5 Folders and sub-folders

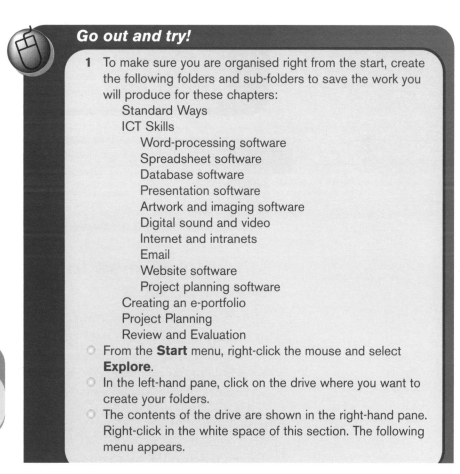

Go out and try!

1 To make sure you are organised right from the start, create the following folders and sub-folders to save the work you will produce for these chapters:
   Standard Ways
   ICT Skills
      Word-processing software
      Spreadsheet software
      Database software
      Presentation software
      Artwork and imaging software
      Digital sound and video
      Internet and intranets
      Email
      Website software
      Project planning software
   Creating an e-portfolio
   Project Planning
   Review and Evaluation

○ From the **Start** menu, right-click the mouse and select **Explore**.

○ In the left-hand pane, click on the drive where you want to create your folders.

○ The contents of the drive are shown in the right-hand pane. Right-click in the white space of this section. The following menu appears.

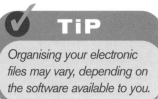

TiP

Organising your electronic files may vary, depending on the software available to you.

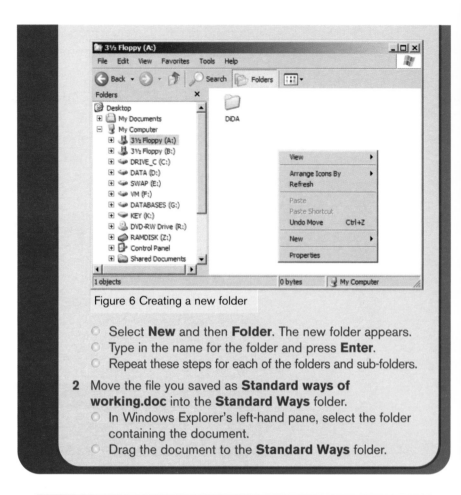

Figure 6 Creating a new folder

○ Select **New** and then **Folder**. The new folder appears.
○ Type in the name for the folder and press **Enter**.
○ Repeat these steps for each of the folders and sub-folders.

2 Move the file you saved as **Standard ways of working.doc** into the **Standard Ways** folder.
   ○ In Windows Explorer's left-hand pane, select the folder containing the document.
   ○ Drag the document to the **Standard Ways** folder.

Open your file saved as 'Standard ways of working'. Create a new bold heading called '**SW Activity 2**' and write a short paragraph describing the skills you have demonstrated in this activity.
▣ Save the file.

Limiting access to confidential or sensitive files

Most files saved on home computers are not particularly confidential or sensitive, but business data held on a computer can often be very confidential or sensitive. For example, medical records should not be accessible to the cleaning staff in a doctor's office or a hospital. Sometimes files in business may be confidential because the company is developing a new product and does not wish its competitors to know its plans.

There are several ways to protect confidentiality.

Using an ID and password to access the computer

Business systems are usually protected by passwords. Users should be prompted to change their passwords regularly. You will notice that when you enter the password, it is displayed as a series of asterisks (**************). This is to hide the characters and prevent anyone reading your password as it is shown on the screen.

Using a password to view data

Modern software systems also allow the use of passwords when saving files. You can set a password to open the file, or a password to modify it. Some people will be able to open the file to *read* it, but they will not be allowed to make any changes.

Many organisations *rank* data files according to their degree of confidentiality. Staff can be given different security levels or privileges which limit access to only *some files* or *some fields* within a file. This is a common method of protecting data and maintaining confidentiality.

Using additional security measures

Internet banking uses a series of security methods to ensure that customers' banking details are kept safe from unauthorised access. Apart from the usual login ID and password, the customer might have to choose another password or some memorable data. This time only certain characters are entered, changing each time the customer accesses the account. This helps to protect against *key loggers*.

For example, suppose the extra password is 'England'. You will see from Figure 7 that on this occasion only the first, fourth and fifth letters of the password are requested from the customer.

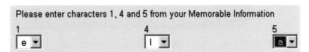

Please enter characters 1, 4 and 5 from your Memorable Information

1 — e ▼   4 — l ▼   5 — a ▼

Figure 7 Memorable data to protect confidentiality when using Internet banking

Another security measure is to limit the time that the file or web page can stay open for if it is not used. This ensures that the user's details are not left open on the computer if he or she forgets to close the file. A timeout message will appear (Figure 8).

Time out warning

You are not currently using Internet banking and for security reasons are about to be logged off.

Figure 8 A time-out warning

TiP

You can use this method to set a password in most Microsoft Office applications.

Go out and try!

1   Open a new file in Word and enter the text 'Setting a password to open and modify a file'.
2   Set a password for the file.
    ○   Select **Save As** from the **File** menu.
    ○   From the **Tools** drop-down menu, select **General**, **General Options** or **Security Options** (Figure 9).
    ○   Now enter the password 'England' in both boxes (Figure 10).
    ○   You will be asked to enter the password again to ensure that the text you entered is correct.

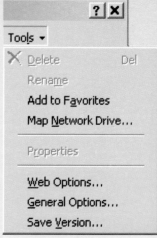

Figure 9 Select General Options on this drop-down menu to set a password

File sharing options for "STANDARD WAYS OF WORKING.doc"

Password to open:
`*******`

Password to modify:
`*******`

☐ Read-only recommended

Figure 10 Setting a password for a file in Word

3   💾 Save and close the document.
4   Open the document. What happens if you type the wrong password?

Open your file saved as 'Standard ways of working'. Create a new bold heading called '**SW Activity 3**' and write a short paragraph describing the skills you have demonstrated in this activity. 💾 Save the file.

Using effective virus protection

A computer virus is a small program that has been developed by someone either for general mischief or to attack a particular organisation. The virus copies itself without the user intending it to, or even being aware of it happening until something goes wrong. Sometimes, in an attempt to prevent detection, the program will mutate (change) slightly each time it is copied.

Viruses can be spread by
- downloading software from the Internet
- opening an attachment to an email
- transferring files from one computer to another via a floppy disk
- using pirated software that is infected.

Your computer system is far less likely to be at risk if you
- use floppy disks only on one system
- delete emails from unknown sources, especially if they have an attachment
- regularly update your virus protection software.

Viruses can spread very quickly via email. A virus may cause problems such as clearing screens, deleting data or even making the whole computer unusable. Organisations treat the risk of infection very seriously, controlling emails and not allowing staff to take disks between work and home. Anti-virus software is therefore essential, both in business and for the home user.

Anti-virus software

Anti-virus software works by scanning files to discover and remove viruses, a process known as *disinfecting*. There are thousands of viruses waiting to attack your computer. More viruses are being written all the time, so it is essential to keep your anti-virus software up to date. As soon as a new virus appears, the anti-virus companies work to produce a *pattern* file, which tells the software how to discover and stop the virus. Symantec (Norton), McAfee, Dr Solomon's and Panda are some of the companies providing anti-virus software.

Using Readme files

Readme files are files on a CD that give an explanation about how to use the software on that CD. For example, the Readme file might

- explain how to install the software
- describe important points
- give specific information that might apply to your particular setup
- say how much hard disk space is needed to install and run the software effectively
- contain late-breaking information that reveals how reported problems with the software can be solved.
- link to additional resources.

Personal effectiveness

To ensure your own personal effectiveness in preparing your project, you must

- select appropriate tools and techniques
- customise settings
- create and use shortcuts
- use available sources of help
- use a plan to organise your work and meet deadlines.

We will look at each of these skills in turn.

Selecting appropriate tools and techniques

TiP

Before you decide how to present the summative project for your e-portfolio, it is very important to think about the tools that are available to you.

If you decide to use video editing in your project, but have access to a video camera and the video editing software for only one hour a week, you are not likely to be able to finish the project. Although it might be a very interesting, exciting project about which you are really enthusiastic, if you can't resolve the problem of access to the equipment it is better to think again and choose an alternative project or presentation style.

Once you have decided on the tools to use, you should then think about suitable, effective techniques that you could apply. For example, if you are fortunate enough to have a video camera and video editing software available, you may need advice on the best techniques to use when making the film. No matter how great your expertise in editing

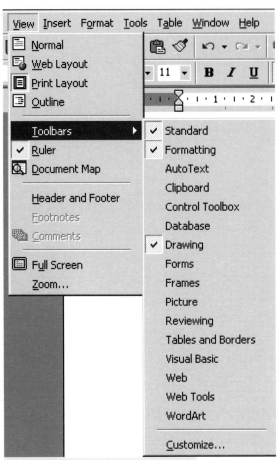

Figure 11 Toolbars available in Word

the film, if the original material is poor because there has been too much zooming in and out, and the sweeps across the views were too fast, then the end product is unlikely to be successful.

Customising settings

You can use the Control Panel to personalise your computer in numerous ways, for example by

- changing the appearance and colour scheme of your screen
- choosing a screen saver
- selecting the date, time and language settings
- changing the mouse buttons for a left-handed person.

Software applications, such as Word, Excel and Access, come with default settings pre-installed during manufacture, but there are many ways to customise the settings to suit your needs. For example, you would probably find the *Standard*, *Formatting* and possibly *Drawing* toolbars to be visible. As you can see from Figure 11, in Word there are 16 toolbars in total – but if most or all of them were shown at once, the screen would be far too cluttered, with not much room left for the page you were working on! Instead, select the ones most useful to you. Word is often set with a default font of Times New Roman 10pt, which is too small for everyday use, so you might wish to set the default to a different size and style.

Go out and try!

Investigate the Control Panel on your PC to find out how to customise the settings.

- From the **Start** menu, select **Control Panel**.
- Investigate how to customise the **Date and Time**, **Display**, **Keyboard** and **Sound** settings.

Open your file saved as 'Standard ways of working'. Create a new bold heading called '**SW Activity 4**' and copy the table shown below. Include a screen shot of the item with an explanation of how to change the settings. 🖫 Save the file.

Desktop setting	Screen shot	Explanation of how to change the settings
Mouse		
Volume control		
Icons		
Cursor		
Colour scheme		
Resolution		
Screen saver options		
Date and time		
Office Assistant		

Figure 12 Record of your customised settings

(a)

Creating and using shortcuts

Every time you click on an icon on a toolbar – such as save 🖫 or print 🖨 – you are using a *shortcut*. Using the print icon allows you to print the document in a single step. If you use **File**, **Print** and **OK** it is at least three steps – but you might want to choose this method if you want to print two or more copies, or only certain pages.

Each of the toolbars has a list of shortcut icons, but only those most frequently used are automatically visible. You can choose to add any others that you find useful. For example, if you frequently send documents as attachments to an email, you might wish to add the relevant icon 📧 to the toolbar.

Shortcuts can also be placed on the desktop. No doubt you are familiar with using shortcuts to software applications – see Figure 13(a). However, you can also choose to create shortcuts to files or folders that you use regularly. For example, a shortcut to the folder containing your work for this qualification might prove useful – see Figure 13(b).

(b)

Figure 13 (a) Shortcuts on the desktop to software installed on the computer. (b) A shortcut to files for this book

Go out and try!

1 Add icons and shortcuts to your toolbar.
   - Open Word and from the **Tools** menu, select **Customise**.
   - Select the **Commands** tab.
   - From the **Categories** menu, select **File**.
   - Scroll down to **Mail Recipient (as Attachment)** by highlighting the icon and dragging it onto the toolbar.
   - Follow the same method to add a **Go To** button (under the **Edit** category) and **Full Screen** button (under the **View** category) to your toolbar.
2 Select three other icons of your own choice to add to the toolbar.
3 Customise your desktop by adding shortcut items to software applications that are not already available.
   - From the **Start** menu, select **Programs, Microsoft Office** and then whatever program you wish to create a shortcut to.
   - Hold down the **Ctrl** key and drag the icon onto the desktop.
   - Release the **Ctrl** key and a shortcut is created.
4 Customise you desktop by adding shortcuts to files or folders you use frequently.
   - In **My Computer**, find the file or folder for which you wish to create a shortcut.
   - Right-click on the icon and select **Create Shortcut**.
   - A shortcut will be created in the same folder.
   - You can now move the shortcut to the desktop by dragging it from the folder onto your desktop.

Open your file saved as 'Standard ways of working'. Create a new bold heading called '**SW Activity 5**' and write a short paragraph describing the skills you have demonstrated in this activity. Save the file.

Assessment Hint

Don't be afraid to ask for help, but do remember that the project must be your own work. On the other hand, don't embark on a project that is too complex in case you can't find the help you need.

Getting help

There will be a variety of sources of help available to you, and it is a good idea to take advantage of them. You may find help through

- software help files
- textbooks
- your teacher
- specialist staff within your school or college

- your peers (who may be more knowledgeable about some aspects of the software, whereas you may know more about other aspects and can offer them help in return)
- family or friends who are experienced in the project you are undertaking.

Using a plan to organise work and meet deadlines

In order to complete your e-portfolio you will have to undertake a number of tasks, gradually building up the content. All the various sections of the e-portfolio will need to be completed to a deadline.

When the final deadline is a long time ahead, it is all too easy to keep thinking there is no rush, and then find you are trying to do ten things at once and cannot possibly finish everything in time! Therefore it is essential to think about all the various items that will go into the e-portfolio and then plan a schedule of your work.

Remember that *it always takes longer than you think*, so make sure you plan to finish well before the final deadline, to allow for all those unexpected delays!

Skills check ▶▶

Information on how to plan and organise your work is presented in more detail in the chapter on project planning (page 490).

Quality assurance

To ensure that your work is accurate and effective, you will need to
- use tools such as spelling and grammar checks, and Print Preview
- proofread your work
- seek the views of others
- check your research.

Using spelling and grammar checks and Print Preview

Spellcheckers

Spelling errors spoil your work, so always use a *spellchecker* to detect words spelt incorrectly and repeated words (for example, 'and and'). Spellcheckers are available not only in word processors, but also in most other applications such as spreadsheets and email programs. Spellcheckers compare the words you have written against a list in the computer's dictionary, then any words not matching are queried and possible alternatives are suggested.

TiP

Be aware that many computer programs use American spellings of words. These are often slightly different from the British spellings.

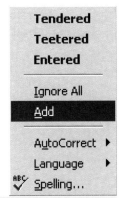

Figure 14 Adding a word to the spellchecker dictionary

But beware! Although the spellchecker is an excellent tool, it does not understand what you are trying to say and so it can be wrong. This means that *it is still important for the operator to have a reasonable level of spelling!* For example, it will not correct 'whether' for 'weather', or 'to', 'too' or 'two' used in the wrong place.

Sometimes a spellchecker will suggest that a word is incorrect when you know that it is correct. The dictionary will include common names such as 'Smith' but not unusual names such as 'Tenterden', which is a village in Kent. For this the dictionary suggested three alternatives (Figure 14), but the name was spelt correctly.

If you are likely to use a particular word frequently, then it is worth adding it to the dictionary. You can right-click on the word and select the **Add** option. In future the spelling checker will accept the word.

Sometimes words are indicated as incorrect because the language of the spellchecker is set to English (US) not English (UK), so it's worth checking. Select **Tools, Language, Set Language** and choose **English (UK)** and **Default** (Figure 15).

Figure 15 Setting the language that Word will use for its spellchecker

Grammar checker

The *grammar checker* can be more complicated and difficult to use than a spellchecker, and therefore tends to be rather less popular. As a starting point, the best way to use a basic grammar checker is as a tool to draw your attention to possible mistakes. It can be very useful for finding typing errors; such as the one shown in Figure 16, where

Figure 16 The grammar checker showing that there is no space after the bracket

there is no space after the closing bracket. At other times the suggestions may not be clear, so *think about* the suggestions made – the final decision is yours.

Print Preview

Before sending your work to the printer, it is a good idea to check it in Print Preview, which you will often identify poor layout that can be corrected before printing. This saves time and prevents you wasting paper.

When the author of this chapter used Print Preview at this point, it revealed a blank page that hadn't been noticed, which would have interfered with page numbering. It was an easy matter to delete the page before printing the file.

Proofreading your work

Even though you read your work on the monitor screen, it is surprising how often errors can be missed that the spelling or grammar checks have not shown up. In addition, you often find that although you were clear in your mind what you wanted to say, on re-reading the text you realise it is muddled, or you haven't fully explained the topic.

As authors of this book we received the proofs (the first copy of the book as it would look when finally printed) and we had to check that everything was correct, including the page layouts. At this stage we made some changes to our original work, not because it was necessarily wrong, but because it wasn't as clear as we wanted it, or it needed to be a little more detailed.

Seeking the views of others

Once you have an idea about the project you wish to undertake, it is excellent practice to ask other people what they think of the idea.

When writing this book, we discussed the syllabus and decided which of us was going to undertake which sections. We also brainstormed ideas about what should be included, and the presentation. Each one of us came up with ideas and suggestions, and together we produced (we hope!) a better result than if we had worked separately.

We also read each other's material and often asked colleagues to read what we had written. As an author you can be 'too close' to your own project to spot minor errors, whereas someone independent

TiP

If your work is web-based, make sure you check it using different browser software on several computers. Is it always displayed as you had intended?

TiP

Proofreading isn't the most popular task, but it is important. You might discover quite silly errors, or an explanation that doesn't quite say what you intended. Correcting it before handing in your assignment or coursework might make all the difference to your final grade.

TiP

Do ask someone else's opinion of the work you have produced for your e-portfolio – and do take note of the comments made. A critical evaluation of your project should be viewed as helpful advice to enable you to improve what you have done, not as a negative criticism.

notices odd little mistakes, or a paragraph that is not clear. These can be edited to improve the final version. It is very important to keep draft versions of your work so you can show changes made as a result of comments from others.

Authenticating your work – checking your research

In general, textbooks are likely to contain reliable information because they will have been written to provide students with the information they need for a course they are studying, and are published by reputable companies. If it became obvious that an author or publisher was producing unreliable textbooks, they would soon go out of business: no one would buy their books.

Probably, by the time you read this book, information such as the amount of data a memory stick can hold will have changed. This does not mean that it contains deliberate misinformation – it's just that technology advances. If you do make use of that kind of data given in a book then it would be wise to check whether it is still accurate.

Figure 17 Discussing your work with other people

As you are well aware, the Internet is an amazing tool to use when researching almost any topic you could think of. It is, however, all too easy to drop into the trap of *believing everything on the Internet is accurate and reliable.* Unfortunately, that is not the case. Anyone can set up a website and put information on that site. Sometimes the author genuinely believes that the information posted is authentic or accurate, but sometimes the author wishes to deliberately mislead. Therefore, when using websites to obtain information, it is very important to use sites – such as those of the BBC or other well-known organisations – where it is likely that information given will be authentic.

Legislation and codes of practice

To ensure that you comply with legislation and codes of practice relating to the use of ICT, you will need to

- acknowledge your sources
- avoid plagiarism
- respect copyright
- protect confidentiality.

Acknowledging your sources and avoiding plagiarism

In order to complete your portfolio evidence you will need to undertake research. This may be from books, from newspapers or journals, from the Internet, or from people through surveys, questionnaires or face-to-face discussions. It is essential that you acknowledge where you obtained this information – your *sources*.

In some cases you may have to gain permission from the author, artist or relevant organisation to use the material. You should also include a *bibliography* of books, journals, articles and websites that you have found useful in your research.

People may copy original work and present it as their own. This is much easier to do from ICT systems (and especially from the Internet) than it is from a paper-based source such as a textbook. This is called *plagiarism* and, because it breaks copyright law (explained opposite), it is a serious offence.

It is quite acceptable to *quote* a reasonable amount of someone else's work, as long as you put inverted commas (" ") at the beginning of the text and at the end, and identify the original author, the book, web address or newspaper where you found the information.

Think it over...

Check out the sources that we might have used when writing this textbook.

Open your file saved as 'Standard ways of working'. Create a new bold heading called '**SW Activity 6**' and write a short paragraph explaining what you have learned about plagiarism and acknowledging sources. Save the file.

Respecting copyright

You are probably familiar with *copyright* warnings at the beginning of books, rental videos and DVDs, when there is a statement along the lines of '*All rights reserved. No part of this publication may be reproduced or transmitted, in any form or by any means, without the prior permission of the publisher.*' This is also true for most computer programs, published text and images.

- The Copyright Designs and Patents Act 1988 was originally set up in order to protect the work of authors, artists and composers from being reproduced or copied without permission.

- Current European copyright law extends for 70 years after the death of the author/creator. During this period, the work (book, work of art, software, photograph, music score, etc.) may not be reproduced without permission.

- This original Copyright Designs and Patents Act was in existence long before computers were invented. It has subsequently been extended to include computer software, making it illegal to copy applications without permission from the copyright holder.

Figure 18 Facts about the Copyright Designs and Patents Act

Check for the symbol ©, followed by a date and sometimes a name, as shown at the beginning of this book. This indicates that the work is covered by copyright. It is very important to understand what copyright means and to respect copyright law (Figure 18).

When you buy computer software it generally comes with a *licence* that allows you to install, use, access, display or run just one copy of the software on one computer and one notebook. Your school or college will have purchased a network licence in order to be granted permission to run the software on all of its machines.

Imagine a small business that started with just one computer. The owner bought the software for that computer and will have the necessary licence. As the business expands, he might decide to install a network and use the same software on the network, forgetting to buy a new licence. He has in fact broken the law, even though it was not intentional.

This law affects everyone who owns a computer. You must not let other people borrow your software to install on their computers. Similarly, you should not borrow software from a friend and install it on your computer. The software houses have, after all, invested a great deal of time and money in order to develop the software, so you are stealing from them by not paying for the software. It's no different from going into a shop and stealing a box of chocolates or a DVD.

> *In order to help protect software copyright, the Federation Against Software Theft (FAST) was set up in 1984 to investigate software piracy. The federation will prosecute when instances of illegal copying of software come to their attention. Be warned!*

Go out and try!

In Word, click the **Help** menu and choose **About Microsoft Word**. Here you will find details of the licence holder and a product registration number. It also carries a strong warning. What does the warning say?

Open your file saved as 'Standard ways of working'. Create a new bold heading called '**SW Activity 7**' and write a short paragraph explaining what you have learned about copyright. Save the file.

Protecting confidentiality

The Data Protection Act of 1994, which was updated in 1998, was introduced to deal with the increasing amount of personal data being held on computers and the potential misuse of that personal data. Think of the many different organisations that hold computerised records containing details of our personal lives, school records, employment history, financial and medical records, criminal activities, etc. Under the Data Protection Act, these organisations must ensure that the data remains confidential. They must also allow people to access the data that is being held about them, in return for a small administration fee.

Both employers and employees have a responsibility under the Act to ensure that personal information is not disclosed, however

Skills check ▶▶

The information on confidential or sensitive files on page 228 is also relevant here.

- Passwords should be kept secret. A note stuck to the side of your computer is not a sensible way to remember your password!

- Personal information should not be passed on to third parties at any time. Imagine a situation where an insurance company employee had access to personal information. Think of the consequences if a list of addresses and details of valuable house contents fell into the wrong hands.

- Staff working with confidential data must be very careful not to disclose personal information during a conversation, however innocently.

- Computer screens in public places – such as a doctor's surgery – should not be visible to the general public. It could be very unfortunate if somebody waiting at the reception desk read personal and confidential information about another patient.

Figure 19 Facts about passwords

innocently. Staff must be aware of straightforward things they can do to protect the confidentiality of the data. Examples are described in Figure 19.

Apart from personal information, a commercial organisation will want to keep information about the company confidential. They do not want their competitors finding out how well or badly they are doing, and what new products or designs are being prepared.

Organisations have always been at risk from dishonest staff, but the main difference since the arrival of computers is that it is so much easier to obtain the information – you do not even need to be in the room or the building! Inevitably there has to be trust in and reliance on the users of ICT, especially in a business environment. In fact most people are honest and have no intention of defrauding their employer or disclosing confidential information.

It is essential to take security issues seriously, so that you do not *unintentionally* give someone else access to uncensored or private materials. Also, if you *accidentally* discover uncensored or private materials, you must not take advantage of the opportunity, and it may be appropriate to report that a breach of security has occurred.

Naturally we all chat about our jobs, but it is important to know which information should be kept to ourselves, and when it is OK to talk about something to a friend or relative. If in doubt then keep quiet.

Working safely

Employers are responsible for promoting health and safety in the workplace. However, each employee also has the duty to take sensible precautions. For example, if you spend a lot of time using a computer, you may tend to develop backache, eyestrain or repetitive strain injury, but good working practices will greatly reduce the risk of suffering from such problems. It is important to

- ensure that the positioning of hardware, cables and seating is correct
- check that the lighting is appropriate
- take regular breaks
- handle and store media correctly.

Positioning hardware, cables and seating

Desks should have a non-reflective surface and be at the correct height with sufficient space for a computer, mouse mat, telephone and supporting documents. There should be enough space around the desk for you to change position and vary your movements. It may be beneficial to use a wrist rest to support your wrists.

The ideal working position is to sit with your eyes level with the top of the screen, the small of your back against the chair, and your feet flat on the floor (Figure 20).

Figure 20 The fundamentals of good posture at a computer workstation

Since we all come in different shapes and sizes, it is important to use a chair that can be adjusted to suit the user. A good computer chair will have five feet with castors to increase stability and to allow freedom of movement. You will be able to adjust the height of the seat to suit your own height, as well as the position and tilt of the backrest in order to support your back. If you are short and your feet don't reach the floor, you can ask for a footrest to be provided so that you can support your feet and legs.

Cables should be correctly and safely positioned where no one can fall or trip over them. They should be securely fastened, usually inside trunking that is attached to the walls. They should *never* be trailing across the floor.

Using appropriate lighting

The ideal position for the computer monitor is at right-angles to a window. In order to keep sun off the screen and help reduce glare, blinds should be provided at the windows. If glare is a problem then an anti-glare shield can be fitted. The office should be well lit and the lighting should offer a contrast between the screen and surrounding area. If the light is too dim, documents will be hard to read, leading to eyestrain. If necessary, adjust the brightness of the screen in response to changes in light.

Taking regular breaks

Bad posture is the main cause of backache. If you work *continuously* at a computer monitor you should be allowed to take a short break (say 5–10 minutes) away from the screen after an hour's *uninterrupted* screen or keyboard work. Ideally your job will involve a variety of tasks so that this situation will not arise in the first place.

Handling and storing media correctly

Think it over ...

How safe is your working environment at home? What could you change to improve it?

It is important to know how to protect the media you are using, by handling and storing them correctly. Care should be taken when handling floppy disks, CDs and DVDs in order to protect the data. Store them in protective cases to keep them clean, away from dust and moisture. Avoid touching the surfaces, and keep them away from extremes of temperature.

Open your file saved as 'Standard ways of working'. Create a new bold heading called '**SW Activity 8**' and insert a table with three columns, headed 'Health and Safety', 'Good Practice' and 'Bad Practice'. In the first column, enter a checklist of the health and safety issues identified in this section of the chapter. Check out the computer lab at school or college and tick the relevant column where health and safety issues are good or need to be improved.

For any items that you have put in the bad-practice column, explain what the problem is and what needs to be done. You might like to work in pairs for this activity.

Save the file.

Section 2 ICT skills

Word-processing software

If somebody asked you 'What is word-processing?' you would probably describe it as *the process of creating, storing and editing text-based documents*. While you would be quite right in saying this, in fact word-processing offers so much more.

Word-processing is one of the most effective ways of communicating information to other people through paper-based documents such as letters, reports, leaflets, newsletters, posters and flyers. In fact, effective word-processing skills also underlie successful communication through on-screen publications such as presentations or web pages.

Your word-processing skills are a valuable asset that you will make use of throughout your student and adult life. Word-processing is more than just sitting down at a computer and producing a document without a second thought. It is the skill of designing a document to convey specific information to different groups of people.

LEARNING OUTCOMES

You need to learn about

✓ entering, cutting, copying, pasting and moving text
✓ formatting text
✓ using paragraph formatting features
✓ using page formatting features
✓ using tables
✓ creating, selecting and inserting components
✓ using images/objects
✓ using spelling and grammar checkers
✓ using mail merge.

Entering, cutting, copying, pasting and moving text

Entering text

Text is keyed in (or *entered*) via the keyboard. When a word will not fit on the end of a line, it is moved on to the next line. This feature is called *word wrap,* and the word processor automatically inserts *soft returns* at the end of each line. These soft returns are adjustable and will move within the document if necessary – such as when you insert an extra word or two in a paragraph or decide to delete some text.

You only need to use the **Enter** key when you want to start a new line, perhaps after a heading or at the start of a new paragraph. The returns that *you* put into a document are called *hard returns* and they are not adjustable by the software. If you display the formatting marks in a document by selecting the **Show/Hide** icon on the *Standard* toolbar, the ¶ character identifies all hard returns.

As you enter text, there are some basic steps you can take to improve the general presentation of the document:

- For most text-based documents, a font size of 11pt or 12pt will be appropriate.
- Remember to leave one clear line space (achieved by pressing the **Enter** key twice) after a heading and between each paragraph. Look at Figure 21, where the ¶ symbol shows that the **Enter** key has been used.
- Nowadays it is common practice when using a word processor to leave only one space following a sentence. However, in the days of the typewriter, it was standard practice to leave two spaces following any punctuation at the end of a sentence. There are many people today who feel that using two spaces between sentences makes your text easier to read because the sentences stand out clearly. You must make your own decision or follow the guidance from your teacher/tutor.
- Leave one space after all other punctuation.
- If possible, use a *fully blocked* style of presentation when producing letters, reports, etc. This means that everything starts at the left-hand margin. Figure 21 is an example of fully blocked working.

Jargon buster

A manual typewriter has a **carriage return key**, which the typist must press between lines to return the carriage to the left of the paper. Because of this the **Enter** key is sometimes called the **Return** key, and the hidden characters it inserts into documents are called **returns**.

Skills check ▶▶

Refer to page 251 for more detailed information on font sizes.

✔ TiP

You can use styles (see page 284) to add space after headings and between paragraphs automatically.

```
Travelbug¶
¶
17·London·Road¶
Whychton¶
TO9·3WN¶
¶
Tel:  → 543·2134·5678¶
Fax: → 543·2134·5679¶
Email:→travelbug@userve.co.uk¶
¶
¶
¶
There·is·so·much·to·see·and·do·in·Brussels·that·a·weekend·just·won't·be·long·enough!¶
¶
There·are·over·30·museums·to·visit,·fine·restaurants·and·bars,·shops·selling·anything·
from·high·fashion·to·antiques·to·sophisticated·chocolate·creations.··Browse·the·open-air·
markets·or·stroll·around·the·magnificent·cobbled·Grand·Place.¶
¶
A·visit·to·Brussels·isn't·complete·without·a·visit·to·the·famous·Manneken·Pis·which·can·
be·guaranteed·to·draw·a·crowd.¶
¶
Travel·by·Eurostar·from·Waterloo·and·arrive·in·Brussels·in·2·hours·20·minutes.··Selected·
services·also·available·from·Ashford·International·Station·in·Kent.¶
¶
Prices·start·at·£125.00·for·2·nights.¶
```

Figure 21 An example of work presented in a 'fully blocked' style

Cut, copy, move and paste

A significant benefit of word processors is that they let you cut, copy, move and paste text. These features allow you to edit (change) the on-screen text without having to retype the whole document.

It is easy to get muddled over the meaning of the terms *cut*, *copy*, *move* and *paste*.

- **Cut** deletes the selected text and places a copy onto the *Clipboard* (a special part of the computer's memory) from where it can be retrieved.

- **Copy** copies the selected text onto the Clipboard, without deleting it. It can then be placed elsewhere in the document.

- **Move** means to cut selected text from one place and immediately paste that text elsewhere in the document.

- **Paste** inserts the text from the Clipboard elsewhere in the document, or even into a different document.

Go out and try!

1. Type out the text showing in Figure 21 in a new document.
   - Open Microsoft Word and key in the text.
   - Proofread what you have typed.
   - Position the cursor at the start of the document and click on the **Spelling and grammar** button.
   - The *Spelling and grammar* dialogue box appears.
   - If the word is incorrect, select the correct spelling from the suggestions and click on **Change** to accept it.

2. Locate the **Show/Hide ¶** button on the *Standard* toolbar and click on it to display the formatting in the document. Notice how the spaces between words are shown as a small dot raised above the typing line.
   Have you got two dots at the end of each sentence to indicate that you have put in two spaces?

3. Copy the text and paste a second copy underneath.
   - Select all the text.
   - Click on the **Copy** button. The text will be saved onto the Clipboard.
   - Position the cursor at the end of the first piece of text and click on the **Paste** button.

4. Make the following changes to the second copy.
   - In the first paragraph add 'break' after 'weekend' and notice how the original text moves on to a new line to accommodate the additional word.
   - In the second paragraph, delete the words 'and bars' and notice how the original text moves up to close the gap.
   - Copy 'Travelbug' at the top of the document to the very end.
     - Select the word 'Travelbug'.
     - Click on the **Copy** button.
     - Position the cursor at the very end of the document and click on the **Paste** button.
   - Move the paragraph beginning 'Travel by Eurostar' so that it becomes the second paragraph.
     - Select the paragraph beginning 'Travel by Eurostar'.
     - Click on the **Cut** button.
     - Position the cursor immediately before the second paragraph, where you want the text to appear.
     - Click on the **Paste** button.

5. Save this document as 'WP Activity 1' in your 'Word-processing software' sub-folder.

TiP

Whenever you cut, copy or move text, remember to check the spacing to make sure you still have one clear line between paragraphs and the correct spacing between sentences. It is very easy to end up with extra lines, or no clear lines, particularly when you cut and move text.

Create a file called 'Word-processing software'. Insert a bold heading called '**WP Activity 1**' and write a short paragraph describing the skills you have demonstrated in this activity.
Save this file in your 'Word-processing software' sub-folder.

Formatting text

Font type and font size

A *font* is the name given to describe the style of typeface you are using. Two popular styles frequently used in the preparation of business documents are Times New Roman and Arial.

○ This is an example of Times New Roman. It is referred to as a *serif* font because of the 'little feet' at the bottom of each letter.

○ This is an example of Arial. It is referred to as a *sans serif* font because it does not have the 'little feet'.

Your default font will generally be Times New Roman, and the size is likely to be somewhere between 10 and 12 points. *Point* refers to the size of the character – the higher the number, the larger the font. A point size of 72 would give you a letter approximately 2.54 cm (1 inch) tall.

Go out and try!

1 Investigate different font sizes and types.
   ○ Open a Word document and type your name three times.
   ○ Select the text you have just typed and click on the down arrow in the *Font Size* box.
   ○ Select **72** points.

Figure 22 Setting the font size

   ○ Highlight one copy of your name and click on the down arrow in the *Font* box.
   ○ Select **Arial**.

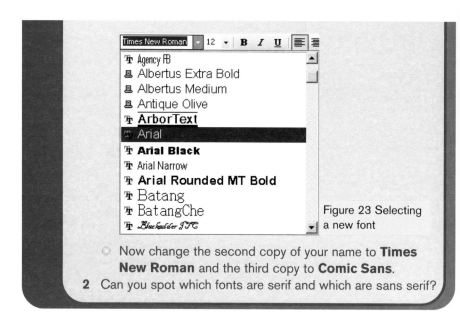

Figure 23 Selecting a new font

○ Now change the second copy of your name to **Times New Roman** and the third copy to **Comic Sans**.

2   Can you spot which fonts are serif and which are sans serif?

It is important that you choose a style and size of font to suit the task you are doing. Some font styles are rather elaborate and difficult to read, so you should use them with care. Similarly, choose a suitable font size.

For example, text contained in a poster will probably need to be quite large so that it is eye-catching and can be read from a distance. In contrast, a leaflet or newsletter might contain fairly large headings, with the body text printed in a smaller font.

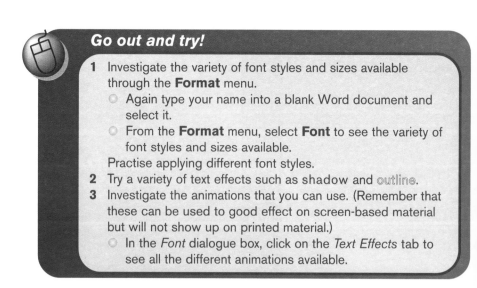

Go out and try!

1   Investigate the variety of font styles and sizes available through the **Format** menu.
    ○ Again type your name into a blank Word document and select it.
    ○ From the **Format** menu, select **Font** to see the variety of font styles and sizes available.
    Practise applying different font styles.
2   Try a variety of text effects such as shadow and outline.
3   Investigate the animations that you can use. (Remember that these can be used to good effect on screen-based material but will not show up on printed material.)
    ○ In the *Font* dialogue box, click on the *Text Effects* tab to see all the different animations available.

TiP

Most business documents will rely on the use of capital letters, bold, underline or italic to emphasise any key points to be made.

Bold, underline and italic

In addition to using different font styles and sizes, you can also use **bold**, <u>underline</u> or *italic* to emphasise text. <u>***However, it is not generally a good idea to apply all three to the same text!***</u>

Go out and try!

Investigate the effect of making text bold, italic and underlined.
○ Type your name three times into a document.
○ Select the first name and click on the **Bold** [B] button.
○ Select the second name and click on the **Italic** [*I*] button.
○ Select the third name and click on the **Underline** [U] button.

Using colour

Colour is not generally applied to text in standard documents, such as letters or reports, but it can be very effective in leaflets, posters, flyers, etc. However, for it to be effective you should use it in moderation – otherwise your document will be messy, difficult to read and therefore may not be fit for the purpose intended.

Your word-processing software has a selection of standard colours (Figure 24(a)). It also has the facility to customise a colour, (Figure 24(b)), which can be useful if you need to match an existing colour. For example, some companies have 'corporate colours' that they replicate on their logo, advertising material, brochures, on-screen presentations, and so on.

The **custom colour** option makes it possible to create a colour of your own choosing. Figure 24(b) shows a white cross-hair shape that can be dragged around to find the colour match. Each colour is made up of a unique combination of red, green and blue (RGB) numbers. If you know the RGB numbers you can enter them to give you an exact colour match.

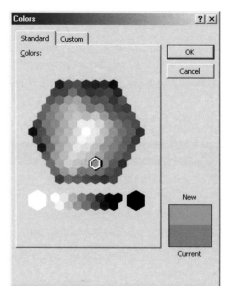
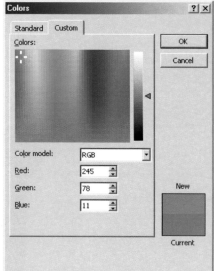

Figure 24 The standard colour palette and the custom colour option

Go out and try!

Apply different colours to fonts.

- Open a document and key in some text.
- Select the text that you wish to apply colour to.
- Click on the down arrow to the right of the **Font Color** button to show the choices (Figure 25).

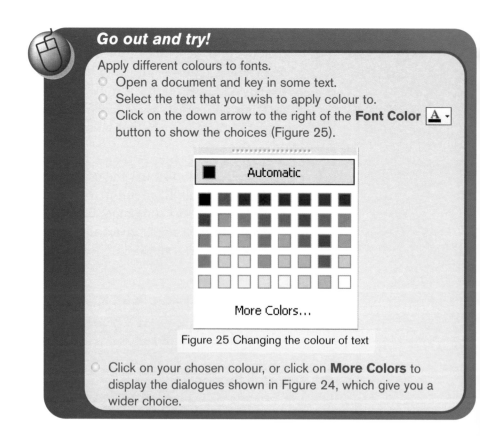

Figure 25 Changing the colour of text

- Click on your chosen colour, or click on **More Colors** to display the dialogues shown in Figure 24, which give you a wider choice.

Go out and try!

1 Start a new document in Word.
2 Look at Figure 26 and list the headings given on the left.
3 Under each heading give at least three examples.
4 Using the skills you have learned, format the example to match the style, colour etc.

One example of each has been given to start you off.

Headings	Examples
Serif font	Times New Roman
Sans serif font	Comic Sans MS
Font size	20 point
Font effect	SMALL CAPITALS
Animated text effects	Marching Red Ants
Colour	Dark blue
Emphasis	<u>Underline</u>

Figure 26 Examples of font options

5 Save this document as 'WP Activity 2' in your 'Word-processing software' sub-folder.

Open your 'Word-processing software' file. Create a new bold heading called '**WP Activity 2**' and write a short paragraph describing the skills you have demonstrated in this activity.
Save the file.

Using paragraph formatting features

Alignment

When you completed WP Activity 1, did you notice how your text automatically lined up against the left-hand margin, leaving the right-hand margin uneven (or *ragged*)? This is because the default style of paragraph alignment is *left aligned*. Word-processing software offers you alternative styles of paragraph format, such as *justified* or *centred*.

Here the text is **left-aligned** and the right-hand margin is uneven or *ragged*. This is the default setting. The spaces between words are equal.

Here the alignment is **justified** and both the left and right margins are straight. The program automatically adjusts the spaces between words to distribute the text evenly between the margins. The spaces between words are not equal.

Here the text is **centred** between the margins. This is generally used for presentation and display rather than letters or notes.

Figure 27 Text left-aligned, justified and centred

The default setting of left alignment is quite acceptable for most text-based documents and on-screen presentations. However, there are occasions when justified alignment may be more appropriate. For example, a newsletter produced in columns looks more professional with justified margins (Figure 28(a)). Lines of text in a poster may be centred between the margins; and, in order to balance the presentation, paragraphs in the same poster look neater if they are justified leaving an equal space against the left and the right margins (Figure 28(b)).

Figure 28 A newsletter and a poster

Go out and try!

Create a poster to demonstrate centred and justified paragraph alignment.

- Open the file you saved as 'WP Activity 1'.
- Copy the edited text and paste it into a new document.
- Select the text that you want to centre.
- Click on the **Center** ☰ button.
- Select the text that you want to justify and click on the **Justify** ☰ button.
- Apply suitable font styles and sizes to make the poster more interesting. Will 'white space' make the poster more effective?
- 💾 Save this document as 'WP Activity 3' in your 'Word-processing software' sub-folder.

Open your 'Word-processing software' file. Create a new bold heading called '**WP Activity 3**' and write a short paragraph describing the skills you have demonstrated in this activity.
💾 Save the file.

Bullets and numbering

Bullet points are used to make items in a list stand out. The standard bullet point is represented by the character symbol ●, but you can choose different symbols. For example

- � a bullet point chosen from the standard selection in Bullets and Numbering (Figure 30)

- 💣 a bullet point customised from a selection in Wingdings

- ♪ a bullet point customised from a selection in Webdings.

As you can see from these examples, the standard bullet point is the clearest and is the style most commonly used in the preparation of paper-based documents.

Sometimes different styles of bullet point are used to indicate different 'levels' in a list. For example:

- Fully-inclusive holidays
  - » Full-board
  - » Half-board
  - » Self-catering
- Activity holidays
  - » Skiing
  - » Water sports

The important thing to remember is that you should use a style of bullet that is fit for the purpose of the document. Use the decorative or picture bullets only for more informal documents, on-screen presentations or web pages.

Sometimes it is preferable to number a list rather than using bullets. The *Numbered* tab illustrated in Figure 30 offers a variety of options – such as **1, 2, 3** or **a), b), c)**. Figure 29 shows both bullets and numbering used in a document.

TRAVELBUG CRUISE CLUB

Our Cruise Club is totally independent and we can therefore offer a varied range of cruises from all leading cruise line operators. Our knowledgeable staff are on hand 7 days a week to help you plan the perfect trip.

Membership is free and Cruise Club members have the following advantages:

- 2 for 1 cruise offers
- Services of our specially trained staff
- Monthly newsletter with the latest information and offers
- Cabin upgrades and on-ship spending vouchers
- Exclusive visits to see the ships whilst docked in the UK
- Specially discounted rates

How to join

1. Call us for an application form or download from our web site
2. Complete the application form
3. Return to us in Whychton
4. Your application membership pack will be sent out by return post

Figure 29 The use of bullet points and numbering

Go out and try!

1. Copy the text shown in Figure 29 to a new document and apply bullets and numbering.
2. Insert a page break at the foot of the document.
   ○ Press **Ctrl** and **Enter** to insert a page break.
3. Make a copy of page 1 and paste it onto the second page.

4 Customise the bullets to a style of your choice.
  ○ Select the bulleted text
  ○ From the **Format** menu, select **Bullets and Numbering**. Select the new style of bulleted list and click on **OK**.

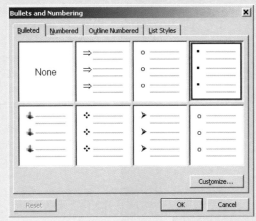

Figure 30 Different bullet styles

  ○ Select the numbered list.
  ○ Change the style of the numbered list by selecting **Bullets and Numbering** from the **Format** menu.
  ○ Select the **Numbered** tab, click on the new style of numbered list and then press **OK**.

5 Insert a further page break at the end of the document.

6 On the third page enter the following text as a list against the left margin: France, Accommodation, Travel, Weather, Summer, Winter, Spain, Accommodation, Travel, Weather, Summer, Winter.

7 Apply a numbered list style to the text you have just entered and then indent it.
  ○ Highlight the text you entered in Step 6.
  ○ From the **Format** menu, select **Bullets and Numbering**.
  ○ In the **Bullets and Numbering** dialogue box select the **Outline Numbered** tab and select the option shown in Figure 31.

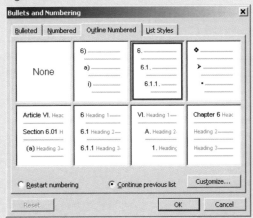

Figure 31 A section numbering style

Your list will now be numbered from 1 to 12.

○ Position the cursor to the right of the number 2 (to the left of the word 'Accommodation') and click the **Increase Indent** button on your *Formatting* toolbar. Number 2 should change to 1.1.

○ Position the cursor to the left of 'Travel' and then 'Weather' and in each case click the **Increase Indent** button once.

○ Now position the cursor to the left of 'Summer' and then 'Winter' and in each case click the **Increase Indent** button twice. The start of your list should look like this:

1. France
   1.1. Accommodation
   1.2. Travel
   1.3. Weather
      1.3.1. Summer
      1.3.2. Winter

○ Do the same again for the headings under Spain.

○ 💾 Save your work as 'WP Activity 4' in your 'Word-processing software' sub-folder.

Open your 'Word-processing software' file. Create a new bold heading called '**WP Activity 4**' and write a short paragraph describing the skills you have demonstrated in this activity. 💾 Save the file.

Tabs

The **Tab** key is located to the left of the letter Q on your keyboard. Every time you press the **Tab** key the cursor jumps across the page. The **Tab** key is used to place and align text on the page. In the example in Figure 32, tabs have been used to position the three columns headed 'Coffee', 'Beer' and 'Meal for 2 people'. The tabs are represented by the → symbol which appears on screen when viewed with the Show/Hide options.

Approximate costs

→	→	Coffee	→	Beer→	→	Meal for 2 people
France→	→	£1.40→	→	£2.50→	→	£44.00
Italy→	→	£0.70→	→	£1.45→	→	£27.50
Spain→	→	£0.80→	→	£1.00→	→	£20.00

Figure 32 The use of tabs to form a simple table

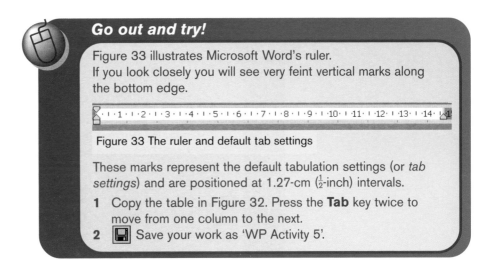

Go out and try!

Figure 33 illustrates Microsoft Word's ruler.
If you look closely you will see very feint vertical marks along the bottom edge.

Figure 33 The ruler and default tab settings

These marks represent the default tabulation settings (or *tab settings*) and are positioned at 1.27-cm ($\frac{1}{2}$-inch) intervals.

1   Copy the table in Figure 32. Press the **Tab** key twice to move from one column to the next.
2   Save your work as 'WP Activity 5'.

Open your 'Word-processing software' file. Create a new bold heading called '**WP Activity 5**' and write a short paragraph describing the skills you have demonstrated in this activity. Save the file.

Tab styles

The default tab settings are known as *left tabs* because the text is left-aligned with the tab. There are three other useful tab settings illustrated in Figure 34:

- right – text is right-aligned with the tab
- centre – text extends either side of the tab setting
- decimal – text before the decimal point extends left and after the decimal point extends right.

4 STAR OFFERS

Date	*Place*	*Hotel*	*No. of Nights*	*Cost*
10 October	Derby	Broadmeadow	4	£210
16 November	Chester	Lodge Gate	6	£249.50
23 November	Edinburgh	Monterry	5	£265.99
6 December	Brighton	Hurlingham Park	1	£75
13 December	London	Stretford	2	£150

Left   Right   Centred   Decimal

Figure 34 Column alignments in a tabbed table

Go out and try!

1 Open a new document and set the following tabs:
    left tab setting = 3 cm
    right tab setting = 8.5 cm
    centre tab setting = 10.5 cm
    decimal tab setting = 13 cm.

○ From the **Format** menu, select **Tabs**.
○ In the *Tabs* dialogue box, key in the first tab stop position in the *Tab stop position* box. Ensure *Alignment* is set to **Left**. Click on **Set**.
○ Repeat for each tab, remembering to change the alignment and to press **Set** after each one.

2 Type the table in Figure 34 into this document.

3 [💾] Save your work as 'WP Activity 6' in your 'Word-processing software' sub-folder.

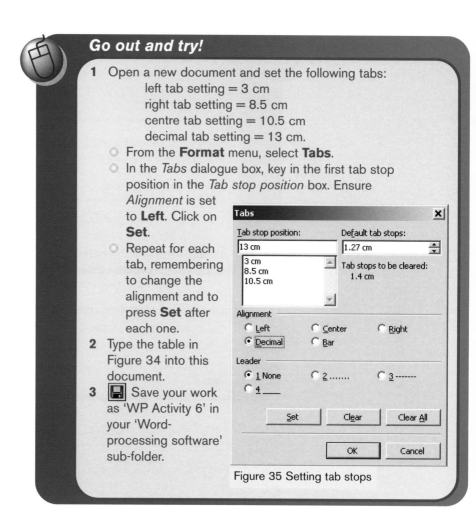

Figure 35 Setting tab stops

Open your 'Word-processing software' file. Create a new bold heading called '**WP Activity 6**' and write a short paragraph describing the skills you have demonstrated in this activity.
[💾] Save the file.

Indents

Paragraph indents can be used to make paragraphs stand out. Indents can be applied by selecting **Format, Paragraph** from the menu, or by dragging the indent markers on the horizontal ruler (Figure 36). Figure 37 shows some examples of paragraph indents in a leaflet.

 ← First line indent
← Hanging indent

Figure 36 Indent markers on the horizontal ruler

TRAVELBUG CITY BREAKS

Luxury coach tours
5 nights from £139.00
Nationwide pick-up points

Take advantage of the special deals we have negotiated with Whychton Coach Company and travel to one of your favourite European destinations by luxury, air-conditioned coach. All coaches have facilities for refreshments, WCs and videos and for your safety 2 qualified coach drivers accompany all journeys.

Paris is a shopper's paradise and is renowned as a city of culture. Your first stop must be the Louvre to see the Mona Lisa and Pei's glass pyramid. If Art Nouveau and Impressionism are more to your liking, then a visit to the Musée d'Orsay is a must.

Barcelona is the place to go to see the unmistakable works of Gaudi. Visit his distinctive houses in the Paseo de Gracia or the awe-inspiring church of the Sagrada Familia. Stroll through Las Ramblas to the busy port and Gothic Quarter.

Venice is a beautiful city and an unforgettable experience. Everybody goes about their business on the broad canals and narrow waterways. The famous Rialto Bridge is lined with shops selling glass, lace and carnival masks. St. Mark's Square is the place to be seen.

Florence represents the cultural heart of Italy and is packed with splendid architecture and fine art, including Michelangelo's famous statue of David and paintings by Raphael, Botticelli and da Vinci.

17 London Road	Whychton	TO9 3WN
Tel: 543 2134 5678		www.travelbug.co.uk
Fax: 543 2134 5679		Email: info@travelbug.co.uk

Figure 37 Examples of indents on a newsletter

Go out and try!

1 Open the file you saved as 'WP Activity 1' and copy the four paragraphs that describe the trip to Brussels.
2 Paste these paragraphs into a new document.
3 Create hanging indents on the first two paragraphs.
- Select the first two paragraphs.
- From the **Format** menu, select **Paragraph**.
- Ensure the *Indents and Spacing* tab is selected.
- In the *Special* box, select **Hanging**.

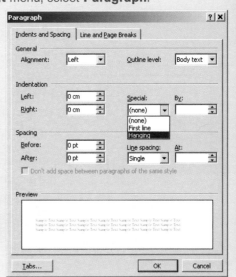

Figure 38 Setting a hanging indent

4 You are now going to indent the third paragraph by 2.54 cm from the left and right margins.
  ○ Select the third paragraph.
  ○ In the *Paragraph* dialogue box (Figure 34), click in the *Left* box and key in **2.54 cm**.
  ○ Repeat in the *Right* box.
  ○ In the *Special* box, ensure that **(none)** is selected.
  ○ Click on **OK**.

5 Create a first-line indent on the last paragraph.
  ○ Select the last paragraph and follow the instructions in Step 4, selecting **First line** in the *Special* box instead.

6 Save your work as 'WP Activity 7' in your 'Word-processing software' sub-folder.

Open your 'Word-processing software' file. Create a new bold heading called '**WP Activity 7**' and write a short paragraph describing the skills you have demonstrated in this activity. Save the file.

Using page formatting features

Margins

The *margin* is the area around the edge of the page that generally remains free of text. The default margins leave approximately 2.54 cm (1 inch) at the top and bottom of the page, and 3.17 cm (1.25 inches) on the left and right sides (Figure 39). For most everyday word-processing tasks these margins are quite appropriate.

Sometimes, however, it is sensible to change one or more of the margin settings. If you are producing a document that is to be bound, such as a report or brochure, then a *gutter* ensures that sufficient space is left so that the binding does not block out the text.

If you are creating a double-sided document, *mirror margins* ensure that the margins on the left page are a mirror image of those on the right page.

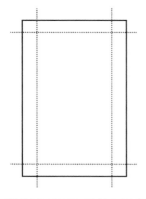

Figure 39 An A4 page showing the margin settings

Portrait

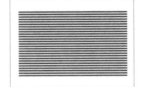

Landscape

Landscape

Landscape

Page orientation

Most documents containing text are produced using the default page orientation of *portrait*. However, there are times when you might want or need to turn the page the other way round, to *landscape* (Figure 40).

The margin settings and page orientation (sometimes called alignment) are generally changed through **File**, **Page Setup** (Figure 41). However, dragging the left and right margin markers on the ruler is an alternative way to change margins.

Go out and try!

1 Look at the default margin settings in Word and change the page orientation from portrait to landscape. What effect does changing the page orientation have on the left and right margin settings?
- From the **File** menu, select **Page Setup**.
- Change the *Orientation* from **Portrait** to **Landscape**.

Figure 41 Page Setup dialogue for Landscape orientation

2 What happens to the preview of the page when you increase or decrease the default settings of the left and right margins?
- In the *Page Setup* dialogue box, delete the measurements in the *Top*, *Bottom*, *Left* and *Right* margin boxes and increase and decrease the values.

3 Set the left and right margins to 3 cm (30 mm) and set the gutter to 1.5 cm (15 mm). What do you notice?
- Reset the page to portrait.
- In the *Page Setup* dialogue box, type in **3 cm** in the *Left* and *Right* boxes and **1.5 cm** in the *Gutter* box.

4 Reset the *Gutter* to **0**. Set the left margin to 5 cm (50 mm) and the right margin at 3 cm (30 mm). What happens to the preview if you select mirror margins?
- With the *Page Setup* dialogue box open, type in **5 cm** in the *Left* box and **3 cm** in the *Right* box.
- Under *Multiple pages*, select **Mirror margins**.

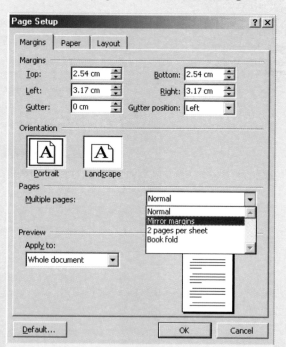

Figure 42 Page Setup dialogue for mirror margins

 Open your 'Word-processing software' file. Create a new bold heading called '**WP Activity 8**' and write a short paragraph describing the skills you have demonstrated in this activity.
 Save the file.

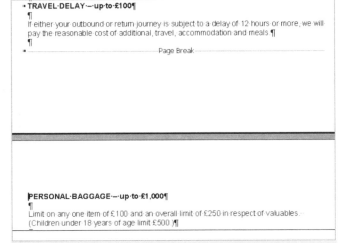

TRAVEL DELAY – up to £100

If either your outbound or return journey is subject to a delay of 12 hours or more, we will pay the reasonable cost of additional, travel, accommodation and meals.

PERSONAL BAGGAGE – up to £1,000

Limit on any one item of £100 and an overall limit of £250 in respect of valuables. (Children under 18 years of age limit £500.)

PERSONAL MONEY – up to £200

(Children under 18 years limit £50.)

Figure 43 A soft page break has been inserted by the program, but immediately under a heading

TRAVEL·DELAY·—·up·to·£100¶
¶
If either your outbound or return journey is subject to a delay of 12 hours or more, we will pay the reasonable cost of additional, travel, accommodation and meals ¶
¶
─────────────Page Break─────────────

PERSONAL·BAGGAGE·—·up·to·£1,000¶
¶
Limit on any one item of £100 and an overall limit of £250 in respect of valuables. (Children under 18 years of age limit £500)¶

Figure 44 The user has inserted a hard page break to prevent the heading from being separated from the text beneath it (compare this with Figure 43)

Page breaks

When you are working on a long document and you run out of space on the page, the text automatically runs onto the next page. Your word-processing software has inserted a *soft page break* and forced the remaining text on to a new page. A soft page break is flexible – rather like the soft returns we looked at on page 248. If you delete a section of text in front of a soft page break, text on the following page moves up to fill the gap.

Usually when this occurs we don't have to worry about it. However, look at Figure 43. The soft page break has left the heading 'PERSONAL BAGGAGE' on one page and the paragraph that should be with it is on the following page. This is not acceptable.

In situations like this you can use a *hard* (or *manual*) *page break* to push the heading onto the next page (Figure 44). A hard page break is not flexible – it will always force a new page at the point you have inserted it, even if text is later inserted or deleted.

There are two ways to insert a hard page break. Whichever way you choose, position the cursor immediately in front of the text that is to move onto the next page. Either

- select **Insert, Break, Page break**; or
- use key strokes – hold down **Ctrl** and at the same time press **Enter**.

By using the **Show/Hide** ¶ option you can see where the hard page break has been inserted.

Headers and footers

Anything inserted as a *header* or *footer* will appear on every page of the document in the same position (Figure 45).

- The document *header* is the space in the top margin above the first line of text on a page. You might find a company name or the title of the document inserted in the header area.

Figure 45 The header and footer areas in a document

○ The document *footer* is the space at the bottom of the page after the last line of text. The date, page number and file reference are often inserted in the footer.

When you use the word processor to produce any work at school or college, it is a good idea to put your name in the header or footer. There is a selection of options available through **Insert AutoText** in the header and footer areas (Figure 47). From this selection you can choose to show in the header or footer a variety of information, such as filename and path. This will help you to locate a document easily at a later date. *Last printed* is also useful to check that you are looking at the most recent copy of a printed document.

Page numbers

When producing a multi-page document, it is very sensible to number the pages. Page numbers can be placed in the header or footer area of the page either through **View, Header and Footer** or through **Insert, Page Numbers**.

Go out and try!

1 Open the file you saved as 'WP Activity 4'. At the very beginning of the document insert a page break so that the first page is now empty and the following three pages show the work you carried out on bullets and numbering.
2 Design a suitable title page on the new first page.
3 In the right-hand corner of the header area, insert page numbers. Format them so that there is no page number showing on the title page.
   ○ Move the cursor to the beginning of the document.
   ○ From the **Insert** menu, select **Page Numbers**.
   ○ Set the *Position* to **Top of the page (Header)** and the *Alignment* to **Right** (see Figure 40).
   ○ Uncheck the **Show number on first page** box (see Figure 46).

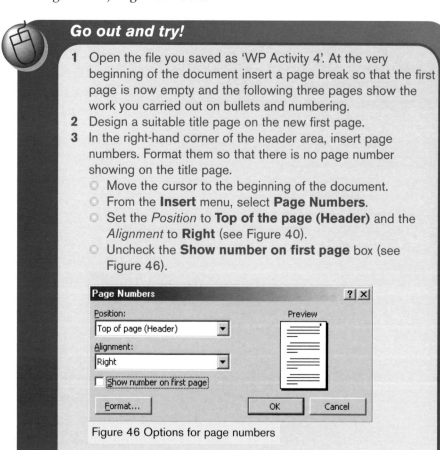

Figure 46 Options for page numbers

4 In the footer of the document, insert the filename and path against the left-hand margin and the date against the right-hand margin.

- Move the cursor to the beginning of the document.
- From the **View** menu, select **Header and Footer**.
- In the *Header and Footer* box select ⊞ **Switch Between Header and Footer** to switch to the footer.
- Ensure the cursor is at the left of the *Footer* box and, from the **Insert AutoText** menu, select **Filename and path**.

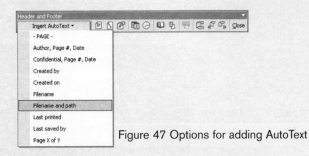

Figure 47 Options for adding AutoText

- Tab the cursor to the right-hand margin of the *Footer* box and click on the ▦ **Insert Date** button.

5 💾 Save your work as 'WP Activity 9' in your 'Word-processing software' sub-folder.

Open your 'Word-processing software' file. Create a new bold heading called '**WP Activity 9**' and write a short paragraph describing the skills you have demonstrated in this activity. At the same time check the pagination in your 'Word-processing software' file and number the pages.

💾 Save the file.

Line spacing

The distance between each line of text in a paragraph is known as the *line spacing*. The default setting in your word processor will produce text in single line spacing. However, there are occasions when it is useful to leave a larger space between the lines. For instance, you might want to make a section of text stand out, or to leave room between lines to make handwritten notes (Figure 48).

This example of text has been produced in **single line spacing**. This is the default setting and is probably the most commonly used.	This example shows text in **one and a half line spacing**. It is used to make sections of text stand out and therefore become easier to read.	This example shows text produced in **double line spacing**. It is particularly effective if you wish to write notes between the lines, as on a draft document.

Figure 48 Examples of single, 1.5 and double line spacings

Go out and try!

1 Open the file you saved as 'WP Activity 1'.
2 Change the left and right margins to 5 cm (50 mm). (Refer back to pages 264–266 if you have forgotten how to do this.)
3 Change the first two paragraphs to one-and-a-half (1.5) line spacing.
- Select the first two paragraphs.
- From the **Format** menu, select **Paragraph**.
- In the *Paragraph* dialogue box ensure that the **Indents and Spacing** tab is selected.
- In the *Spacing* section of the *Line Spacing* box, click on the down arrow and select **1.5 lines**, as shown in Figure 49.
- Click on **OK**.

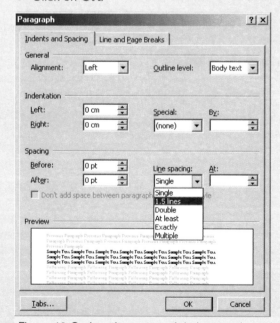

Figure 49 Options for paragraph indents and spacing

4 Change the remaining paragraphs to double line spacing. Use the instructions in Step 3 but select **Double** in the *Line Spacing* box instead.

5 Save your work as 'WP Activity 10' in your 'Word-processing software' sub-folder.

Open your 'Word-processing software' file. Create a new bold heading called '**WP Activity 10**' and write a short paragraph describing the skills you have demonstrated in this activity. Suggest one occasion when you might use 1.5 line spacing and one occasion when you might use double line spacing. Save the file.

Using columns

Word makes it easy to set up multiple columns on the same page. This is particularly useful if you are writing a newsletter.

The easy way to set up columns is to use the **Columns** icon on the *Standard* toolbar. This pops up an area that lets you choose how many columns you want (see Figure 50).

Figure 50 Setting two columns

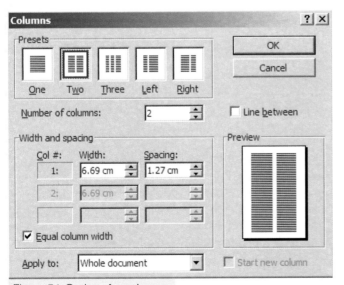

Figure 51 Options for columns

If you need to use more advanced features, such as uneven column widths, you can select **Format, Columns** from the menu. This displays the *Columns* dialogue box shown in Figure 51.

Go out and try!

1. Open the file you saved as 'WP Activity 1'. Make a copy of the text and paste it into a new document.
2. Select the five paragraphs at the foot of the page and display the text in two columns using the **Columns** button on the *Standard* toolbar. Justify the text.
3. Use the **Undo** button to remove the justification and columns.
4. Select the text again and use **Format**, **Columns** from the menu to display the text in three columns. Justify the text again.
5. Use the **Undo** button to remove the justification and columns.
6. Turn the page to landscape and repeat steps 2 to 5.
7. Decide which of the four versions you prefer and reformat the text to that style.
8. Save your work as 'WP Activity 11' in your 'Word-processing software' sub-folder.

Open your 'Word-processing software' file. Create a new bold heading called '**WP Activity 11**' and write a short paragraph describing the style of columns you preferred and justifying your reasons for choosing this style.
 Save the file.

Tables

We have already seen on page 260 that columns of data can be presented tidily by using tabs. A more powerful option, which can help you to display information effectively, is to use *tables*.

Tables consist of rows and columns that form individual boxes (or *cells*) – rather like a spreadsheet. Each individual cell may contain any amount of text, a picture or even a mathematical formula.

Figure 52 shows a basic table prepared by Travelbug to tell their customers the price of overnight accommodation in France.

Hotel stopovers
Prices shown in £s per room

Category	Accommodation	Weekend	Extra Child
Room only	Twin/double	£35	N/A
	Family	£45	2 free
Bed and Breakfast	Twin/double	£55	1 free
	Family	£75	2 free

Figure 52 A basic table layout

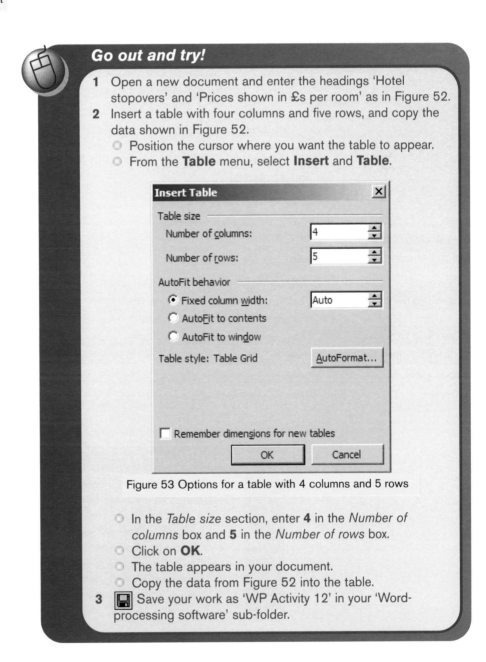

Go out and try!

1 Open a new document and enter the headings 'Hotel stopovers' and 'Prices shown in £s per room' as in Figure 52.
2 Insert a table with four columns and five rows, and copy the data shown in Figure 52.
   ○ Position the cursor where you want the table to appear.
   ○ From the **Table** menu, select **Insert** and **Table**.

Figure 53 Options for a table with 4 columns and 5 rows

   ○ In the *Table size* section, enter **4** in the *Number of columns* box and **5** in the *Number of rows* box.
   ○ Click on **OK**.
   ○ The table appears in your document.
   ○ Copy the data from Figure 52 into the table.
3 Save your work as 'WP Activity 12' in your 'Word-processing software' sub-folder.

Open your 'Word-processing software' file. Create a new bold heading called 'WP Activity 12' and write a short paragraph describing the skills you have demonstrated in this activity. Save the file.

Borders and shading in tables

There are additional features in your word-processing software that give you the opportunity to enhance or improve the general appearance of a table. For example you can apply borders and shading, and introduce colour.

Figure 54 shows the table from Figure 52 with the addition of some features.

Hotel stopovers
Prices shown in £s per room

Category	Accommodation	Weekend	Extra Child
Room only	Twin/double	£35	N/A
	Family	£45	2 free
Bed and Breakfast	Twin/double	£55	1 free
	Family	£75	2 free

Figure 54 The table in Figure 52 with the addition of an outside border, shading and colour

Go out and try!

1 Open the file you saved as 'WP Activity 12'.
2 Change the outside border to a double line.
  - Click anywhere within the table.
  - From the **Table** menu, choose **Select** then **Table**.
  - From the **Format** menu, select **Borders and Shading**.
  - In the *Borders and Shading* dialogue box, select the **double line** option in the *Style* box and **Box** in the *Settings* box. Ensure **Table** is selected in the *Apply to* box.

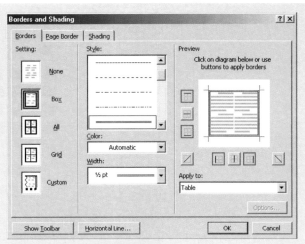

Figure 55 A double-line table border

3 Shade the cells containing the column headings.
- Select the cells containing the column headings and right-click on them.
- In the pop-up menu, select **Borders and Shading**.
- With the *Shading* tab selected, choose a colour.
- Click on **OK**.

TiP

Make sure the shading you choose is in contrast to the colour of the text so that you can still read it. If you choose a light shade keep the text dark. If you choose a dark shade consider changing the text to a lighter colour.

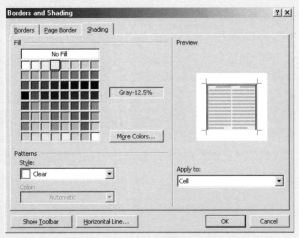

Figure 56 Options for shading

4 Add a coloured background to the cells showing the row headings, and apply a contrasting font colour.
- Select the row headings and follow the instructions in Step 3 to apply shading to the cells.
- With the row heading cells selected, click on the arrow next to the ⬛ ▾ **Font Color** button to show the colours available.

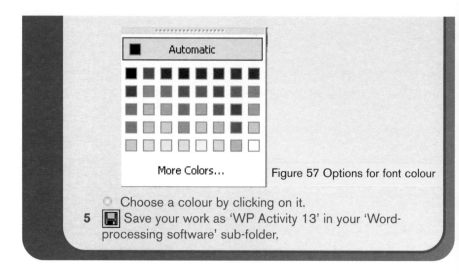

Figure 57 Options for font colour

○ Choose a colour by clicking on it.

5 Save your work as 'WP Activity 13' in your 'Word-processing software' sub-folder,

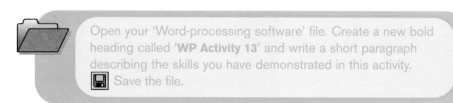

Open your 'Word-processing software' file. Create a new bold heading called '**WP Activity 13**' and write a short paragraph describing the skills you have demonstrated in this activity. Save the file.

Modifying row and column sizes

The columns showing prices for weekends and extra child details are wider than they need to be. The column width can be modified by picking up the arrow shape ⇔ and dragging the column border to a new position. The effect of doing this is shown in Figure 58.

You can also modify the row height by picking up the arrow shape ⇕ and dragging up or down.

Hotel stopovers
Prices shown in £s per room

Category	Accommodation	Weekend	Extra Child
Room only	Twin/double	£35	N/A
	Family	£45	2 free
Bed and Breakfast	Twin/double	£55	1 free
	Family	£75	2 free

Figure 58 Compare this with Figure 54: the column widths have been adjusted

Go out and try!

1 Open the file you saved as 'WP Activity 13'.
2 Carefully move your cursor across the rows and columns to see it change shape as it rests on row and column boundaries.
3 Reduce the column widths for 'Weekend' and 'Extra Child'.
   ○ Select the column showing 'Weekend'.
   ○ Place your cursor over the right column border and, when it changes to a double-headed arrow, drag it to the correct position.
   ○ Do the same for the 'Extra Child' column.
4 💾 Save your work as 'WP Activity 14' in your 'Word-processing software' sub-folder. Leave the file open.
5 Apply Autofit to the 'Weekend' column.
   ○ Position the cursor on the column border between 'Weekend' and 'Extra Child'.
   ○ Double-click on the border to see what happens to the width of the 'Weekend' column. The column width should automatically reduce to fit the text within it.
   ○ Try it again on the outside column border.
   ○ Close the file without saving these changes.

Open your 'Word-processing software' file. Create a new bold heading called '**WP Activity 14**' and write a short paragraph describing the skills you have demonstrated in this activity.
💾 Save the file.

Inserting and deleting columns and rows

In Figure 59 an extra column has been added to the table to show the midweek prices. Extra rows have also been added to enable the headings to become part of the table and to separate the two different categories of accommodation. Extra columns and rows can be inserted by selecting **Table, Insert**.

HOTEL STOPOVERS				
ALL OFFERS SUBJECT TO AVAILABILITY				
Category	**Accommodation**	**Weekend**	**Midweek**	**Extra Child**
Room only	Twin/double	£35	£35	N/A
	Family	£45	£45	2 free
Bed and Breakfast	Twin/double	£55	£60	1 free
	Family	£75	£80	2 free
Prices shown in £s per room				

Figure 59 Compare this with Figure 58: the table now has an extra column, and four additional rows have been inserted

Go out and try!

1 Open the table you saved as 'WP Activity 14'.
2 Insert a new column between Weekend and Extra Child and head the column 'Midweek'.
   ○ Select the Extra Child column and right-click on it.
   ○ From the pop-up menu, select **Insert Columns**.
   ○ Type in **Midweek** as the column heading.
3 Insert two rows above the cell headed 'Category'.
   ○ Select the row containing the heading category.
   ○ From the **Table** menu, select **Insert**, then **Rows Above**.
   ○ Repeat to add a second row.
4 Using the method described in Step 3, insert a new row above 'Bed and Breakfast'.
5 Add an extra row at the foot of the table.
   ○ Click in the last cell in the table.
   ○ Press the **Tab** key.
   ○ An extra row should appear.
6 For each of the four new rows you are going to merge the cells.
   ○ Select each of the new rows, one at a time.
   ○ From the **Table** menu, select **Merge Cells**.
   ○ The four rows should each appear as one cell running the width of the table.
7 Complete the table with the additional information (from Figure 59).
8 [💾] Save the file as 'WP Activity 15' in your 'Word-processing software' sub-folder.

Open your 'Word-processing software' file. Create a new bold heading called 'WP Activity 15' and write a short paragraph describing the skills you have demonstrated in this activity. [💾] Save the file.

Text boxes

A *text box* is a drawing object that contains text. You can format the text in a text box in the same way as any other text in your document, but because it is contained in a box you can resize it and move it. You can use a text box to realign text and can add shadow and 3-D styles.

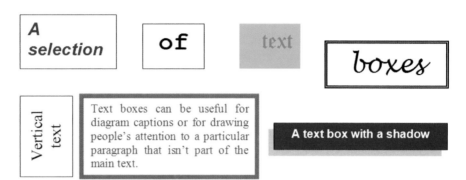

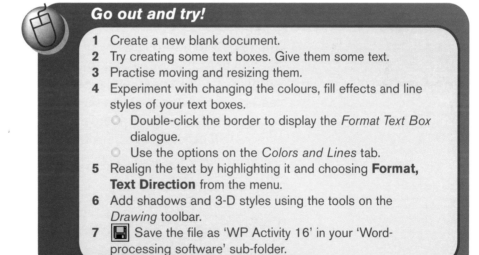

Figure 60 A selection of text boxes

You can add a text box by selecting **Insert, Text Box** from the menu, or by using the **Text Box** icon on the *Drawing* toolbar. You must then click and drag your mouse over the area in which you want the text box to appear.

Go out and try!

1 Create a new blank document.
2 Try creating some text boxes. Give them some text.
3 Practise moving and resizing them.
4 Experiment with changing the colours, fill effects and line styles of your text boxes.
  - Double-click the border to display the *Format Text Box* dialogue.
  - Use the options on the *Colors and Lines* tab.
5 Realign the text by highlighting it and choosing **Format, Text Direction** from the menu.
6 Add shadows and 3-D styles using the tools on the *Drawing* toolbar.
7 Save the file as 'WP Activity 16' in your 'Word-processing software' sub-folder.

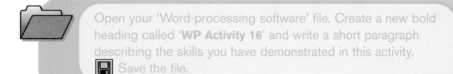

Open your 'Word-processing software' file. Create a new bold heading called '**WP Activity 16**' and write a short paragraph describing the skills you have demonstrated in this activity. Save the file.

Creating, selecting and inserting components

Types of components

Many of the publications you produce may comprise more than one component, such as

- images
- lines and simple shapes
- tick boxes
- comments
- hyperlinks.

You must remember that whatever you include in a publication should be there because it improves the effectiveness of that publication and not just because you felt like putting something in.

Images

Images used to illustrate a topic can certainly help people to understand the topic and generally make a publication more interesting for the reader. However, you should only include images that are fully relevant to the topic and that serve a purpose by being included.

You may search through a picture library to find a relevant image, but you must be very careful to obtain permission to use the image if it is protected by copyright laws. Images taken with a digital camera can be inserted directly from the camera. Photographs and images in books and magazines or photographs you take with a traditional camera will need to be scanned into the document.

Remember to record full details of the sources of all images you include in your work.

Lines and simple shapes

You will find it very useful to investigate the *Drawing* toolbar and to experiment with the variety of lines and shapes that are available for you to use. Move your mouse pointer over the toolbar to see the names given to the various tools.

Figure 61 The Drawing toolbar

TiP

*If you find it difficult to place one object in front of another use the **Order** option in the Draw menu to send an object in front or behind another.*

TiP

*If you hold down the **Ctrl** key whilst using the arrow directional keys you can 'nudge' the lines and shapes across the screen in very small steps. If you increase the zoom on the screen to 200% or 500% you can see very clearly when lines and shapes are in the right position.*

The arrow tool is very helpful if you need to label a diagram. Other shapes can be built up to form a variety of objects.

The image of the train in Figure 62 is made up from approximately 30 lines and shapes. Some have been copied, some have been filled with colour and all lines have been made thicker.

Figure 62 A train constructed from simple shapes

Go out and try!

1 Open the *Drawing* toolbar on your screen and spend a few minutes investigating the selection of features it offers.
2 Draw some simple shapes and lines and experiment with the fill colour, line colour and line style options.
3 Move the shapes across the screen with the arrow directional keys.
4 Use a variety of lines and shapes and produce an image of your choice.
5 💾 Save your work as 'WP Activity 17' in your 'Word-processing software' sub-folder.

Grouping and ungrouping

You have produced an image that is made up of many different lines and shapes. If you try to move the image, it will be impossible to keep all the shapes together unless you *group* them. Grouping allows you to treat a group of objects as a single object that can be rotated, resized or flipped. Any group of images can be *ungrouped* and treated as a number of separate objects again.

1 Use the **Select Objects** tool (the arrow) and drag a large rectangle around the complete image you have formed. You will see that every component of the image becomes selected.
2 From the *Draw* menu select **Group**. The image can now be treated as a single object.
3 Experiment with the **Rotate or Flip** options.
4 Try to resize the image by double-clicking it and choosing the Size tab. Ensure the **Lock aspect ratio** box is selected and re-size by changing the dimensions.
5 Save your work as 'WP Activity 18' in your 'Word-processing software' sub-folder.

Figure 63 The Draw menu

Borders

You already know how to place a border round text (see page 274) but you may sometimes wish to place a border round a full page, for example on a poster. You will find a wide choice of artwork and line styles available in **Format, Borders and Shading, Page Border**.

You can use the *Rectangle* tool to place a border around an image or object. Draw the rectangle shape over the image with the **Rectangle** tool on the *Drawing* toolbar. The image will disappear under the rectangle but you can double-click the rectangle, remove the 'Fill' colour and choose a suitable line style and colour. You can resize the rectangle as necessary.

Go out and try!

1 Open the image you created in the previous activity.
2 Place a border round the image.
3 Choose a line style and colour to enhance the image.
4 Save your work as 'WP Activity 19' in your 'Word-processing software' sub-folder.

Tick boxes

Tick boxes are useful on questionnaires and surveys if you are
supplying a set of choices and you want people to tick one or more
boxes. You will find a selection of tick (or check) boxes through
Insert, Symbol, Wingdings. To increase their size, treat them like any
other character symbol.

Figure 64 Characters useful for tick boxes

Comments

You know it is essential that your work is reviewed regularly by a
wide range of people and that you should consider carefully any
comments your reviewers make. Sometimes it may be convenient to
ask your reviewer to look at a printed version of your work. In that
case your reviewer might write his or her comments down or talk
them over with you.

However, there may be occasions when you send a copy of your
work by email if the reviewer is not nearby, for example if he or she
is a member of a specialist group or team. The reviewer can use the
'comments' feature of the word processor to insert his or her
thoughts directly into the document file. The file can then be emailed
back to you and the comments will be on-screen for you to consider.
This can save a lot of time for a reviewer.

You will also find comments useful for you to use as your projects
develop. If you have a change of mind about something, you can
insert a comment into the document explaining and justifying your
reasons. This can then be presented as evidence in your e-portfolio.

Go out and try!

1 Open the file you saved as WP Activity 9. This is a multi-
page file containing several features such as bullets and
numbers, page breaks, and headers and footers.
2 Insert comments into the document describing the features
contained within it.
3 Place the cursor against the first feature (or highlight a
particular section of text if this is relevant) and select **Insert,
Comment**.

4   Your comments can be entered into the comment boxes.
5   Look at the toolbars on display on your screen. Has the *Reviewing* toolbar appeared? If not, display it through **View**, **Toolbars**. Place your mouse pointer over the toolbar and investigate the options offered.
6   Save your work as 'WP Activity 20' in your 'Word-processing software' sub-folder.

Hyperlinks

You have learnt how to insert and use hyperlinks in web pages. You can insert hyperlinks in word-processed documents too. For example in your e-portfolio you might have a series of versions of a document showing all of its development stages; you can use hyperlinks to take you from one version of the document to another. Imagine how effective it will be for your assessors to follow the progress and read your comments as each element of your project is considered.

Go out and try!

1   Open your Word-processing software file. Create a new bold heading '**WP Activities 17 to 20**'. Write short paragraphs explaining what you have learnt about lines and simple shapes, tick boxes, comments and hyperlinks. Resave the file in your 'Word-processing software' sub-folder.
2   Select the heading **WP Activity 1** and insert a hyperlink that will automatically open the file 'WP Activity 1', as follows.
○   Select the text that indicates the hyperlink position.
○   From the menu, select **Insert**, **Hyperlink** and browse your files.
○   Double-click on the file name you wish the hyperlink to open – in this example 'WP Activity 1'.
3   Insert a second hyperlink in that file that will return you to the 'Word-processing software' file.
4   Repeat this activity with several of the headings.
5   Resave the file.

Styles

When you open your word processor, you know that some things will always be the same. For example

○   the first letter is always positioned in the same place on the page
○   the font size and style is always the same
○   the line spacing is always single
○   paragraph alignment is always left aligned or left justified.

This style of presentation is the default or *Normal* style, which always presents itself when you open a new document.

The current style is displayed through the *Style* button ![Normal style button] and if you click on the button you will be able to see the styles that are available.

A style can be any combination of formatting characteristics that you name and store as a set, such as font style, font size, margin settings and page orientation. When you apply a style, all the formatting instructions in that style are applied at one time. Any style can be created and saved to suit the requirements of a particular document. For example, if certain documents must always be set up in Comic Sans 14 pt, double line spacing with centre justification then it would be sensible to set a style so that you don't have to reformat the standard features every time you need to create such a document. You would just select the style from the stored list.

You could set a style to add a defined space after headings and paragraphs. Choose Format, Paragraph and insert the required point-sized space against 'After'. For example, a 6 pt space after all headings is the equivalent to ½ clear line space if you are working in 12 pt font size.

Use styles to improve the overall appearance of your documents, to help retain consistency of presentation throughout and to make them smarter.

Go out and try!

1 Open a new document and enter the following text:

> What can I do in my school holidays?
>
> Are you looking for some ideas to help fill the long, summer days? Travelbug are sponsoring a series of events in Whychton Park throughout the summer. Entrance is free to all children aged 5 to 12 years but you must be accompanied by an adult.
>
> Treasure Hunt
>
> Come and unscramble the clues to find the hidden treasure. Monday, 31 July at 10.00 am and 2.00 pm for children aged 7–12.
>
> Bouncy Castles
>
> Visit Whychton Park from Monday 7 August until Friday

11 August and have fun on the inflatables. Open from 10.00 am to 5.00 pm for children aged under 10.

Archery

Sign up for one of the following sessions according to your age and experience.

Beginners

We will run a series of introductory sessions for boys and girls on Tuesday, 1 August and Wednesday, 2 August.

Intermediates

If you have completed the beginners session, come along and improve your technique any time on Thursday 3 August and Friday 4 August.

2 Open the *Styles and Formatting* task pane through the *Format* menu and apply the following styles:
   ○ **Heading 1** to the main heading
   ○ **Heading 2** to Treasure Hunt, Bouncy Castles and Archery
   ○ **Heading 3** to Beginners and Intermediates.
3 Decide on a style of your own choice for the paragraphs in the document you have just produced. For example Comic Sans, Red, 14 pt font and one-and-a-half line spacing.
4 Create a new style based on your choice through the *Styles and Formatting* task pane and call the style 'My Style'. Position the cursor in each paragraph and click on 'My Style'.

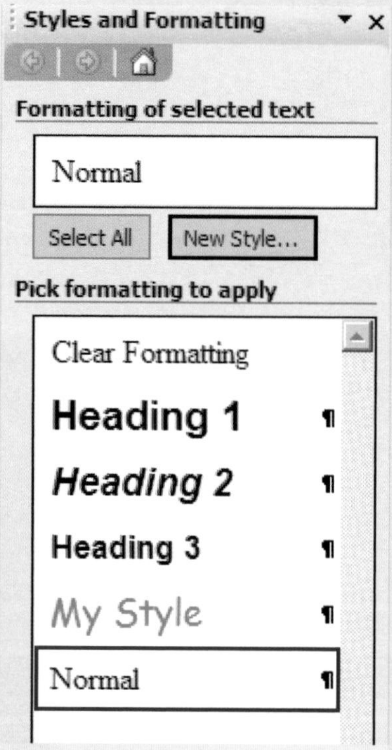

Save the file as 'WP Activity 21' in your 'Word-processing software' sub-folder.

Styles and Formatting ▼ ✕

⊕ | ⊕ | ⌂

Formatting of selected text

Normal

Select All | New Style...

Pick formatting to apply

Clear Formatting

Heading 1 ¶

Heading 2 ¶

Heading 3 ¶

My Style ¶

Normal ¶

Figure 65 The Styles and Formatting task pane

TRAVELBUG WATER SPORTS

Departing 20 June
Travel by luxury coach from Whychton
14 nights half-board accommodation in 3-star hotel

A fantastic opportunity to experience a variety of water sports including:

Windsurfing

Learn the basics of windsurfing, including rigging, equipment care, sailing across the wind and self-rescue. Advanced skills include instruction on topics such as water starts, harness use, and shortboards. Wetsuits and windsurfing gear are provided.

Snorkelling

For many people the water's edge is the limit of their activity and knowledge. Learn to snorkel and enjoy the world that lurks beneath the surface of the water. You will be introduced to snorkelling equipment including the mask, flippers and snorkel and will learn how to move safely in the water.

Water skiing

If you are a complete beginner you will start on land and learn the fundamentals of body position, technique and safety. Once you and your instructor are confident in understanding the basics on land, you move to the water. First-time skiers will use the static boom on the side of the boat to offer stability. When you have mastered the boom, then it is off to the long line! Who knows, you may be able to Slalom, Trick or Jump before the end of your holiday!

£585 per person
(based on two people sharing a room and fully inclusive of all equipment and tuition)

17 London Road   Whychton   TO9 3WN

Tel: 543 2134 5678   www.travelbug.co.uk
Fax: 543 2134 5679   Email: info@travelbug.co.uk

Using images and objects

Many documents and on-screen presentations contain illustrations. These are included to help simplify the information contained in the text, or simply to provide decoration. In this book many types of illustrations have been used: pictures, photographs, charts, graphs, screen prints, text boxes, clip art, WordArt, etc. Collectively these are referred to as *objects*.

Sensible use of images will greatly improve a document and make it more appealing to the target audience. Figure 66 is an example.

An image or object can be inserted by selecting the **Insert** drop-down menu.

Figure 66 Sensible use of images will greatly improve a document and make it more appealing to the target audience

Positioning images and objects

Any image in a document should be there to serve a specific purpose, and its positioning is therefore very important. The position of the cursor when the image is inserted into the document will determine where it appears. Figure 67 shows an example. After the image was inserted, the text was pushed down the page.

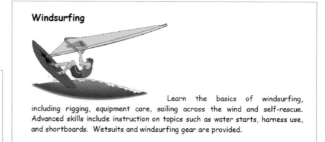

Windsurfing

Learn the basics of windsurfing, including rigging, equipment care, sailing across the wind and self-rescue. Advanced skills include instruction on topics such as water starts, harness use, and shortboards. Wetsuits and windsurfing gear are provided.

Figure 67 An example of text before the insertion of an image, and the same text with an image: notice how the text has been pushed down the page

Wrapping text around an image

As you can see from Figure 67, although an image has been placed in the document, its inclusion does not really improve the document because it is positioned on the left with empty space at the side. In order to make the document more interesting and the image more manageable, you can format the image and select a *wrapping style* to improve the layout. Figure 68 shows two examples.

Figure 68 A 'square' wrapping style, and a 'tight' wrapping style in which the text hugs the edges of the image

TiP

You should make sure that any images you include in your documents improve their appearance and are not included just because you fancied putting them in!

Wrapping of an image can be achieved by selecting the **Format**, **Picture** (or **Object**), **Layout** drop-down menu.

Images and objects that are formatted to wrap text can also be moved more easily within the document by clicking and dragging them to a new position.

Sizing an image

Sometimes the size of an image or object should be restricted because of the amount of available space on the page. Any object can be resized by selecting the object to show the selection handles and dragging one of the handles with the mouse.

Figure 69 Images that have been resized without retaining the original proportions: inclusion of these images would not improve a document!

Cropping an image

From time to time an image we require might be part of a larger image. We can 'crop' the unwanted area from the image by using the **Crop** tool ⊞ in the *Picture* toolbar.

(a)

(c)

(b)

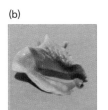

Figure 70 (a) A clip art image of a sea shell on the beach. (b) The sea shell has been 'cropped', removing the surrounding area. (c) The cropped image can then be resized if necessary.

Go out and try!

1 Write four paragraphs describing different activities you like to do in your spare time. Each paragraph should cover about six lines on the page.

2 Find four clip art images that relate to the activities you have described.
   ○ Place your cursor where you want your image to appear.
   ○ From the **Insert** menu, select **Picture** then **Clip Art**.
   ○ In the *Insert Clip Art* task pane, type in to the *Search For* box words that describe your activities.
   ○ Click on **Search**.

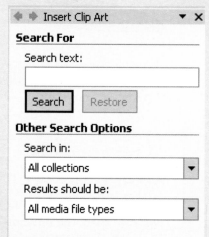

Figure 71 Clip art search options

   ○ Click on your selection to insert the clip art into your document.
   ○ Repeat to insert the other three images.

3 Resize the images to fit into the paragraphs.
   ○ Click on the image to select it. It will have handles on the corners and at the sides.
   ○ Hover over a handle until a double-sided arrow appears. Drag a corner handle to resize the image.

4 Find one more image that you can crop to leave only part of the image on display. Insert the image at the end of the document and crop as required.

5 Save the file as 'WP Activity 22' in your 'Word-processing software' sub-folder.

Go out and try!

1   Incorporate the images within the paragraphs by selecting different text wrapping styles.
    ○   Double-click on one of the images you have inserted to access the *Format Picture* dialogue box.
    ○   Select the *Layout* tab and choose the *Wrapping style* you want to use.

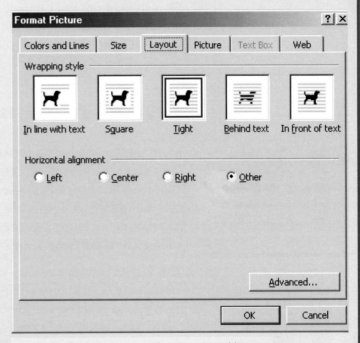

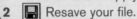

Figure 72 Options for wrapping text around images

    ○   Click **OK** to apply it to your document.
2   Resave your file.

Open your 'Word-processing software' file. Create a new bold heading called '**WP Activity 22**' and write a short paragraph describing the skills you have demonstrated in this activity. Save the file.

Using spelling and grammar checkers

The importance of using spelling and grammar checkers has been stressed in Standard Ways of Working (on page 236) and in Unit 1 (on page 35).

As a student on an IT course, you have no excuse for submitting work which contains spelling and grammar errors – the tools to help you check the accuracy of your work are at your fingertips. Make sure nothing is left unchecked!

Using mail merge

Jargon buster

Mail merge is used when an organisation wishes to send the same letter to a large number of people.

Many of the letters that arrive in the post at your home will have been prepared using a process called *mail merge*. The letters will appear to have been addressed personally to their recipients, but in fact each letter will probably have been produced as part of a large batch of many letters, all containing exactly the same message but addressed to different people.

This is a very quick and easy way of contacting customers, whose details may be held on a company database. These letters are often sent from banks, building societies, insurance companies, large retail stores, utility companies, credit card companies and other financial businesses.

? Think it over ...

Think of five occasions your family might have received letters produced using mail merge.

How are the letters produced?

The letters are produced in two stages.

- First, a *data file* which contains the personal information of the recipients is required. This may be an existing database, or it might be produced in a word-processing or spreadsheet file for a one-off mail merge operation. It will contain details such as name, address, telephone number and account number.

- Second, a *standard letter* is produced. This will contain the text of the message. Instead of being addressed in the usual way, it will contain what are called *merge fields*.

Jargon buster

Merge fields are the points at which the individual personalised details will be inserted in each letter.

Go out and try!

Step 1

○ From the **Tools** menu, select **Letters and Mailings, Mail Merge Wizard**.
○ In the task pane's *Select document type* section, select **Letters.**

Mail Merge

Select document type

What type of document are you working on?

⦿ Letters
○ E-mail messages
○ Envelopes
○ Labels
○ Directory

Letters

Send letters to a group of people. You can personalize the letter that each person receives.

Click Next to continue.

Figure 73 Mail merge: select the document type

○ Click on **Next: Starting document**.

Step 2

This gives you a choice of preparing the letter from a document (or blank document) on the screen, a letter saved in a file, or a template.

○ In the *Select starting document* section, select **Use the current document**.

Mail Merge

Select starting document

How do you want to set up your letters?

⦿ Use the current document
○ Start from a template
○ Start from existing document

Use the current document

Start from the document shown here and use the Mail Merge wizard to add recipient information.

Figure 74 Mail merge: select the starting document

○ Click on **Next: Select recipients**.

Step 3

○ In the *Select recipients* section, select **Type a new list**.

Mail Merge

Select recipients

○ Use an existing list
○ Select from Outlook contacts
⦿ Type a new list

Type a new list

Type the names and addresses of recipients.

 Create...

Figure 75 Mail merge: the address list can be customised to suit you needs

○ Click on **Create**.
○ A *New Address List* dialogue box appears.

TiP

If you have the names and addresses in an existing data file, you can link that file to the letter by browsing through your files and opening the file that contains the data. It may be in a word-processing, spreadsheet, database or email application.

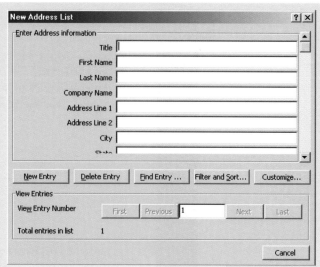

Figure 76 Entry screen for an address list

You can customise your address list to suit your needs and delete any unwanted information.

○ Click on the **Customize** button.
○ Delete any unwanted fields (e.g. company name).
○ Make your list the same as in Figure 77.

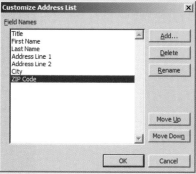

Figure 77 Mail merge: this address list has been customised

Create three entries in the revised list.

○ Enter your own details in the appropriate boxes as the first entry.
○ Click on **New Entry** and enter the two records shown in Figure 80 on page 296.
○ Click on **Close**.

Save your address list with a suitable filename.

○ In the **Save As** dialogue box, save your address list with a suitable filename, such as 'Mail merge addresses', in your 'Word-processing software' sub-folder.
○ Click on **Next: Write your letter**. The *Write your letter* task pane appears.

Figure 78 Mail merge: write your letter

Step 4

You are now ready to write your letter

○ Copy the letter shown in Figure 79.

○ Where you see merge fields such as <<Title>>, <<First_Name>> and <<Last_Name>>

   ● click on the **More items** link.

   ● select the merge field from the list and click on **Insert**.

○ When you have inserted all the merge fields, click on **Close**.

NB Remember to insert spaces between <<Title>>, <<First_Name>> and <<Last_Name>> and to press **Enter** at the end of each line of the address.

Insert the current date

«Title» «First_Name» «Last_Name»
«Address_Line_1»
«Address_Line_2»
«City»
«ZIP_Code»

Dear «Title» «Last_Name»

Thank you for your interest in the forthcoming weekend visit to northern France.

I enclose your tickets and confirm the coach will pick you up at «City» station at the time indicated on the ticket.

I hope you have an enjoyable visit to France.

Yours sincerely

Figure 79 Mail merge: the skeleton letter template with fields highlighted

○ 💾 Save your letter as you go along in your 'Word-processing software' sub-folder, with a suitable filename such as 'Mail merge letter'.

○ Click on **Next: Preview your letters**.

○ Click on **Next: Complete the merge**.

You will now have three letters, each personally addressed – and you only had to type the letter once! The merged letters should be similar to those in Figure 80.

Insert the current date

Mr John Gray
23 Deepfield House
Deepfield Way
Linfield
TO6 5DC

Dear Mr Gray

Thank you for your interest in the forthcoming weekend visit to northern France.

I enclose your tickets and confirm the coach will pick you up at Linfield station at the time indicated on the ticket.

I hope you have an enjoyable visit to France.

Yours sincerely

Insert the current date

Miss Jean Smith
4 Glebe Gardens
Whychton
TO7 3FD

Dear Miss Smith

Thank you for your interest in the forthcoming weekend visit to northern France.

I enclose your tickets and confirm the coach will pick you up at Whychton station at the time indicated on the ticket.

I hope you have an enjoyable visit to France.

Yours sincerely

Figure 80 Examples of two letters produced by mail merge

? Think it over ...

Remember that in business the data file will probably have hundreds of entries. Imagine the time it will save to produce hundreds of letters in this way.

Open your 'Word-processing software' file. Create a new bold heading called '**WP Activity 23**' and write a short paragraph describing the skills you have demonstrated in this activity. Save the file.

Spreadsheet software

You will almost certainly have used a spreadsheet for your schoolwork. You will know that the main purpose of a spreadsheet is to enter, edit and manipulate *numerical* data, and to *make calculations* using this data. As part of your e-portfolio evidence for your coursework, you will need to gather and analyse data to produce meaningful information, some of which will be in the form of spreadsheets and graphs or charts.

Spreadsheet programs make it much easier to perform financial tasks such as calculating staff wages, profit made on goods sold, VAT (value-added tax) returns for the government, and bank accounts. A spreadsheet program is an invaluable tool to all kinds of organisations, from small ones such as a neighbourhood card shop, to your own school or college, or huge companies such as Top Shop, Microsoft or government organisations such as the National Health Service.

On a personal level you might use a spreadsheet to keep track of how much income you receive, what expenses you have and how much is left to save.

LEARNING OUTCOMES

You need to learn about

✓ entering, cutting, copying, pasting and moving data

✓ formatting cells to match data types

✓ using operators

✓ replicating formulas using relative cell references

✓ replicating formulas using absolute cell references

✓ inserting or deleting rows and columns

✓ using simple functions

✓ sorting data

✓ producing fully customised charts and graphs

✓ using headers and footers

✓ printing selected areas

✓ inserting comments

✓ filtering data

✓ linking sheets.

Entering, cutting, copying, pasting and moving data

> **Jargon buster**
>
> Spreadsheet files are known as **workbooks**. Each workbook may include several **worksheets** (pages) all related to the main purpose of that file.

Let's look at the structure of spreadsheets in more detail, beginning with a very basic example.

The spreadsheet worksheet is divided into *rows* and *columns*, creating a *grid of cells*. Each row and column in a spreadsheet is given a unique number or letter, so each cell can be identified rather like a map reference – A1, B6, C12 etc.

	A	B	C	D
1				
2				
3				
4				

Cell C2

Figure 81 Spreadsheet cell references

> **Jargon buster**
>
> The **default size** of a spreadsheet cell is the width and height already set by the software.

The data – a row or column heading, text or number – is entered into a cell. However, the default size of a cell is quite small. If the data entered into the cell is too wide it will overlap into the next cell; but as soon as data is entered into the adjacent cell, some of the original data becomes hidden (not lost). You will then need to decide the best method of overcoming the problem, and this is discussed later.

After you start using a spreadsheet you may need to make changes because

- you have identified some improvements you could introduce
- you have learned more about the spreadsheet program's facilities
- the needs of the business have altered.

You can cut, copy, paste and move data between cells, rows and columns. Look back at page 249 – you will see that the icons and keystrokes work in exactly the same way in Excel.

Formatting cells to match their data types

Unless formatting techniques (use of bold, colour, borders, fill or shading) have been used, the spreadsheet can be very difficult to read – especially if it is very large, covering many rows and columns. So it is very important to consider the *appearance* of the spreadsheet as well as the data and the formulas.

Just as in word-processing software, you can enhance the text in a spreadsheet by

- using bold, italic or underlined text
- varying the font size for main headings or sub-headings
- using different font styles.

In addition you can improve the appearance of the spreadsheet by

- formatting a heading at an angle or vertically within cells
- centring a heading horizontally within a cell or across two or more columns
- centring a heading vertically within a cell (i.e. centred from top to bottom)
- wrapping text within a cell to avoid having an extremely wide column
- adjusting the cell width or height
- highlighting significant cells (e.g. ones with totals) with borders or colours.

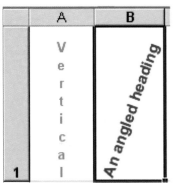

Figure 82 Angled headings

You should also pay attention to the following when formatting numerical data:

- How many decimal places do you need, if any? For example, if you have a column for the number of students in different tutor groups, you would not have $\frac{1}{2}$ or 0.5 of a student! However, if you are listing the sales of fruit or vegetables, you might well have $\frac{1}{2}$ or 0.5 of a kilo. In the first case you do not need any decimal places, but in the second you might well want to show two decimal places.
- If the data is the cost of the item, do you wish to show the currency symbol, or is it enough to format the money to two decimal places? What would be suitable for house prices?
- If the currency symbol is used, is it too cluttered to show the £ sign everywhere, or might it be better to use it just for the totals?
- Do you wish to show negative numbers in red? If so, this can be set automatically.

Columns marked A, B, C etc.

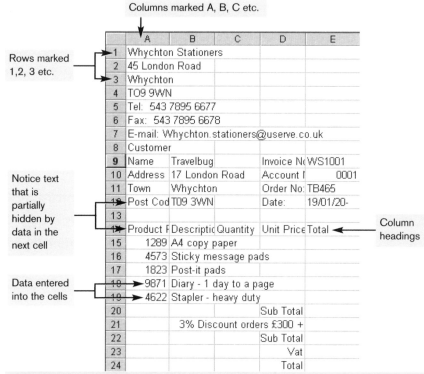

Rows marked 1,2, 3 etc.

Notice text that is partially hidden by data in the next cell

Column headings

Data entered into the cells

	A	B	C	D	E
1	Whychton Stationers				
2	45 London Road				
3	Whychton				
4	TO9 9WN				
5	Tel: 543 7895 6677				
6	Fax: 543 7895 6678				
7	E-mail: Whychton.stationers@userve.co.uk				
8	Customer				
9	Name	Travelbug		Invoice No	WS1001
10	Address	17 London Road		Account I	0001
11	Town	Whychton		Order No:	TB465
12	Post Cod	TO9 3WN		Date:	19/01/20-
13					
14	Product F	Descriptic	Quantity	Unit Price	Total
15	1289	A4 copy paper			
16	4573	Sticky message pads			
17	1823	Post-it pads			
18	9871	Diary - 1 day to a page			
19	4622	Stapler - heavy duty			
20				Sub Total	
21		3% Discount orders £300 +			
22				Sub Total	
23				Vat	
24				Total	

Figure 83 Whychton Stationers invoice to Travelbug: a very basic spreadsheet layout before quantity, unit price and formulas have been entered

Go out and try!

Thomas Tripp of Travelbug likes to give business to the local shops and has placed an order with Whychton Stationers, which has recently opened. When businesses place orders with each other, they do not usually pay for the goods immediately, but are sent an invoice – the bill – at a later stage.

Figure 83 shows the invoice to Travelbug from Whychton Stationers, but as you can see the invoice form is badly laid out and there has been no attempt to format the spreadsheet. Peter Paperly, the manager of Whychton Stationers, realises that the invoice template needs to be improved before it can be used for customers.

1 Study the spreadsheet shown in Figure 83. Look back at the tips on formatting spreadsheets and list any improvements you could make. Think about the formatting techniques described and whether the company address should be set out like a letterhead.

2 Enter the data into your spreadsheet program. The words you can't quite read because of overlapping cells should be
cell D9 – Invoice No:
cell D10 – Account No:
cell A12 – Post Code
cell A14 – Product Ref:

3 Format the layout, including the improvements you have identified.
  ○ To make columns wider, move the mouse pointer to the line between the column header on the right side of the column, click and drag it to the required width.

	A	B	C	D
1		**Whychton Stationers**		
2		45 London Road		
3		Whychton		

Figure 84 Resizing a column

4 Add in the quantities and prices as follows:

A4 copy paper	40	5.99
Sticky message pads	12	3.99
Post-it pads	24	2.99
Diary – 1 day to a page	2	12.99
Stapler – heavy duty	1	24.99

5 Think about
  ○ how to format the numerical data
  ○ the calculations (formulas) you will need for column E.
  See if your formulas match those in Figure 85.
6 💾 Save the file as 'Travelbug invoice' in your 'Spreadsheet software' folder. Make sure you save all your work for this chapter in the same folder.

Start a new word-processing file called 'Spreadsheet software'. Create a new bold heading called '**SS Activity 1**' and write a short paragraph describing the skills you have demonstrated in this activity. 💾 Save the file.

Entering and using formulas

Jargon buster

In a spreadsheet, a **formula** always starts with an equals sign (=). It is the **method** to make a calculation, but it is not the answer. The **result** of using the formula is the answer.

If you go into a sweetshop and buy three bars of chocolate at 50p each, you know that the total cost will be £1.50, but how would you work that out? You multiplied 3 by 50, and that was your *formula*.

Using operators

The important point to remember is that in Excel *a formula always starts with an equals sign*. This tells Excel that it needs to perform a calculation. In order to tell the spreadsheet what kind of calculation you need, you use the following *arithemetic operators*:

- adding +
- subtracting –
- multiplying *
- dividing /

The spreadsheet will calculate formulas using *values*, such as

	Formula	Result
Formula using values	=40*5.99	239.60

More typically, *cell references* are used in formulas. For example, in cell E15 in Figure 83 (page 300) you would use the formula '=C15*D15' to calculate the cost of the A4 copy paper

	Formula	Result
Formula using cell references	=C15*D15	239.60

The big advantage with using cell references in formulas, rather than the actual numbers, is that the spreadsheet will automatically do a recalculation if any changes are made in the data. For example, if the price of the paper changes to £6.50, you enter the new price in cell D15 and the total cost will be automatically recalculated (£260).

Go out and try!

Figure 85 shows the Travelbug invoice from Figure 83 (page 300) with the formulas inserted in column E.

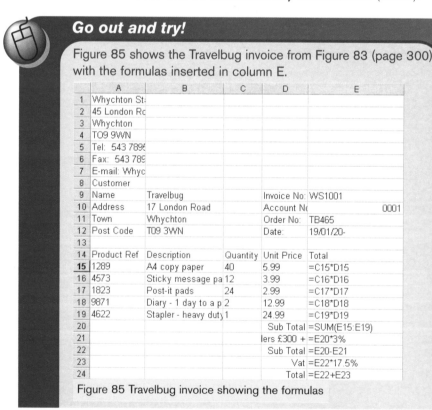

	A	B	C	D	E
1	Whychton St:				
2	45 London Rc				
3	Whychton				
4	TO9 9WN				
5	Tel: 543 7895				
6	Fax: 543 789				
7	E-mail: Whyc				
8	Customer				
9	Name	Travelbug		Invoice No:	WS1001
10	Address	17 London Road		Account Nc	0001
11	Town	Whychton		Order No:	TB465
12	Post Code	TO9 3WN		Date:	19/01/20-
13					
14	Product Ref	Description	Quantity	Unit Price	Total
15	1289	A4 copy paper	40	5.99	=C15*D15
16	4573	Sticky message pa	12	3.99	=C16*D16
17	1823	Post-it pads	24	2.99	=C17*D17
18	9871	Diary - 1 day to a p	2	12.99	=C18*D18
19	4622	Stapler - heavy duty	1	24.99	=C19*D19
20				Sub Total	=SUM(E15:E19)
21				lers £300 +	=E20*3%
22				Sub Total	=E20-E21
23				Vat	=E22*17.5%
24				Total	=E22+E23

Figure 85 Travelbug invoice showing the formulas

1　Open the file you saved as 'Travelbug invoice' and enter the formulas into column E as shown in Figure 85.
　○　Click into cell E15 and type **=C15*D15**. Press the **Enter** key or click the green tick on the toolbar to accept the formula.
　○　Enter the rest of the formulas in the same way.
2　It is very easy to assume that because the computer has worked something out for you *it must be right*, so check the results of these formulas by using a calculator. Do they match? If not, why not? It might be a simple error such as entering a minus sign (–) when you should have entered a plus sign (+).
3　 Save the file 'Travelbug invoice'.

Open your file 'Spreadsheet software'. Create a new bold heading called '**SS Activity 2**' and write a short paragraph describing the skills you have demonstrated in this activity. Save the file.

Jargon buster

A **relative cell reference** is one which changes automatically when its formula is copied to the next cell.

Replicating formulas

Using relative cell references

The spreadsheet designed for Whychton Stationers had only a few formulas, so it did not take long to enter them into the cells. However, as already mentioned, spreadsheets used by business organisations can be huge, and it would be very tedious to enter the same formula across 100 rows or down 100 columns:

```
=SUM(C5:E5)
=SUM(C6:E6)
...
...
=SUM(C105:E105)!
```

One of the advantages of using a spreadsheet is the facility to *replicate* (i.e. copy) a formula across columns or down rows, rather than having to keep entering it again and again. If you need to have totals down several rows or across several columns, you can enter the formula into the first cell and then replicate the formula across to the last column or down to the last row. The spreadsheet will automatically change the formula to give the correct cell references.

Look back at Figure 85, where you can see the formula in cell E15 to calculate the total is '=C15*D15'. You could then enter the formula on the next row by keying in '=C16*D16', and so on down each row. However, once the formula is entered into cell E15, as it is copied down the rows the software automatically changes the cell references to '=C16*D16', '=C17*D17' and so on.

Using absolute cell references

Sometimes you wish to refer to a particular cell address many times. Therefore when you replicate the formula, the *cell address needs to remain the same*. The technical term for this is *absolute reference*.

Figure 86 illustrates this point. Travelbug have a number of villas for holiday rentals in different parts of Europe. As more and more customers are making enquiries via the Internet, Travelbug realised that it was important to quote prices in both pounds and euros. The price in euros is calculated by multiplying the price in pounds by the rate of exchange. The rate of exchange is entered in one cell: D2. In this case, as the formula is copied down the rows, the cell reference for the price in sterling needs to change from row to row, *but the cell reference for the rate of exchange – D2 – needs to remain the same*.

You will notice that the formulas in column E show $ signs before the D and 2 (note $D$2 in Figure 86). These signs are used in Excel to instruct the program that, when copying the formula, this cell reference must *not* be changed. Although in the small example shown it would be easy to key in the formula on each new line, as mentioned already, in a commercial spreadsheet you might replicate

	A	B	C	D	E
1			**Travelbug Villas**		
2			of Exchange £ to €	1.4	
3	**Destination**	**Resort**	**Name of Villa**	**Price per week Sterling**	**Price per week Euros**
4	Algarve	Bordeira	Casa Luz	799	=D4*$D$2
5	Algarve	Lagos	Casa Limoa	849	=D5*$D$2
6	Algarve	Estol	Casa Marco	719	=D6*$D$2
7	Algarve	Carvoeiro	Sete Estrelo	899	=D7*$D$2
8	Cyprus	Latchi	Irene	859	=D8*$D$2
9	Cyprus	Coral Bay	Villa Olivia	809	=D9*$D$2
10	Cyprus	Polis	The Vines	909	=D10*$D$2
11	Costa Blanca	Denia	Casa Moura	779	=D11*$D$2
12	Costa Blanca	Javea	Las Palmmares	829	=D12*$D$2
13	Costa Blanca	Calpe	Casa Alana	779	=D13*$D$2
14	Costa Blanca	Albir	Villa Marlene	649	=D14*$D$2
15	France	Dordogne	Eva	2225	=D15*$D$2
16	France	Dordogne	Chateau Alexa	1490	=D16*$D$2
17	France	Cote D'Azur	La Marina	2720	=D17*$D$2
18	France	South West Coast	Villa Zivia	1660	=D18*$D$2
19	France	West Coast - Charentes	La Belle Vacance	965	=D19*$D$2

Figure 86 The formula view of the price list for renting Travelbug villas: notice that the cell reference D4 changes to D5, etc., but the cell reference $D$2 does not

the formula down hundreds of rows. The other benefit is that, when the rate of exchange alters, it is a simple matter to enter the new rate in cell D2 and all prices in column E will change automatically.

Figure 87 shows the spreadsheet after the calculations have been done by the software.

	A	B	C	D	E
1		**Travelbug Villas**			
2		**Rate of Exchange £ to €**		**€ 1.40**	
3	**Destination**	**Resort**	**Name of Villa**	**Price per week Sterling**	**Price per week Euros**
4	Algarve	Bordeira	Casa Luz	£799	€ 1,119
5	Algarve	Lagos	Casa Limoa	£849	€ 1,189
6	Algarve	Estol	Casa Marco	£719	€ 1,007
7	Algarve	Carvoeiro	Sete Estrelo	£899	€ 1,259
8	Cyprus	Latchi	Irene	£859	€ 1,203
9	Cyprus	Coral Bay	Villa Olivia	£809	€ 1,133
10	Cyprus	Polis	The Vines	£909	€ 1,273
11	Costa Blanca	Denia	Casa Moura	£779	€ 1,091
12	Costa Blanca	Javea	Las Palmmares	£829	€ 1,161
13	Costa Blanca	Calpe	Casa Alana	£779	€ 1,091
14	Costa Blanca	Albir	Villa Marlene	£649	€ 909
15	France	Dordogne	Eva	£2,225	€ 3,115
16	France	Dordogne	Chateau Alexa	£1,490	€ 2,086
17	France	Cote D'Azur	La Marina	£2,720	€ 3,808
18	France	South West Coast	Villa Zivia	£1,660	€ 2,324
19	France	West Coast - Charentes	La Belle Vacance	£965	€ 1,351

Figure 87 The data view of the price list for renting Travelbug villas

Go out and try!

1 Key in the spreadsheet shown in Figure 86.
2 Format cells D4 to D19 to currency with the £ symbol and 0 decimal places and cells E4 to E19 with the € symbol with 0 decimal places.
3 Make sure you use a formula for the price in euros as shown in the next step. At first do not include the dollar signs.
   ○ In cell E4 enter the formula '=D4*D2'.
4 Copy the formula down to row 19.
   ○ Position the mouse pointer over the bottom right-hand corner of the cell and, when the white cross turns to a black cross, press the left mouse button and drag down the column.
   You will notice that there are errors in the results. Why is this? Look at the cell references to see whether you can find the problem.

Price per week Euros
=D4*D2
=D5*D3
=D6*D4
=D7*D5
=D8*D6
=D9*D7

5 Go back to cell E4 and change the formula to '=D4*$D$2'.
6 Copy the formula down to row 19. This time you should find the prices in euros do match those in Figure 87.
7 Make sure the prices in columns D and E are formatted to 0 decimal places.
   ○ Click and drag over the prices in columns D and E to select them.
   ○ From the menu, select **Format**, **Cells**.
   ○ The *Format Cells* dialogue appears. Make sure the *Number* tab is displayed.
   ○ Choose the **Currency** option and set the decimal places to **0** for column D.
   ○ For column E choose the **Euro** from the *Symbol* drop down list.

Price per week Euros
=D4*$D$2
=D5*$D$2
=D6*$D$2
=D7*$D$2
=D8*$D$2
=D9*$D$2

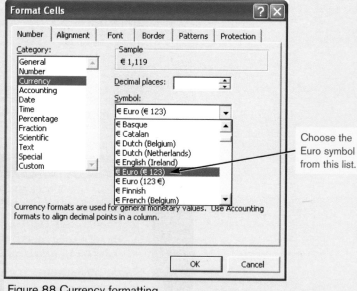

Choose the Euro symbol from this list.

Figure 88 Currency formatting

8   Save the file as 'Villas' in your 'Spreadsheet software' sub-folder.

Open your 'Spreadsheet software' file. Create a new bold heading called '**SS Activity 3**' and write a short paragraph describing the skills you have demonstrated in this activity.
Save the file.

Inserting or deleting rows and columns

Spreadsheet software makes it easy to add or delete rows or columns. To delete cells, select them and then use the **Delete** command on the right-click menu. To insert cells, select the location where you want to add them and use the options on the **Insert** menu.

Go out and try!

1 Open the file saved as 'Villas'.
2 The villa Eva has been sold, so delete row 15.
   ○ Right-click in the row number box.
   ○ Choose **Delete** from the shortcut menu that appears.

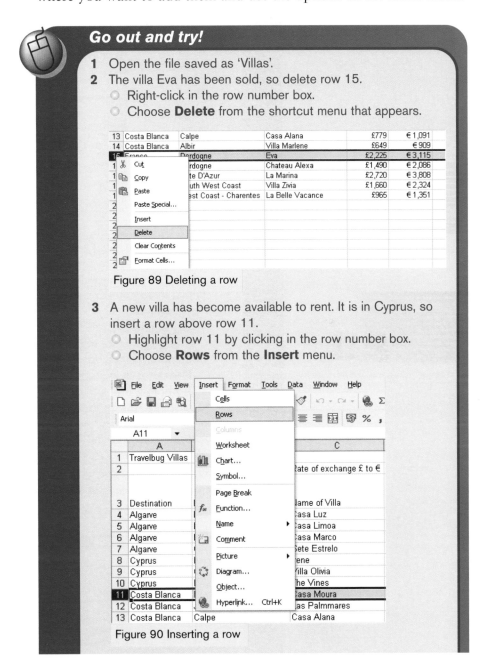

Figure 89 Deleting a row

3 A new villa has become available to rent. It is in Cyprus, so insert a row above row 11.
   ○ Highlight row 11 by clicking in the row number box.
   ○ Choose **Rows** from the **Insert** menu.

Figure 90 Inserting a row

The villa is in the resort of Angaka, is called Agathi and costs £859. Check that the price in euros has been calculated – if not, copy the formula.

4   Thomas Tripp has realised that the spreadsheet is showing only the prices for the high season and this is putting people off renting the villas in the low season. Insert two new columns before column D.

   ○ Highlight the two columns D and E
   ○ Choose **Columns** from the **Insert** menu.

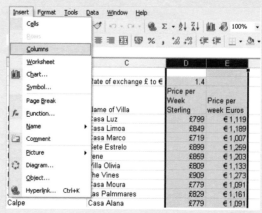

Figure 91 Inserting two columns

5   This should insert two columns, since you had selected two columns. If you only selected one then repeat the process so that there are two new columns.

6   The rate of exchange – €1.40 – is no longer next to the words, but has moved from cell D2 to cell F2.

   ○ Place the cursor in cell F2 and cut the data (**Edit**, **Cut**).
   ○ Place the cursor in cell D2 and paste the data (**Edit**, **Paste**) back in the right place.

7   Highlight row 3 (containing the headings 'Destination', etc.) and insert a row above it (**Insert**, **Rows**).

8   In cell D3, enter the heading 'Low Season' and centre it across columns D and E.

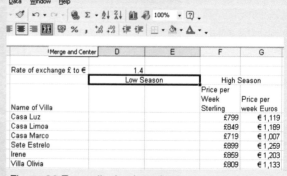

Figure 92 Two cells that have been merged and centred

○ Highlight D3 and E3

○ Click on the **Merge and Center** ⊞ icon on the toolbar.

○ In cell F3, enter the heading 'High Season' and centre it across columns F and G in the same way as before.

10 Highlight cells F4 and G4 and copy the data to the clipboard in the usual way. Place the cursor in cell D4 and paste the selection.

11 Key in the prices for the low season – see Figure 93.

12 In cell E5, enter the formula to convert the prices to euros and replicate it down the rows. Check your results with Figure 93.

	A	B	C	D	E	F	G
1			Travelbug Villas				
2		Rate of Exchange £ to €		€ 1.40			
3				Low Season		High Season	
4	Destination	Resort	Name of Villa	Price per week Sterling	Price per week Euros	Price per week Sterling	Price per week Euros
5	Algarve	Bordeira	Casa Luz	£559	€ 783	£799	€ 1,119
6	Algarve	Lagos	Casa Limoa	£594	€ 832	£849	€ 1,189
7	Algarve	Estol	Casa Marco	£503	€ 704	£719	€ 1,007
8	Algarve	Carvoeiro	Sete Estrelo	£629	€ 881	£899	€ 1,259
9	Cyprus	Latchi	Irene	£601	€ 841	£859	€ 1,203
10	Cyprus	Coral Bay	Villa Olivia	£566	€ 792	£809	€ 1,133
11	Cyprus	Polis	The Vines	£636	€ 890	£909	€ 1,273
12	Cyprus	Argaka	Agathi	£629	€ 881	£859	€ 1,203
13	Costa Blanca	Denia	Casa Moura	£545	€ 763	£779	€ 1,091
14	Costa Blanca	Javea	Las Palmmares	£580	€ 812	£829	€ 1,161
15	Costa Blanca	Calpe	Casa Alana	£545	€ 763	£779	€ 1,091
16	Costa Blanca	Albir	Villa Marlene	£454	€ 636	£649	€ 909
17	France	Dordogne	Chateau Alexa	£1,043	€ 1,460	£1,490	€ 2,086
18	France	Cote D'Azur	La Marina	£1,904	€ 2,666	£2,720	€ 3,808
19	France	South West Coast	Villa Zivia	£1,162	€ 1,627	£1,660	€ 2,324
20	France	West Coast - Charentes	La Belle Vacance	£675	€ 945	£965	€ 1,351

Figure 93 Low- and high-season prices for Travelbug villas

TiP

When you move a cell using cut and paste, any references to the original cell are automatically updated.

13 The rate of exchange has changed to €1.45. Change the rate in cell D2 and check that the prices in euros are automatically recalculated.

14 No, there is a mistake – the rate of exchange is still €1.40. Change it back again. Once again the prices in euros are automatically recalculated.

15 Customers need to know the number of bedrooms and the number of people the villa can sleep. Insert two columns before column D in the same way as before. The rate of exchange is now in cell F2, so move it back to cell D2 using cut and paste.

16 Add the data in Figure 94 to show the number of bedrooms and the number of people the villa can accommodate for sleeping.

Name of villa	No. of bedrooms	Sleeps up to
Casa Luz	3	6
Casa Limoa	3	6
Casa Marco	2	4
Sete Estrelo	4	8
Irene	4	8
Villa Olivia	3	6
The Vines	5	10
Agathi	4	8
Casa Moura	4	8
Las Palmmares	4	8
Casa Alana	3	6
Villa Marlene	2	4
Chateau Alexa	4	8
La Marina	5	10
Villa Zivia	4	8
La Belle Vacance	2	4

Figure 94 Data for your *Go out and try!* task

17 Save the file.

 Open your 'Spreadsheet software' file. Create a new bold heading called '**SS Activity 4**' and write short paragraphs describing the skills you have demonstrated in this activity, under the following headings:

- ○ *Insert and delete rows or columns*
- ○ *Cut, copy and paste*
- ○ *Replicate formulas*
- ○ *Change the rate in the absolute cell reference.*

Save the file.

Using simple functions

When you open an Excel worksheet and click on the function icon fx, you will see that there are very many functions available. We shall look here at two frequently used functions – SUM and AVERAGE.

The SUM function

Look back at Figure 85 on page 302 and the formula in cell E20. Remember that the formula could have been written as

'=E15+E16+E17+E18+E19'. That becomes very tedious if you have to add up 100 rows or columns, and it is easy to make mistakes, but by using the SUM function you can add up the range of cells without having to enter each cell reference.

You can use the SUM function by keying in a formula – in this case '=SUM(E15:E19)'. The colon (:) tells the program to add up all the cells in the range from E15 to E19.

It can be quicker to use the **Autosum** icon ⌷Σ⌷ on the *Standard* toolbar.

Usually the correct range of cells will be selected, but do be careful when using **AutoSum**: sometimes cells are included that are not required.

Look at Figure 95, where the **AutoSum** command was used in cell F5 to calculate the total number of weeks reserved. The range selected was 'B5:E5', but *this includes the cost of weekly rental* as well as the weeks reserved in each of the three months. To calculate the total number of weeks, only the range 'C5:E5' is necessary. To correct the error you can either enter '=SUM(C5:E5)' yourself, or select cells C5 to E5 by dragging with the mouse. You can then copy the formulas down the rows using relative cell references, as you learned earlier.

AutoSum command

	A	B	C	D	E	F	G
1			**Travelbug Villas**				
2	**Quarterly Rentals**						
3	**Low Season**		**Number of weeks reserved**				
4	**Name of Villa**	**Cost of weekly rental**	**Jan**	**Feb**	**Mar**	**Total No Weeks Reserved**	**Total Value of Bookings**
5	Casa Luz	£559	2	0	3	=SUM(B5:E5)	
6	Casa Limoa	£594	1	2	3	SUM(**number1**, [number2], ...)	
7	Casa Marco	£503	1	1	4	6	£3,018
8	Sete Estrelo	£629	3	1	2	6	£3,774
9	Irene	£601	3	2	4	9	£5,409
10	Villa Olivia	£566	4	4	3	11	£6,226
11	The Vines	£636	2	2	3	7	£4,452
12	Agathi	£629	1	2	2	5	£3,145
13	Casa Moura	£545	3	0	2	5	£2,725
14	Las Palmmares	£580	2	1	3	6	£3,480
15	Casa Alana	£545	2	2	1	5	£2,725
16	Villa Marlene	£454	3	1	3	7	£3,178
17	Chateau Alexa	£1,043	1	0	0	1	£1,043
18	La Marina	£1,904	0	0	1	1	£1,904
19	Villa Zivia	£1,162	0	1	2	3	£3,486
20	La Belle Vacance	£675	1	2	3	6	£4,050

1st Quarter / 2nd Quarter / 3rd Quarter / 4th Quarter /

Figure 95 The AutoSum command and four worksheets in the workbook: the status line near the top shows the incorrect formula '=SUM(B5:E5)' selected by the AutoSum command

Quite often, students enter '=SUM' as part of a formula when it is not necessary. Look back at Figure 85 (page 142). The formula in cell E24 is '=E22+E23', but students sometimes enter '=SUM(E22:E23)'. This will work, but it is *not* required in this case.

Go out and try!

1 Create a new spreadsheet file as shown in Figure 95. Enter the headings given in rows 1 to 4.

2 Instead of entering the names of all the villas again, reopen the file you saved as 'Villas'. Highlight cells C5 to D20 and copy the names of the villas and the low-season costs of rental. Switch back to the new spreadsheet, click in cell A5 and paste the data into the new file.

3 Copy the data for the number of weeks reserved for January, February and March from Figure 95.

4 Add a formula into column F to add up the number of weeks.
 - Click in cell F5.
 - Click on the **AutoSum** button.
 - Highlight the correct cells (to exclude the cost cell) and press **Enter**.
 - Copy down to the other rows.

5 Calculate the total value of bookings.
 - Click in cell G5.
 - Key in '=B5*F5'.
 - Copy down to the other rows.

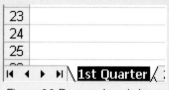

Figure 96 Renamed worksheet

6 Save the file as 'Villa Rentals' in the 'Spreadsheet software' sub-folder.

7 Name the worksheet '1st Quarter'.
 - Double-click on the 'Sheet 1' worksheet tab and enter the name '1st Quarter'.
 - Press **Enter**.

8 Make a copy of your worksheet.
 - Right-click with the mouse on the worksheet tab.
 - Choose **Move or copy**.
 - Select (**move to end**) and click in the **Create a copy** checkbox.

9 Repeat twice more so that you have three new worksheets. Rename them

Figure 97 Creating a copy of a worksheet

'2nd Quarter', '3rd Quarter' and '4th Quarter'. 🖫 Save your work.

10 Select the 2nd Quarter sheet and change the months to 'April', 'May' and 'June'. This is the high season so change the heading in cell A3 to 'High Season'.

11 The rental costs need to be changed to the high season rates.
    ○ Open the file saved as 'Villas'.
    ○ Copy the high season rates from H5 to H20.
    ○ Switch back to the 'Villa Rentals' file and its '2nd Quarter' worksheet.
    ○ Place the cursor in cell B5 and use **Paste** 🖫.
    The high season rates will replace the low season rates and the value of bookings will automatically be recalculated.

12 Highlight cells C5 to E20 and press the **Delete** key to remove the data.

13 Select the '3rd Quarter' worksheet, which is also high season, and change the months to 'July', 'August' and 'September'. Also change the heading in A3 to 'High Season'. Repeat steps 11 and 12 for the '3rd Quarter' worksheet.

14 Select the '4th Quarter' worksheet, which is low season, and change the months to 'October', 'November' and 'December'. Because this is low season the rates do not need to be changed. 🖫 Save your work.

15 Enter the data in Figure 98 into the 2nd, 3rd and 4th Quarter worksheets. Notice that the total number of weeks reserved and the total value of bookings automatically recalculate as you enter the new data. 🖫 Save the file.

Name of villa	April	May	June	July	Aug	Sept	Oct	Nov	Dec
Casa Luz	2	3	4	4	4	3	2	2	2
Casa Limoa	3	2	3	4	4	3	3	3	4
Casa Marco	2	3	4	4	4	4	4	2	3
Sete Estrelo	1	2	3	4	4	2	3	2	3
Irene	3	3	3	4	4	4	3	3	4
Villa Olivia	4	3	4	4	4	3	4	3	4
The Vines	3	3	4	4	4	3	3	4	4
Agathi	4	2	4	4	4	4	3	2	3
Casa Moura	4	2	4	4	4	4	3	2	3
Las Palmmares	3	3	3	4	4	3	4	2	2
Casa Alana	1	3	3	4	4	3	4	3	3
Villa Marlene	3	2	4	4	4	3	4	3	0
Chateau Alexa	2	2	3	4	4	3	3	1	0
La Marina	1	2	3	4	4	3	2	0	4
Villa Zivia	1	3	2	4	4	4	2	0	3
La Belle Vacance	2	3	4	4	4	4	4	3	2

Figure 98 Data for your *Go out and try!* task

The AVERAGE function

When you calculate the average, you are trying to establish the typical value of a group or situation. You do this by adding up all the relevant items and dividing by the number of items. For example, if you wanted to find out the average rental price of the villas, you would add up all the prices and divide by the number of villas in the list.

Look at Figure 99. The formula '=AVERAGE(F5:F20)' is entered into cell F21, and this calculates the average cost to rent a villa for a

	A	B	C	D	E	F	G	H	I
1				Travelbug Villas					
2			Rate of Exchange £ to €	€ 1.40					
3						Low Season		High Season	
4	Destination	Resort	Name of Villa	No of bedrooms	Sleeps up to	Price per week Sterling	Price per week Euros	Price per week Sterling	Price per week Euros
5	Algarve	Bordeira	Casa Luz	3	6	£559	€ 783	£799	€ 1,119
6	Algarve	Lagos	Casa Limoa	3	6	£594	€ 832	£849	€ 1,189
7	Algarve	Estol	Casa Marco	2	4	£503	€ 704	£719	€ 1,007
8	Algarve	Carvoeiro	Sete Estrelo	4	8	£629	€ 881	£899	€ 1,259
9	Cyprus	Latchi	Irene	4	8	£601	€ 841	£859	€ 1,203
10	Cyprus	Coral Bay	Villa Olivia	3	6	£566	€ 792	£809	€ 1,133
11	Cyprus	Polis	The Vines	5	10	£636	€ 890	£909	€ 1,273
12	Cyprus	Argaka	Agathi	4	8	£629	€ 881	£859	€ 1,203
13	Costa Blanca	Denia	Casa Moura	4	8	£545	€ 763	£779	€ 1,091
14	Costa Blanca	Javea	Las Palmmares	4	8	£580	€ 812	£829	€ 1,161
15	Costa Blanca	Calpe	Casa Alana	3	6	£545	€ 763	£779	€ 1,091
16	Costa Blanca	Albir	Villa Marlene	2	4	£454	€ 636	£649	€ 909
17	France	Dordogne	Chateau Alexa	4	8	£1,043	€ 1,460	£1,490	€ 2,086
18	France	Cote D'Azur	La Marina	5	10	£1,904	€ 2,666	£2,720	€ 3,808
19	France	South West Coast	Villa Zivia	4	8	£1,162	€ 1,627	£1,660	€ 2,324
20	France	West Coast - Charentes	La Belle Vacance	2	4	£675	€ 945	£965	€ 1,351
21				Average price of weekly rental		£727	€ 1,017	£1,036	€ 1,450

Figure 99 Spreadsheet showing calculated average weekly rentals

week. You will notice that none of the villas costs £727 to rent, but this was the *average* or typical cost in the low season.

If you were working out the average cost of rental yourself, you would need to add up the cost to rent all the villas (£11 629), and divide by the number of villas in the list (16) to find the average (£727). The advantage of using the AVERAGE function is that these various stages are all worked out automatically for you.

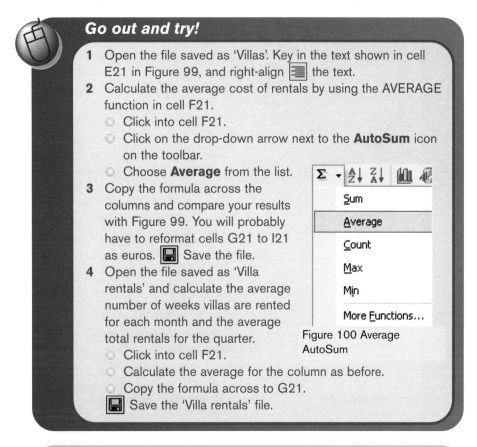

Go out and try!

1 Open the file saved as 'Villas'. Key in the text shown in cell E21 in Figure 99, and right-align ⊟ the text.
2 Calculate the average cost of rentals by using the AVERAGE function in cell F21.
   ○ Click into cell F21.
   ○ Click on the drop-down arrow next to the **AutoSum** icon on the toolbar.
   ○ Choose **Average** from the list.
3 Copy the formula across the columns and compare your results with Figure 99. You will probably have to reformat cells G21 to I21 as euros. 🖫 Save the file.
4 Open the file saved as 'Villa rentals' and calculate the average number of weeks villas are rented for each month and the average total rentals for the quarter.
   ○ Click into cell F21.
   ○ Calculate the average for the column as before.
   ○ Copy the formula across to G21.
   🖫 Save the 'Villa rentals' file.

Figure 100 Average AutoSum

Open your 'Spreadsheet software' file. Create a new bold heading called '**SS Activity 6**' and write a short paragraph describing the skills you have demonstrated in this activity, under the heading Average. 🖫 Save the file.

Sorting data

It can often be useful to sort the data in the spreadsheet *alphabetically* (from A to Z or from Z to A), or *numerically* (from lowest to highest or from highest to lowest).

DiDA

Go out and try!

Figure 101 The Sort dialogue box

1 Open the file saved as 'Villas'. Try sorting the data by the Low Season price.
   ○ Highlight cells A4 to I20.

   It is essential to highlight the whole section. Otherwise you risk sorting only one column, which jumbles the data.

   ○ Click on the A–Z icon.

   Notice that Excel assumes you want to sort by the first column – 'Destination' – so highlight cells A4 to I20 again.

   ○ Choose **Sort** from the **Data** menu.
   ○ Select **(1) Price per week Sterling**, as in Figure 101.
   ○ Save your file.
2 Now practise sorting the data
   ○ highest to lowest – select **Descending**
   ○ by the number of bedrooms.
3 Save the 'Villas' file.
4 Open the file saved as 'Villa rentals' and sort the data as follows:
   ○ 1st Quarter – Total no weeks reserved, descending
   ○ 2nd Quarter – Total value of bookings, descending
   ○ 3rd Quarter – Total no weeks reserved, ascending
   ○ 4th Quarter – Total value of bookings, ascending
5 Save the file.

	A	B	C	D	E	F	G	H	I
1			**Travelbug Villas**						
2		Rate of Exchange £ to €		€ 1.40					
3						**Low Season**		**High Season**	
4	**Destination**	**Resort**	**Name of Villa**	**No of bedrooms**	**Sleeps up to**	**Price per week Sterling**	**Price per week Euros**	**Price per week Sterling**	**Price per week Euros**
5	Costa Blanca	Albir	Villa Marlene	2	4	£454	€ 636	£649	€ 909
6	Algarve	Estol	Casa Marco	2	4	£503	€ 704	£719	€ 1,007
7	Costa Blanca	Denia	Casa Moura	4	8	£545	€ 763	£779	€ 1,091
8	Costa Blanca	Calpe	Casa Alana	3	6	£545	€ 763	£779	€ 1,091
9	Algarve	Bordeira	Casa Luz	3	6	£559	€ 783	£799	€ 1,119
10	Cyprus	Coral Bay	Villa Olivia	3	6	£566	€ 792	£809	€ 1,133
11	Costa Blanca	Javea	Las Palmmares	4	8	£580	€ 812	£829	€ 1,161
12	Algarve	Lagos	Casa Limoa	3	6	£594	€ 832	£849	€ 1,189
13	Cyprus	Latchi	Irene	4	8	£601	€ 841	£859	€ 1,203
14	Cyprus	Argaka	Agathi	4	8	£629	€ 881	£859	€ 1,203
15	Algarve	Carvoeiro	Sete Estrelo	4	8	£629	€ 881	£899	€ 1,259
16	Cyprus	Polis	The Vines	5	10	£636	€ 890	£909	€ 1,273
17	France	West Coast - Charentes	La Belle Vacance	2	4	£675	€ 945	£965	€ 1,351
18	France	Dordogne	Chateau Alexa	4	8	£1,043	€ 1,460	£1,490	€ 2,086
19	France	South West Coast	Villa Zivia	4	8	£1,162	€ 1,627	£1,660	€ 2,324
20	France	Cote D'Azur	La Marina	5	10	£1,904	€ 2,666	£2,720	€ 3,808
21			**Average price of weekly rental**			**£727**	**€ 1,017**	**£1,036**	**€ 1,450**

Figure 102 Spreadsheet sorted by price per week sterling

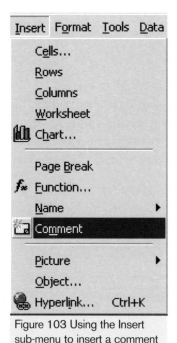

Figure 103 Using the Insert sub-menu to insert a comment

Inserting comments

Sometimes it can be helpful to add comments to the spreadsheet. These comments do not print, but are an on-screen guide to help the user. This would be a useful method to remind Whychton Stationers' administrator to call the customer if the order is less than £300 (Whychton Stationers offer a discount on orders over £300).

In order to add a comment in Excel, place the cursor in the cell where you wish the comment to appear and select **Insert, Comment** (Figure 103). A box will appear in which you can write a suitable message (Figure 104).

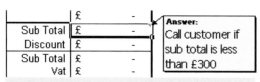

Figure 104 The box in which to write your comment

A small red triangle in the corner of the cell shows that the cell contains a comment. The default setting usually shows the indicator only, but the message appears when the mouse pointer is over the cell. However, you can choose to show the indicator (the small red triangle) and the message by selecting **Tools, Options** and then the **View** tab (Figure 105).

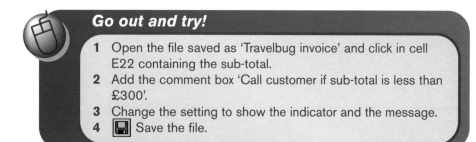

Figure 105 To show the comment as well as the indicator, click in the circle

Go out and try!

1 Open the file saved as 'Travelbug invoice' and click in cell E22 containing the sub-total.
2 Add the comment box 'Call customer if sub-total is less than £300'.
3 Change the setting to show the indicator and the message.
4 Save the file.

Filtering data

The *filter tool* 🔽= is a method of displaying more precisely the information you require just at that moment. For example, you might wish to find items in a certain category or to a specific value, or the top ten items in a list. By using the filter to select the relevant criteria, the spreadsheet will filter out everything that does not match the criteria.

Imagine that your phone bill arrives and is much higher than usual. You want to find out exactly how much you have spent on calling landlines, on foreign calls and on mobile numbers. You could scan the bill into the spreadsheet and then use the filter tool to separate the various charges.

D	E	F
DESTINATION ▼	**TIME** ▼	**COST** ▼
UK Mobile	00:43:21	£1.97
Freephone	00:00:06	£0.00
UK Mobile	00:25:03	£2.96
Usa	00:01:37	£0.05
Local	00:09:15	£0.00
UK Mobile	00:02:18	£0.34
Freephone	00:08:56	£0.00
UK Mobile	00:01:03	£0.29
UK Mobile	00:10:19	£1.25
UK Mobile	00:00:27	£0.14
Local	00:01:04	£0.04
Usa	00:28:31	£0.74
Local	00:06:33	£0.15
Local	00:00:53	£0.02
UK Mobile	00:00:04	£0.15
UK Mobile	00:05:19	£0.68
Usa	00:25:47	£0.66
Local	00:09:55	£0.00
Local	00:06:51	£0.00
Local	00:00:34	£0.00
National	00:29:09	£0.64
Local	00:18:19	£0.00
Usa	00:22:54	£0.59
Local	00:00:04	£0.00
Local	00:00:49	£0.00
UK Mobile	00:00:21	£0.11
Local	00:01:20	£0.00

Figure 106 A small part of an itemised phone bill

Click here to select the type of filter to apply.

Look at the row numbers. See how they jump from 1 to 5 to 13 etc., because all rows not containing the text Usa are now hidden.

	D	E	F
1	**DESTINATION** ▼	**TIME** ▼	**COST** ▼
5	(All)	00:01:37	£0.05
13	(Top 10...)	00:28:31	£0.74
18	(Custom...)	00:25:47	£0.66
24	Australia	00:22:54	£0.59
29	Freephone	00:00:41	£0.03
30	Local	00:16:47	£0.43
	National		
54	UK Mobile	00:00:34	£0.03
	Usa		
62	Usa	00:13:11	£0.36
96	Usa	00:00:58	£0.03
114	Usa	00:13:09	£0.36
115	Usa	00:00:03	£0.03
116	Usa	00:00:52	£0.03
127	Usa	00:05:15	£0.15
128	Usa	00:00:59	£0.03
129	Usa	00:00:09	£0.03
131	Usa	00:00:27	£0.03
146	Usa	00:17:02	£0.41
147	Usa	00:17:02	£0.05
149	Usa	00:00:39	£0.03
150	Usa	00:00:45	£0.03
151	Usa	00:02:19	£0.08
153	Usa	00:17:10	£0.46
167	Usa	00:20:31	£0.54
172	Usa	00:04:45	£0.13
184	Usa	00:02:58	£0.08
203	Usa	00:00:40	£0.03
204	Usa	00:00:33	£0.03
205	Usa	00:00:28	£0.03
206	Usa	00:00:34	£0.03
234	**Total**	**215 Mins**	**5.43**

Figure 107 The list of calls has been filtered to show only those made to the United States

Figure 106 shows a small section of a telephone bill that runs to 219 rows in total. The total bill for the month is £38.37. By clicking on the arrow next to the destination, it is possible to select 'Usa' (United States), with the result that only calls to the United States will be shown. Figure 107 illustrates the result – the total cost was £5.43.

Go out and try!

1. Open the spreadsheet file saved as 'Villa rentals'. You want to identify which villas are having very few rentals in the first quarter. Whilst this is easy to see with such a small spreadsheet, it would be much more difficult if the company were letting a large number of villas.

2. Select the worksheet for the 1st Quarter and highlight the column headings in row 4 – cells A4 to G4. Click on the filter icon ▽=; if it is not available then select **Data**, **Filter**, **AutoFilter** from the menu. Notice that arrows appear next to each of the column headings, as shown in Figure 108.

	A	B	C	D	E	F	G
1			Travelbug Villas				
2	Quarterly Rentals						
3	Low Season		Number of weeks reserved				
4	Name of Villa ⏷	Cost of weekly rental ⏷	Jan ⏷	Feb ⏷	Mar ⏷	Total No Weeks Reserve ⏷	Total Value of Booking ⏷
5	Villa Olivia	£566	4	4	3	(All)	£6,229
6	Irene	£601	3	2	4	(Top 10...) (Custom...)	£5,412
7	The Vines	£636	2	2	3	1	£4,454
8	Villa Marlene	£454	3	1	3	3 5	£3,180
9	Casa Limoa	£594	1	2	3	6	£3,566
10	Casa Marco	£503	1	1	4	7 9	£3,020
11	Sete Estrelo	£629	3	1	2	11	£3,776
12	Las Palmmares	£580	2	1	3	89	£3,482

Figure 108 First-quarter worksheet showing the filter options for the number of weeks reserved

3. To identify those villas with only one week reserved, click on the down arrow in column F and then select **1**. All other villas will be filtered out.

4. Select the worksheet for the 2nd Quarter and this time click on the down arrow in column G and then select **(Top 10...)** (Figure 109) and **OK**. The top ten values will be filtered.

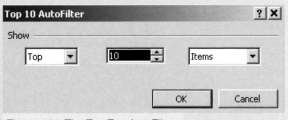

Figure 109 The Top Ten AutoFilter

5   Select the worksheet for the 3rd Quarter and identify those villas that were not booked for the full 12 weeks. To do this, click on the down arrow in column F and then select **(Custom...)**. Select **is less than** and **12** and click **OK** (Figure 110). All villas booked for 12 weeks will be filtered out.

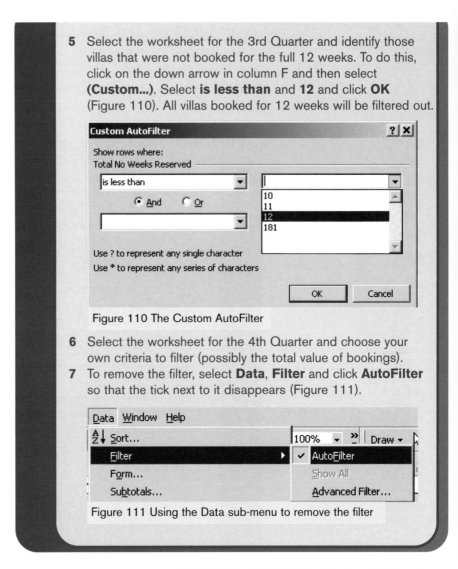

Figure 110 The Custom AutoFilter

6   Select the worksheet for the 4th Quarter and choose your own criteria to filter (possibly the total value of bookings).

7   To remove the filter, select **Data**, **Filter** and click **AutoFilter** so that the tick next to it disappears (Figure 111).

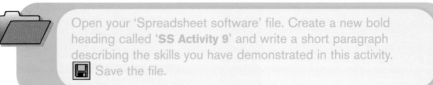

Figure 111 Using the Data sub-menu to remove the filter

Open your 'Spreadsheet software' file. Create a new bold heading called '**SS Activity 9**' and write a short paragraph describing the skills you have demonstrated in this activity. Save the file.

Linking worksheets

It can often be useful to *link worksheets* so that a value on one worksheet is carried forward to another. The advantages of linking the data, rather than copying it into a new sheet, are that there is no risk of making a copying error and if the original data changes then the cells in the linked sheets will be automatically updated.

Go out and try!

TiP

To create a new worksheet, right-click any of the worksheet tabs and select **Insert** *from the menu that appears. With* **Worksheet** *selected, press* **OK**. *Double-click the new tab to rename it.*

1 Open the spreadsheet file 'Villa rentals' and select each quarter's worksheet in turn. *Make sure that the filters are removed from all the worksheets.* Sort each worksheet into alphabetical order of the name of the villa.
  ○ Highlight cells A4 to G20.
  ○ Click on the A–Z sort icon ⚄ on the *Standard* toolbar.
  ○ Repeat these two steps for each of the quarterly worksheets and then 💾 save the file.

2 Start a new worksheet named 'Summary' and enter the headings shown in Figure 112. Now you are going to create links between the Summary worksheet and the quarterly worksheets.

	A	B	C	D	E	F	G	H	I	J	K
1		Travelbug Villas									
2		1st Quarter		2nd Quarter		3rd Quarter		4th Quarter		Year	
3	Name of Villa	Total No Weeks Reserved	Total Value of Bookings	Total No Weeks Reserved	Total Value of Bookings	Total No Weeks Reserved	Total Value of Bookings	Total No Weeks Reserved	Total Value of Bookings	Total No Weeks Reserved	Total Value of Bookings

Figure 112 Headings for the Summary worksheet

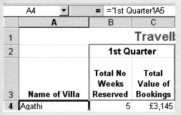

Figure 113 Formula for the link between worksheets

3 On the Summary worksheet, click on cell A4 and type an equals sign (=). Do **not** press **Enter** yet.

4 Click on the 1st Quarter worksheet tab, then on cell A5, and press **Enter**. The formula will be **='1st Quarter'!A5**, but the name of the villa (Agathi) will appear in the cell (Figure 113). Copy the formula down the rows until the name of the last villa appears – Villa Zivia.

5 Repeat this process for the total number of weeks reserved and the total value of bookings for each of the four quarters. Figure 114 will start you off.

	A	B	C	D
1				Travelbug Villa
2		1st Quarter		2nd Q
3	Name of Villa	Total No Weeks Reserved	Total Value of Bookings	Total No Weeks Reserved
4	='1st Quarter'!A5	='1st Quarter'!F5	='1st Quarter'!G5	='2nd Quarter'!F5
5	='1st Quarter'!A6	='1st Quarter'!F6	='1st Quarter'!G6	='2nd Quarter'!F6
6	='1st Quarter'!A7	='1st Quarter'!F7	='1st Quarter'!G7	='2nd Quarter'!F7

Figure 114 Section of the spreadsheet showing the formulas for columns A to D

?

◦ **Think it over ...**

What formulas will you need to calculate the total for the year? Be careful – you cannot use the AutoSum icon **Σ** to total across the rows.

6 Enter formulas to calculate the total number of weeks reserved and the total value of bookings for the year for each villa. Then calculate the grand totals.

7 The Summary spreadsheet should now look like the one shown in Figure 115.

	A	B	C	D	E	F	G	H	I	J	K
1		**Travelbug Villas**									
2		**1st Quarter**		**2nd Quarter**		**3rd Quarter**		**4th Quarter**		**Year**	
3	**Name of Villa**	**Total No Weeks Reserved**	**Total Value of Bookings**	**Total No Weeks Reserved**	**Total Value of Bookings**	**Total No Weeks Reserved**	**Total Value of Bookings**	**Total No Weeks Reserved**	**Total Value of Bookings**	**Total No Weeks Reserved**	**Total Value of Bookings**
4	Agathi	5	£3,145	11	£9,449	12	£10,308	5	£3,145	33	£26,047
5	Casa Alana	5	£2,725	7	£5,453	11	£8,569	10	£5,450	33	£22,197
6	Casa Limoa	6	£3,564	8	£6,792	11	£9,339	10	£5,940	35	£25,635
7	Casa Luz	5	£2,795	9	£7,191	11	£8,789	6	£3,354	31	£22,129
8	Casa Marco	6	£3,018	9	£6,471	12	£8,628	9	£4,527	36	£22,644
9	Casa Moura	5	£2,725	10	£7,790	12	£9,348	8	£4,360	35	£24,223
10	Chateau Alexa	1	£1,043	7	£10,430	11	£16,390	4	£4,172	23	£32,035
11	Irene	9	£5,409	9	£7,731	12	£10,308	10	£6,010	40	£29,458
12	La Belle Vacance	6	£4,050	9	£8,685	12	£11,580	9	£6,075	36	£30,390
13	La Marina	1	£1,904	6	£16,320	11	£29,920	6	£11,424	24	£59,568
14	Las Palmmares	6	£3,480	9	£7,461	11	£9,119	8	£4,640	34	£24,700
15	Sete Estrelo	6	£3,774	6	£5,394	10	£8,990	8	£5,032	30	£23,190
16	The Vines	7	£4,452	10	£9,090	11	£9,999	11	£6,996	39	£30,537
17	Villa Marlene	7	£3,178	9	£5,841	11	£7,139	7	£3,178	34	£19,336
18	Villa Olivia	11	£6,226	11	£8,899	11	£8,899	11	£6,226	44	£30,250
19	Villa Zivia	3	£3,486	6	£9,960	12	£19,920	5	£5,810	26	£39,176
20									**Grand total**	533	£461,515

Figure 115 The Summary worksheet

8 Return to the 1st Quarter worksheet and increase the number of weeks reserved by 1, *for each of the villas*. Notice that the Summary worksheet automatically changes.

9 Undo the changes you made at Step 8 and then save your work.

Open your 'Spreadsheet software' file. Create a new bold heading called '**SS Activity 10**' and write a short paragraph describing the skills you have demonstrated in this activity. Save the file.

Producing graphs and charts

Graphs and charts can be very helpful tools to illustrate numerical data in a visual format, and spreadsheet programs provide easy-to-use facilities to create the graphs and charts.

Probably the most frequently used examples are

- column charts
- bar charts
- pie charts.

A well-presented graph or chart might include

- a *main title*
- *axis titles* – used on bar and column charts to show what the axes represent
- *data labels* – which can show the actual value or a percentage figure
- a *legend* (sometimes referred to as a *key*) to explain the segments of a pie chart or two or more sets of data in a column or bar chart.

You can see quite clearly in Figure 116 that the 3rd Quarter has the highest number of weeks reserved. However, do you think that Figure 117 might be more useful because it shows the actual values at the end of the bars? Figure 118 shows the value of bookings as a percentage, which indicates that the income in the 3rd Quarter is nearly half of the income for the year. These three charts provide useful graphical representation of different aspects of the data relating to the bookings and income of the villas.

When creating graphs or charts, it is essential to be absolutely clear about what data you wish to illustrate. When you have completed the graph or chart, ask yourself these questions:

- Is the chart style effective?
- Are the titles suitable?
- Do you need axis titles?
- Do you need a legend?

Axis label

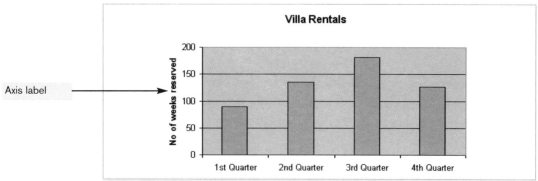

Figure 116 Column chart showing the total number of weeks for which villas were reserved each quarter

Data label

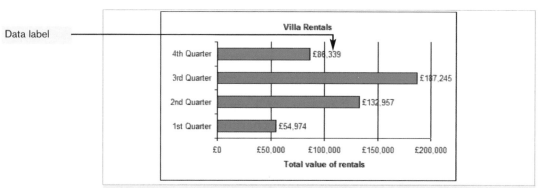

Figure 117 Bar chart showing the total value of bookings for each quarter

Legend or key

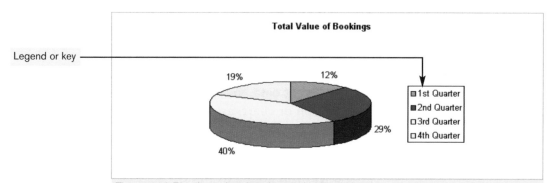

Figure 118 Pie chart showing the total value of bookings for the year, as percentages per quarter

Go out and try!

1 Open the file saved as 'Villa rentals'.

2 Insert a new worksheet and rename it 'Totals'.

○ From the menu, select **Insert**, **Worksheet**.

○ Drag the worksheet tab after the '4th Quarter' worksheet.

○ Double-click the **Sheet1** tab to rename it 'Totals'.

3 Key in the totals for each quarter, as shown in Figure 119.

4 Create a column chart from cells A2 to B6 similar to the one in Figure 116.

○ Highlight cells A2 to B6.

○ Click on the Chart wizard .

○ Select **Column** from the *Chart type* list and click **Next**.

	A	B	C
1		Travelbug Villas	
2		Total No weeks reserved	Total Value of Bookings
3	1st Quarter	89	£54,974
4	2nd Quarter	136	£132,957
5	3rd Quarter	181	£187,245
6	4th Quarter	127	£86,339

Figure 119 Data for your *Go out and try!* task

	A	B	C
1		Travelbug Villas	
2		Total No weeks reserved	Total Value of Bookings
3	1st Quarter	89	£54,974
4	2nd Quarter	136	£132,957
5	3rd Quarter	181	£187,245
6	4th Quarter	127	£86,339

Figure 120 Selected cells

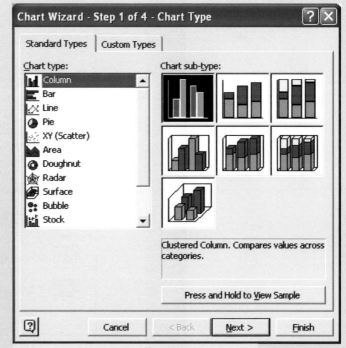

Figure 121 Chart Wizard: setting the chart type

- Click **Next** – Step 2 should be OK if the correct cells were highlighted.
- Type in the *Chart title* 'Villa Rentals'.
- Type in the *Value (Y) axis* title 'No of weeks reserved'.

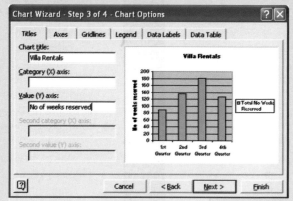

Figure 122 Chart Wizard: setting titles

- Click on the **Legend** tab and remove the tick from the **Show legend** checkbox – the legend needs to be removed as it serves no useful purpose when there is only one set of data.

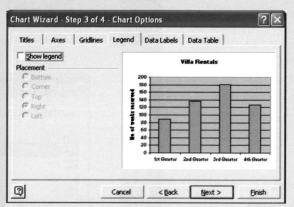

Figure 123 Chart Wizard: removing the legend

- Click **Next**.
- Click in the **As new sheet** option and then click **Finish**.

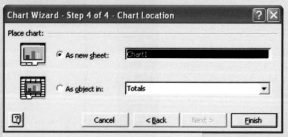

Figure 124 Location for the new chart

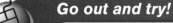

Go out and try!

1 Create a bar chart similar to the one in Figure 117 (page 324) from cells A2 to A6 and C2 to C6.
- ○ Highlight cells A2 to A6.
- ○ Hold the **Ctrl** key down and highlight cells C2 to C6.
- ○ Click on the **Chart Wizard** icon on the toolbar.
- ○ Select **Bar** from the *Chart type* list and click **Next** twice.
- ○ Key in a title and a y-axis title.
- ○ Remove the legend as before and click **Next**.
- ○ Click in the **As new sheet** option and click **Finish**.

2 Create a pie chart from cells A2 to A6 and C2 to C6 similar to Figure 118 (page 324).
- ○ Highlight cells A2 to A6.
- ○ Hold the **Ctrl** key down and highlight cells C2 to C6.
- ○ Click on the **Chart Wizard** icon on the toolbar.
- ○ Select the **Pie** option from the *Chart type* list.
- ○ Choose the *Chart sub-type* at the top of the second column (**Pie with a 3-D visual effect**).
- ○ Click **Next** twice.
- ○ Leave the title as it is.
- ○ Click on the **Data labels** tab.
- ○ Click in **Percentage** and then click **Next**.
- ○ Click in **As new sheet** and then click **Finish**.

TiP

*Holding down the **Ctrl** key allows you to highlight non-adjacent cells (cells that are not next to each other).*

Open your 'Spreadsheet software' file. Create a new bold heading called '**SS Activity 11**' and write a short paragraph describing the skills you have demonstrated in this activity, under the following headings:

- ○ *Creating a column chart*
- ○ *Adding a chart title*
- ○ *Adding an axis label*
- ○ *Creating a bar chart*
- ○ *Adding data labels*
- ○ *Creating a pie chart showing percentages.*

 Save the file.

TiP

When you create spread-sheets for your e-portfolio, it will be an excellent plan to include your own name, the filename and date in the footer. You might want to include other information as well.

Headers and footers

Just as in a word processor, you can include a header or footer in your spreadsheet. In Excel you can choose to have the page number, the sheet name, filename and date inserted automatically.

If the worksheet covers more than one page, the header or footer will automatically appear on all the pages. However, if you have more than one worksheet in your workbook, then you will need to put the footer on all the worksheets.

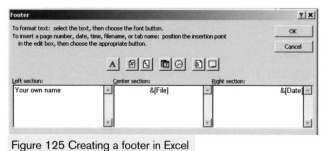

Figure 125 Creating a footer in Excel

To insert a footer into a worksheet, select **View**, **Header and Footer** and then **Custom Footer**. The dialogue box shown in Figure 125 will appear. The filename was automatically inserted in the centre section by clicking on the Excel icon, and the date in the right section by clicking on the date icon. The date will be updated each time you make changes to the file. When the spreadsheet is printed, the actual filename and date will be shown.

Printing a spreadsheet

To print from Excel you can either click on the familiar **Print** icon (🖨) or you can select **File**, **Print** and press **OK**.

However, it is well worth checking **Print Preview** before sending the file to print, to make sure the printout will *look* as you want it. Do remember that with spreadsheets the layout is usually wide, so landscape orientation is more common than portrait.

As with Microsoft Word, through the *Page Setup* dialogue box you can
- change margins
- select portrait or landscape
- include a header or footer.

You can also print the spreadsheet
- with or without gridlines
- with or without row and column headings
- showing the values or the formulas.

Businesses rarely print the row and column headings, but your teacher or tutor may want them included in your coursework, since it makes it easier to check your formulas.

Spreadsheets used in business are often very large – one worksheet in Excel allows you to use hundreds of columns and more than 10,000 rows! We have never used a worksheet that large, and you probably won't either, but even with much smaller worksheets you are likely to want to print just a part of it. Excel allows you to do this very easily.

Jargon buster

The **print area** is the actual part of the worksheet that you want to print. This may mean selecting all the data without any surrounding blank cells. Alternatively it might involve selecting just a part of the worksheet that you wish to print.

Go out and try!

1 Open the file you saved as 'Travelbug invoice'.
2 Set the print area.
- Highlight from cell A1 to the last cell used in column E –
  probably around row 27 or 28.
- From the menu, select **File**, **Print Area**, **Set Print Area**.

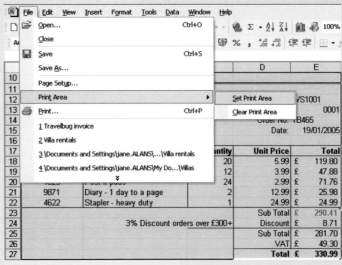

Figure 126 Setting the Print Area

- From the menu, select **File**, **Print Preview**. Check that it
  shows the correct area, then close it.
3 Open the *Page Setup* dialogue box (**File**, **Page Setup**) and
  study each of the tabs in turn. Find out how to do the following:
- *Add gridlines*. Are they helpful in your printout? In some
  cases it is better to omit them, perhaps because borders
  are used to divide the cells.
- *Adjust the margins*. You can drag the margin markers or
  give an exact width or height. In this case set the left and
  right hand margins to 1.5 cm.
- *Centre the spreadsheet*. Try this vertically and horizontally
  on the page.
- *Change from portrait to landscape*. Decide whether you
  need to change to landscape, perhaps because the
  spreadsheet is wide.
- *Create the header or footer*. Create a footer as shown
  earlier in Figure 112, putting your name in the left-hand box.
- *Fit the spreadsheet to the page*.
- *Show row and column headings*.
4 Print the spreadsheet.
5 Print the spreadsheet showing the formula view.
- Hold down the **Ctrl** key and press the backwards quote
  key (`), which is above the **Tab** key and left of the **1** key.
- Repeat to return to normal view.

TiP

*A quick way to show the
formulas in Excel is to
press the **Ctrl** key with the
key to the left of the **1** key.*

Open your 'Spreadsheet software' file. Create a new bold
heading called '**SS Activity 12**' and write short paragraphs
describing the skills you have demonstrated in this activity,
under the following headings:

- *Page setup*
- *Margins setup*
- *Headers and footers.*

 Save the file.

Database software

If you were asked to explain what a database is, you might say that it is a way of keeping names, addresses and telephone numbers on a computer. That is true, but a database is a file of any set of *related* data. Other examples of databases are

- records of stock held in a shop or warehouse
- school or college examination results
- attendance and punctuality records
- records of customers and suppliers.

Every business, large or small, needs to store and access databases of information. For example, the publisher of this book (Heinemann) will have information on its authors, customers (such as your own school or college), staff who work for the company, and printers who produce the books, as well as details of the stock held in the warehouse.

In today's world, more databases than we are even aware of will hold information about us, because it is so much easier to store and transfer data held on a computer than it was when all databases were handwritten. Your school or college will have a database of student records, and each record will contain the same *fields*, such as *ID number, last name, first name, address, telephone number* and *date of birth*. Heinemann's stock records will include *book title, author(s), ISBN number* and *price*.

Jargon buster

A **field** is part of a database record that contains a single item of data.

LEARNING OUTCOMES

You need to learn about:

✓ creating simple flat-file database structures
✓ setting and modifying field characteristics
✓ creating validation rules
✓ entering, editing and deleting records
✓ importing data sets
✓ designing data entry forms that facilitate data entry
✓ creating data entry forms
✓ sorting on one field
✓ sorting on two fields
✓ creating and using searches to extract relevant information
✓ producing customised reports
✓ exporting information from a database into other applications.

So what are the benefits of storing the data in a computerised database, compared with using a paper-based system such as an address book? Figure 127 provides some answers to that question.

Advantages of a computerised database	Disadvantages of a paper-based database
A vast amount of data can be stored on one disk.	You would need many, many files to store the same quantity of data.
Records are entered only once, but can be searched in all kinds of ways (e.g. alphabetically, numerically, selectively, by date).	If student details are stored alphabetically, but you also wanted to store them in order of date of birth, you would have to photocopy all the forms and file them again in date order. You would then have the problem of making sure both sets were kept up to date.
Searching for information is fast, even in a huge database.	Searching for information can be very slow.
Although data can be lost, you should be able to get it back if you keep backups.	When a paper form is removed from the file, it is easily mislaid, filed in the wrong place, lost or damaged.
It is easy to update details (e.g. a change of address).	It is easy to write a new address in an address book, but eventually the book wears out and you have to rewrite all the data in a new book.
It can perform calculations. You could search the database to check the dates of birth of all students and provide a list of those aged over 18. The report will be produced almost immediately.	To search the paper-based system, each form must be checked and then the relevant names copied on to a separate sheet. If the school or college has hundreds or even thousands of students this would be very slow and tedious.

Figure 127 Highlighting the advantages of using a computerised database

You will notice that Figure 127 refers to both *data* and *information*; so what is the difference?

- The details such as the students' names and dates of birth form the *data*.
- A list of all those students aged over 18 is an example of *information* obtained from the data.

Creating simple flat-file database structures

A *database* consists of a file, containing many records. Each record will include the *fields*, into which will be entered the appropriate data. Each record will contain the same fields, but sometimes a field is left empty in a particular record (for example, if there is no email address the field for 'email' will be left blank). A flat-file database is a fairly simple one consisting of only one table.

Tables and forms

A database is usually designed through a *table*. Once the table design is complete, a form is usually created. The data entry clerk will use the form to enter new data or to look at existing data on the screen.

The on-screen layout can be designed in a variety of styles, just as paper forms for different purposes are laid out differently. You may wish to view one record at a time on screen, or you might want to see all records listed under the different field names. A computerised database provides great flexibility in the way you look at the data, and it is easy to switch between viewing a list of all records in a table or one record on a form.

This is illustrated in Figures 128 and 129, which show the records of Travelbug's database of Cruise Club members.

Jargon buster

A database **table** is a grid with one row for each record (see Figure 128).

A database **form** shows only one record on the screen at once (see Figure 129).

Member's ID	Title	First Name	Last Name	Street	Town	Post/Zip Code	Country	E-mail	Phone No	Date joined
1	Miss	Sharon	Weeks	16 Glebe Way	Whychton	TO7 3GH	UK	S.Weeks@userve.co.uk	543 1111 2222	26/09/2005
2	Mr	Otto	Mortensen	Grasvej 9	Helsinge	3489	Denmark	Otto.M@danebank.de	300 4555 3456	29/09/2005
3	Mrs	Kristelle	Mortensen	Grasvej 9	Helsinge	3489	Denmark	Otto.M@danebank.de	300 4555 3456	04/10/2005
4	Mr	Jason	Jarrett	28 Rue Moliere	Margon	34276	France	J.Jarrett@servez.fr	400 3377 3727	05/10/2005
5	Mrs	Naomi	Harrison	28 Rue Moliere	Margon	34276	France	J.Jarrett@servez.fr	400 3377 3727	06/10/2005
6	Mrs	Elizabeth	Cambridge	3108 Crown Walk	Santa Barbara	Ca 92373	USA	Liz.Cam@service.com	600 6789 6789	07/10/2005
7	Mr	James	Cambridge	3108 Crown Walk	Santa Barbara	Ca 92373	USA	Jim.Cam@service.com	600 6789 6789	07/10/2005
8	Mr	Paul	Cambridge	3108 Crown Walk	Santa Barbara	Ca 92373	USA	Paul.Cam@service.com	500 6789 6789	07/10/2005
(AutoNumber)										

Figure 128 A table in Microsoft Access showing the data relating to the Cruise Club members

Figure 129 Form showing one record from the Cruise Club members database

Setting and modifying field characteristics

Before you design a database, it is important to think about the characteristics that will be most useful and suitable for the fields. It would be perfectly possible to create every field as text, because text allows you to enter letters, numbers and symbols into the field. However, if you did use all text fields, you would not be able to

- make calculations, such as finding out the value added tax (VAT) on the price of an item
- search for orders placed in a specific month, or before or after a particular date, or students in a certain age range
- search easily for a particular category, such as male or female, or a particular item of stock (e.g. skirts, blouses, trousers, T-shirts).

In order to do these things

- the field design for the price of the item must be *numerical*
- the field design for the date an order is placed or a date of birth must be in *date format*.

Also, it will be much easier to find a category if the categories are specified in a choice field. Let's look at this in more detail.

Setting up a computerised database

Once you know the purpose of your database, you have to decide several things.

The fields you need

You must decide the names of the fields (e.g. Student ID, First Name). The name of each field indicates which data should be entered into it.

The primary key

This field provides a unique reference for each record. No doubt when you enrolled at school or college you were given a student ID number, which is different for every student. It is essential that the primary key be unique; for example, a *surname* field would not make a good primary key. Records are automatically sorted in order of the primary key.

The data type for each field

You could just use text for everything, because text will accept letters, numbers and symbols. However, as we have just seen, your database would be much less effective when it comes to searching, and it would not be possible to make any calculations.

The size of the fields

How many characters do you need in a particular field? With fields such as names and addresses, obviously you need to allow enough space to enter a long name or long street reference, although it is possible to increase the length of the field later if necessary.

For numerical data you must decide whether the field can be an *integer* (whole number) or whether you need decimal places, and if so how many. You would not design a field with decimal places for the price of a house, as house prices are not quoted as £100,789.58. However, the price of grocery items ranges from less than a £1 upwards, so two decimal places would be necessary. Similarly, you might fix the length of the field for a house price at seven digits, which would allow a price up to £9,999,999. For items sold by a supermarket, you would probably fix the length at three digits to the left and two to the right of the decimal point, which would allow prices up to £999.99.

The format of the field

As with word-processing, you can format the font type, size and colour. It is tempting to select fancy fonts, which may look attractive, but are not necessarily easy to read.

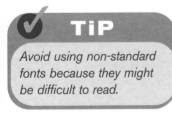

TiP

Avoid using non-standard fonts because they might be difficult to read.

Field data types

Figure 130 lists some typical fields, which are useful in a database. Note, however, that you may not find all these data types available in the database program you are using.

Type of field	Purpose	Advantages/possible uses
Text/character: Sometimes called *alphanumeric*	Any data – letters, numbers or symbols on the keyboard – can be entered into a text field.	• Names/addresses • Where you might include extra detail/description
Numerical – **integer**	A whole number	• Restricts data entry to whole numbers • Can restrict the number of digits • Reduces the risk of errors • Can be sorted in numerical order • Can also ask for list of items above/below/equal to a specific number • Reduces space for storage and display
Numerical – **decimal**	A number with decimal places	• Suitable for money where prices include pence – £13.67 • Measurements – 4.25 km
Numerical – **currency**	Can be set as an integer or with decimal places	• Suitable for money and would show the currency specified; e.g. £3.67, $287, €18
Numerical – **counter** or **AutoNumber**	A numeric value As each new record is entered the counter automatically selects the next number in the sequence.	• Suitable for a member ID, student ID, account number etc. • The operator does not have to enter the number, and if a number has already been used, the computer will not allow you to use it again • Ensures that each member ID, account number etc. remains unique

Date	Storing dates	• Restricts data entry to 1–31 for the day, and 1–12 for the month
		• Reduces the risk of errors
		• Can be used to calculate a person's age, which will automatically update once his/her birth date has passed
		• Can search for
		  – birthdays in a given month
		  – those older or younger than a given age
		  – birthdays between particular dates
		  – orders placed before, after or on a given date

Time	Storing times	Might be used where employees are paid by the hour: • Hours worked can be calculated from time clocked on and off • Wages can be calculated as length of time worked multiplied by the hourly rate
Choice: male/female true/false red/blue/green/yellow	Data entry is limited to the selection that has been pre-determined Choice fields can also be encoded; e.g. M for male, F for female, R for red	• Speeds up data entry • Can search for specific entries, such as 'male', 'true', or 'green' • Reduces space for storage and display

Figure 130 Typical database fields and their characteristics

List/combo boxes and check boxes

List/combo boxes and check boxes are facilities provided by the database program to make data entry easier and more accurate.

List boxes or *combo boxes* are used where the data is limited to a particular selection – for example

- male/female
- child/adult
- red/blue/yellow/green
- part-time/full-time
- Mr, Mrs, Miss, Ms.

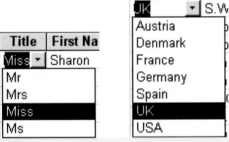

Jargon buster

A **combo box** is a *combination* of a list box and a text edit field. You can either make your choice from the list or type it in.

Figure 131 Examples of combo boxes

Figure 131 gives examples of combo boxes from the Cruise Club members database, showing the drop-down lists. The data entry clerk can either key in the words or simply click on the correct choice, which speeds up data entry and reduces the risk of error.

When designing a combo box it is usually important to select 'Limit to List', as in Figure 132. This prevents the data entry clerk keying in any data not in the list.

General	Lookup	
Display Control	Combo Box	
Row Source Type	Value List	
Row Source	Austria;Denmark;France;	← Possible values
Bound Column	1	
Column Count	1	
Column Heads	No	
Column Widths		
List Rows	8	
List Width	Auto	
Limit To List	Yes ←	Do not allow any other values

Figure 132 Design of a combo box to limit data entry

Non-smoking

| ☑ |
| ☐ |
| ☐ |
| ☐ |
| ☐ |
| ☑ |

Figure 133
Example of a check box

Check boxes are used where there is a yes/no option. The data entry clerk clicks in the box to indicate 'Yes' and a ✓ appears. The clerk leaves the box blank to indicate 'No'. For example, the Cruise Club members are asked if they require a smoking or non-smoking cabin, and the tick indicates those who want non-smoking (Figure 133).

∘∘ Think it over ...

When planning the design of the database for Cruise Club members, think carefully about the different field types. Taking trouble at the design stage will make data entry easier and quicker, and searching more effective. You may wish to work in pairs to plan your design.

Go out and try!

1 Create a table in Word (or on paper) in two columns. List the column headings shown in Figure 128 on page 333 – Member's ID, Title, etc. – and, next to the field names, decide
   ○ the most suitable data type – look back at Figure 130 on page 336
   ○ field size
   ○ field format – font size, style – which will usually be the same for all the fields.
2 Compare your design with other students' designs and discuss it with your teacher.
3 Did you modify your design after you compared your work with other people's? If so, explain your changes.

Create a new word-processing file called 'Database software'. Create a new bold heading called '**DB Activity 1**' and write a short paragraph explaining field types – including the *primary key*, *text*, *number* and *combo box*. Save the file.

Go out and try!

Once you are confident that your field design is suitable, you are ready to create the database file.
1 Design the database table for Cruise Club members using the field types you have chosen. Save the database as 'Cruise Club Members'.
   ○ Start Access and choose **New**, **Blank Database** from the *New File* task pane.

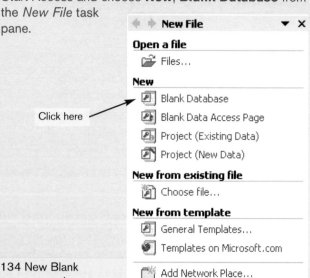

Figure 134 New Blank Database command

Click here

2 Name the database 'Cruise Club Members'.

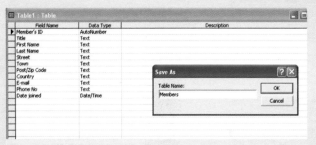

Figure 135 Naming a new database

3 Create a table for the members' details. Double-click on **Create table in Design view**. Enter the field names and data types you have chosen. Don't forget the primary key.

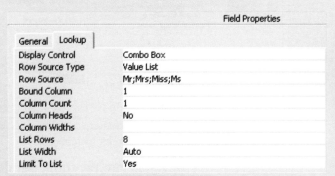

Figure 136 Saving a table

4 To set up a combo box for the *title* field, do the following steps.
- Click into the *Title* field.
- Click the *Lookup* tab in the properties section of the window.
- Change the *Display Control* to read **Combo Box**.
- Change the *Row Source Type* to **Value List**.

Field Properties

General	Lookup	
Display Control	Combo Box	
Row Source Type	Value List	
Row Source	Mr;Mrs;Miss;Ms	
Bound Column	1	
Column Count	1	
Column Heads	No	
Column Widths		
List Rows	8	
List Width	Auto	
Limit To List	Yes	

Figure 137 Properties for the Title field

○ In the *Row Source* box key in 'Mr,Mrs,Miss,Ms' (separated by commas).
○ Change *Limit To List* to **Yes**.
○ Save the design.

To set up a short date, do the following steps.

○ For the *Date joined* field select *Date/Time* as the data type.
○ Click into the *Format* property and change it to *Short Date* from the drop-down list.
○ Save the design.

5 Save the table as 'Members'. Close the table.
6 Open the table by double-clicking on the name in the database window view.
7 Enter the data given in Figure 128 on page 333.

○ Click into the cell for Member's ID.
○ Tab to the next field cell and key in 'Miss'.
○ Tab across the row and enter the details.
○ At the end of the row press **Tab** again to go to the beginning of the next row.
○ Continue until you have entered all eight records.

Open your word-processing file called 'Database software'. Create a new bold heading called '**DB Activity 2**' and write a short paragraph explaining the skills you have learned in designing a table and entering records. Did you have any problems, and if so how did you overcome them? Save the file.

Designing data entry forms

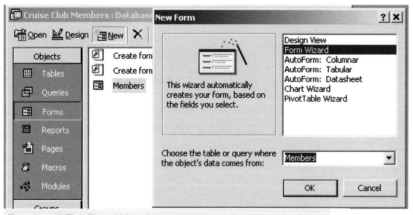

Figure 138 The Form Wizard to create a new form for members

As already explained (see page 333), the data in the database can be presented in table view or form view. Once you have created the table you can then create the form from the table. The easiest way to do this is to use the *Form Wizard* (Figure 138).

It is very convenient to use the wizard so that all the fields are transferred from the table into the form, but do customise it afterwards. You may wish to rearrange the fields into a more appropriate layout, change the font style and size, and add text boxes or navigation buttons.

Go out and try!

1 Using the *Form Wizard,* create a form for the 'Members' table.
- Choose **Forms** from the *Objects* list.
- Double-click on **Create form by using wizard**.
- Ensure your table is selected in the *Tables/Queries* list.
- Click on the double chevron (**>>**) to transfer all the records to the *Selected fields* box.

Jargon buster

A **wizard** is a guide available in the software to take you step-by-step through the process of a specific task.

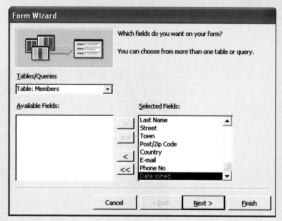

Figure 139 Form Wizard showing all fields selected

- Click **Next**.
- Select **Columnar** and click **Next**.
- Choose a style for your form and click **Next**.
- Enter a name for your form and click **Finish**.

Once the form is created, you will find that all the records are automatically available in the form view.

2 While in form view, add in your own details as if you were a new member.
- Click on the new record navigation button (▶✱) at the bottom of the form.
- Enter your details, pressing the **Tab** key to move from one field to the next.

3 Check whether your record is shown in the table.
- Close the form.
- Choose **Tables** from the **Objects** list.
- Open the table to view all the records.

Open your word-processing file called 'Database software'. Create a new bold heading called '**DB Activity 3**' and write a short paragraph explaining the skills you have learned in designing a form and entering a record using form view. Did you prefer to use the table or the form to enter records? 💾 Save the file.

Although the *Form Wizard* makes it very easy to create a form from the table, the result will probably be in columns, where all fields are listed one under the other (as shown in Figure 129 on page 334). All the right-hand side of the window is wasted, and the form may not fit in the screen window. Another common ready-prepared format is tabular, where all the field names are listed across the screen with the data in rows underneath. This is not much different from table view.

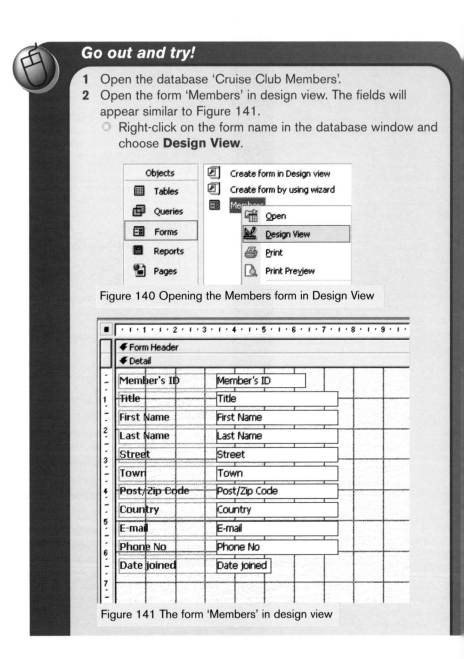

Go out and try!

1 Open the database 'Cruise Club Members'.
2 Open the form 'Members' in design view. The fields will appear similar to Figure 141.
   ○ Right-click on the form name in the database window and choose **Design View**.

Figure 140 Opening the Members form in Design View

Figure 141 The form 'Members' in design view

4 Experiment with moving the fields to see if it improves the layout.
   - Select a control (the field) and position the mouse pointer until it becomes a hand (✋) and then drag the control to a new position.
5 Experiment with the font style and colour, or place a border around the fields.
   - Select the control to change.
   - Right-click and choose **Properties** from the menu that appears.
   - There are properties for font, font size, font colour, border, alignment, etc. Options are available on drop-down lists in each property.
6 Add the heading 'Cruise Club Members' using the **Label** tool from the *Toolbox* (Figure 142).

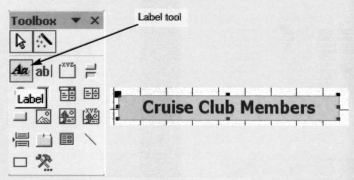

Figure 142 Adding a heading using the Toolbox

   - Switch to design view for the form.
   - Click on the **Label** tool.
   - Drag a heading box to the size you want in a space at the top of your form.
   - Type in the heading.
   - Press **Enter**.
   - With the control still selected, you can format the font, size, alignment, colour, etc. from the *Formatting* toolbar.
7 Add buttons for navigating to the previous and next records.
   - Click on the **Command Button** tool from the *Toolbox* (Figure 143).

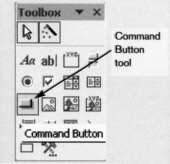

Figure 143 The Toolbox

   - Drag out a shape for the button on your form. The *Command Button Wizard* should start.

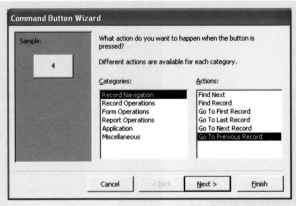

Figure 144 Choice of navigation action

○ Select **Record Navigation** from the *Categories* list
and **Go To Previous Record** from the *Actions* list.
Click **Next**.

○ Click in the option button for **Text** and click **Next**.

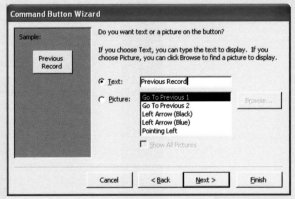

Figure 145 Setting a title for the button

○ Give the button a name and click **Finish**.

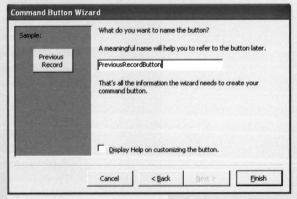

Figure 146 Naming the button

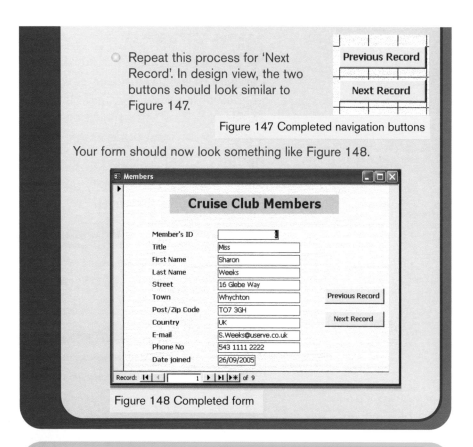

Figure 148 Completed form

 Open your word-processing file called 'Database software'. Create a new bold heading called '**DB Activity 4**' and write a short paragraph explaining the skills you have learned in improving the form layout. Save the file.

Creating validation rules

The word 'valid' means *suitable*. Planes, boats and cars are all forms of transport, but if you want to cross a lake it is no use trying to drive across – you need a boat! That is a silly example, but in this case the car is not suitable – not valid.

Two very important validation checks used in computerised databases are

- type checks
- range checks.

If invalid or unsuitable data is entered into the field, the database program will indicate an error – such as the ones shown in Figure 149.

Type checks

We have looked at the various data types that may be used in a database. If a field has been designed for numbers, the computer will not accept letters in that field. If a field has been designed to accept a choice of titles – Mr, Mrs, Miss, Ms – by using a combo box, it will not accept any other title in that field.

Clearly, it is still possible for the data entry clerk to make errors, but some errors will immediately be apparent – often by a beep and an error message on the screen.

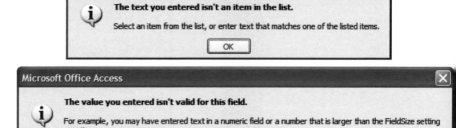

Microsoft Office Access	
The text you entered isn't an item in the list.	
Select an item from the list, or enter text that matches one of the listed items.	
OK	

Microsoft Office Access	
The value you entered isn't valid for this field.	
For example, you may have entered text in a numeric field or a number that is larger than the FieldSize setting permits.	
OK	

Figure 149 An error message when text not listed in the combo box was entered, and one when the date entered was 29/13/2005 – because there are only 12 months in a year

Figure 150 shows the effect of using a type check.

Data to be entered	Data actually entered	Data valid	Data correct
25	25	✓	✓
25	52	✓	✗ – but it is accepted because it is of the *correct type*
25	q5	✗	✗ – because 'q' is not a number – i.e. the *wrong type*
Mr	Mr	✓	✓
Mr	Mrs	✓	✗ – but it is accepted because Mrs is one of the titles listed in the combo box – i.e. the *correct type*
Mr	Doctor	✗	✗ – because Doctor is not one of the titles listed in the combo box – i.e. the *wrong type*

Figure 150 The effect of using a type check

Range checks

A number field may include a further check as well as the type check. The field can be limited within a set *range,* by giving a minimum or maximum figure or both.

For example, a date field will include an automatic range so that 13 will not be accepted as a month, and 31 will not be accepted as a day for the months of February, April, June, September and November. The effect of using a range check is demonstrated in Figure 151.

Data to be entered	Data actually entered	Data valid	Data correct
29/09/2005	29/09/2005	✓	✓
29/09/2005	29/08/2005	✓	✗ – but it is accepted because it is within the correct *range*
29/09/2005	29/13/2005	✗	✗ – computer immediately signals an error, because there are only 12 months in the year – 13 is outside the *range*

Figure 151 The effect of using a range check

Go out and try!

1 Open the database 'Cruise Club Members'. Test out the range and type checks given in Figures 150 and 151. If invalid data is accepted then check the field design.

2 Try entering the following. If the data is accepted, check your field design again.
   - **Senor** in the field for *Title.*
   - **Mongolia** for the field for *Country.*
   - **five43 1111 2222** in the field for *Phone no.*
   - **31/02/05** in the field for *Date joined.*

Think it over ...

Why might a number field **not** be appropriate for telephone numbers?

Open the word-processing file called 'Database software'. Create a new bold heading called '**DB Activity 5**' and write a short paragraph explaining what happens when invalid data is entered into the fields. ▪ Save the file.

Entering, editing and deleting records

As you have already discovered, it is usually much easier to edit a computerised database than a manual system. From time to time you may need to

- add a new record – e.g. a new customer
- delete a record – e.g. a product item that is discontinued
- edit a record – e.g. if an address changes
- add new fields or change existing ones.

To add a new record to the database, you either click on the next row in the table, or select a blank form and add in the new details. If the primary key is an AutoNumber, the next number available will be chosen and the new record will automatically be filed in correct order of the primary key.

With the small sample of records available in the 'Cruise Club Members' database, it does not take long to look at each one in turn if you need to find a particular record. However, this would be very time-consuming if the database had hundreds of records. You can 'ask' the computer to search the database by selecting **Edit, Find,** clicking on a specific field and entering what you are looking for into the *Find What* box. Click on **Find Next** and, if the data matches one of the records in the database, the record will be located.

TiP

*You can also click on the binoculars icon 🔍 to access the **Find What** box.*

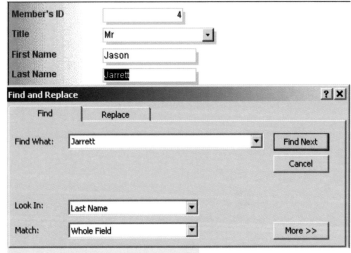

Figure 152 Finding a specific record

In Figure 152 the cursor was placed in the *Last Name* field, **Jarrett** was entered into the *Find What* box and, when **Find Next** was selected, the correct record was found.

When you have found a record, you can then either delete the record, change the data, or simply look up the information you need.

Go out and try!

1 Using the *Find and Replace* facility, find the record for Jarrett.
- Open the table in either form view or datasheet view.
- Click into the *Last Name* field.
- From the menu, select **Edit**, **Find**.
- Enter 'Jarrett' in the *Find What* box and click **Find Next**.

2 Select the 'Members' table and add a new field for Non-smoking, designed as a check box.
- Open the table in Design view.
- Click into the first empty *Field Name* box and key in 'Non-smoking'.
- Tab into the *Data Type* column and set the type to **Yes/No**.
- Save the design (the default setting is for a check box).

3 Select non-smoking for Sharon Weeks and the Cambridge family.
- Switch the table to Datasheet view.
- Click into the check boxes for Sharon Weeks and the three members of the Cambridge family.

4 You now need to add the field to your 'Members' form.
- Open the form in Design view.
- Select **View**, **Field List**.
- Drag the field for *Non-smoking* on to the form (you may need to make room by dragging the bottom boundary of the design area).

Change to Form view to see that the records have been updated.

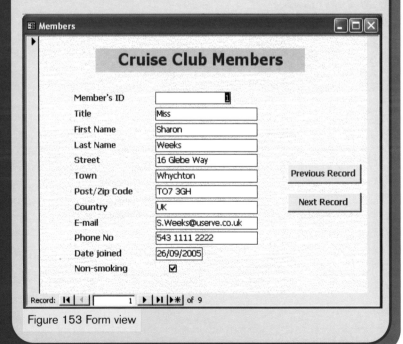

Figure 153 Form view

Open your word-processing file called 'Database software'.
Create a new bold heading called '**DB Activity 6**' and write a
short paragraph explaining *how to*

- *find a specific record*
- *add a check box field to your database table and form.*

 Save the file.

Sorting a database and using searches

As you saw earlier, records in the database are automatically saved *in the order of the primary key field*. However, you may wish to present the data in a particular order – e.g. alphabetical, numerical, chronological (order of date).

In Figure 154, Travelbug have created another database with details of the cruises, shown here sorted in order of price.

⊞ Cruise details : Table

Cruise Ref	Destination	Rating	Duration in days	Price
AI01	Atlantic Islands	Budget	8	£875
ME04	Mediterranean	Budget	10	£950
NO12	Norway	Luxury	7	£1,100
GI10	Greek Islands	Standard	8	£1,150
FA07	Falklands	Budget	7	£1,500
TE03	Tenerife	Luxury	7	£1,999
BA11	Bahamas	Standard	12	£2,050
SP05	South Pacific	Standard	11	£2,100
AU06	Australia	Standard	14	£2,975
CA09	Caribbean	Luxury	12	£3,400
NZ02	New Zealand	Luxury	14	£3,750

Figure 154 A sorted Travelbug database

The order can be *ascending* (lowest to highest – A to Z or 1 to 100), or *descending* (highest to lowest – Z to A or 100 to 1).

If you wish to sort the database on one field only, then highlight the field name and click either the A–Z button (🔼) or the Z–A button (🔽) on the toolbar. However, if you wish to sort on one field and then on a secondary field, you will need to design a *query*, as explained in the next section.

Creating and using searches to extract relevant information

Searching the database to find specific information is known as a *query*. The query defines the *parameters*: what you want to find out. The result of your query may be presented on the monitor screen or printed on paper. You will need to know how to design a variety of different queries:

- sorting on one field with a secondary sort on another field
- using a single criterion or multiple criteria
- using relational operators
- using logical operators.

We shall now look at some examples.

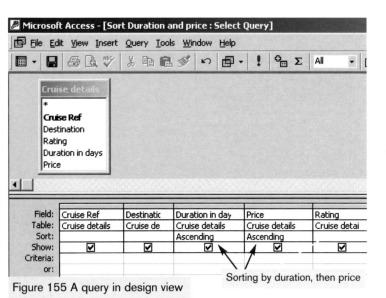

Figure 155 A query in design view

Sorting by duration, then price

Sorting on one field with a secondary sort on another field

A Travelbug customer would like to have a list of cruises sorted by duration and then by price. To design the query, Thomas Tripp first selects the table and then the fields he wishes to include. The field *Duration in days* must be listed before the field *Price* and both must be set to sort in ascending order. This is shown in Figure 155. The result of the search will then be sorted in the right order, as in Figure 156.

	Cruise Ref	Destination	Duration in days	Price	Rating
	NO12	Norway	7	£1,100	Luxury
▶	FA07	Falklands	7	£1,500	Budget
	TE03	Tenerife	7	£1,999	Luxury
	AI01	Atlantic Islands	8	£875	Budget
	GI10	Greek Islands	8	£1,150	Standard
	ME04	Mediterranean	10	£950	Budget
	SP05	South Pacific	11	£2,100	Standard
	BA11	Bahamas	12	£2,050	Standard
	CA09	Caribbean	12	£3,400	Luxury
	AU06	Australia	14	£2,975	Standard
	NZ02	New Zealand	14	£3,750	Luxury

Figure 156 Result of running a query to sort the database on two fields

TIP

If you tend to confuse the signs for greater than and less than, try to remember that less than (<) points to the left.

Relational operators

If you search a database using relational operators, you will be looking for a number *greater than*, *less than* or *equal to some value*. There are signs that are used to represent these relationships:

- < less than
- > greater than

- = equal to
- <> not equal to
- <= less than or equal to
- >= greater than or equal to.

Another Travelbug customer wishes to find cruises costing less than £2000. Figure 157 shows the design for this query, and Figure 158 shows the result.

Field:	Cruise Ref	Destination	Rating	Duration in day	Price
Table:	Cruise details	Cruise details	Cruise detail:	Cruise details	Cruise detail
Sort:					Ascending
Show:	☑	☑	☑	☑	☑
Criteria:					<2000
or:					

Figure 157 Search for a single criterion

Cruise Ref	Destination	Rating	Duration in days	Price
AI01	Atlantic Islands	Budget	8	£875
ME04	Mediterranean	Budget	10	£950
NO12	Norway	Luxury	7	£1,100
GI10	Greek Islands	Standard	8	£1,150
FA07	Falklands	Budget	7	£1,500
TE03	Tenerife	Luxury	7	£1,999

Figure 158 Result of running a query to find cruises costing less than £2000

Logical operators

The logical operators – *and, or,* and *not* – let you chain together multiple conditions in the same query.

Suppose a Travelbug customer enquires about luxury cruises under £2000. To get the list you need to query the records where *Price < 2000* **and** *Rating = 'luxury'*. In Access you do this by adding both criteria, as shown in Figure 159. There are just two cruises suitable, as revealed in Figure 160.

Field:	Cruise Ref	Destination	Price	Rating
Table:	Cruise deta	Cruise details	Cruise details	Cruise details
Sort:				
Show:	☑	☑	☑	☑
Criteria:			<2000	="luxury"
or:				

Figure 159 Search for multiple criteria – 'less than £2000' and 'luxury'

	Cruise Ref	Destination	Price	Rating	Duration in days
	TE03	Tenerife	£1,999	Luxury	7
	NO12	Norway	£1,100	Luxury	7

Figure 160 Result of running the query in Figure 159

A Travelbug customer would like to go on a cruise for seven or eight days. Figure 161 shows the query criteria, and Figure 162 shows the result.

Field:	Cruise Ref	Destination	Duration in day	Price	Rating
Table:	Cruise details	Cruise details	Cruise details	Cruise details	Cruise detail
Sort:				Descending	
Show:	☑	☑	☑	☑	☑
Criteria:			=7		
or:			=8		

Figure 161 Design of a query to select cruises for seven or eight days

TiP

To do a **not** search, use the <> operator in one or more of your criteria.

	Cruise Ref	Destination	Duration in days	Price	Rating
	TE03	Tenerife	7	£1,999	Luxury
	FA07	Falklands	7	£1,500	Budget
	GI10	Greek Islands	8	£1,150	Standard
	NO12	Norway	7	£1,100	Luxury
	AI01	Atlantic Islands	8	£875	Budget

Figure 162 Result of running the query in Figure 161

Go out and try!

1 Set up a new database with details of the cruises as shown in Figure 154 (page 350). Take care when deciding on the field types.
2 Enter the data.
3 Practise designing queries as shown in Figures 155 to 162
   ○ Close the table.
   ○ Choose **Queries** from the *Objects* list.
   ○ Double-click on **Create query in design view**.
   ○ Click **Add** to add the table and then close the *Show table* box.
   ○ Click into the first field cell in the design grid and, using the drop-down list, choose **Cruise Ref**.
   ○ Tab into the next field cell and set it to **Destination**.
   ○ Continue until you have entered all the required fields for the query shown in Figure 155.
   ○ Click into the *Sort* cell for the field you want to sort (in this case) and choose *Duration in days* **Ascending** .
   ○ Repeat for the *Price* field.
   ○ Click on the **Run** icon (!) on the toolbar and compare your results with Figure 156.
   ○ Repeat these steps for the other queries, changing the criteria as appropriate.

Open your word-processing file called 'Database software'. Create a new bold heading called '**DB Activity 7**' and write a short paragraph explaining what is meant by

○ *a query*
○ *relational operators*
○ *logical operators.*

 Save the file.

Producing customised reports

Less 2000 and luxury

Cruise Ref	TE03
Destination	Tenerife
Price	£1,999
Rating	Luxury
Duration in days	7
Cruise Ref	NO12
Destination	Norway
Price	£1,100
Rating	Luxury
Duration in days	7

The result of a query is presented in table format, but you may wish to present your query more professionally. To do this you need to design a *report*.

Figure 160 showed the query result for 'luxury' cruises 'less than £2000' in table format, whereas Figure 163 shows the same result in report format. You can choose various options in the report design, and wizards are available to help you design the report layout quickly and easily.

Figure 163 The report view of the same query shown in Figures 159 and 160

Go out and try!

Create reports for all the queries you have made in the Cruise database.

○ Click on **Reports** in the *Objects* list
○ Double-click on **Create report by using wizard**.
○ From the *Tables/Queries* drop-down list, choose the query to use for the report.
○ Click on the **>>** button to move all the fields to the *Selected Fields* box.

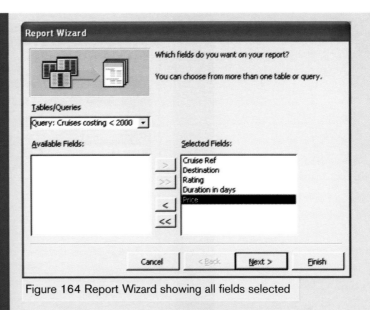

Figure 164 Report Wizard showing all fields selected

- Click **Next**.
- Don't add any grouping. Click **Next**.
- Add any sorting required and click **Next**.
- Click in the option for **Columnar** and select **Portrait**.

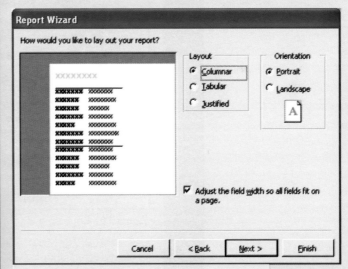

Figure 165 Settings for a columnar portrait report

- Click **Next**.
- Choose a style and click **Next**.

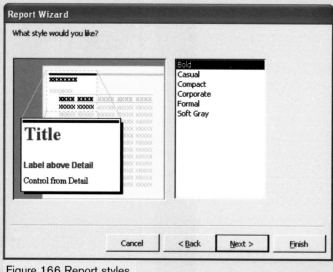

Figure 166 Report styles

○ Enter a title for your report and click **Finish**.

Figure 167 Entering a report title

○ Your report should look something like the one in Figure 163 (page 354).

Open your word-processing file called 'Database software'. Create a new bold heading called '**DB Activity 8**' and write a short paragraph describing the difference between a query and a database report. ▣ Save the file.

Exporting data for use in other applications

It is possible to export data held in the database for use in other software applications, and a particularly good example is exporting names and addresses for mail merge (see page 292).

One of the advantages of a computer is the facility to write one letter but send it out to a large number of people using mail merge. Instead of creating a data file in Word, if the names and addresses are already held in a database file then they can be exported to the word processor.

Go out and try!

1 Open the file saved as 'Members' and select the 'Members' table. Select **File**, **Export** and select the 'Members' table (Figure 168).

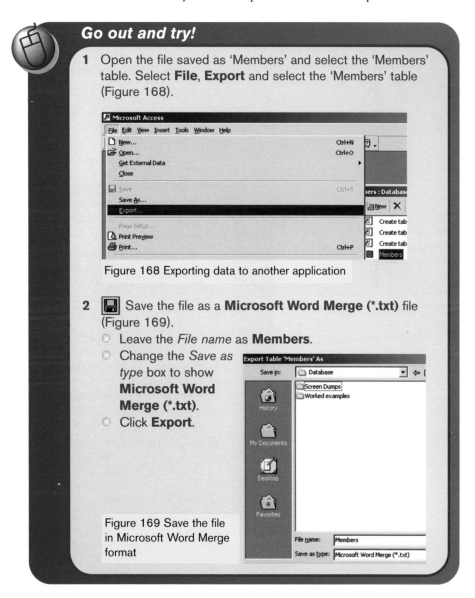

Figure 168 Exporting data to another application

2 💾 Save the file as a **Microsoft Word Merge (*.txt)** file (Figure 169).
- ○ Leave the *File name* as **Members**.
- ○ Change the *Save as type* box to show **Microsoft Word Merge (*.txt)**.
- ○ Click **Export**.

Figure 169 Save the file in Microsoft Word Merge format

Importing data sets

As well as being able to export data, Access can import data from other applications in a variety of common formats, such as text or spreadsheet files. When a suitable set of data that is already available is imported into Access, the field names and field types are automatically assigned by the software.

If you have created the spreadsheet file saved as 'Villa Rentals', you can practice importing data from the spreadsheet into the database. If at this stage you have not created this file, but have a different spreadsheet file available, then you could use that one instead.

Go out and try!

1   Open the file saved as 'Villa Rentals' and resave it as 'Villas to export'.
2   You will need to delete rows 1–3 on all four worksheets, but make sure you keep row 4 containing the column headings – Name of Villa, Cost of Weekly Rentals etc. Access will use this row for the field names. Close the file.
3   Open a new database file in Access and call it 'Villas'.
4   From the menu, select **File**, **Get External Data**, **Import**. The *Import* dialogue box appears.
5   Set the *Files of type* drop-down list to **Microsoft Excel (*.xls)** and find the file 'Villas to export.xls'.
6   Click on the file and then press **Import**.
7   Select the **1st Quarter** worksheet and then click **Finish** (Figure 170).
8   Press **OK** on the confirmation dialogue, and open the new *1st Quarter* table to check that the contents are OK. You may find you have some blank rows or columns, which you should delete.

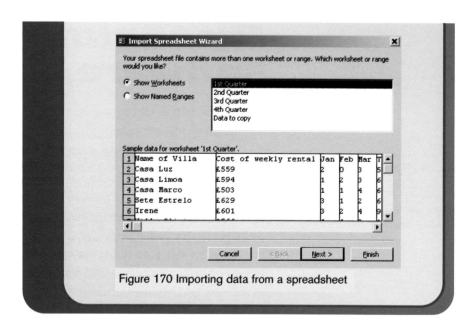

Figure 170 Importing data from a spreadsheet

Open your word-processing file called 'Database software'.
Create a new bold heading called '**DB Activity 10**' and write a
short paragraph explaining what is meant by importing data.
Save the file.

Presentation software

Presentations can be in a variety of forms. At school or college your teacher may present information using an overhead projector and slides. A cinema's booking office could use a computer to show a series of pictures about forthcoming films; this would also be a presentation.

Travelbug could use Microsoft PowerPoint to create a presentation of its products and services to show prospective clients. You will probably be asked to deliver a PowerPoint presentation during your school or college studies, and you may even be asked to deliver one when you go for a job interview. Learning to use PowerPoint effectively will therefore provide you with a skill that you will find useful both now and in the future.

LEARNING OUTCOMES

You need to learn about

✓ designing and creating the structure and navigation route of a presentation

✓ selecting and creating colour schemes

✓ creating and using a corporate style

✓ creating and selecting components – text, graphics, video and sound

✓ using master slides and templates

✓ using frames

✓ editing text – fonts, aligning, bullets, line spacing

✓ editing graphics – aligning, rotating, flipping, cropping and resizing, changing colour and resolution

✓ using transparency

✓ optimising file size

✓ adding lines and simple shapes

✓ using text wrap

✓ inserting animation

✓ creating slide transitions

✓ producing speaker notes and handouts to accompany slide shows

✓ rehearsing and checking timings of a slideshow

✓ packing a presentation for transfer to another computer.

Designing and creating the structure of a presentation

A PowerPoint presentation is made up of individual parts, called *slides*. You can build up a series of slides to create a presentation. Often you will see a PowerPoint presentation displayed through a digital projector on to a screen. You may have experienced your teachers doing this in lessons. Alternatively the presentation could be shown on a computer screen as an on-screen display – for example the presentation about forthcoming films.

It is essential to plan a presentation before creating it. This includes creating a *storyboard* that shows the layout and content of each individual slide. You should also plan the structure of the presentation, making sure you show the *navigation route*. There is an opportunity to learn more about storyboards and structures in Unit 2 of the qualification.

Jargon buster

A **storyboard** is a series of pictures that is used by multimedia developers to illustrate the proposed content, structure and navigation of the end product. For example, storyboards can be used to plan presentations, websites, films or videos.

Go out and try!

Plan a PowerPoint presentation about yourself and your friends. Create a storyboard to show the structure. You should plan a presentation that will allow you to practise all the skills you will learn about in this chapter.

Create a new word-processed file called 'Presentation software' and save it in your Presentation sub-folder. Create a bold heading '**PS Activity 1**' and write a short paragraph describing the skills you have demonstrated in this activity. Save the file.

Using wizards, templates and master slides

Wizards

You may already be familiar with the wizards used in applications such as Microsoft Access. PowerPoint also provides a wizard to simplify the creation of a presentation. In PowerPoint this is called the *AutoContent Wizard* (Figure 171). If you want to create a

Figure 171 The AutoContent Wizard

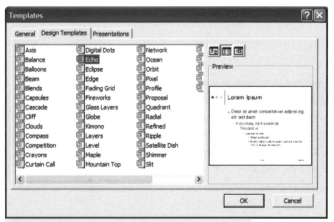

Figure 172 The Design Template window

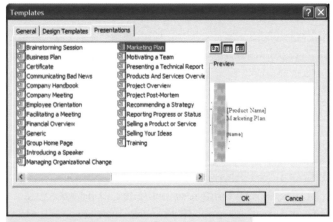

Figure 173 The Presentation Templates window

presentation quickly and be guided step by step, this is an ideal feature.

Templates

PowerPoint also makes creating a presentation easier by providing a wide range of design and presentation *templates* (Figure 172).

A design template is a file that has been designed with special backgrounds and layouts ready to use. It includes styles for the type and size of bullets and fonts. Using a design template is another timesaving feature, and, if you are not particularly artistic, can be invaluable.

The design template always has two slide designs – one used for the title slide (the first slide in a presentation) and one used for the remaining slides. This means that the title slide will have a slightly different design from the remaining slides in a presentation.

Presentation templates are pre-structured presentations that you can choose to suit a specific purpose (Figure 173). For example, Thomas Tripp from Travelbug could use the marketing plan template to create a presentation to market holidays to prospective clients.

If you don't want to use one of the templates supplied with PowerPoint, you can find different themes and design templates on the Internet, many of which you can download without charge.

The slide master

Each design template comes with a *slide master* on which you can put any graphics or text that you want to appear on every slide, and an optional *title master* where you can make changes to slides in your presentation that use the title slide layout. For example, Travelbug can put their logo on the slide master so that it will appear on every slide (Figure 174).

Figure 174 The slide master

If you wish to divide your presentation into several sections, each starting with a title slide, you can create a separate title master. You edit the slide masters and title masters to set the default text formats and styles for all slides in your presentation. You can also number each slide, include a footer, and show the date a presentation was created.

Selecting and creating colour schemes

Colours are used for the background, text and lines, shadows, title text, fills, accents, and hyperlinks on a slide. Together they are called the presentation's *colour scheme*.

If you choose to use an existing template for your presentation, one useful feature is that if you do not like the colour scheme then you can change it easily (Figure 175). A design template will include a default colour scheme for the presentation, together with additional alternative schemes to choose from.

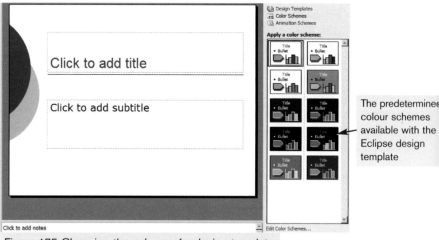

The predetermined colour schemes available with the Eclipse design template

Figure 175 Changing the colours of a design template

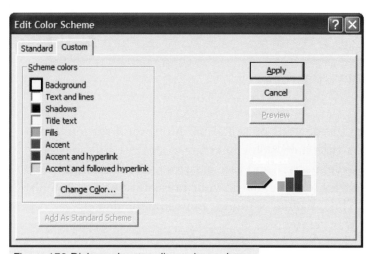

Figure 176 Dialogue box to edit a colour scheme

You can even change certain aspects of a default colour scheme. For example, suppose Thomas Tripp of Travelbug wants to create a PowerPoint presentation to be shown at a travel exhibition. Because he wishes to ensure that the colour scheme uses the Travelbug house style, he can choose to modify the design template to reflect this. As PowerPoint allows you to change the colour for all or only certain elements of a colour scheme, Thomas Tripp could change the colour for text and lines, but leave the other elements unchanged (Figure 176).

Colour schemes can be applied to one slide, selected slides or the entire presentation. If you are creating the template yourself for a presentation, you can apply colour schemes in the same way you would if you were using an existing design template.

Go out and try!

1 Choose a template that is appropriate the presentation you planned in Activity 1.
  - Start PowerPoint.
  - Click on **From Design Template** in the *New Presentation* task pane.
  - Choose a design from *Apply a design template*.
2 Choose a colour scheme.
  - Click on **Color Schemes** at the top of the task pane.
  - Select a colour scheme for your design layout.
3 Modify the colour scheme.
  - Click on **Edit Colour Schemes** at the bottom of the task pane.
  - Click on an item in the *Scheme colors* list (Figure 176), then use the **Change Color** button to change the colour of that item.
  - Repeat the previous step for any other items you want to change.
4 💾 Save your presentation.

Open your 'Presentation software's file. Create a new bold heading '**PS Activity 2**' and write a short paragraph describing the skills you have demonstrated in this activity when selecting and creating colour schemes for a PowerPoint presentation. 💾 Save the file.

Viewing your slides

There are three main ways of viewing slides.

- *Normal view*. This is the main view used for editing. It displays three areas. On the left-hand side there are tabs which alternate between slide and outline view, the slide pane and the notes pane. You can adjust the pane sizes by dragging the pane borders. Slides are displayed individually and you can work on the slides in this view. The notes pane allows you to enter notes that you want to make about a slide, which will assist you when making a presentation.

- *Slide sorter*. This allows you to view all the slides in miniature form. Not only can you delete slides, change the order of slides or insert new slides in slide sorter view, you can also copy existing slides and paste them into the desired positions very easily.

- *Slide show*. You can view your presentation by clicking on the Slide Show icon () in the bottom-left.

Creating, selecting and using text and graphics components

Slide layout

Slide Layout ▼ ✕

⊕ | ⊕ | ⌂

Apply slide layout:

Text Layouts

Content Layouts

Text and Content Layouts

☑ Show when inserting new slides

Figure 177 The slide layout options

It is possible to design your own slides from scratch, or to choose one of the layouts provided by PowerPoint. The *Slide Layout* option will display the different layouts from which you can choose. By pointing to each picture you can see a description of the slide.

The layouts are divided into different categories – *Text Layouts*, *Content Layouts*, *Text and Content Layouts*, and *Other Layouts*. Figure 177 shows the different layouts, which allow a range of components to be included in a slide: text (including bulleted lists), charts, graphics, sound and video (referred to as *media clips*).

PowerPoint allows you to click on icons to add the appropriate content for a slide. For example, Thomas Tripp would click on the **Insert Picture** icon to insert a digital photograph in his presentation (Figure 178).

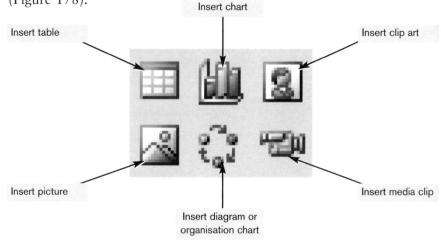

Insert table

Insert chart

Insert clip art

Insert picture

Insert diagram or organisation chart

Insert media clip

Figure 178 The components available

Using boxes/frames

The design of each slide is broken down into areas called *boxes* (sometimes referred to as *frames*). Each box/frame holds an object. The object can be, for example, a list, a title, text, a piece of clip art, or a chart. A box can be copied, moved and resized in the same way as you would a piece of clip art, and can even be rotated.

You can either use one of the slide layouts provided by PowerPoint, or start with a blank slide and insert objects wherever you like on the slide. These objects are automatically held in boxes.

Editing text on slides

Many of the features that you may be familiar with from using other applications – such as Word or CorelDraw – can be applied to text in PowerPoint by selecting **Format** on the *Standard* toolbar (Figure 179). You can format text to bold, italic, underlined or shadowed, and align text to the left, centre, right or justify it. You can change the colour of text and choose from a wide range of fonts and sizes.

Skills check

Refer to page 251 for information on formatting text.

TiP

PowerPoint includes a spellchecker. All Microsoft Office applications use the same dictionary file to check spellings. If you add a word to the dictionary in Word, PowerPoint will also recognise it.

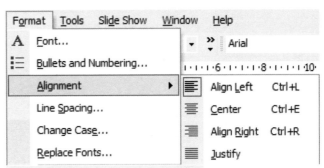

Figure 179 The Format menu options

Using the *Line Spacing* dialogue box from the **Format** menu, you can adjust the line spacing, not only between lines, but before and after paragraphs, just as you can in Word.

Some slide layouts allow for text areas that are specifically for lists. When you start typing in one of these, a bullet will appear before the text. You can format the bullets to different styles, in the same way as you would in Word.

Skills check

Refer to page 257 for information on formatting bulleted and numbered lists.

TiP

Take care always to use a font size that can be read easily. Font size 24 or above is a good size to read. Font size 12 or 14 may be fine for a handout, but it would be impossible to read from the back of a room!

Go out and try!

Format the first slide for the presentation you planned in Activity 1.
- From the menu, select **Format**, **Slide Layout**. The *Slide Layout* task pane appears (see Figure 177).
- Choose an appropriate layout for your first slide. *Title and Text* is often a good choice.
- Type in a title and some descriptive text based on the first slide in your plan. Use formatting (e.g. bold) where appropriate.

Open your 'Presentation software' file. Create a new bold heading called '**PS Activity 3**' and write a short paragraph describing the skills you have demonstrated in this activity when editing text in a PowerPoint presentation. 💾 Save the file.

Skills check ▶▶

The Artwork and Imaging skills section of this book covers editing techniques which you can use when modifying images for a PowerPoint presentation.

Editing and using graphics

The graphics you include in a presentation could be a photograph taken with a digital camera, some clip art, a drawing, or perhaps a logo such as the Travelbug logo.

? Think it over ...

Have you heard the expression 'a picture is worth a thousand words'? Including graphics in a presentation will ensure that it is more interesting, often easier to understand and – most importantly – more memorable.

Skills check ▶▶

Positioning, cropping, resizing, grouping and borders are controlled in the same way as in Microsoft Word. See page 287 for details.

You may decide to use a specialist editing package or the *Picture* toolbar in PowerPoint (Figure 180) to edit a graphic. For instance, Thomas Tripp might decide to adjust the colour and resolution of a digital photograph using Coral Photo-Paint or Microsoft Photo Editor rather than use the more limited options supplied with PowerPoint.

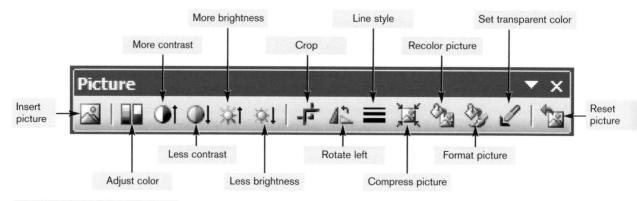

Figure 180 The Picture toolbar

Transparency

You can use the **Set transparent color** tool to remove one colour from your picture and let whatever is behind it show through. This is typically used to remove a coloured background from an image. Some graphics formats, such as GIF, can be saved with transparent areas.

Inserting clip art

Inserting clip art into a slide is very easy – PowerPoint comes with a gallery (Figure 181). If you have an Internet connection, you can click on the **Clips Online** button on the menu bar. This will connect you to Microsoft's database of free clip art. You can also buy a CD-ROM full of pictures you can use.

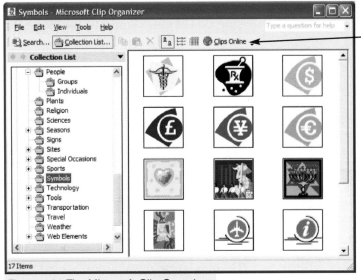

Click here to access Microsoft's Clips Online.

Figure 181 The Microsoft Clip Organizer

✔ **TiP**

*The Internet is a wonderful source of graphics that you can download. However, whatever the source of your graphics, it is important to remember to check that you are allowed to use them. If the creator says that a picture is in the **public domain**, then this means that the copyright on it has been waived and it is free to use. Otherwise you may have to get permission.*

✔ **TiP**

*You can combine a number of images together to make a new image using the **Group**, option on the Drawing toolbar (see page 281).*

Go out and try!

Build a new slide which forms part of the presentation you planned in Activity 1. Include a graphic.
- Click on the **New Slide** button in the *Formatting* toolbar.
- Change the layout to one of the *Content Layouts* using the *Slide Layout* task pane.
- To add some clip art, click the **Insert Clip Art** button (or double-click the area, depending on which version of PowerPoint you are using).
- Double-click the image you would like to use.
- You may decide to insert a photograph and use the editing techniques you have learned to crop and adjust the colour and resolution within PowerPoint.
- Display the *Picture* toolbar (click on an image in your presentation or select **View**, **Toolbars**, **Picture** from the menu).
- Click the **Insert Picture** button (see Figure 180).
- Navigate to the picture you want to add, then double-click it.
  Save your work.

TiP

Double-click the picture to display the Format Picture *dialogue box. On the* Picture *tab, press the* **Compress** *button to display the* Compress Pictures *dialogue box shown in Figure 182. Select the required options and press* **OK** *to perform the compression.*

Optimising the file size of an image

One aspect you should be aware of when creating a PowerPoint presentation that includes a range of images is that the overall file size can quickly become huge. A very useful feature of PowerPoint 2002 and later versions is that you can compress images and remove unneeded data (Figure 182). For example, it will delete cropped areas of pictures from the file.

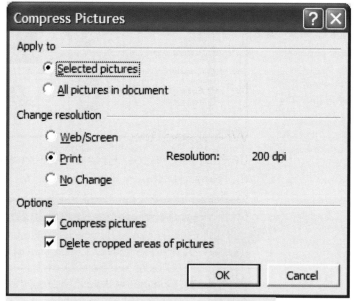

Figure 182 Dialogue box to compress image files

Adding more features

Inserting lines and simple shapes

There are many ways to improve a PowerPoint presentation. You can add lines and shapes, fill the shapes with colour, outline them and make them look three-dimensional. The **Autoshapes** button on the *Drawing* toolbar provides a menu of types of shape, each type having its own sub-menu showing all the shapes available. There are over 150 different shapes to choose from!

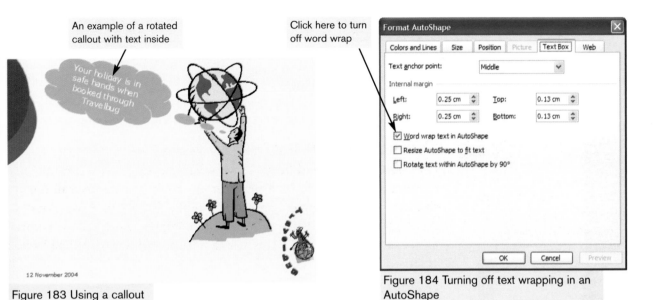

An example of a rotated callout with text inside

Click here to turn off word wrap

Figure 183 Using a callout

Figure 184 Turning off text wrapping in an AutoShape

Callouts are designed to hold text within the shape. They can be simple boxes with lines pointing from them or 'word and thought' balloons (Figure 183). As with other text boxes, you can resize a callout, and rotate and format its text.

Wrapping text

By default, text inside a shape is wrapped so that it does not spill over the border. If you need to turn this setting off, double-click the shape to display the *Format AutoShape* dialogue, and untick the **Word wrap text in AutoShape** option in the *Text Box* tab (see Figure 184).

Inserting WordArt

As with other Microsoft Office programs, such as Word and Excel, you can use the *WordArt* tool to create a logo, or to make text more interesting. One very useful feature is that a design you make in one Office application can be used in any of them. Therefore, if you have used WordArt in Word to create a logo, for example, you could use the same logo in a PowerPoint presentation.

Think it over ...

Look at the two sample slides in Figure 185. One of these has WordArt for the text, and the other does not. Which do you think looks more appealing?

WordArt used for text

Normal text

Figure 185 A comparison of WordArt and normal text

1 Build a new slide which forms part of the presentation planned in Activity 1. Include lines or shapes.
○ Click on **New Slide**.
○ Choose a *Blank* or *Title Only* slide layout.
○ If the drawing toolbar is not visible, select **View**, **Toolbars**, **Drawing**.
○ Click on **AutoShapes** on the *Drawing* toolbar and choose a shape.
○ Drag out the shape on the slide.
○ Use the formatting icons on the toolbar to change the colour, border, shadow style and 3-D style until you are happy with the result.

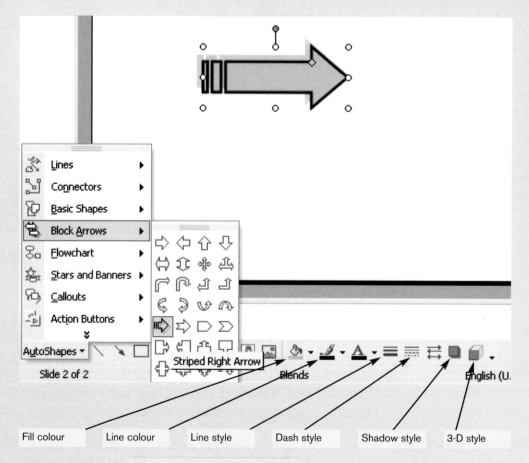

Figure 186 The Drawing toolbar

2 Build a second slide which includes WordArt.
○ Click on **New Slide**.
○ Click on the **WordArt** button on the *Drawing* toolbar. The *WordArt Gallery* dialogue appears.

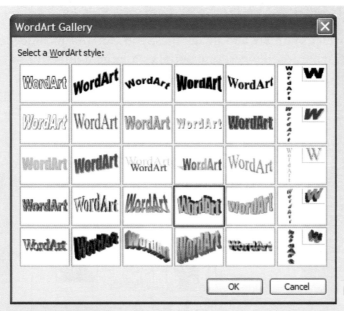

Figure 187 WordArt styles

○ Click on a style and then click **OK**. The *Edit WordArt Text* dialogue appears.

 (a)

 (b)

Figure 188 (a) Before and
(b) after setting the WordArt text

○ Type your text and then press **OK**.
○ Use the handles to move, resize and rotate the WordArt as necessary.
    Save your work.

Open your 'Presentation software' file. Create a new bold
heading '**PS Activity 5**' and write a short paragraph describing
the skills you have demonstrated in this activity when using
simple lines, shapes and WordArt in a PowerPoint presentation.
Save the file.

Inserting a video file

As well as clip art and image files, you can also include video files in a presentation. PowerPoint supplies a large number of media clips that you can use to enhance a presentation. For example, Thomas Tripp has decided to use a media clip of a cruise liner to illustrate the slide which gives details of the Travelbug Cruise Club (Figure 189).

(a)

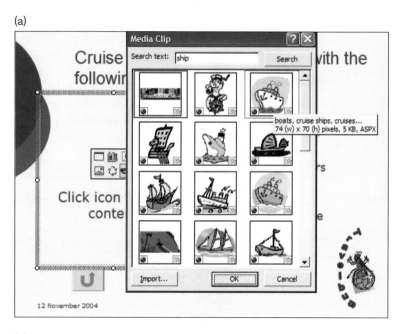

(b)

Figure 189 (a) Inserting a media clip, and (b) the completed slide with the clip inserted

Inserting sounds

Sound can enhance a presentation when used carefully. You can use one of the sound clips provided with PowerPoint, record your own sounds, play sounds off a CD to accompany your presentation, or download sounds from the Internet.

You can add sound effects to your animations. If you wish to, you can even record your own commentary. You cannot, however, use a pre-recorded commentary and another form of recorded sound at the same time.

The final enhancement Thomas Tripp makes to his slide for the Cruise Club presentation is to insert sound. He has chosen 'Sailing' sung by by Rod Stewart. On searching the Internet he finds a free midi (sound) file which he can save to his computer and then insert into the presentation.

Go out and try!

Build up a new slide which forms part of the presentation planned in Activity 1. Include a sound clip and a video clip using the following steps:

○ From the menu select **Insert**, **Movies and Sounds**, **Sound From File**.

○ Navigate to the sound file you want to add, select it and press **OK**.

○ You will be asked whether you want the sound to play when the slide loads or when the user clicks the sound icon. Make your choice.

○ Test your slide show to make sure that the sound plays as you expected.

○ From the menu select **Insert**, **Movies and Sounds**, **Movie from Clip Organiser**.

○ Click one of the movies that has appeared in the *Clip Art* task pane to insert it into your slide.

○ Test that the movie plays when you run your slide show.

○ Save your work.

Open your 'Presentation software' file. Create a new bold heading '**PS Activity 6**' and write a short paragraph describing the skills you have demonstrated in this activity when using simple video and sounds in a PowerPoint presentation.
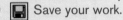 Save the file.

Navigation between slides

The default navigation route of a PowerPoint presentation is linear. However, the Action Settings feature will allow you to link to another slide further on in your presentation, to another PowerPoint presentation, to a file, or even to a website (Figure 190). You can add settings to text or to an object in your presentation.

Figure 190 Dialogue box for action settings

The **AutoShapes** button on the *Drawing* toolbar also includes a number of action buttons which you can include on slides. This feature can be useful when you wish to move to another part of your presentation, or even to another file.

Thomas Tripp has built a slide which gives examples of what Travelbug can offer their customers (Figure 191). He has also used the action settings facility to link to slides in a different part of the presentation (Figure 192).

By clicking here, the presentation moves out of sequence to show the Cruise Club slide.

Figure 191 Slide with links to different parts of the presentation

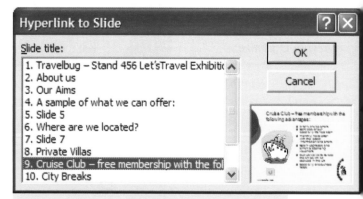

Figure 192 Adding a hyperlink from slide 4 to slide 9

Finally, Thomas has included an action button which he has set to return to the last slide viewed.

Go out and try!

Use the Action Settings feature of PowerPoint to assist in the navigation between slides in your presentation.
- Use the *Drawing* toolbar to insert an AutoShape on the slide you want to link from.
- Right-click the AutoShape and choose **Action Settings** from the menu that appears.
- Select the **Hyperlink to** option and choose which slide you want to link to. Choose **Slide** to link to a particular slide, or **First Slide** to jump back to the beginning of the presentation.
- Test your slide show to make sure that the navigation works as expected.
- 💾 Save your work.

Open your 'Presentation software' file. Create a new bold heading '**PS Activity 7**' and write a short paragraph describing the skills you have demonstrated in this activity when using actions settings in a PowerPoint presentation.
💾 Save the file.

Using animation

PowerPoint has a clever feature that will allow you to make words and pictures on your slides appear and disappear when you want. This is called *animation*. Instead of being visible immediately when the slide appears, the object that you animate – text, a picture, or a piece of clip art for example – comes in afterwards, appearing in a special way.

Animation controls how an object is brought on to the slide. An object can appear automatically, or wait until the user clicks the mouse button before appearing. If you have more than one animated object on a slide you can control the order in which they appear. The object will always end up where you put it when you were designing the slide.

The simplest way to animate your presentation is to use one of the animation schemes that PowerPoint provides. You have a choice from such things as *Appear and Dim* (Figure 193), *Dissolve In*, and *Spin*. PowerPoint lets you preview how the animation of your text and objects will appear for one slide or for the whole presentation.

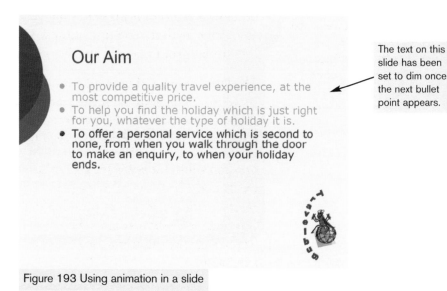

The text on this slide has been set to dim once the next bullet point appears.

Figure 193 Using animation in a slide

TiP

You will need to experiment to find out how these animations appear on the screen.

For the more adventurous, there is the *Custom Animation* option, which provides more control of your animations. You can use a lot more animation effects, pick the sound that goes with each animation, choose the order in which animations take place, and set the amount of time to wait between animations. You can decide what happens to an object once it appears, such as making it disappear or change colour.

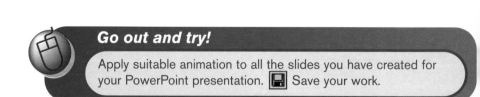

Go out and try!

Apply suitable animation to all the slides you have created for your PowerPoint presentation. Save your work.

Open your 'Presentation software' file. Create a new bold heading '**PS Activity 8**' and write a short paragraph describing the skills you have demonstrated in this activity when using animation in a PowerPoint presentation. Save the file.

Think it over ...

You will have seen examples of transitions all the time, without realising it. For example, a transition happens when you are watching the television and the scene changes from one shot to another.

Creating slide transitions

When you are showing a PowerPoint presentation and move from one slide to the next, this is referred to as *slide transition*. When you design a PowerPoint presentation, each slide has a transition associated with it. The transition will tell PowerPoint how to change the display from one slide to the next.

The latest version of PowerPoint offers over 50 different transition styles from which to choose – examples are *cut*, *dissolve* and *wipe right*. If you prefer, you can choose a random transition, so that a different style and direction will be used each time you move on to a new slide.

You can adjust the speed for slide transitions to be slow, medium or fast. Furthermore, you can make the transitions occur on the click of a mouse or automatically after a set period of time. You can even set up a presentation to show continuously until the **Esc** key is pressed. Thomas Tripp could use this feature for the slide show he wants to show at a travel exhibition.

Go out and try!

Apply suitable slide transitions to all the slides you have created for your PowerPoint presentation. 🖫 Save your work.

Open your 'Presentation software' file. Create a new bold heading '**PS Activity 9**' and write a short paragraph describing the skills you have demonstrated in this activity when applying slide transitions to a PowerPoint presentation. 🖫 Save the file.

TiP

You have learned the skills necessary to adjust the timings for a PowerPoint presentation. However, be careful when adding timings to a presentation. There is nothing worse than sitting watching a slide show where the timings are too fast or too slow.

Rehearsing and checking timings of a slideshow

Before you give a PowerPoint presentation, it is important to rehearse and check the timings carefully. Consider these points:

- Is the timing correct between objects appearing on a slide?
- Are the transition timings for slides correct?

TiP

*It is possible to blank the screen when running a presentation. This is useful if you want to catch the audience's attention. By pressing **B** on the keyboard the screen will turn black, and on pressing **W** the screen will turn white. You just press these keys again to return to the presentation.*

- If you have set timings for objects or slide transitions to appear automatically, rather than on the click of a mouse, have you allowed sufficient time to say everything you want to at a reasonable pace?

- Will the audience have time to read text before the next bullet point or object appears?

Producing speaker notes and handouts

Speaker notes

PowerPoint has a facility called *speaker notes*, which allows you to include notes with a slide. This feature gives a text display for each slide. You can add anything you want in these notes (Figure 194). For example, Thomas Tripp of Travelbug can use this facility to give

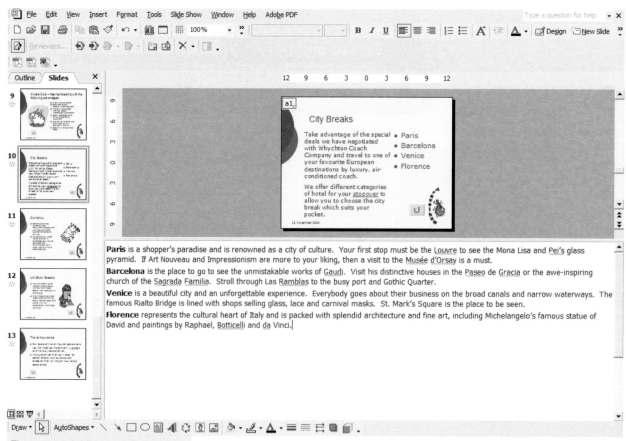

Figure 194 Adding speaker notes

extra details on the different cities shown on the City Breaks slide of his presentation. The slide, together with the notes, can be printed out to give to prospective customers.

Handouts

Another feature of PowerPoint is that you can print a presentation as a *handout*. You have the option of choosing how many slides per page to print, up to a maximum of nine. If you choose three slides per page, as shown in Figure 195, PowerPoint automatically adds lines to the right-hand side of each slide so that the audience can write their own notes during the presentation.

<table>
<tr><td valign="top">

✔ TiP

PowerPoint is a very versatile package, and not all of its features have been discussed in this chapter. You should experiment and learn to use even more of its features.

✔ TiP

It can be tempting to incorporate many different features within a presentation to show off your newly acquired skills. Remember that doing so can distract from the actual content of the presentation!

</td><td valign="top">

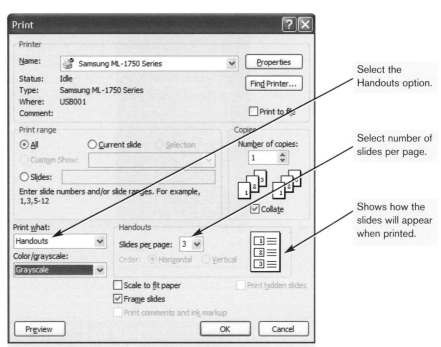

Select the Handouts option.

Select number of slides per page.

Shows how the slides will appear when printed.

Figure 195 Options to choose from when printing handouts

</td></tr>
</table>

Go out and try!

Use the skills you have learned to produce Speaker Notes and Handouts to accompany your presentation. 💾 Save your work.

Open your 'Presentation software' file. Create a new bold heading '**PS Activity 10**' and write a short paragraph describing the skills you have demonstrated in this activity when producing Speaker's Notes and Handouts. 💾 Save the file.

Pack and Go

The travel exhibition where Travelbug have booked a stand is providing computers for exibitors. However, Thomas Tripp is uncertain whether PowerPoint will be installed on the machines.

Rather than take the risk that PowerPoint will not be available, Thomas decides to use the *Pack and Go* feature in PowerPoint. By choosing the option to include the PowerPoint Viewer (Figure 196), Thomas will be able to run the presentation in PowerPoint format even if the computer does not have the program installed.

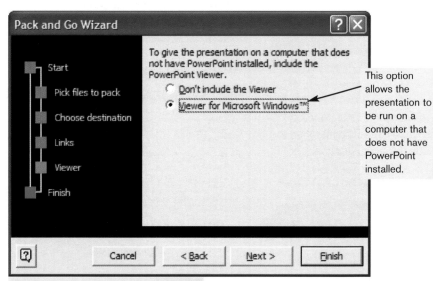

Figure 196 The Pack and Go Wizard

Go out and try!

Use the Pack and Go feature so that your presentation can run on any computer, irrespective or whether it has the software installed on it. Save your work.

TiP

PowerPoint is a very versatile package, and not all of its features have been discussed in this chapter. You should experiment and learn to use even more of its features.

Open your 'Presentation software' file. Create a new bold heading '**PS Activity 11**' and write a short paragraph describing the skills you have demonstrated in this activity. Save the file.

Artwork and imaging software

With the power of the modern computer and its ability to select, capture or modify images, you don't have to be an artist to create interesting, imaginative and effective artwork. This book contains a variety of images and artwork: some are screen prints of the computer, some are photographs and some are drawings; some are in black and white and others are in colour. They are all intended to make the book more interesting to read and to help you understand the topics you are studying.

Sometimes a graphical representation can stand alone without any words at all, and at other times the image makes the words much easier to understand, or vice versa. For example, it would be very difficult to describe charts and graphs just in words.

LEARNING OUTCOMES

You need to learn about
- ✓ selecting and capturing images
- ✓ modifying images
- ✓ choosing appropriate resolutions and file formats
- ✓ optimising file sizes and formats for print and digital applications
- ✓ creating simple animations.

Selecting and capturing images

Skills check ▶▶

See page 433 for information about downloading images from the Internet.

There are a variety of methods to select and capture images that can then be used to improve the presentation of your e-portfolios. You can select images that are already prepared (such as clip art), create your own using drawing tools, or acquire images electronically by scanning them or downloading photos from a digital camera.

Using clip art and library images

Images can be imported into your documents from libraries on CD-ROM, the Internet, or packaged with the software. Word contains its own selection of images, but far more are available from other sources. Many of these clip art libraries are free.

You can enter a topic in the search field and the computer will find relevant pictures available in the library. A search for 'Australia' produced many results. The search was then refined to show only images first in clip art format and then in photo format. Two images of Sydney Opera House were selected, and copied and pasted into the text for this chapter (Figure 197).

Figure 197 Sydney Opera House in clip art format, and in photo format

Go out and try!

Find two images (one from clip art and one from a photo library) to represent a European country of your choice.

- Open a new blank document in Word.
- From the menu, select **Insert**, **Picture**, **Clip Art**. The *Insert Clip Art* task pane appears.
- In the search field, key in the name of your chosen European country (Figure 198).
- Select one suitable image and insert it into your document.
- Search for a photo of your chosen country, from a photo CD or the Internet. Insert the photo using **Insert**, **Picture**, **From File**.
- 💾 Save the document containing the images as 'Graphic images 1' in your 'Artwork and imaging software' sub-folder.

Figure 198 Clip art search

Start a file called 'Artwork and imaging software'. Create a bold heading '**AIS Activity 1**' and write a short paragraph describing the methods you used to capture these images. Save this file in your 'Artwork and imaging software' sub-folder.

Using a scanner

Figure 199 A scanner

A *scanner* allows you to add pictures from other sources – such as a magazine, book or photograph – into your documents (Figure 199). The scanner reads the information and converts it into digital format.

The document is placed inside the scanner. Once the image has been scanned, it can be stored in the computer and used intact or edited as required. The scanned image is stored in picture format, even if it is text – unless text recognition software is available, in which case the text is stored as data that can be edited using a word processor.

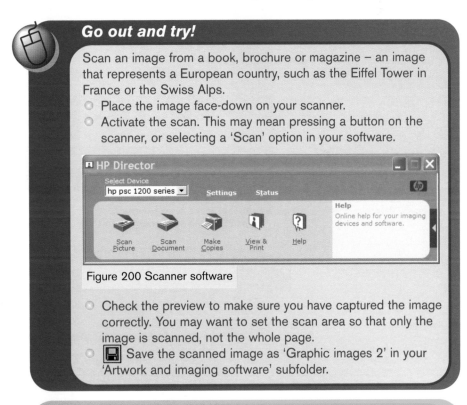

Go out and try!

Scan an image from a book, brochure or magazine – an image that represents a European country, such as the Eiffel Tower in France or the Swiss Alps.
- Place the image face-down on your scanner.
- Activate the scan. This may mean pressing a button on the scanner, or selecting a 'Scan' option in your software.

Figure 200 Scanner software

- Check the preview to make sure you have captured the image correctly. You may want to set the scan area so that only the image is scanned, not the whole page.
- Save the scanned image as 'Graphic images 2' in your 'Artwork and imaging software' subfolder.

Open your file called 'Artwork and imaging software'. Create a new bold heading called '**AIS Activity 2**' and write a short paragraph describing how you scanned the image and viewed it on screen. Save the file.

Using a digital microscope

A digital microscope includes a built-in camera that makes it possible to view specimens on a TV or a computer. Magnified images can be saved on to the computer, together with live video or time-lapsed film of objects such as insects or plant life. It is then possible to manipulate these images by adding text or special effects, or to incorporate them into another document.

Go out and try!

If you have access to a digital microscope (Figure 201), select an item, such as a leaf or flower, to study under the microscope. Transfer the image to the computer. Write a short description of the detail, not visible to the naked eye, that you can observe through the microscope. Add the image to your description and label the different parts of the image.

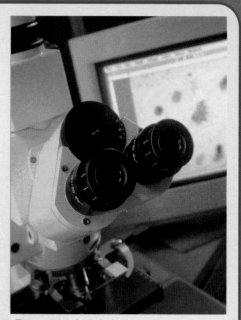

Figure 201 A digital microscope

Open your file called 'Artwork and imaging software'. Create a new bold heading '**AIS Activity 3**' and write a short paragraph describing what you have learned when using a digital microscope. Save the file.

Using a digital camera and downloading images

Digital cameras look very similar to traditional cameras (Figure 202), but most of them allow you to view the image on a small liquid-crystal display (LCD) screen built into the camera. As soon as you take a picture, you can view it on the screen and decide whether to

Figure 202 A digital camera

keep it or to retake the shot. With a traditional camera the picture is recorded on film, so you have no idea how good or bad the photograph is until the film has been processed.

With a digital camera, light intensities are converted into a digital form that can be stored on a memory card or stick. The images can then be downloaded into the computer, viewed on screen, saved and imported into a document or printed on special photographic-quality paper. The digital images can also be taken to photographic shops and printed in the same size formats as standard photographs taken on film.

Go out and try!

1 Use a digital camera to take a picture of a friend, and ask your friend to take a picture of you.
   ○ Make sure you are happy with the pictures. Delete them and retake them if necessary.
   ○ Transfer the images from the digital camera to your computer (following your manufacturer's instructions). The software will assign numbers to each shot, e.g. Img_0822.
2 🖫 Save each image in your 'Artwork and imaging' subfolder.
3 Open a new document and insert both photos into the document.
4 🖫 Save the document as 'Graphic images 4' in your 'Artwork and imaging' subfolder.

Open your file called 'Artwork and imaging software'. Create a new bold heading '**AIS Activity 4**' and write a short paragraph describing how you captured and downloaded the images. 🖫 Save the file.

TiP

When grouping images, if you click on an image to highlight it and then click on another image, you lose the first highlight. In order to group two or more images, click on the first image, hold down the **Shift** key (the up arrow under the **Caps Lock**), click on each other image in turn, then select **Group** from the Drawing toolbar.

Modifying images

Once an image has been captured electronically, it is possible to modify the image to suit your purpose exactly.

Grouping and ungrouping

Several different images can be combined to make a new image. The logo designed for Travelbug (Figure 203) was created using WordArt for the text, combined with two clip art images: the world plus an insect sitting on top!

Once the two images were positioned correctly, they were grouped together using the *Drawing* toolbar (Figure 187). The WordArt was resized, rotated to fit around the image, and the colour of the letters changed to blend in. All three elements of the logo were then grouped together.

When the images have been grouped in this way they can be manipulated as one image. If you then wish to change part of the image, you can click on the image and this time select **Draw**, **Ungroup** from the *Drawing* toolbar. After the necessary changes have been made, the individual images can be regrouped to make one image. It is much easier to work with a grouped image because all the elements move together and can be resized in proportion.

Figure 203 WordArt and clip art images are highlighted and grouped to make the logo

Go out and try!

Using clip art and WordArt, combine three separate components to create a logo for a travel company specialising in holidays to your chosen European country.

- Open a new document.
- Use WordArt to create one component for a logo for the travel company.
- Insert two clip art images that suit the name of the travel company.
- Position the three components into a single logo image.
- Group the three images into one logo: click on one, and holding down the **Shift** key, click on the other two. Then right-click on one of the images and select **Group**.
- Save the logo file as 'Graphic images 5' in your 'Artwork and imaging software' subfolder.

Open your file called 'Artwork and imaging software'. Create a new bold heading '**AIS Activity 5**' and write a short paragraph describing how you grouped the images to create your logo. Save the file.

✓ **TiP**

Images can be reduced or enlarged by dragging the 'handles' at their corners.

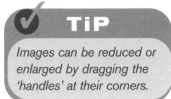

Cutting, pasting, cropping, trimming and resizing images

Sometimes you find that what you require is part of a bigger picture. For example, the Sydney Opera House scene shown in Figure 197 (page 384) included a lot of water and sky. If you wanted only the actual opera house, you could cut out that section by using the ⊞ crop (trim) tool to remove the unwanted sections (Figure 204).

Figure 204 Sydney Opera House cropped and resized

Another method of cropping an image is to use the mask tools (▢ ○ ◇) that are typically available in graphics software.

- The first mask enables you to draw a rectangular shape around the area you wish to keep.
- The second mask enables you to draw a circle around the area you wish to keep.
- The third mask enables you to draw a freehand shape around the area you wish to keep.

Once the area to be kept has been identified, the image can be cropped to the mask.

To obtain the image of these mask tools, a screen print was made showing the toolbars in Corel Photo-Paint (Figure 205). The rectangular mask was used to select the mask icons and, once the image was 'cropped to mask', the rest of the screen print was removed leaving just the three mask tools.

Figure 205 Corel Photo-Paint toolbars

Go out and try!

Choose two images from those you have already saved. Copy each of the images into one new file. Crop or trim one image, and resize the second image.

○ Open a new document.

○ Insert the two images you have chosen.

○ Crop one of the images: select the image and clip on the crop tool 🔲, then drag the edges to cut off the part of the image you want to lose.

○ Resize the other image:

  ● Select the image and drag the corner handles of the image until it is the size that you want.

  ● If you want to be more precise, right-click the image and choose **Format Picture**. In the dialogue box, on the *Size* tab, enter the dimensions for *either* the **Height** or **Width**, tick **Lock aspect ratio** and **Relative to original picture size**, and click **OK**.

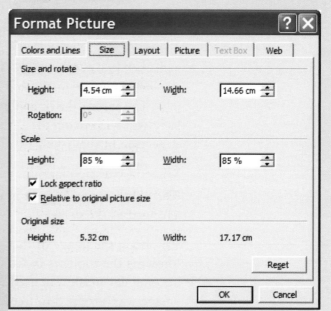

Figure 206 Resizing a picture

💾 Save your document as 'Graphic images 6' in your 'Artwork and imaging software' subfolder.

Open your file called 'Artwork and imaging software'. Create a new bold heading '**AIS Activity 6**' and write a short paragraph describing how you copied and edited the images. 💾 Save the file.

Aligning, rotating, and flipping images

Aligning an image

The **Align or Distribute** options on the *Drawing* toolbar allow you to place an image in a particular position on the page (Figure 207).

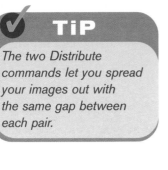

TiP

The two Distribute commands let you spread your images out with the same gap between each pair.

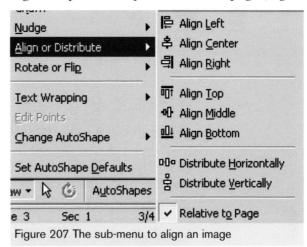

Figure 207 The sub-menu to align an image

This facility can be very useful if, for example, you wish to position the image exactly in the middle of the page, which is quite difficult just by dragging the image into position. Click on the image, select **Relative to Page** and then **Align Middle** – the image will be placed in the centre of the page.

When drawing a diagram, you may wish to draw a series of boxes the same size and then arrange them to line up evenly on the page. It can be quite difficult to do this just by dragging the boxes into position (Figure 208). Instead, select the boxes and choose **Draw, Align or Distribute, Align Left** from the *Drawing* toolbar.

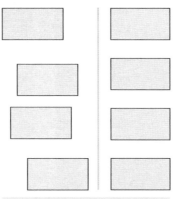

Figure 208 Boxes unaligned, and then aligned and spaced evenly

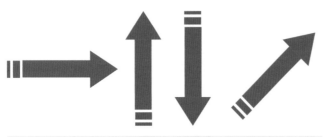

Figure 209 The AutoShape arrow rotated in various directions

Rotating an image

An image can be rotated to the left, to the right or freely. The *AutoShape arrow* points to the right, but suppose you need an arrow pointing upwards. Select the arrow and rotate left, which changes the direction to point up. If you select free rotate, then the arrow can be angled to any direction you choose (Figure 209).

Flipping an image

If you flip an image, you reverse the direction in which the image is pointing. For example, suppose you need a picture of a horse facing to the right. You have found a good picture but the horse is pointing to the left. You can use the picture and flip it to the right (Figure 210) using **Draw, Rotate or Flip, Flip Horizontal**.

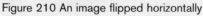

Figure 210 An image flipped horizontally

You can also flip an image vertically so it turns upside down (Figure 211).

Figure 211 An image flipped vertically

Go out and try!

1 Open the file called 'Graphic images 5'; it should contain your logo for a travel company specialising in holidays in your chosen European country.

2 Copy the image and paste *one* copy into a new file. Insert a page break and paste *four* more copies on to the second page. The steps are as follows.

　○ Copy the logo into the clipboard.
　○ Close the file called 'Graphic images 5'.
　○ Create a new document and paste the logo.
　○ Select **Insert**, **Break** and select **Page break**.

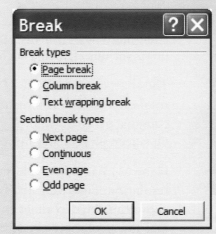

Figure 212
Inserting a page break

　○ Paste the logo four times on to page 2.

3 Align the logo on page 1 so that it is centred on the page, as follows.
　○ Use the **Draw**, **Align or Distribute** menu on the *Drawing* toolbar. You may need to turn on **Relative to Page**.

4 On page 2, rotate the first logo to the left; rotate the second logo to the right; rotate the third logo using the free rotation tool; and flip the fourth logo.
　○ Use the **Draw**, **Rotate or Flip** menu on the *Drawing* toolbar.

5 On page 2, align the four logos so they are vertically distributed and in the centre of the page, as follows.
　○ Select all four logos.
　○ Use the **Draw**, **Align or Distribute** menu on the *Drawing* toolbar.

6 Save the file as 'Graphic images 7' in your 'Artwork and imaging software' subfolder.

Open your file called 'Artwork and imaging software'. Create a new bold heading '**AIS Activity 7**' and write a short paragraph describing the skills you have learnt. Save the file.

Choosing appropriate image resolutions and file formats

Optimising image resolution for print and digital publications

There are two basic types of images on a computer:

- bitmaps
- vectors.

Bitmaps

A *bitmap* image is made up of dots, whereas a *vector* image is made up of various elements such as lines, curves, circles and squares.

The sharpness or clarity of a bitmap image is determined by its *resolution*, which is measured by the number of *pixels* (or dots) it contains per inch (dpi). A general 'rule of thumb' is to use 72dpi for on-screen images and up to 300 or 600dpi for printed images.

Figure 213(a) shows a bitmap image of a bird with a clear resolution. Figure 213(b) shows the same image increased to approximately 3.5 times the original size, and you can see clearly that the resolution has deteriorated. Figure 213(c) shows an enlarged section of the bird's beak. Notice that the edge of the beak is now looking very ragged and uneven. Figure 213(d) shows the same enlargement including the gridlines. The individual pixels are clearly visible, which is very useful if you wish to edit a picture.

TiP

As a bitmap image is enlarged, the quality becomes poorer. There will be a point beyond which the quality is unacceptable for all normal uses.

TiP

If you want to create an image as a bitmap then it is important to design it at the size it should be printed.

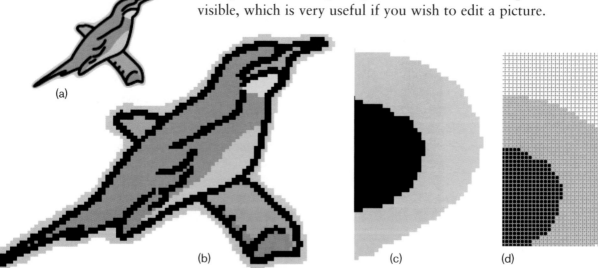

Figure 213 (a) Bitmap image of a bird. (b) The same image enlarged about 3.5 times. (c) An enlarged section of the beak. (d) An enlarged section of the beak showing the individual pixels and gridlines

Vector graphics

In vector graphics, objects are treated as collections of lines rather than patterns of individual dots. This makes it easier to enlarge the image without reducing its sharpness or quality (Figure 214). However, many people believe that bitmap images provide more subtlety in shading and texture.

Figure 214 A vector image: notice that the enlargement retains the quality

Go out and try!

1 Choose a vector/clip art image, such as the one shown in Figure 214, and insert it into a new Word File.
2 Copy the image in Word, open Paint and paste in the copied image. (This turns the vector image into a bitmap image.)
3 Select **View**, **Zoom**, **Large Size** from the menu in Paint.
4 Select **View**, **Zoom**, **Show Grid**. You will now see the individual pixels.
5 Use the Select tool to select just the image, then copy it to the clipboard.
6 Paste the bitmap into the Word file under the vector image.
7 Enlarge each of the images and compare the clarity. You should find that curved and diagonal lines are jagged in the enlarged bitmap image and smooth in the enlarged vector image.
8 Save the Word file as 'Graphical images 8' in your 'Artwork and imaging software' subfolder.

TiP

You can find the Paint *program by clicking on the Windows* **Start** *menu, and selecting* **Programs**, **Accessories**, **Paint**.

Open your file called 'Artwork and imaging software'. Create a new bold heading '**AIS Activity 8**' and write a short paragraph describing the quality of the four resized images. What conclusions can you draw from this? Save the file.

Optimising file size

Graphical images, especially photographs downloaded from a digital camera, are often very large. For example, a camera with 3 million pixels (3 megapixels) produces images of file size up to 1.5 MB, and a 5-megapixel camera may produce images more than 2 MB in size. At those sizes it can be very slow, or sometimes impossible, to download a photograph via the Internet. Therefore, it is important to think about the best way to save the file so that the file size is as small as possible without affecting the quality of the image too much.

Figure 215 The resize dialogue box in Microsoft Photo Editor

The Microsoft Windows XP operating system includes Microsoft Photo Editor software, which can be used to resize an image. Double-click on your photograph, which will open in Microsoft Photo Editor. Select **Image**, **Resize** and change the 'units' from centimetres to pixels in the dialogue box (Figure 215). Reduce the size to 50 per cent of the original.

This *physically reduces the size of the picture*, so it appears smaller on screen. However, the quality looks just about as good, even though the file size is dramatically reduced. This will will be much quicker to send.

Another way of reducing the size of the image file is to *compress* it. Select **File**, **Save as** and then click on the **More>>** button in the dialogue box (Figure 216). Reduce the scale for the quality factor at the botton of the box. A JPEG file becomes much smaller, but the trade-off is a noticeable reduction in quality.

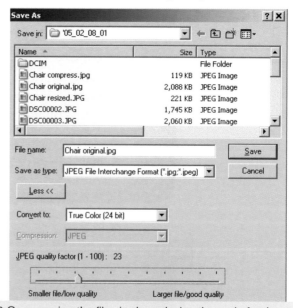

Figure 216 Compressing the file size by reducing the scale for the quality factor

Look at the photographs of a kitchen table and chair taken on a 5-megapixel digital camera (Figure 217). Note the differences in the quality of the pictures depending on the method of reducing the file size.

The photograph resized. The quality is the same and the file size is now 566 KB.

Photograph in the original size downloaded from a 5 megapixel camera. The file size is 2088 KB.

The photograph compressed. The quality has degraded – the file size is 127 KB.

Figure 217 Comparison of three versions of the same image

Go out and try!

1 Open the file containing the photograph you took of your friend. Resize it and save it again with 'resized' included in the filename.
2 Open the original photograph again. This time compress the file size and save it again with 'compressed' included in the filename.

Open your file called 'Artwork and imaging software'. Create a new bold heading '**AIS Activity 9**' and write a short paragraph comparing the differences in file size and quality of the saved images. Save the file.

Optimising file formats for print and digital publications

The screen shots for this book were saved in TIFF format, as it supports 16.7 million colours. TIFF graphics are very flexible. They can be be any resolution, and can be greyscale or full colour. It is the preferred format for desktop publishing as it produces excellent printing results. Figure 218 shows other file formats that might be chosen in certain circumstances.

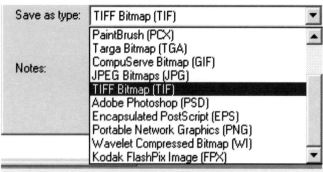

Figure 218 File formats available in this graphics software

Name ▲	Size	Type
Sydney Opera House 2.jpg	20 KB	JPEG Image
Sydney Opera House 2.tif	138 KB	Corel PHOTO-PAINT 7.0 Image
Sydney Opera House.bmp	1,696 KB	Bitmap Image

Figure 219 File size comparison

Windows has traditionally used bitmap images (with the file extension '.bmp') for graphics. The colour quality is as good as TIFF files, but BMP files are very large in size, and – unlike TIFF files – they cannot be compressed. The picture of Sydney Opera House saved as a bitmap file is 1696 KB, whereas the same image saved in TIFF format was only 138 KB (Figure 219).

As the name suggests, the format devised by the Joint Photographic Experts Group (*JPEG*, pronounced J-peg) is the most suitable format for scanned photographs – full-colour photographs or greyscale images with large variations in the colour. The format is not so effective for text, cartoons or black and white line drawings.

The JPEG format uses the full 16.7 million colours. Images taken with a digital camera are saved as JPEG files (with the '.jpg' extension in Microsoft applications). Image files saved in the JPEG format are considerably compressed. The Sydney Opera House saved as a JPEG file was only 20 KB.

The Graphics Interchange format (*GIF*, pronounced Jif) supports only 256 colours, which is a huge difference from the JPEG format. However, GIF is significantly better for images with just a few distinct colours, where the image has sharp contrasts – black next to white, or cartoons and animations. The format compresses images even more than the JPEG format.

Go out and try!

Open the file 'Graphic images 1' that you created earlier and change both images to greyscale. Resave the file as 'Graphic images 10'.

Open your file called 'Artwork and imaging software'. Create a new bold heading '**AIS Activity 10**' and write a short paragraph describing the effect greyscale has had on both images, and comparing the sizes of the two files 'Graphic images 1' and 'Graphic images 10'. Save the file.

Go out and try!

Choose any one of the images you have created in this chapter. Save it in all the following file formats so that you can compare the overall file sizes: bitmap, TIFF, JPEG and GIF.

Open your file called 'Artwork and imaging software'. Create a new bold heading '**AIS Activity 11**' and record the results of saving an image file in four different formats. Save the file.

Creating animations

Jargon buster

Animation creates an illusion of movement by displaying a series of progressively changing images in quick succession.

In its simplest form, animation can be used to draw attention to something on the screen. A more complicated animation might be used to illustrate a complex process, such as the workings of the human body.

A great many of the websites that you will have investigated included some form of animation. It might have been something very simple, such as blinking text, or rather more elaborate such as an object moving across the screen. The rollover buttons that often provide the links from one page to another are animated – as you point or click on the button it changes in appearance.

You will find a wide selection of animated clip art freely available on the Internet, in the same way as the standard clip art images you are familiar with. It is always a very sensible idea to keep a record of the sources of any images and animations you use, so that you can acknowledge your sources in your work.

There are several specialist animation software packages available, but you do not have to use this software if you only need to create a very simple animation. An animated image is composed of a number of frames, where each frame contains an image that has been slightly manipulated to make it different from the previous image. When you run the frames in quick succession you get the impression that the image is moving.

To illustrate this we have used PowerPoint to create an animation that consists of a series of slides (Figure 220). However, PowerPoint is not specifically designed to produce animated images and the timing is not so effective. The images in our example change at one-second intervals, whereas professional animations run at 24 frames (or more) per second.

Shape, position, size and colour

Animation software offers a selection of predefined shapes together with a toolbox to help you create your own shapes and effects.

If you look closely at Figure 220 you will see the image is positioned in an identical position on each slide – the only element that moves is the tail. When the animation is viewed, the dog will appear to be sitting in the same place.

If an animation is representing a moving car, for instance, each frame will show the image of the car nudged slightly further across each frame. Specialist animation software offers a feature called 'tweening'. For example, in a sequence of ten frames the designer creates the first and last frames and the animation software will automatically fill in the frames in between.

The use of colour can make the difference between a successful or unsuccessful image. Animations tend to be based on cartoon-type graphics with limited colours, and this makes the components of the image clearer to see. Using too many colours may detract from the animated effect.

User control

Be careful you don't get too carried away with animating objects. Using large animations, or too many of them, can be irritating to the user and can detract from the information contained on the page. If your animation is looped to run continually, you could consider adding an option to enable the user to turn it off.

? Think it over ...

The simple animations you create will be two-dimensional – drawn in height and width only. Professional animators use three dimensions – in addition to height and width they also specify the depth of the image.

Step 1: A clip art image is inserted into PowerPoint.

Step 2: The image is copied into a second slide and ungrouped.

Step 2: The dog's tail is selected.

Step 4: The Free Rotate tool is used to drag the end of the tail down slightly.

Step 5: The new image is copied and pasted into a new slide and the tail dragged down a little more.

Step 6: This is repeated until the tail is level with the table.

:01   1

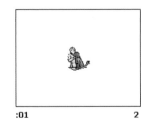

:01   2

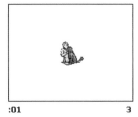

:01   3

:01   4

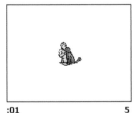

:01   5

:01   6

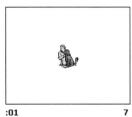

:01   7

Step 7: Further slides can be made by pasting copies of the images in reverse order to return the tail to the original position. You can set up a slide show to run in a continuous loop or you can copy and paste the complete sequence to run for a limited time. Set the shortest possible timings and run the presentation. Hey Presto – simple animation!

Figure 220 The construction of a simple animation in PowerPoint

Publishing for use in websites or as standalone animations

The GIF format was originally designed for the fast transfer of data over modems and has always been the most popular format for storing standalone animated files. The 256 colours available make the format ideal for images such as logos, cartoons and animations. A large number of animations published on the Internet are in GIF format. However, the format is protected by copyright, and in some cases royalties can be payable for the use of GIF files. In addition, GIF files are not viewable in all browsers.

More recently the Portable Network Graphics format (*PNG*, pronounced 'ping') was created to avoid the royalties. PNG offers better compression than GIF and supports millions of colours. It is ideal for websites but is not well suited to printed graphics, and it does not support animation.

An alternative format for published animations on web pages is *Macromedia Flash* (or *Shockwave*). Download times are very fast. As it is vector based, it has the advantage that images can be resized without affecting the image quality

> ✓ **TiP**
>
> *To embed your animation in a web page you could save it from PowerPoint as a series of images (one for each slide) and then use Microsoft Movie Maker to convert the images into a movie. You will learn how to use Microsoft Movie Maker in the next chapter (see page 409).*

Go out and try!

Create your own animation in PowerPoint by following the steps in Figure 220.

Open your file called 'Artwork and imaging software'. Create a new bold heading '**AIS Activity 12**' and write a short paragraph describing how you created an animation in PowerPoint.
Save the file.

Digital sound and video

Skills check ▶▶

The website authoring and presentation skills chapters have information on how to add sound to websites or presentations.

In the early days of the World Wide Web, websites consisted of text, but little else. DVDs and CD–ROMs were unheard of, and 40 MB of storage capacity was exceptional. Newer technologies have led to audio, video and other multimedia being used on many websites and other platforms such as DVDs and CD–ROMs.

LEARNING OUTCOMES

You need to learn about

✓ capturing sound clips

✓ editing and using sound clips

✓ capturing video footage

✓ editing and using video footage.

Capturing sound clips

Jargon buster

A **WAV file** (with extension '.wav') is the most common format for sound files. All recent browsers can open WAV files. However, these files can be very large: a one-minute WAV file is over 10MB.

Figure 221 Headset, microphone and connectors

If your computer has a sound card, you will be able to capture sound in a digital format and create a *WAV file*. You can use Microsoft Sound Recorder to do this very easily. The source of the sound can be from any playback device, such as a CD player, DVD player, tape recorder and so on. Alternatively you can record the sound live from a microphone or several microphones using a mixing device.

If you want to include a WAV file on a website, it is best to *compress* it. MPEG 3 (MP3) is a popular audio compression that will compress a WAV file to about one-tenth its original size.

You will need to connect the source of the sound to the sound card. In Figure 221 you will see an example of a headset, microphone and two connectors. The pink connector has a picture of a microphone on it and the green connector has a picture of the earphones. You will need to plug these into the correct sockets on your sound card, which are normally at the back of your computer. If you using a microphone to record speech, the speech will go through the pink connector into the sound card and be played back through the green connector to the headset.

Recording a sound file

Microsoft Sound Recorder allows you to record, mix, play and edit sounds. A mixer, such as the one shown in Figure 222, will allow you to adjust the level to ensure that the sound is not too high and distorted, or too low and hard to hear. The vertical sliders allow you to control the volume of the sound: move them up to increase the volume of the signal or down to decrease it. The Balance controls allow you to adjust the sound between left and right.

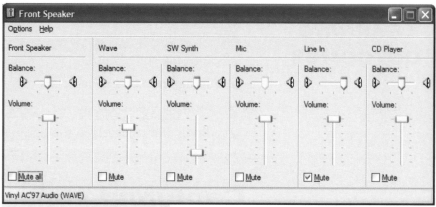

Figure 222 A mixer panel

To record a sound, simply make sure you have an audio input device, such as a microphone, connected to your computer and then select **File, New** to create a new file (Figure 223). Click on the start button to commence recording, click on the stop button when you have finished, and finally remember to save the file.

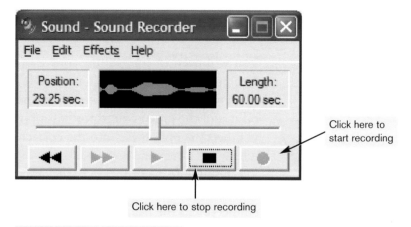

Figure 223 Recording a sound

Go out and try!

Select a sound from a suitable source such as CD, DVD, or voice input via microphone). Using Microsoft Sound Recorder, record the sound, adjusting the balance for the sound using the mixer supplied with Microsoft Windows if necessary. 💾 Save the sound file with a suitable name.

Create a new file called 'Digital video and sound and video' and save it in your 'Digital sound and video' sub-folder. Create a new bold heading called '**DSV Activity 1**' and write a short paragraph describing the skills you have demonstrated in this activity. 💾 Save the file.

Editing and using sound clips

Editing a sound file

Once you have recorded a sound, you are able to edit the file in a number of ways. You can

- add sounds to the file
- delete part of the file
- change the playback speed
- change the playback volume
- change the playback direction
- add an echo
- change or convert the sound file type.

Figure 224 Editing options with Sound Recorder

If you wish to mix the sound file with another sound file, you will need to select **Edit, Mix with File** (Figure 224). Alternatively, by moving the slider to the place in the file you want to cut, you can choose to delete all the sound before the current position or after the current position. You can also add echo to an uncompressed sound file by selecting **Effects, Add Echo**.

If you wish to insert a different sound file, move the slider to where you would like to insert the file and select **Edit, Insert File**. You can only insert a sound file into an uncompressed sound file. When there is no green line in Sound Recorder, the file is compressed and you cannot modify it unless you first adjust the sound quality (Figure 225).

This file has been compressed, therefore there is no green line here.

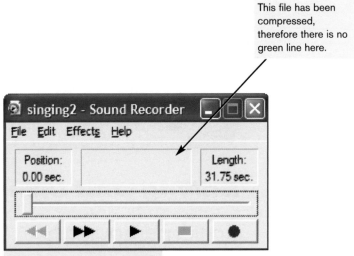

Figure 225 A compressed file

When you are satisfied with your recording, you can compress the file by saving it in a different format, such as MP3. Sound Recorder allows you to save in several different formats (Figure 226).

Jargon buster

Compressing a file means reducing the file size so that it requires less storage space. This will allow it to be transmitted over the Internet more quickly. Unfortunately, the more you compress a digital sound or video file, the more the quality is reduced.

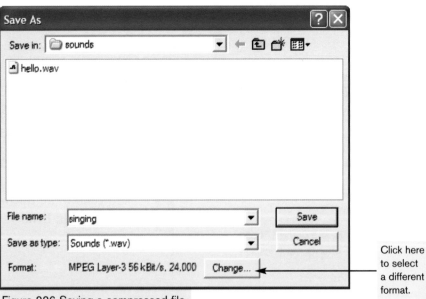

Click here to select a different format.

Figure 226 Saving a compressed file

Using alternative audio software

Microsoft Sound Recorder is an ideal way to record and edit a sound track when you are first starting out. However, as you become more experienced, you will no doubt find that it can be limiting in its features. It is possible to download free audio editing software such as Audacity – see www.heinemann.co.uk/hotlinks (express code 0069P) for more. You can use this software to edit sound in a wide variety of ways. Figure 227 shows the Audacity window.

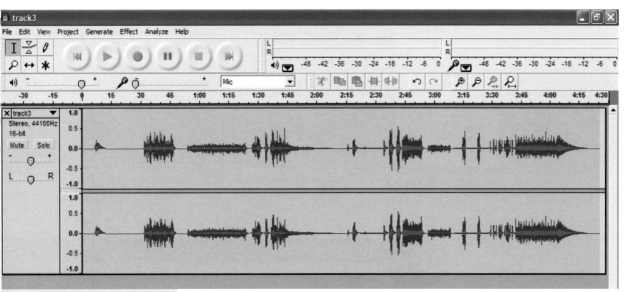

Figure 227 The Audacity window

This software programme includes two excellent online tutorials to work through, which will equip you with the skills to do more advanced editing of sound tracks.

Figure 228 shows a sound track that has been highlighted prior to an effect being applied to it. As you can see, there are a large number of possible effects available with this software.

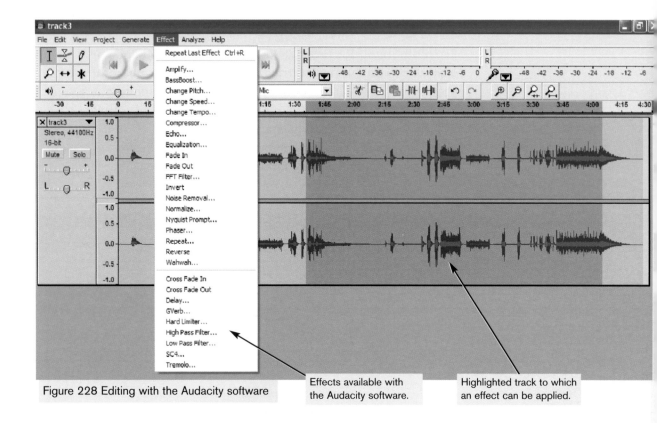

Figure 228 Editing with the Audacity software

Effects available with the Audacity software.

Highlighted track to which an effect can be applied.

Go out and try!

Using some or all of the techniques you have learned, edit the sound file you recorded in Activity 1. You may decide to record another sound and then mix it with this file, add echo, or increase or decrease the speed. Add the sound file to the presentation or website created for your project. Save your work.

Open your 'Digital sound and video' file. Create a new bold heading '**DSV Activity 2**' and write a short paragraph describing the skills you have demonstrated whilst modifying a recorded sound. Save the file.

Video footage

To be able to download digital video clips, you will need a digital video camera, a *Firewire card*, a cable to connect your computer to the camera, and video editing software such as Microsoft Movie Maker.

Alternatively, the Internet can be a source of videos that you can download and edit, but often there is a charge for this.

About Microsoft Movie Maker

Microsoft Move Maker will allow you to

- add narration to a film
- add a soundtrack to the start and end of a film
- add sound throughout a film
- create transitions between scenes, such as fade in and wipe out
- add titles and subtitles
- slow down parts of the film
- add special video effects
- capture still photo images from a frame in a film
- import a still picture and add it between clips
- create a slide show using still pictures.

When you first open Movie Maker, you will see the screen shown in Figure 229. Figure 230 explains some of the features to look out for. The Movie Tasks pane is shown in Figure 231.

Starting a new project

Before you download a video to your computer, you should start a new Movie Maker project by selecting **File**, **New Project**. The project will hold all the aspects that will help you produce your edited video: the clips, the transitions between clips, the audio, the video effects and any titles and credit.

Capturing a video

Once you have shot a video with a digital video camera, you must download (or *capture*) it to your computer for editing. Connect the camera to your computer's Firewire card using a cable, then load the *Video Capture Wizard* from the **File** menu in Movie Maker. This wizard will take you step by step through the process of downloading a video.

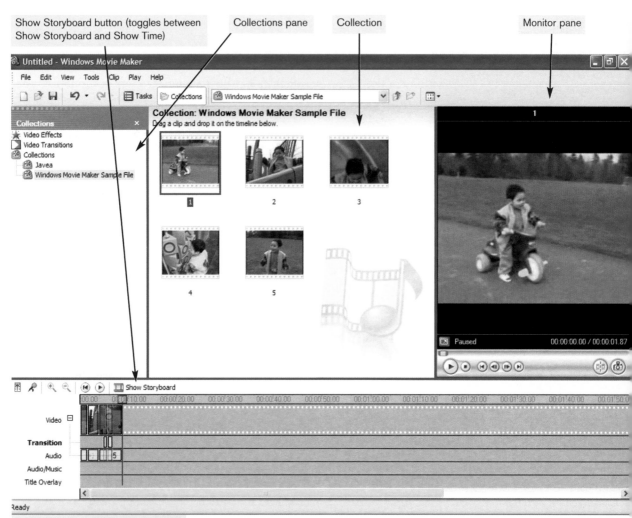

Figure 229 The Movie Maker screen

Collections pane	This contains all the items available to create a video: videos that have been captured from a camera, together with video transitions and video effects that you can add.
Collection	This contains a captured video, broken into clips. You can then choose which clips to include in your movie.
Monitor pane	This is used to preview clips, pictures, special effects, transitions and completed movies.
Storyboard	This shows the order and content of clips in a movie, but does not show the timing. It is useful for viewing the overall sequence of a movie.
Timeline	This consists of a row of clips that make up the order and timing of a movie. You can add and delete clips, sounds, transitions and special effects.
Video, transition, audio, audio/music and title overlay tracks	When you add special effects such as transitions, background music, a title or audio narration, these appear in the appropriate track on the timeline.
Movie Tasks pane (as shown in Figure 231)	By selecting **Tasks pane** from the **View** menu, the *Movie Tasks* pane will replace the *Collections* pane. This is a useful tool for prompting you on the various tasks that you will need to take into account when creating your video.

Figure 230 Meanings of Movie Maker terms

Movie Tasks pane

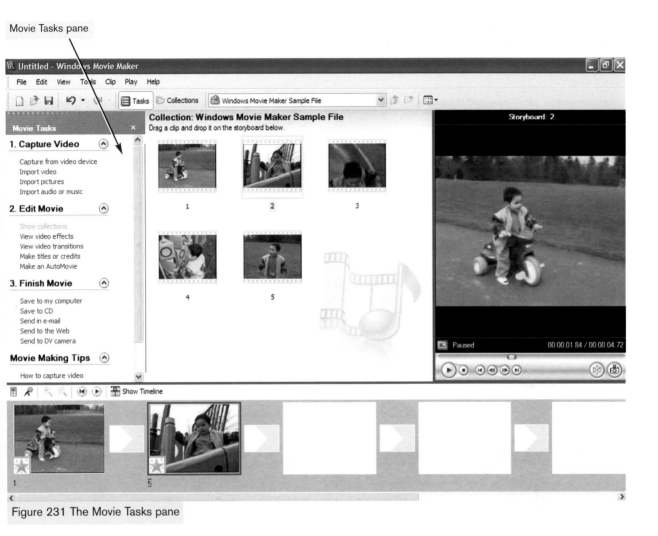

Figure 231 The Movie Tasks pane

The *Video Setting* dialogue box, shown in Figure 232, allows you to specify the quality of the captured film.

- If you are going to mainly play back the video on a computer, then you should select the **Best quality for playback on my computer** option.
- If you are going to play the video on another device, such as a DVD player, then you will need to click the option labelled **Other settings** and select the quality that matches the device you are going to use (Figure 233).

As you select the different output settings, the dialogue box will show details of the file type (e.g. Windows Media Player with the '.wmv' file extension), the bit rate, the display size in pixels and the numbers of frames played per second of video.

Setting details

Video file size details

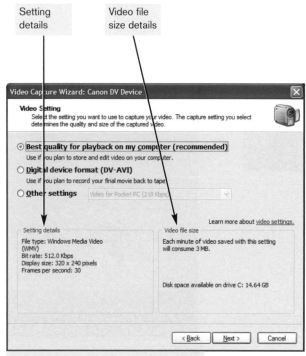

Figure 232 Setting the capture quality

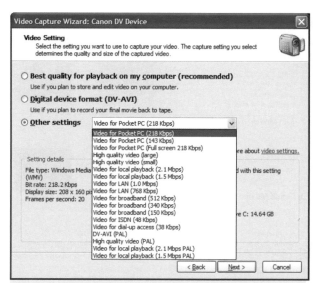

Figure 233 The 'Other settings' list of choices for quality

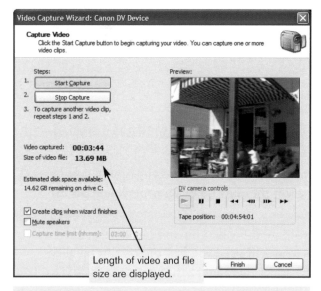

Length of video and file size are displayed.

Figure 234 The progress of capturing the video is displayed

Movie Maker allows you to capture all or part of a video and to preview the video whilst you are capturing it. You can start and stop the capture at any time and even rewind to capture part of the video that you may have missed. During this process, the length of the video and the file size are displayed (Figure 234).

The final part of the capture process is to import the file into a new 'collection'. For example, Thomas Tripp of Travelbug has decided to include a video of a private villa in Javea in his PowerPoint presentation and on the new Travelbug website. He therefore goes through the process of capturing the video using Movie Maker and then imports the file into the new collection called 'Javea' (Figure 235). As the file is being imported, Movie Maker automatically creates the clips to display in the collection pane (Figure 236).

Jargon buster

Bit rate refers to the number of bits used per second of video. For example, the bit rate in Figure 232 is 512.0 Kbps.

Pixel is short for 'picture element'. It represents the smallest dot of resolution in your video. The more pixels allocated to video, the smoother it will appear, but it will also take up more disk space.

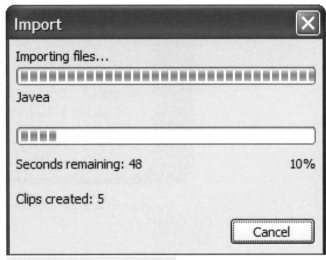

Figure 235 Importing video files

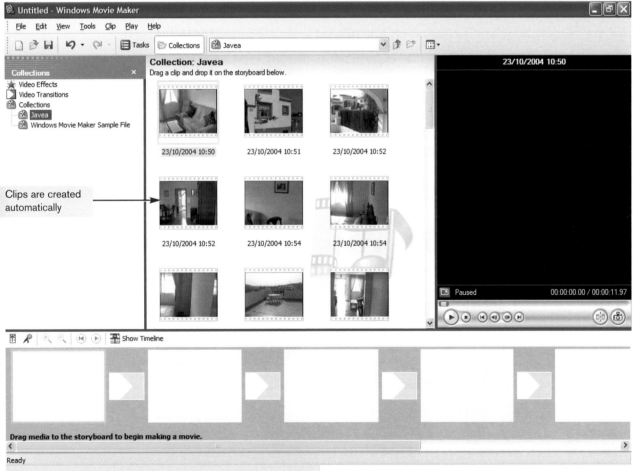

Figure 236 A video that has been captured into Movie Maker

413

Open your 'Digital sound and video' file. Create a new bold heading '**DSV Activity 3**' and write a short paragraph describing the skills you have demonstrated whilst starting a new project in Movie Maker and capturing a video. Save the file.

Creating an edited movie

You are now ready to start creating your edited movie. You can drag the clips into the *storyboard*, and change the order if necessary. You can always remove a clip from the storyboard if you decide, at a later stage in the video production, that you do not wish to include it. Figure 237 shows some of the clips that Thomas Tripp has decided to include in his video.

Once the clips have been dragged to the storyboard, you are able to click on timeline view in order to trim them if necessary (Figure 238).

Figure 237 Clips on a storyboard

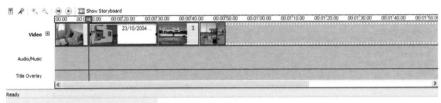

Figure 238 The timeline view

Adding video effects

It is possible to add video effects to your video production by selecting the chosen effect and dragging it on to the clip in the storyboard. Video effects change the way a clip plays back, such as blurring or fading in from black. Thomas Tripp has included effects on some of his clips – in Figure 239, the blue star on the clip indicates that a video effect has been added.

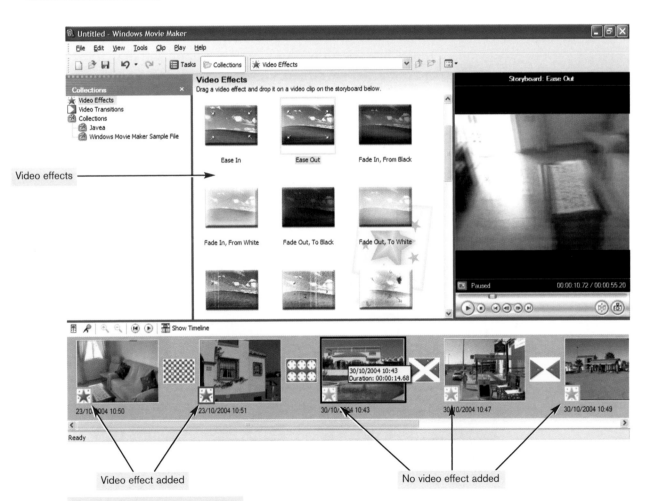

Figure 239 Adding a video effect

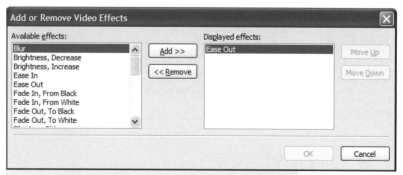

Figure 240 Dialogue box to add or remove video effects

It is even possible to add multiple video effects to a clip by right-clicking on the clip in the storyboard and selecting the **Video Effects** option. The *Add or Remove Video Effects* dialogue box allows you to select the effects you require (Figure 240).

Setting transitions

In the same way as you can add transitions to a PowerPoint presentation, you can include different transition effects that are played when one clip moves to another clip. The clips will then show a gradual change from one clip to the next as the first clip fades into the next one using the selected transition pattern.

Movie Maker provides a large number of transitions from which to choose. Just select the transition you require and drag it between the clips in the storyboard, as shown in Figure 241.

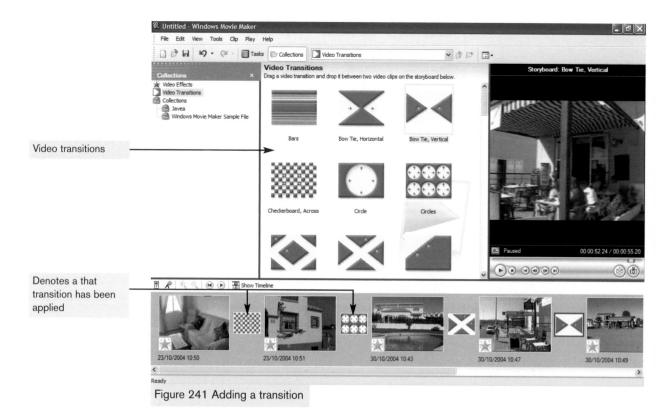

Figure 241 Adding a transition

Adding a title

Movie Maker allows you to add titles and credits to a video in a number of ways: at the beginning of the video, before, on or after a clip, or as credits at the end of the video (Figure 242). Titles and credits always appear in text that fades in and out, or scrolls on to the screen. You can even select the style (font and colour) of text to be used.

Choices of where to add the title ⟶

Figure 242 Adding a title

As you can see in Figure 243, Thomas Tripp has included a title at the beginning of the video.

Figure 243 A title has been added to the video

Adding sound

You cannot edit or delete sound that you import with a video. However, you can add an audio clip, such as the sound file you created whilst learning about Microsoft Sound Recorder earlier in

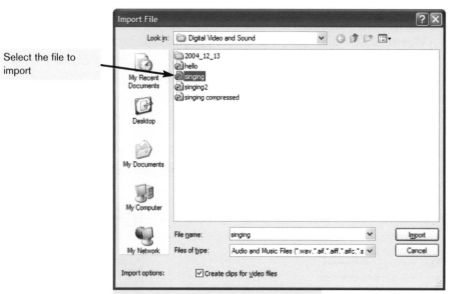

Select the file to import

Figure 244 Dialogue box to import a file

this chapter. By choosing the **Import Audio or Music** option from the *Movie Tasks* pane, the *Import File* box appears (Figure 244).

The file is then added to the collection and can be dragged to the *Audio/Music* track in the timeline. You can right-click on the file in the timeline in order to change the volume or set the sound to fade in or out (Figure 245).

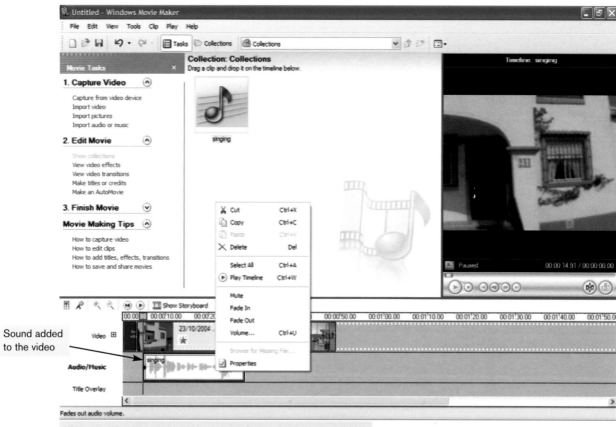

Sound added to the video

Figure 245 Adding sound to a video (right-click menu shown)

Saving the video

Having edited your video, the last step is to save it as a movie. The *Save Movie Wizard* guides you through the steps of saving. It prompts you to give the movie an appropriate name and then to select the location (Figure 246). In most instances you will choose the option to save to the *My Videos* folder.

Finally, the *Save Movie Wizard* allows you to compress the file. The option **Best quality for playback on my computer** is selected by default (Figure 247).

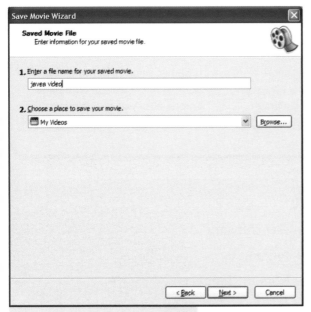

Figure 246 The Save Movie Wizard

Figure 247 Setting the video quality

Go out and try!

Use the skills you have learned in this chapter to create a movie. Add appropriate video effects, transitions between clips, sound and titles. Show a prototype at each stage of the production to a group of friends. Take their feedback into account to make any necessary changes to the project. When you are satisfied with the end product, 💾 save the movie.

Open your 'Digital sound and video' file. Create a new bold heading '**DSV Activity 4**' and write a short paragraph describing the skills you have demonstrated editing a video using Movie Maker. 💾 Save the file.

Internet and intranets

In your studies you will need to research information from a wide variety of sources. A huge amount of information can be obtained if you carry out a search on the Internet or an intranet. However, be warned: there are millions of websites on the World Wide Web (WWW) and, unless you have the skills to carry out an effective search, you may find it difficult to find the exact information you need.

Jargon buster

The **Internet** is the world's largest computer network, connecting millions of organisations and people across the globe.

An **intranet** uses the same technology as the Internet but is an internal communication system for a particular organisation or company. It can be accessed only by authorised users. It allows secure email communication and distribution of data.

The **World Wide Web** is a part of the Internet. Multimedia documents are connected together using **hyperlinks**. Each document is called a **web page** and a set of web pages make up a **website**.

LEARNING OUTCOMES

You need to learn about

✓ using features of browser software

✓ using search engines and portals

✓ downloading images from the Internet.

Jargon buster

Broadband is the general term given to the latest in high-speed Internet access technology, which is much faster than using a dial-up modem. An Asymmetric Digital Subscriber Line (ADSL) is an example of always-on broadband technology. It uses an ordinary telephone line to allow you to access the Internet and talk on the telephone at the same time.

Using features of your browser software

The special software which enables you to search the Internet or an intranet is known as a *web browser*. A web browser enables you to view web pages and to click on links – known as *hyperlinks* – to other web pages and websites. The most common web browsers are Microsoft Internet Explorer and Netscape Navigator.

When you double-click on your browser to start it up, you can access web pages only if you are connected to the Internet via your *Internet Service Provider* (ISP). You may have an 'always on' *broadband connection*, or you may have a 'dial-up' connection (which means that your modem has to dial to your ISP before you can access the Internet).

Jargon buster

A **modem** is a device that converts the digital signals from a computer into analogue signals that can be sent down a phone line. These analogue signals are then converted back to digital signals by a modem at the receiving end.

Jargon buster

A web page has its own unique identification or address known as a **uniform resource locator** (URL). Every address is constructed in the same manner and usually starts with 'http://www'. For example, the web address of the publishers of this book is http://www.heinemann.co.uk (Figure 249).

The home page

When you launch a web browser while connected to the Internet, the default web page – the *home page* – will be loaded and appear on screen. This can be the intranet of the company whose computer you are using, the website of your ISP, or any website you have chosen.

Finding a website

If you know the *website address* (URL) you can go directly to it by typing it in the Address box of the browser and clicking on **Go**. If you don't know the address of a company or organisation, try guessing. It is often possible to guess correctly, as organisations usually try to include their name in the address. You don't even have to type 'http://www' because the browser will add that for you. Figure 248 shows the toolbar and Address box in Internet Explorer.

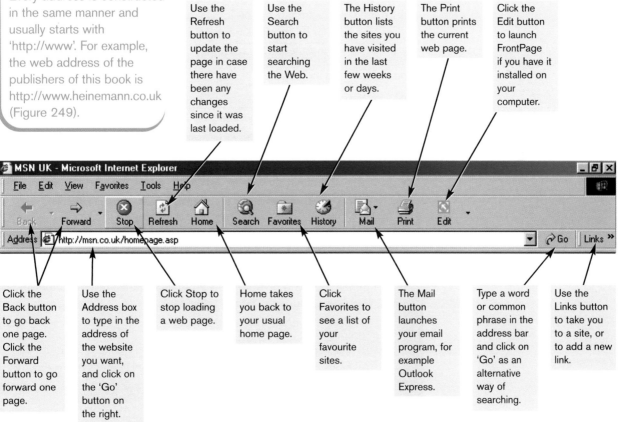

Use the Refresh button to update the page in case there have been any changes since it was last loaded.

Use the Search button to start searching the Web.

The History button lists the sites you have visited in the last few weeks or days.

The Print button prints the current web page.

Click the Edit button to launch FrontPage if you have it installed on your computer.

Click the Back button to go back one page. Click the Forward button to go forward one page.

Use the Address box to type in the address of the website you want, and click on the 'Go' button on the right.

Click Stop to stop loading a web page.

Home takes you back to your usual home page.

Click Favorites to see a list of your favourite sites.

The Mail button launches your email program, for example Outlook Express.

Type a word or common phrase in the address bar and click on 'Go' as an alternative way of searching.

Use the Links button to take you to a site, or to add a new link.

Figure 248 The Internet Explorer toolbar

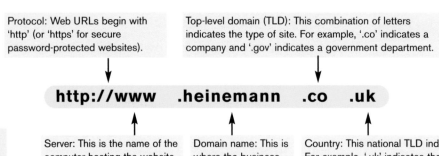

Figure 249
The Heinemann
URL explained

Protocol: Web URLs begin with 'http' (or 'https' for secure password-protected websites).

Top-level domain (TLD): This combination of letters indicates the type of site. For example, '.co' indicates a company and '.gov' indicates a government department.

http://www .heinemann .co .uk

Server: This is the name of the computer hosting the website. It is usually 'www'.

Domain name: This is where the business name will appear.

Country: This national TLD indicates the country. For example, '.uk' indicates the United Kingdom, 'ie' indicates Ireland, and 'es' indicates Spain.

Top-level domains (TLDs) indicate the type of site. Examples of useful top-level domains to know are listed in Figure 250.

.ac	A university, college or academic department
.co	A company
.com	A commercial organisation
.uk.com	An alternative area for UK registrations, often used if the .com or .co.uk name is not available
.gov	A government department
.me	An individual
.mil	A military site
.net	A network-related site
.org	generally a charity or non-profit-making organisation
.sch	A school
.tv	The latest domain for television websites

Figure 250 Top-level domains

Go out and try!

Open your web browser and try to find the following companies' websites by guessing their addresses:

1 Argos
2 Pizza Hut
3 Dixons.
○ Start Internet Explorer (or your installed Internet browser program).
○ In the address bar, key in your guess of the website address.
○ Click 'Go' or 'Search' at the end of the address bar.
○ Repeat for each website address.

Start a new file called 'Internet and intranets' and save it in your 'Internet and intranets' sub-folder. Create a new bold heading called '**II Activity 1**' and write a short paragraph describing the skills you have demonstrated in this activity. Save the file.

Hyperlinks within websites

Many companies have very large websites, starting with a home page and panning out with many pages about different aspects of their company. These pages are connected together by hyperlinks. When you move your mouse pointer over a hyperlink, the arrow changes to a pointing hand. When you click on the hyperlink you will be connected to this link.

It is very easy sometimes to get lost within a company's website, but a well constructed site will always have a link that takes you back to the home page. There will usually be hyperlinks to return you back to the top of a page and to the other main areas of the site. Figure 251 shows some examples of hyperlinks.

Large organisations, such as the BBC, will usually include a search facility for their own site, so that you can quickly find the information you require. The BBC's site even has a 'search help and tips' page to help you find the information easily. This is a good website to bookmark in your favourites – you will find a host of useful resources to help you with your studies.

Television

- Pick: **Himalaya with Michael Palin**
  9pm **BBC One**

- BBC TV schedules

Popular programmes:
EastEnders | Smile | TOTP | Lottery

Figure 251 Hyperlinks

Bookmarks

In the same way as you can put a bookmark in a book to return to a page quickly and easily, you can bookmark your favourite websites. You can create folders in which to file these bookmarks, in the same way as you organise and save your files on your hard drive.

Favorites	Tools	Help

Add to Favorites...

Organize Favorites...

- digital applications book ▶
- Jenny ▶
- Ian ▶
- Colin ▶
- Ray ▶

Figure 252 Internet Explorer's Favorites folder

Rather than having to remember the address of a website, you can easily return to a site by selecting the name from the favourites list. If there is a specific page within a website that you know you will want to return to on other occasions, you can bookmark that page, rather than the home page of the site.

By using the **Organize Favorites** option, you can add, rename and delete folders. You can also change the order in which you view your favourites so that websites that you visit on a regular basis appear higher in the list.

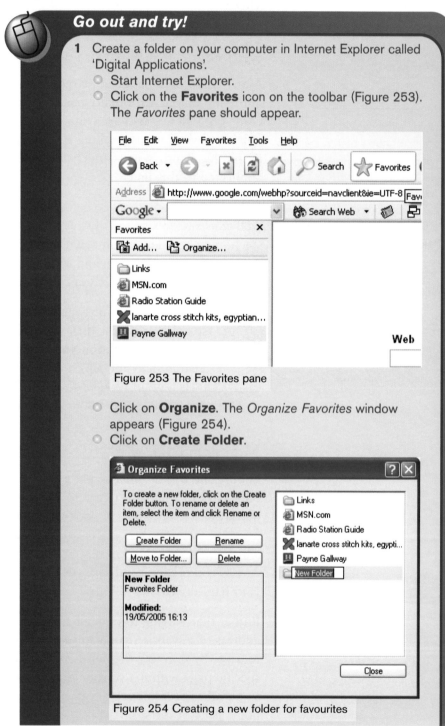

Go out and try!

1 Create a folder on your computer in Internet Explorer called 'Digital Applications'.
- Start Internet Explorer.
- Click on the **Favorites** icon on the toolbar (Figure 253). The *Favorites* pane should appear.

Figure 253 The Favorites pane

- Click on **Organize**. The *Organize Favorites* window appears (Figure 254).
- Click on **Create Folder**.

Figure 254 Creating a new folder for favourites

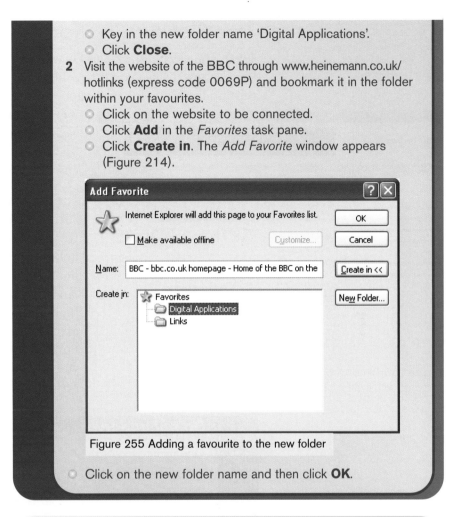

○ Key in the new folder name 'Digital Applications'.
○ Click **Close**.
2 Visit the website of the BBC through www.heinemann.co.uk/
hotlinks (express code 0069P) and bookmark it in the folder
within your favourites.
○ Click on the website to be connected.
○ Click **Add** in the *Favorites* task pane.
○ Click **Create in**. The *Add Favorite* window appears
(Figure 214).

Figure 255 Adding a favourite to the new folder

○ Click on the new folder name and then click **OK**.

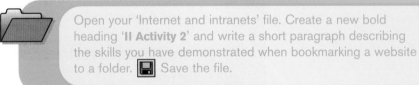

Open your 'Internet and intranets' file. Create a new bold
heading '**II Activity 2**' and write a short paragraph describing
the skills you have demonstrated when bookmarking a website
to a folder. Save the file.

The Back and Forward buttons

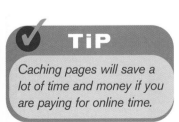

TiP

*Caching pages will save a
lot of time and money if you
are paying for online time.*

All the time you are online, your browser is storing copies of the
pages you have recently used in a memory area called *cache*. If you
wish to return to a page you visited before, click on **Back** until you
reach the page you require. Because the browser program does not
have to go back to the Internet, but simply has to look into its
internal cache, the page will appear more quickly than it did the first
time. You can click on the **Forward** button to return to the web page
you were on before you clicked **Back**.

The Refresh button

When you use the **Back** and **Forward** buttons, any changes that may have occurred since you first visited the relevant page will not appear, because the browser has not gone back to the online web page but has merely loaded that page from its internal cache. Clicking on the **Refresh** button will update the page in case there have been any changes since it was last loaded.

For example, by visiting the British Airports Authority plc's (BAA plc) website through www. heinemann.co.uk/ hotlinks (express code 0069P), it is possible to check when flights have landed. When you first visit the site, the flight may be shown with its expected arrival time (Figure 256). By clicking on the **Refresh** button at regular intervals you will be able to check when it has actually landed.

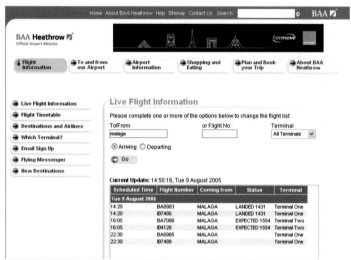

Figure 256 The BAA website, which is being constantly updated with flight information

Go out and try!

Open your web browser and go to the BAA's website via www.heinemann.co.uk/hotlinks (express code 0069P). Choose an airport near you and monitor the progress of a flight which is arriving from Faro in Portugal.

○ Click on an airport in the list on the left.
○ Key in **Faro** in the *From/To* box of the *Live Flight Information* section.

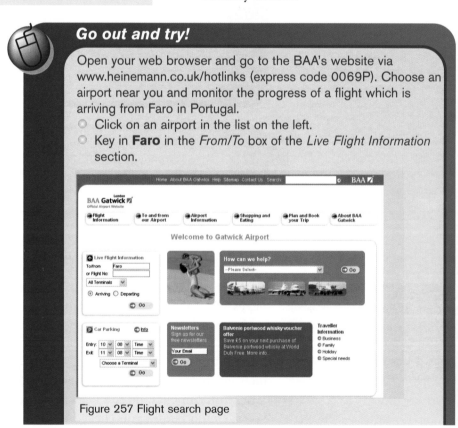

Figure 257 Flight search page

○ Click on **Submit**.

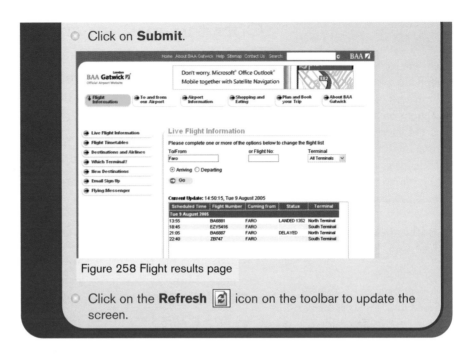

Figure 258 Flight results page

○ Click on the **Refresh** 🔃 icon on the toolbar to update the screen.

Open your 'Internet and intranets' file. Create a new bold heading '**II Activity 3**' and write a short paragraph describing the skills you have demonstrated in this activity. 💾 Save the file.

History

Your browser will store a history of all the websites you have visited over the last few days or weeks. This can be helpful if you have

Figure 259 The History list

forgotten to bookmark a particularly useful site. It is also useful if you have been surfing the net for some time, and you want to return to a page that you previously visited during the current session.

One way to go back to the page is to click the **Back** button, but this can be quite slow if you have visited quite a few pages. Another way is to use the *History* list to select the site (Figure 259).

TiP

Selecting a site from the history list is a quick way of returning to it.

Copying and saving web pages

You can copy text from a website and paste it into another document using the same techniques as you would in Word or Excel. You can also save whole web pages and images from a website on to your computer.

When you save a web page it will be saved in *HTML* (hypertext mark-up language – see page 449). Once you have saved a web page, you can view it through your browser even when you are offline.

Selecting and printing pages

It is also possible to print web pages that you wish to keep for future reference. Many web pages, such as the one shown in Figure 261, include their own print hyperlink. However, you can also print a page by selecting **File, Print** from the menu in the usual way.

The selected text can be printed.

Click here to print the whole page in a printer-friendly format.

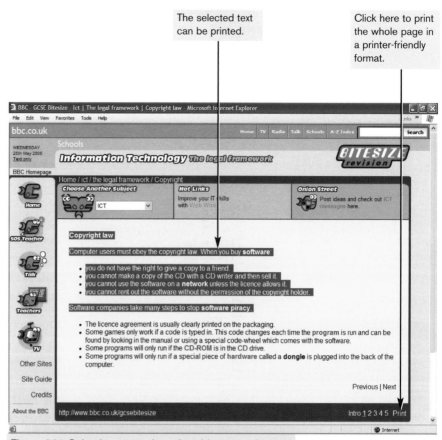

Figure 261 Selecting text to be printed from a web page

Sometimes when you print a web page you find that the material on the right-hand side is cut off. If this happens you will need to change the orientation of the page to landscape using **File, Page Setup** from the menu. You will have practised these skills already with a word processor.

If you want to print a small section of the page, again you can use the skills you have already learned when using other applications such as Word. Select the text you want to print (see Figure 261) and then choose **File, Print** and click on **Selection** before pressing **OK**.

The Go button

You can use the **Go** button on the Address bar to search for web pages. If you type a common name or word in the address bar and click on **Go**, Internet Explorer will either automatically display the web page or list those that are the most likely match.

For example, if you type 'virgin trains' in the Address bar and click on **Go** you will automatically be directed to the Virgin Trains website. However, if you type 'record shops' in the Address bar, a list of possible web pages will be displayed.

Jargon buster

A **portal** is a website that offers news, weather information or other services, set up as an entry point to the Web. Most portals are also search engines.

Using search engines

The Internet is the world's largest source of information. However, as you have probably already discovered, there are millions of websites, so it is sometimes quite hard to find the information you want.

If you want to find a particular company, or a certain piece of information, you will need to use a *search tool*. There are several different search tools, the main types being search engines, subject directories, meta-searches and name directories. Figure 262 explains what these are.

You might well be thinking that not only is there a huge amount of information to search, but also many different ways of searching, and you would be right! Choose one search tool and just use that one for a while. If you are not sure which one to choose, ask your friends or your teacher or tutor. When you are used to how it works and what sort of results you get then try another search tool.

- **Search engines** are indexes that work by keywords and context. Popular search engines include Altavista, Ask Jeeves and Google (see www.heinemann.co.uk/hotlinks (express code 0069P) for more). Search engines use a program called a *spider*, *robot* or *crawler* to index huge collections of Internet files. Use search engines when you want to find large numbers of related documents or specific types of document such as image files, MP3 music files or discussion lists.

- **Subject directories** are similar to search engines, but are smaller collections of Internet files grouped by subject headings. These files are not found by software, but chosen by humans. These directories are ideal if you wish to research a general topic and you want to avoid all the irrelevant files that search engines can find. An example of a search directory is Open Directory Project (see www.heinemann.co.uk/hotlinks (express code 0069P) for more).

- **Meta-search engines** send searches to several search engines at the same time. Within a few seconds, you get back results from all the search engines that were queried. Meta-search engines do not own a database of web pages; they send your search terms to the databases maintained for other search engines. You can download and install a meta-search engine to work alongside your browser. Copernic is an example of a meta-search engine which can be downloaded (see www.heinemann.co.uk/hotlinks (express code 0069P) for more). Use meta-searches when you want to get an overall picture of what the Internet has on your topic and to check whether the Internet really is the best place for you to search.

- **Name directories** such as Yell (see www.heinemann.co.uk/hotlinks (express code 0069P) for more) are used when you want to search for people by name, telephone number, email address, postcode and so on.

Figure 262 Search tools

Successful searching

As mentioned earlier, sometimes searching can be difficult because, if you do not narrow your search in some way, you can be presented with a large number of irrelevant results. There are ways to overcome this, but these differ between search engines: look at their help pages for tips. Check out the number of hits a search produces, and, if necessary, refine your search to limit the number.

Imagine you are searching for a holiday villa to rent in the Dordogne region of France.

- If you entered *holidays* in the search box of a search engine this would be an example of a *single-criterion search*. It is important to choose the words you are searching on very carefully in order to reduce the number of results you are likely to get. This simple search produced more than 21 million results in Google, so it is unlikely that you would find the ideal holiday from using it!

- You could try typing the words *holiday villas to rent*. This *refined search* narrowed the number of hits to 668 000.

- You could reduce the number of hits further by putting double quotations marks before and after the search words. You will get more accurate information by doing so. This will find websites that include the exact phrase *"holiday villas to rent"* rather than any websites that include *any of the words in any order*. This search reduced the number of hits to 12 700.

- You can limit the number of hits further by using the + sign to show that the word must appear in the results. Typing *"holiday villas to rent" +France* reduced the number of hits to 4470. This is an example of *multiple criteria*, the first criterion being *"holidays villas to rent"* and the second being *France*.

- Some of the results included holiday villas in other countries, so typing *"holiday villas to rent" +France –Spain* will exclude all sites that have the word *Spain*. This reduced the number of hits to 1560.

- Finally, adding *+Dordogne* to the search, so that it became *"holiday villas to rent" +Dordogne +France –Spain* reduced the number of hits to 889.

Using wildcards

To make sure that you do not miss a good website by using the wrong words in your search, you can use *wildcard* matches.

You can use right-hand or left-hand wildcard searches. Entering *water** would produce results that include terms such as 'waterside' and 'waterfront'. Entering **bus* would produce results that include terms such as 'bus', 'minibus' and 'trolleybus'.

Figure 263 is a summary of search techniques.

TiP

Google only supports wildcards when searching for missing words in phrases. For example, "holidays in *France" will find holidays in Paris, France and holidays in rural South-West France.

- **Single-criterion searches** – single word searches or words grouped together by the use of quotes.
- **Multiple-criterion searches** – multiple word searches that are not grouped together by the use of quotes, or searches that are refined by using logical operators (+ or –).
- **Wildcards** – some search engines (but not Google) allow the use of * as a wildcard. For example, entering *villa** will search for sites including the words 'villa' and 'villas'.

Figure 263 Summary of search techniques

Open your 'Internet and intranets' file. Create a new bold heading 'II **Activity 4**' and write a short paragraph describing the skills you have demonstrated when searching the Internet. Save the file.

Logical operators

The earlier example of searching for holidays used two logical operators: + and –. Those and other operators are explained further in Figure 264.

Operator	What is does when used in a search	Example	What it means when used in a search
+ (AND)	Place this in front when you want a word to be present in the results of your search.	+Dordogne +France	The words *Dordogne* and *France* must appear somewhere in the results.
– (NOT)	Place this in front when you want to exclude a word from the results of your search.	+Dordogne +France –Spain	The words *Dordogne* and *France* must appear somewhere in the results, but all pages also with *Spain* should be excluded.
OR	Use this when you want either word to be included in the result.	France OR Spain	Web pages are included in the results if either or both search terms appear.
" "	Use this when you want the words to appear together in the same order.	"Holiday villas to rent"	The words must appear in this order.

Figure 264 The principal logical operators you will need to refine searches

It is important to remember that different search engines will produce different results, so it is a useful exercise to compare the results achieved from different search engines. Most search engines will have an advanced search option which will prompt you to refine your search (Figure 265).

TiP

Google also allows you to find synonyms (words with similar meanings) using the tilde (~) character. For example, searching for ~hotel will also return results containing the words inn, accommodation, hoteles (Spanish) and so on.

Figure 265 The Google advanced search tool

Also, some search engines, like Ask Jeeves, will allow you to type in direct questions. For example, you could type in *Where can I find information about holiday villas to rent in the Dordogne region of France?*

Downloading images from the Internet

As well as being useful sources of information, search engines provide easy access to a wealth of images that you can use to illustrate your projects. Most modern search engines will let you search for images on a particular topic, and display thumbnails of the results so that you can easily choose the one you want.

Figure 266 shows Google's Image Search. Notice that you can switch between different types of search – Web, Images, Groups, News, and so on – by clicking the links above the text box. In Figure 266, Thomas Tripp is searching for an image of a French villa.

Figure 266 Searching for an image using Google

Figure 267 shows the first page of results. To save a particular image, click the thumbnail to go to the web page that contains the full-size image, then right-click the image and choose **Save Picture As**.

TiP

You need to be very aware of copyright issues (see page 241) when downloading images from the Internet. Rather than using a general search engine, you might choose to use a site such as Pics4Learning (see www.heinemann.co.uk/ hotlinks (express code 0069P) for more), which contains only copyright-friendly images.

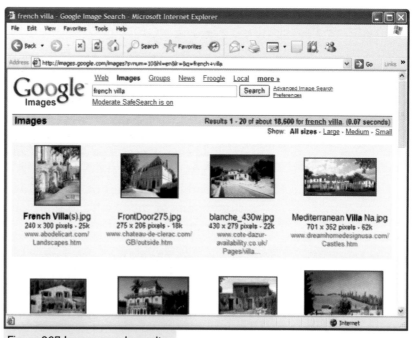

Figure 267 Image search results

Go out and try!

Search the Internet for an image of the Eiffel Tower and download it.

Open your 'Internet and intranets' file. Create a new bold heading '**II Activity 5**' and write a short paragraph describing the skills you have demonstrated when downloading a picture from the Internet. Add a second paragraph explaining who owns the copyright to the picture you downloaded, and anything you would need to do before you could use the picture in your own work. 💾 Save the file.

A warning!

There is no single individual or organisation controlling the information that is published on the Internet. This means that the information you find may not always be correct. It may appear convincing and correct but, in fact, be completely wrong or at least misleading. Protect yourself from inaccurate information in these ways:

- Check whether there is a date on the site, and when it was last updated.
- Look to see whether it is possible to contact the site's developer. Is there an email address to contact?
- Try to work out (or at least be aware of) whether the site was developed by someone or some organisation that wants to put across its message – for example a political (sometimes an extreme political) view.

Email

You will probably have used email at school and often at home. When you start your first job after school or college, or if you go on work experience, you will find that email plays an extremely important role in business and few businesses would be able to function without it.

An email is like an electronic letter, sent in most instances via a computer instead of the postal service. Email is a very sophisticated method of electronic transfer, where messages and documents can be sent from one computer to another using a communications link such as a modem and a telephone line. You can receive and send the electronic equivalent of letters, pictures and sounds, and if you have a webcam attached to your PC you can even send a video email.

Documents prepared on a word processor or other software package, or a document scanned into the computer, can be attached to an email.

LEARNING OUTCOMES

You need to learn about

✓ receiving an email

✓ sending an email

✓ using folders to store and organise emails and attachments

✓ setting the priority of an email

✓ setting up and using an email address book

✓ setting up and using distribution lists.

Hardware and software requirements

To send or receive emails you need

- ○ access to a computer
- ○ a phone line
- ○ a modem (an *analogue modem* if you are using an ordinary phone line, or a *broadband modem* if you have an ADSL line)
- ○ an account with an Internet Service Provider (ISP)
- ○ email communication software, such as Microsoft Outlook Express.

Many businesses use more powerful email programs, such as Microsoft Outlook or Lotus Notes.

The ISP will provide an *email account*, a *password* and a *mailbox* on their server. You will be given an *email address*. The address is a short code, often made up of the user's name, followed by the ISP's domain name – but this can vary. In the example in Figure 268 you will see that three email addresses have been used.

ISP = AOL

ISP = BTInternet

ISP = Freeserve

Text box

Figure 268 Three ISPs represented in this email

When you are connected to the Internet, you can send your email to the ISP's server. From there it is transmitted to the recipient of the message via another server, this time run by the recipient's ISP. It is stored on that server in a *mailbox* until the person you have emailed logs on to check whether he or she has received any new messages.

Many companies have internal email systems so that all their employees can communicate easily with each other. In this case their email address will usually reflect the company name. For example, Thomas Tripp at the Travelbug travel agency has the email address *Thomas.Tripp@travelbugonline.co.uk*.

You may find that the email address of your school or college includes its name (possibly abbreviated) followed by '.ac.uk'. The '.ac' indicates that you are using an academic network that links all colleges and universities in the UK.

Many people have their own web-based email address through companies such as Hotmail – see www.heinemann.co.uk/hotlinks (express code 0069P) for more. By logging on to the Hotmail website and entering a user name and password, you can access your email wherever you are in the world. Also, more and more ISP's will allow you to log on to the same email account that you usually use at home to check your email using any computer with Internet access.

Sending an email

The format of an email depends on the program you are using, but the most basic features of an email message include the following:

- **From:** This is where you enter your own email address.
- **To:** This is where you enter the address of the recipient of the email.
- **Cc:** This is where you enter the address of someone else who you would like to receive a copy of the e-mail.
- **Bcc:** This is where you enter the address of someone else who you would like to receive a copy of the e-mail *without the other recipients knowing that this copy has been sent* (the B stands for 'blind').
- **Subject:** A short description of what your email is about.
- A text box for the body of the message.

Jargon buster

'Cc' means **carbon copy** and is an expression from the days when carbon paper was used to make copies.

This is demonstrated in Figure 269, which shows an email message ready to be sent.

To send an email using software such as Outlook Express, you would do the following.

- Prepare your message offline (to save on telephone charges, unless you have an always-on connection).
- Click on the **Send** button to store it in the *Outbox* (containing outgoing mail).
- Connect to the Internet via your ISP.
- Click on the **Send and Receive** option.
- You may have to enter a password to access your mailbox at your ISP's server. In Outlook Express and most other programs you can configure the software to store and automatically enter the password.

Attach button

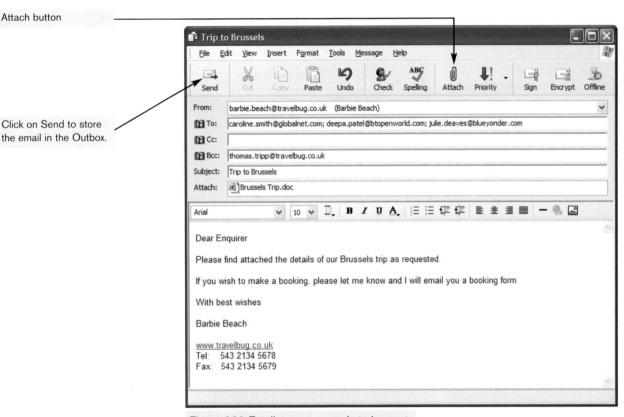

Click on Send to store the email in the Outbox.

Figure 269 Email message ready to be sent

Your email will be sent to the server at your ISP, and from there to the recipient's ISP.

Sending an email to a group of people

In Figure 269 there are several email addresses in the 'To:' line. Email software will allow you to send emails to more than one person at the same time. In the example, Barbie Beach wants to send details of the Brussels trip to three prospective clients. Note that the email addresses are separated by semicolons (;). You can also Cc or Bcc more than one person in the same way.

Sending an attachment

The **Attach** button allows you to attach (i.e. to send with your email) copies of files stored on your computer. The files can be text, sound, graphics, or even video. In the example in Figure 269, a Word document – Brussels Trip.doc – has been attached.

When you click the **Attach** button, a dialogue box appears, allowing you to locate the file you want to attach (Figure 270).

Figure 270 Adding an attachment

Replying to emails

When you receive an email from someone, you might want to reply to it. The simplest way to do this is to click on the **Reply** button (Figure 271). Alternatively, by clicking on the **Reply All** option, your reply could be sent to both the sender and the other recipients of the email – in this case, Molly Wischhusen. In addition, there is usually the option to forward the email on to someone else.

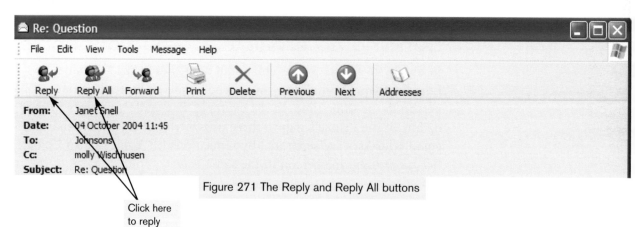

Figure 271 The Reply and Reply All buttons

When replying to an email, you can choose whether or not to include the original message. Most email software packages will let you set up your system so that the original email is automatically included when you click on the **Reply** button.

Go out and try!

1 Find out the email addresses of five of your fellow students. Send three of them a copy of the file 'WP Activity 1', which you created earlier (see page 250). Include a Cc and Bcc to the two other people.

- Start your email program.
- Click on **New Message**.
- In the **To:** box type the email addresses of the three students, separated by semi-colons.
- In the **Cc:** box type the email address of one of the remaining two students.
- In the **Bcc:** box type the email address of the one remaining student.
- In the **Subject**: box type a brief phrase, such as 'See my attached file'.
- In the main part of the window type any message that you want to send to these students.
- Click on the **paperclip** icon on the toolbar to attach the file.
- Locate the file 'WP Activity 1.doc' in your 'Word processing' sub-folder and click **Attach**.
- Click **Send** to send the email to your Outbox.
- Click the **Send/Recv** button to actually send the email over the Internet.

2 When you receive an email from one of your friends, reply using the **Reply All** feature to let them know you received it.

- Open the email.
- Press the **Reply All** button.
- Type a message such as 'thanks for the file'.
- Send the reply as before.

Figure 272 Email before file is attached

Figure 273 Email after file is attached

  Create a new file called 'Email' in your 'Email' sub-folder. Create a bold heading called '**E Activity 1**' and write a short paragraph describing the skills you have demonstrated in this activity.
Save the file.

Storing and organising emails and attachments

Using folders

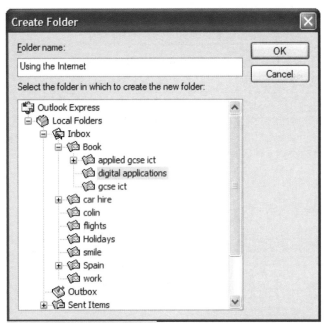

Figure 274 Creating a folder

It is important to create folders to help organise your emails, in the same way as you manage any other files such as word-processed documents. Most email software will allow you to create folders and sub-folders to help you organise your emails.

In Figure 274 a new folder called 'Using the Internet' is being created as a sub-folder in the 'digital applications' folder.

Once a folder has been created, you can transfer any emails to it by clicking on the message in the message list and dragging it to the folder, as shown in Figure 275.

TIP

The more emails you send and receive, the harder it can be to find them. It is good practice to spend some time each week deleting emails that are out of date – for example, an email sent to you by a friend reminding you of a music concert, the date for which has now passed.

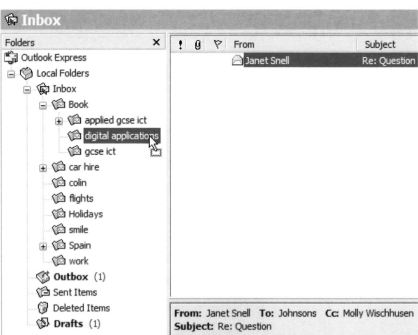

Figure 275 Dragging and dropping to organise emails into folders

To make it easier to locate emails, folders can be sorted by date, name of the sender, or subject. If you sort a folder by sender, you can easily find all the messages from one particular person.

It is possible to set up rules to automatically store received emails directly into folders *at the time they are received*. This means that your Inbox remains tidy, and emails are easy to find.

When you receive an email with an attachment, it is good practice to save the attachment to a folder in the directory where you keep all such files. This folder could be in your user area if you are at school or college, or it could be in *My Documents* on your home computer. In Figure 276 the Edexcel specification is being saved to the folder 'digital applications book'.

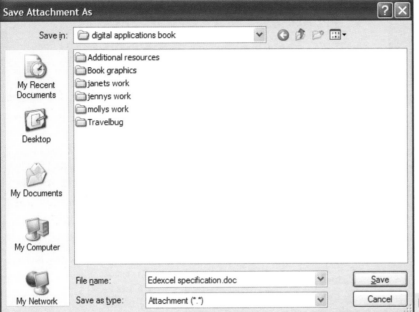

Figure 276 Saving an attachment

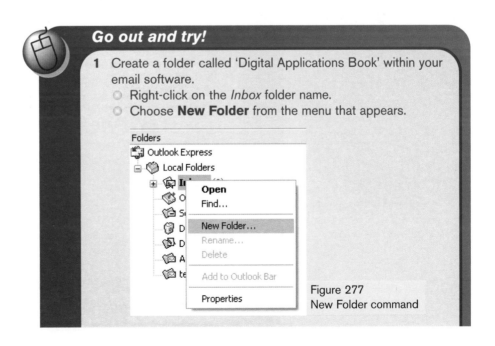

Go out and try!

1 Create a folder called 'Digital Applications Book' within your email software.
 ○ Right-click on the *Inbox* folder name.
 ○ Choose **New Folder** from the menu that appears.

Figure 277
New Folder command

○ Key in the folder name 'Digital Applications Book' and click **OK**.

Figure 278 Naming the new folder

2 Move the emails you received from your fellow students in the first activity to this folder.
   ○ Click on the Inbox to display its contents.
   ○ Drag the emails from the Inbox to the new folder.

3 Save any attachments you received to your 'Email' folder within your user area on the school or college network.
   ○ Open the email with the attachments you want to save.

Figure 279 New folder created under Inbox

   ○ From the menu, select **File**, **Save Attachments**.
   ○ Click on the **Browse** button to specify a folder.

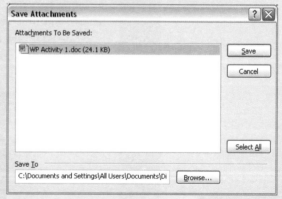

Figure 280 Saving attachments

○ Click the **Save** button.

Open your 'Email' file in the 'Email' sub-folder. Create a new bold heading '**E Activity 2**' and write a short paragraph describing the skills you have demonstrated in this activity. Save the file.

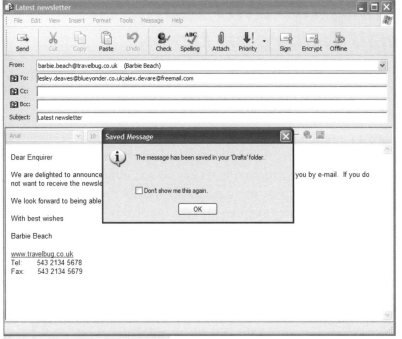

Figure 281 Saving a draft email

Using a drafts folder

If you wish to prepare an email to send sometime later, most email software packages allow you to save it. For example, in Outlook Express you can save to the *Drafts* folder by selecting **File, Save** (Figure 281). This will allow you to review the content of the email and send it when you are ready to do so.

Setting the priority of an email

Outlook Express and other email software will allow you to set the priority of an email (Figure 282). Emails sent as High Priority can usually be identified by a red exclamation mark.

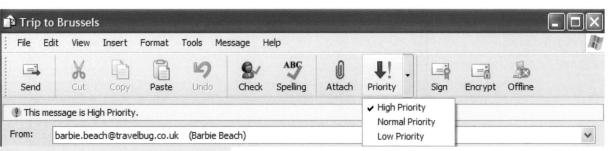

Figure 282 Choosing the priority of an email

✓ **TiP**

It is a good idea not to use the High Priority setting too often. If you send too many emails as high priority, your emails may all be treated in the same way by the recipients.

Jargon buster

An **email contact** is a person or organisation whose details, including name and email address, you have recorded in your email software address book.

The default setting in Outlook Express is Normal Priority, and there is also the option to send emails as Low Priority. Low Priority emails are identified by a blue down arrow.

The priority you choose for an email will *not* affect its speed of transmission over an internal email system or the Internet.

Setting up and using an email address book

You may have noticed that the To:, Cc: and Bcc: options each have an address button. Clicking any of these buttons takes you to your professional and personal address books.

Setting up an email address book will save you time, as you do not have to try to remember the addresses of email contacts. Your address book will save you having to key in someone's full address every time you send him or her a message. Another advantage of address books is that they help to prevent you from making mistakes, such as a wrong spelling or putting the dot in the wrong place, which would mean your email being returned ('bounced') or delivered to the wrong person.

Figure 283 The address book entry for one contact

Most email software, such as Outlook Express, will allow you to save all the details regarding your contacts, including their name, address, email address and phone number (Figure 283).

Outlook Express will also allow you to record other useful information regarding your email contacts, including personal details such as their birthday and even the names of their children.

Another feature is that you can give a contact a 'nickname'. In Figure 283 you can see that the nickname given to the email contact is 'IanJ'. This means that if you wanted to send an email you could enter the nickname in the 'To:' line as an alternative to opening the address book, and Outlook Express would automatically retrieve the full email address.

Go out and try!

Add the details of five of your friends to your email address book on the email system you use at school or college. Give each new email contact an appropriate nickname. Send an email to the five contacts confirming that they have been successfully added to your address book.

Open your 'Email' file. Create a new bold heading '**E Activity 3**' and write a short paragraph describing the skills you have demonstrated in this activity. Save the file.

Setting up and using distribution lists

A *distribution list* will allow you to send an email to several email contacts simultaneously, but without having to type all the email addresses in the 'To:' box, separated by semicolons.

For example, if Thomas Tripp of the Travelbug agency has decided to send an electronic newsletter to all customers on a monthly basis, it would be extremely tedious for him to have to type in all of the addresses each time the newsletter is sent. It would be sensible for Thomas, in this instance, to set up a distribution list (Figure 284).

Jargon buster

Outlook Express calls a **distribution list** a **group**.

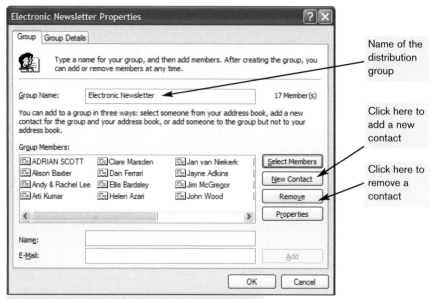

Name of the distribution group

Click here to add a new contact

Click here to remove a contact

Figure 284 Setting up a group in Outlook Express

Go out and try!

Set up a distribution list (group) called 'Friends' and add the email addresses of the five friends you added to your address book in the last activity. Add the email address of another friend, whose email address you have not as yet added to your address book. Send an email to the distribution group informing them that you have created the new group.

Open your 'Email' file. Create a new bold heading '**E Activity 4**' and write a short paragraph describing the skills you have demonstrated in setting up a distribution group for this activity. Save the file.

Assessment Hint

During your studies for this course you will be required to create e-portfolios to present evidence of your achievements, and you may decide to create these using website software.

Website authoring software

Most organisations and businesses would benefit from having a website. The Internet is an extremely good way of advertising goods and services, and many websites allow customers to order goods online. The Travelbug travel agency have decided that it is very important for them to have their own website to promote their business. They will be designing one using Microsoft FrontPage, a very popular website authoring application. This chapter will follow in detail the construction of their site.

LEARNING OUTCOMES

You need to learn about
- ✓ creating simple web pages
- ✓ using colour schemes
- ✓ creating and modifying tables
- ✓ editing text
- ✓ editing graphics
- ✓ adding lines and simple shapes
- ✓ using hyperlinks to link pages
- ✓ using text wrapping
- ✓ including sounds and video
- ✓ using animation options.

Before we consider website authoring software, it is important to understand what a website actually is.

HTML (hypertext markup language)

A *website* is a collection of related web pages. A *web page* is an electronic document that can contain text, images, forms, graphics, and other multimedia elements such as animation. Web pages are created with computer code known as *hypertext markup language* (*HTML*) and then viewed via web browsers, such as Internet Explorer and Netscape.

HTML is in the form of *tags*, which are used around blocks of text to indicate how the text should appear on the screen. The author of a web page designs the page and links all the material together using HTML. When the page is viewed (either by the author or someone viewing a published web page), the web browser software interprets the HTML language and displays the text exactly as the author intended.

HTML enables you to create *hyperlinks* within the text. When the viewer clicks on a hyperlink with a mouse, he or she is taken automatically to another part of the page or to another page on the Internet. A hyperlink might be represented by a word, a button or a picture.

TiP

Figure 286 on page 452 gives a list of common HTML tags.

TiP

Word processors such as Microsoft Word are less effective for writing HTML than basic tools such as Notepad. This is because advanced word processors tend to add extra formatting that interferes with the HTML coding.

Requirements for creating a simple web page

Most modern word processors enable you to produce HTML pages without the need to understand the coding. You can also use *web authoring tools*, such as Microsoft's FrontPage or Macromedia's Dreamweaver. We shall be looking at this method of creating web pages later in this chapter. However, it is important to know the basic concepts of HTML, so we shall first be looking at how Travelbug can create a web page manually.

In order to create a web page, Travelbug will need at the very least a simple text editor (like Notepad) to write the HTML. Alternatively, a dedicated HTML text editor (such as Allaire's HomeSite) could be used. There are many alternatives that they could use, including dedicated authoring tools. They could also use standard application software such Microsoft Word, which includes a 'Save as HTML' option. There are also many online wizards that will guide you step-by-step through the process of creating a web page – many ISPs offer online tools, for example.

Travelbug also needs at least one web browser – a dedicated software application that will enable them to view their own web pages as they are written.

Although it is possible to rely on a web authoring tool to create web pages, it is a good idea to learn the codes (or tags) used to format and structure the text.

Finally, and perhaps most importantly, good design and presentation skills are required.

Go out and try!

Look at a range of websites on the Internet. Find a page that particularly interests you. Read the page to familiarise yourself with its contents.

You can see how the page has been constructed with HTML code by viewing the *source code*: select **View**, **Source** (or **Document**, **Source**) from the menu of your web browser.

Figure 285 The HTML source of a website

The source code is what the author used to design the page. Can you pick out some of the text you read on the actual page? The code will probably look very complicated because it might have been written by an expert in HTML and will include many advanced concepts.

Create a file called 'Website software' in your 'Website software' sub-folder. Create a new bold heading '**WS Activity 1**' and write a short paragraph describing the skills you have demonstrated in the activity. Save the file.

HTML tags

When you viewed the source code, did you notice words or letters inside the < and > marks? These are known as 'tags' and are the way the web browser knows how to display the document. For example, tags tell the web browser where to start a new paragraph or print a line of text.

Tags usually come in pairs, with the second tag of the pair beginning with a slash symbol (/) to show that the effect of the first tag should now stop. As an example, the **<h1>** and **</h1>** tags indicate where a main heading begins and ends.

The first tag of any document is **<html>**, which tells the web browser that you a beginning a page of information written in HTML. The closing tag **</html>** is put at the end of the document. Figure 286 lists some other very common tags.

Tag		What it does
<html>	**</html>**	Indicates the beginning and the end of an HTML page.
<head>	**</head>**	The head section of the web page.
<title>	**</title>**	The text that will appear on the title bar.
<body>	**</body>**	All the text in the document is between these tags.
<h1>	**</h1>**	Inserts a heading in the largest font. Other sizes are h2, h3, h4, h5 and h6, which is the smallest.
****	****	Displays characters in bold.
<i>	**</i>**	Displays characters in italics.
<center>	**</center>**	Everything between these tags is centred.
** **		Inserts a line break.
<p>	**</p>**	The text between these tags is treated as a separate paragraph.

Figure 286 Common HTML tags

Not all tags come in pairs. The **
** tag, used to create a line break, comes on its own. The **</p>** tag (end of paragraph) is optional, but it is good practice to include it.

Jargon buster

A **comment** is something you would use to add a note to remind you or someone else who is looking at your program about something important that you don't want to forget.

Comment tags

If you want to write something in your HTML page that you don't want to appear on your web page, you use a *comment tag*. The tag that turns the comment on is **<!--** and the tag that turns the comment off is **-->**.

Structure of an HTML document

There are always two parts of an HTML document – the *head* and the *body*.

- The first part of any document is always the head. Information in the head is enclosed between the **<head>** and **</head>** tags. Elements in the head area are not displayed in the web page. The most common element is the document's title, bracketed by the **<title>** and **</title>** tags.

- The body of the document begins after the head and is enclosed within the **<body>** and **</body>** tags. The body will contain all the parts of the web page displayed in a web browser's viewing window.

Colour of the background and fonts

You can include between the **<body>** and **</body>** tags different attributes for the style of the text or the background on the web page.

There are 16 colour names that you can choose from (Figure 287). There are also many different combinations of colours that you can achieve by typing what are called alphanumeric codes. Examples of these are **#FFFFCC** for a pale weak yellow, and **#CCCCFF** for a pale weak blue.

TiP

There are far too many colour codes to mention in this book. By searching with the phrase 'HTML colour names' in an Internet search engine, you can find links to websites that list all the codes.

Black	Silver	Green	Lime
Gray*	Olive	Yellow	White
Maroon	Navy	Red	Blue
Purple	Teal	Fuchsia	Aqua

Figure 287 Colour names that can be included in HTML code   *Note the American spelling

TiP

When altering the font, beware not to use strange fonts. If the font does not exist (is not installed) on the computer of whoever is viewing your page, their browser will choose the 'next best' font, which might destroy the effect you wanted to achieve.

Font type and size

Standard headings come in sizes from H1 (the biggest) to H6 (the smallest). It is possible also to choose the font size of standard text. The default size is 3, but using the tag **<font size=4>** will increase the font size.

The default font type in Internet Explorer is *Times New Roman*. By using the tag **<font face=arial>** the font on the web page can be changed to Arial, which is a very popular sans serif font.

Go out and try!

1   Open the text editor *Notepad* on your computer and key in the HTML code in Figure 288, exactly as shown.
   - From the *Start menu*, select **All Programs**, **Accessories**, **Notepad**.
   - Key in the text shown in Figure 288. You will need to press **Enter** to go to a new line.

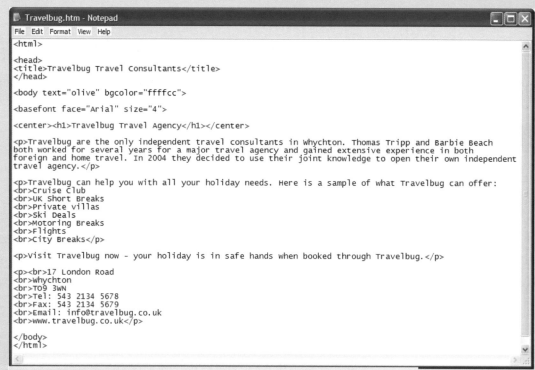

Figure 288 Simple HTML code, written between the <html> and </html> tags

2 Save the file in your 'Website software' sub-folder as 'Travelbug.htm'.
- ○ Select **File**, **Save** and key in 'Travelbug.htm' in the *Filename:* box.
- ○ Click **Save**.

3 View the file in a web browser.
- ○ Browse to the saved file on disk.
- ○ Double-click the file to open it in your web browser.

4 Referring to Figures 286 and 287, which show common HTML tags and colour names, experiment with making changes to the code.
- ○ Edit the 'Travelbug.htm' file in *Notepad*.
- ○ Save the file after each change.
- ○ Click the **Refresh** button in your web browser to see the end result.

TiP

It is sensible to put all your web pages and graphics into a single folder.

Open your 'Website software' file. Create a new bold heading '**WS Activity 2**' and write a short paragraph describing the skills you have demonstrated while creating a simple web page in the activity. 🖫 Save the file.

Skills check ▶▶

There is an opportunity to learn more about storyboards and structures in Unit 2.

Although it is important to understand how to create web pages manually, it is usually quicker to use web-authoring software. The remainder of this unit will show you how to use the features of Microsoft FrontPage to develop web pages.

Jargon buster

The **navigation route** is the way the visitor to the site will be taken (by means of links) to achieve maximum effect.

Establishing the structure of a website

Before you begin creating pages for a multiple-page website, it is important to plan on paper how you want the site to appear. In the same way as when you plan a presentation, you should plan the structure of a website which clearly shows the *navigation route*, and create a *storyboard* that shows the layout and content of each page. A well-designed website will have a clear structure and be easy to navigate.

Using wizards

Most authoring tools will include wizards to make designing a website or web page an easier process. Even a beginner can create a professional looking site by following one of the wizards provided. A wizard will take you step by step through the process, giving you options from which to chose at each stage.

For example, you can see from Figure 289, the *New Web Site* wizard in FrontPage, provides a range of different designs from which to choose. Furthermore, you can create the folder in which to save the *web* at the same time.

Thomas Tripp of Travelbug could decide to use the Personal Web wizard in FrontPage to create a website for the company. This wizard will automatically create a basic website with a home page and several pages that link to the home page. The structure will not necessarily be the same as his paper design, but Thomas will be able to amend it very easily. In *Navigation view* it is possible to add or delete pages and rename existing pages.

Figure 290 shows the navigational structure of the Travelbug website with the pages renamed to meet Thomas's needs. It is the construction of this website that you will be following throughout the remainder of this chapter.

The next step will be for Thomas to build each web page in turn. However, unlike when a website is coded from scratch in HTML, screen prompts are given on how to continue.

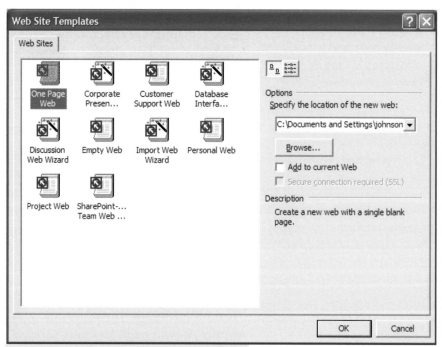

Figure 289 FrontPage's New Web Site wizard

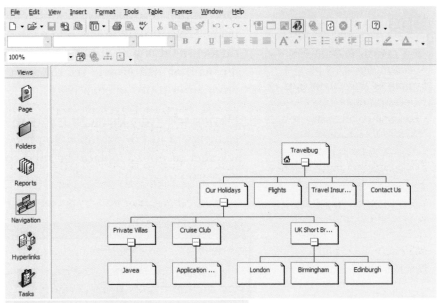

Figure 290 The Navigation view in FrontPage

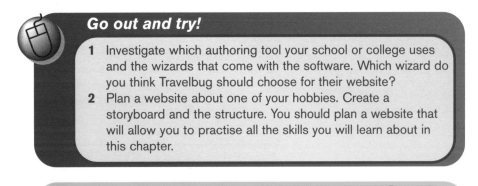

Go out and try!

1 Investigate which authoring tool your school or college uses and the wizards that come with the software. Which wizard do you think Travelbug should choose for their website?
2 Plan a website about one of your hobbies. Create a storyboard and the structure. You should plan a website that will allow you to practise all the skills you will learn about in this chapter.

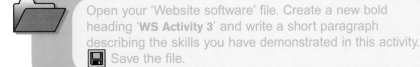

Open your 'Website software' file. Create a new bold heading '**WS Activity 3**' and write a short paragraph describing the skills you have demonstrated in this activity. Save the file.

Using colour schemes

Another benefit of using an authoring tool such as FrontPage is that *templates* or *themes* are included, rather like the design templates supplied with PowerPoint. You can choose the theme for the entire web or for individual pages.

TiP

It is preferable to have a uniform theme, as using a variety of themes will give an overall muddled appearance to a site.

One of the easiest ways to apply colours to a website being built using FrontPage is to use one of the supplied themes. Using a theme like this will provide a consistent feel to the site, which means that visitors will see the same colour scheme and navigation tools on each page.

Having selected a theme, it is a fairly simple task to change certain elements of it. For example, you have the option of deciding whether or not to replace the solid colour *background* with the background graphic included with the theme (Figure 291).

Click here to show the background picture supplied with a theme.

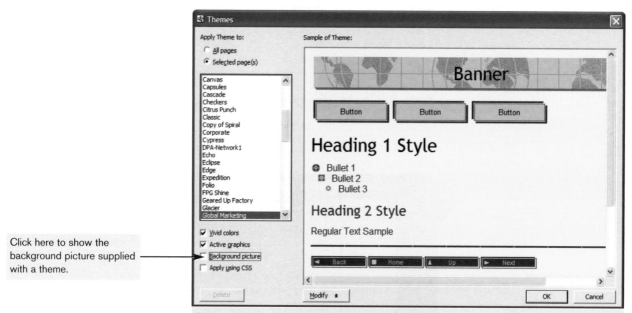

Figure 291 An optional background picture is supplied with each theme in FrontPage

Furthermore, you can modify the *colour scheme* of the elements of a theme as shown in Figure 292. If Thomas Tripp wanted to use a theme supplied with FrontPage for the Travelbug website, he could change the colour of the background of all the pages, or of one individual page, rather than using a graphic as the background.

As well as the background graphics included in a theme, there are also banner, bullet and button graphics. FrontPage allows you to change any or all of these (Figure 293). You can even change the fonts, sizes and font styles (bold, italic) that are used for text on graphic items such as banners and buttons in a theme.

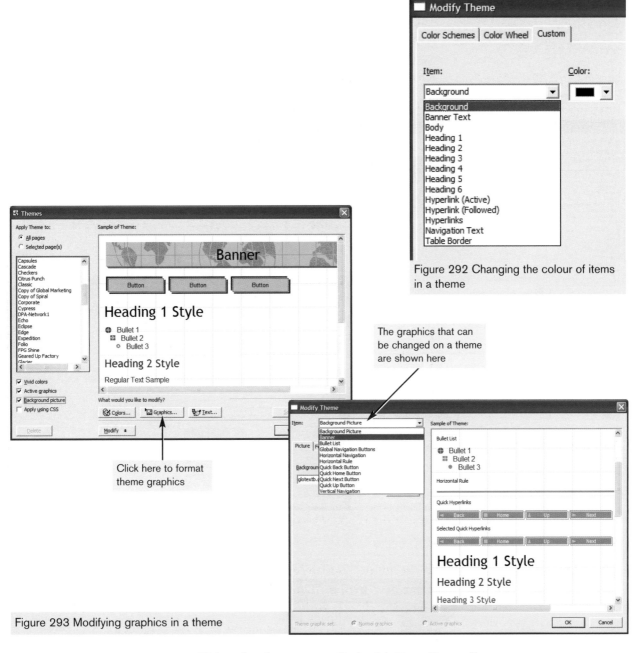

Figure 292 Changing the colour of items in a theme

The graphics that can be changed on a theme are shown here

Click here to format theme graphics

Figure 293 Modifying graphics in a theme

Using the themes supplied with FrontPage allows you to create a consistent website. You can either use the colour schemes as they are or make changes that will be reflected on individual pages or throughout the entire website.

If you prefer not to use one of the themes supplied, you can still easily change the background colour, or even include a graphic, by selecting the **Background** option from the **Format** menu.

459

Also, you can change the text styles used, either in a theme or in a web page you are designing without a theme. For example, if Thomas Tripp decides to change the font style and size for normal text on his website (called 'Body' text), he can click on the **Text** button of the *Themes* dialogue box to do so (Figure 294).

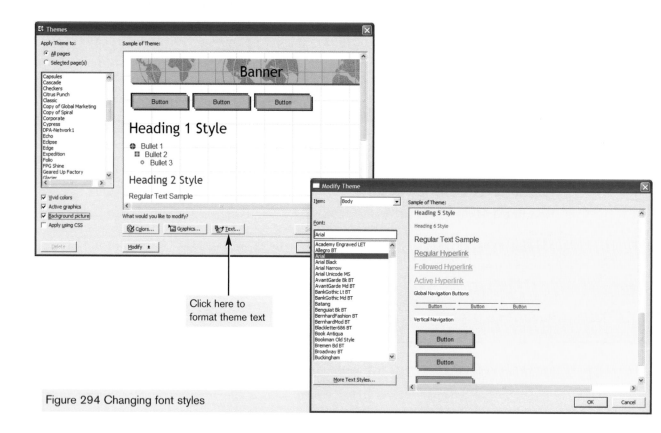

Click here to format theme text

Figure 294 Changing font styles

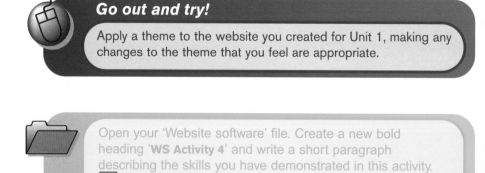

Go out and try!

Apply a theme to the website you created for Unit 1, making any changes to the theme that you feel are appropriate.

Open your 'Website software' file. Create a new bold heading '**WS Activity 4**' and write a short paragraph describing the skills you have demonstrated in this activity. Save the file.

Using and editing text

Whether you have decided to build a web page from scratch, or to use one of the templates supplied with FrontPage, you will need to add text. One of the benefits of using a web-authoring tool is that you do not need to use HTML to add text. You simply enter the text you want and format it using the normal formatting tools, just as you would in Word. As you are doing this, FrontPage is creating the HTML for you.

Once you have keyed in your text, changing the font type, size and colour is far easier than in HTML. Simply select the text and change the font type, size and colour, just as you would do in Word. You can create bulletted lists and change paragraph formatting – justification and line spacing – again, just as you would do in Word. In FrontPage you can choose the option you require from the **Format** menu (Figure 295).

Skills check ▶▶

See page 251 for a reminder of how to format text in Word.

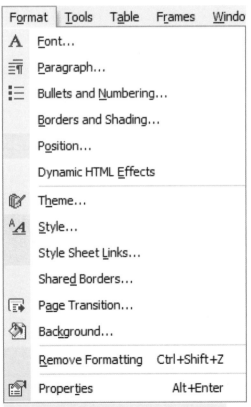

Figure 295 The Format menu in FrontPage

Figure 296 shows FrontPage dialogue boxes used to format text. You will see that they are very similar to those used in other packages – just remember to select the text first before applying the different formatting.

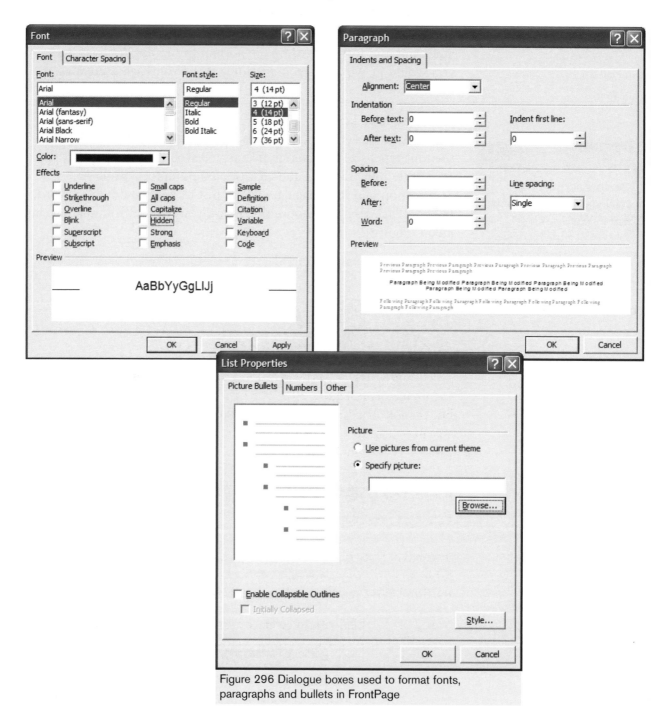

Figure 296 Dialogue boxes used to format fonts, paragraphs and bullets in FrontPage

Figure 297 shows a possible home page for Travelbug's website, which is still under construction. There are three view buttons – **Normal**, **HTML** and **Preview**. Use **Normal** view to edit the page, **HTML** view to view or edit the HTML code, or **Preview** view to see how the page will look in a web browser.

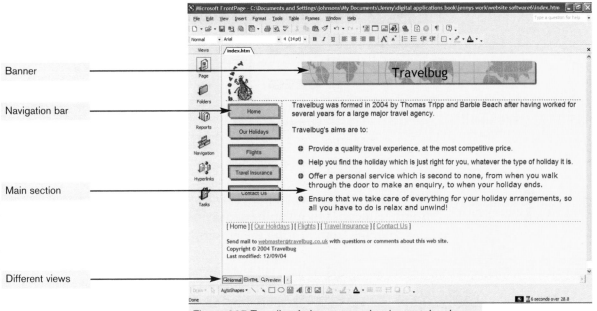

Banner

Navigation bar

Main section

Different views

Figure 297 Travelbug's home page begins to take shape

Page Banner refers to the text and graphic that goes across the top of each page, as in Figure 297. The banner graphic remains the same but the text heading changes on each page. This would be quite a complex task to code using HTML alone, but by using FrontPage the process is extremely simple.

Creating and modifying tables

You have probably guessed by now that if you want to include a table in a web page, it will be more complicated if you do so by writing HTML code than by using FrontPage.

Many of the skills you have learned for creating a table in Word can be applied to FrontPage. You can create a basic structure by using the **Table** menu on the *Standard* toolbar, and then add text or graphics in the cells (Figure 298). You can even include tables within tables! You can merge cells, change their height and width, and apply different borders just as you would in Word.

Skills check ▶▶

See page 272 for a reminder of how to format tables in Word.

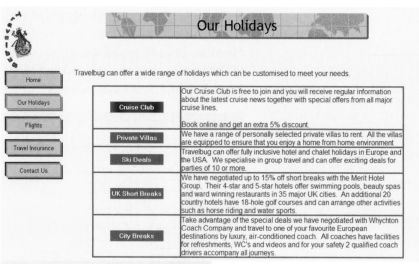

Figure 298 A table created in FrontPage

You can create more complex tables by selecting **Table, Draw Table** from the menu. Once you have drawn a table, you can erase rows and columns from it using the eraser tool.

Tables can be used for arranging information in rows and colums, or for displaying text and graphics on a page. In fact, tables are extremely useful for designing a web page layout. Often tables are used for some or all of a page's layout, although you may not be aware of this when looking at a web page (Figure 299).

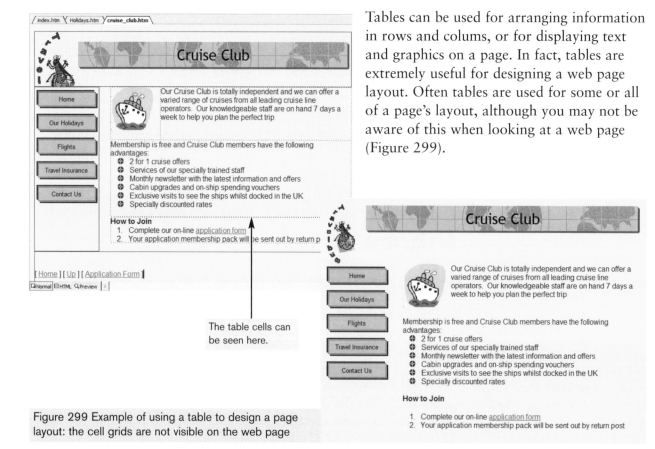

The table cells can be seen here.

Figure 299 Example of using a table to design a page layout: the cell grids are not visible on the web page

Using and editing graphics

Graphics are an important part of any website as they can communicate a lot of information very easily. It is a simple process to insert a graphic into a website being created in FrontPage.

Sourcing the images

The graphics can come from a number of sources, which you will have already learned about in the chapter on artwork and imaging software (page 383).

- Graphics applications allow you to create your own pictures. Examples are CorelDraw, Windows Paint and Adobe Photoshop.
- Clip art is available from various sources.
- You can scan existing photographs or pictures to put into your work.
- Digital still and video cameras allow you to take photos and videos which can be included on your website.

Inserting an image

Thomas Tripp wants to include the Travelbug logo on his newly designed website. To do this he selects **Insert, Picture** from the **File** menu (Figure 300). The **Set Transparent Color** option from the *Picture* toolbar will allow Thomas to remove the white background so that the logo blends nicely into the page.

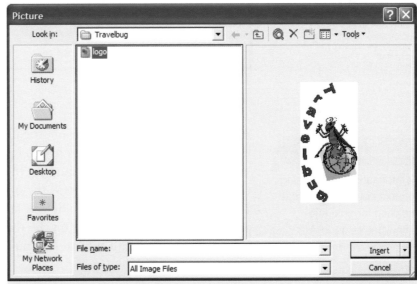

Figure 300 The picture called 'logo' has been selected from the Travelbug folder, and a thumbnail is displayed

Jargon buster

Thumbnails are smaller versions of large images. They are used by graphic designers and photographers to make it easier and quicker to look at and manage a group of larger images.

Just as in other applications, FrontPage's *Picture* toolbar will allow you to make changes to a graphic, such as rotating it, adjusting the brightness or even creating an automatic *thumbnail*. Thumbnails are often used on web pages to decrease download times – the visitor to the website can decide which images to see in full size, usually by clicking on them.

Another useful feature of FrontPage is that you can create a *photo gallery* of pictures very quickly by using **Insert, Web Component** and then selecting **Photo Gallery**. You can choose from four different layouts. In each case, thumbnail images of your files are created automatically (Figure 301).

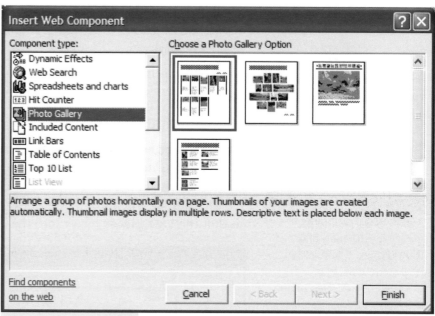

Figure 301 A photogallery

Skills check ▶▶

For information on choosing the most appropriate image resolution for print and screen, see page 394.

An advantage of producing a photogallery automatically with FrontPage is that the file sizes of the images are reduced substantially when the thumbnails are created. In the photogallery in Figure 302, each thumbnail is 4 KB, whereas the original images were all in excess of 1000 KB. Of course, if you keep the original images as part of your web (so that clicking on the thumbnail displays the full-size image) then the overall file size of your project will increase.

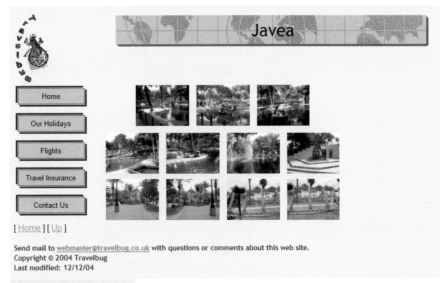

Figure 302 Thumbnails

Wrapping text

You can change the properties of an image to control how text wraps around it.

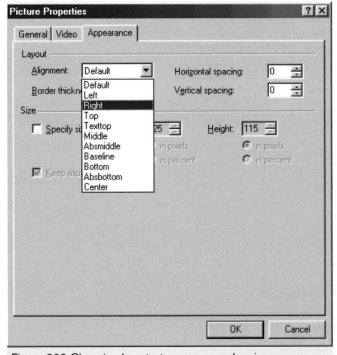

Figure 303 Changing how text wraps around an image

Double-click the image to display its *Picture Properties* dialogue. Click on the *Appearance* tab and make your selection for the **Alignment**, as shown in Figure 303.

Adding lines and simple shapes

You can add lines and shapes, fill the shapes with colour, outline them and make them look three-dimensional. The method in FrontPage is the same as in PowerPoint and the other Microsoft Office tools.

The **Autoshapes** button on the *Drawing* toolbar can be used to add shapes, including lines, a flowchart, stars, banners and callouts. It is possible to add borders to text and objects, as shown in Figure 304: Travelbug have used a *callout* on their Contact Us page, and have used a border around the text on their Insurance page.

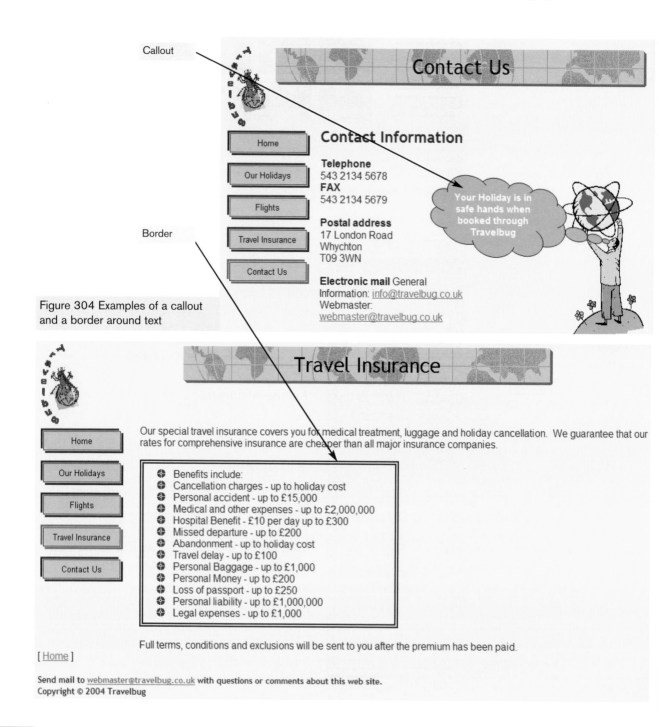

Callout

Border

Figure 304 Examples of a callout and a border around text

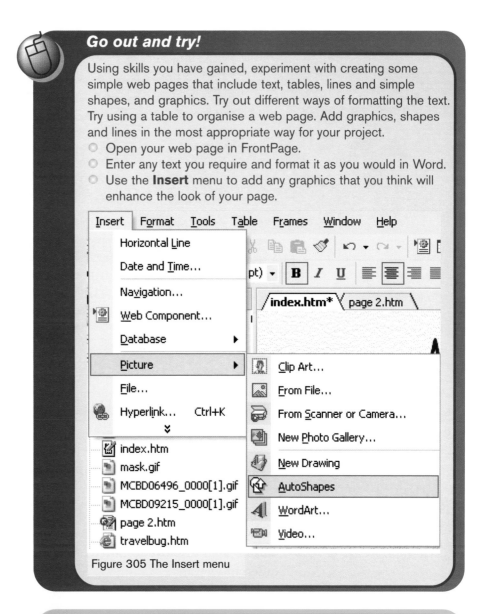

Go out and try!

Using skills you have gained, experiment with creating some simple web pages that include text, tables, lines and simple shapes, and graphics. Try out different ways of formatting the text. Try using a table to organise a web page. Add graphics, shapes and lines in the most appropriate way for your project.
- Open your web page in FrontPage.
- Enter any text you require and format it as you would in Word.
- Use the **Insert** menu to add any graphics that you think will enhance the look of your page.

Figure 305 The Insert menu

Open your 'Website software' file. Create a new bold heading '**WS Activity 5**' and write a short paragraph describing the skills you have demonstrated when using text, tables, shapes/lines and graphics when creating web pages. Save the file.

Adding a rollover

By using the Dynamic HTML option in Frontpage, it was a fairly simple process for Travelbug to include a rollover on the page shown in Figure 306. When the user's mouse pointer is over the picture of the outside of the villa, the picture changes to show the inside.

Figure 306 Adding a rollover

Go out and try!

Try adding some rollovers to the web pages you have created. You might like to try out some other Dynamic HTML options.

Open your 'Website software' File. Create a new bold heading **'WS Activity 6'** and write a short paragraph describing the skills you have demonstrated when using rollovers.

 Save the file.

Inserting hyperlinks

FrontPage will allow you to add *hyperlinks*, which enable visitors to the website to move from one page to another easily. Hyperlinks can also be used to move to different parts of a page or even to a different website.

You have the option of using text, buttons or pictures as hyperlinks. For example, on the Cruise Club web page, Thomas Tripp has created a hyperlink to the online application form (Figure 307). He has done this by typing the text, selecting it and then choosing **Insert, Hyperlink** from the menu.

Furthermore, when you are creating a set of web pages (a 'web') using certain wizards, FrontPage automatically creates a *navigation bar* that has hyperlinks to the other pages in the web. These hyperlinks allow the visitor to move to a different page when the appropriate link is clicked. In Figure 308 the main navigation bar shows user-friendly *button hyperlinks*, whereas the hyperlinks at the bottom of the web page are examples of *text hyperlinks*.

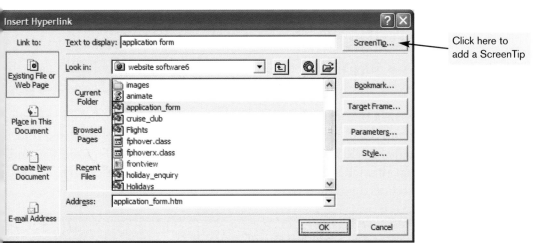

Figure 307 Adding a hyperlink and a ScreenTip

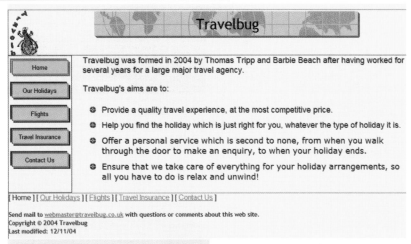

Figure 308 Hyperlinks on a web page

Go out and try!

1 Create a text hyperlink between two web pages.
   ○ Make sure you have at least two web pages. If not, create a copy of an existing page, giving it a different name. Make sure the text is different, so you will be able to tell which page you are looking at.
   ○ Open one of the pages in FrontPage.
   ○ Click where you want to create the link.
   ○ Select **Insert**, **Hyperlink** from the menu. The *Insert Hyperlink* dialogue (Figure 307) will appear.
   ○ Type the link text you want to use, such as 'my other page', in the *Text to display:* area.
   ○ Click on the web page you want to link to, then press **OK**.
2 Open the first page in a web browser, and check that clicking the new link takes you to the second page.
3 Try adding another link from the second page back to the first.

Open your 'Website software' File. Create a new bold heading **'WS Activity 7'** and write a short paragraph describing the skills you have demonstrated when adding hyperlinks between pages in a website.
💾 Save the file.

Using hyperlinks to point to other websites

Thomas Tripp decided to add links on Travelbug's City Breaks page to a another website that gives details of the current weather in each city.

To ensure that the hyperlink is correct, Thomas first found the page he wanted to link to using Internet Explorer. He then selected and copied the URL from the *Address* bar, as shown in Figure 309, and pasted this URL directly into the *Address* box in the *Insert Hyperlink* dialogue box.

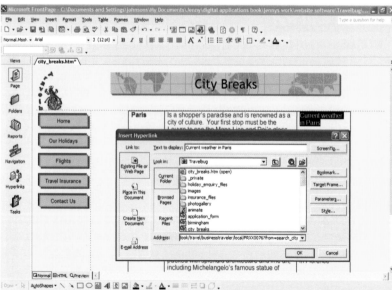

Figure 309 Inserting an external hyperlink

TiP

When you include links in a website, it is very important to check regularly that all the links still work. Failure to do so may result in visitors to your website receiving the message 'The page cannot be found' (Figure 310) – which is not something that will give the visitors confidence in the accuracy of the rest of your website.

Hyperinks that do not work are often referred to as 'broken links'. They can be caused for a number of reasons:

- the external website no longer exists
- the specific page on the external website has been deleted
- there is a temporary problem on the server on which the website is hosted (the web server).

---

i | **The page cannot be found**

The page you are looking for might have been removed, had its name changed, or is temporarily unavailable.

Please try the following:

- If you typed the page address in the Address bar, make sure that it is spelled correctly.
- Open the www.landregistry.gov.uk home page, and then look for links to the information you want.
- Click the ⇐ Back button to try another link.
- Click 🔍 Search to look for information on the Internet.

HTTP 404 - File not found
Internet Explorer

Figure 310 Example of a Page cannot be found error page

Using buttons for hyperlinks

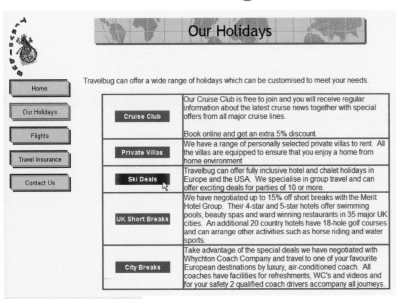

Figure 311 Hover buttons

FrontPage allows you to easily change the display for hyperlinks from text to buttons, which can make a web page more interesting. By selecting **Insert, Web Component,** you can add interactive (hover) buttons which link to other pages. Thomas Tripp has done this (Figure 311) – the buttons change colour when the mouse pointer is over them.

Using hotspots for hyperlinks

Just as pictures can be defined as hyperlinks, you can identify *specific areas of a picture* as separate links. These links are known as *hotspots*. In FrontPage you use the hotspot drawing tools □ ○ ◁ on the Picture toolbar to insert a hotspot.

You need to *select* the picture and then choose the rectangle, circle or polygon hotspot tool to create a border around the exact small area of the picture you want to become the hotspot. You will then be able to insert the URL of the page or website to which you want the hotspot to take the user.

In Figure 312 you can see that Travelbug have included a map of the UK that allows the user to click on areas to view the details of services in Edinburgh, Birmingham and London.

Figure 312 Hotspots inserted on a map of the UK

Using an email hyperlink

FrontPage allows you to create an *email hyperlink*. When activated by a visitor to the website, this link will call up the visitor's email program and open it at a 'new message' window with your email address already inserted in the 'To:' field. In this way, the visitor can easily send you an email message or enquiry.

In Figure 313 you can see that Thomas Tripp has used this facility on Travelbug's Contact Us web page.

Type the email address here

Choose this option to add an email address

Figure 313 Adding an email hyperlink

TiP

WAV files can be very large. If you are going to put a WAV file on a web page, you can keep the size down by making it very short, or by using lower-quality recording settings. You could decide to compress the file into MP3 format.

Open your 'Website software' file. Create a new bold heading '**WS Activity 8**' and write a short paragraph describing the skills you have demonstrated when using a variety of methods to insert hyperlinks on web pages. 💾 Save the file.

Skills check ▶▶

More information on recording sound files can be found on page 403.

Including sounds

FrontPage allows you set a background sound for a web page. With your mouse, right-click on the page area while in Normal view and select **Page Properties** from the pop-up menu. The sound can be set to loop a set number of times, or to play the entire time the user is viewing a page.

Thomas Tripp of Travelbug decided to set the background sound of the company's Cruise Club page to the sound file 'Sailing', which he included in his PowerPoint presentation (see page 375). The *Page Properties* dialogue box he used is shown in Figure 314.

Sound can be attached also to 'hover buttons' and other dynamic effects. If you have a microphone and sound card, you may decide to record the sound in a digital format on your computer using Microsoft Sound Recorder. You might choose to save the recorded sound as a WAV file, which is the most common format for sound files and the easiest for users to play, since all recent browsers can open WAV files.

Figure 314 Adding a sound to a web page in FrontPage

Including video

With FrontPage, adding a video is straightforward. You use the same technique you learned when using PowerPoint (see page 374). You simply select **Insert, Picture** and choose the **Video** option.

It is important to take into account that video files take a large amount of storage space. The video file in Figure 315, which is 1285 KB, has a playing time of only 20 seconds!

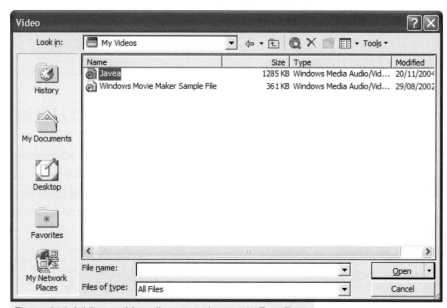

Figure 315 Adding a video clip to a web page in FrontPage

When you include a video on a web page in FrontPage, it will not appear until you view the page through a browser, or the website is published. Instead, a symbol will appear in the location where the video has been added.

Go out and try!

Add a variety of videos to the web pages you have created. Remember to take into account the warnings about file sizes and how this will effect download times.

Open your 'Website software' file. Create a new bold heading 'WS Activity 9' and write a short paragraph describing the skills you have demonstrated for this activity. Save the file.

Including animation (movement)

There are a number of ways in which you can include animation on your website.

Scrolling text

FrontPage allows you to add what it calls *marquees*. These are text areas that will *scroll* across the screen repeatedly. They are useful for getting a message across. Travelbug could include a marquee on its Cruise Club page: 'Don't delay … join now!'

Animated GIFs

You could include an animated GIF file, which consists of a series of static GIF images that are displayed in succession to create the illusion of movement. It is possible to download the Microsoft GIF Animator for free use in order to create animated GIF files for a website.

Dynamic HTML

You can use the *dynamic HTML* facility within FrontPage to animate text in a number of ways. For example, you could animate text to fly in from the right when a page is loaded, or you could format the text to change size when the mouse is moved over it. Figure 316 shows the *DHTML Effects* toolbar.

Allows you to select the event that will trigger the effect.

Available effects are displayed here.

Allows you to set any properties that are available for the effect.

Click here to remove the effect.

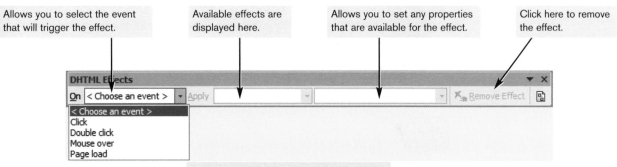

Figure 316 The dynamic HTML toolbar

Using transitions

As in PowerPoint presentations, you can apply transitions. FrontPage allows you to apply transitions to a web page for when a user enters or exits a page, or when the user enters or exits your website. You are able to choose the transition effect that you want, or choose random transition, so that the effect will change each time a user enters or leaves your website or web page (Figure 317).

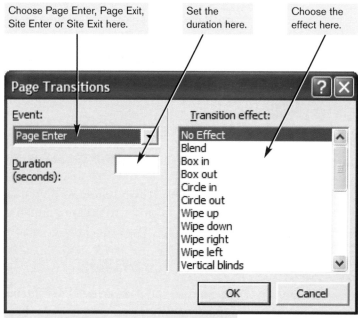

Figure 317 Dialogue box for page transitions

You can also set the time for the transition in seconds by entering a value in the *Duration (seconds)* text box.

Go out and try!

Add a variety of sounds and animations, as appropriate, to the web pages you have created. Remember to take into account the warnings about file sizes and how this will effect download times.

Open your 'Website software' file. Create a new bold heading '**WS Activity 10**' and write a short paragraph describing the skills you have demonstrated for this activity. 💾 Save the file.

Publishing the Web

In FrontPage, a 'web' does not become a website until it has been published and can be viewed by other people. A *web host* is the name given to the company that provides space on a web server for you to publish your site. Many companies will offer to publish websites free of charge on condition that they display some advertising banners at the top of each page. Alternatively, your school or college may have their own web server onto which you can publish your site.

Your own ISP may offer limited free space to publish your site. If you wish to publish your 'web' as it has been created in FrontPage, you need to find out whether your ISP supports FrontPage Server Extensions.

The steps necessary to upload the files that make up your website can vary from one ISP to another, but it is normally quite a simple process.

Project planning software

When you read through the section on project planning (page 490), you will see how important it is to prioritise tasks and to allocate time for each task, while at the same time ensuring you complete everything in the time available. In that chapter we suggest you produce a *mind map* and a *Gantt chart* to help you plan your project. Project planning software is available to help you do this.

Mind mapping software

A mind map is a useful way to organise your ideas in the early stages of a project. See page 496 of the Project Planning section for more information about mind mapping.

Although it is easy to create mind maps on paper (for example, using a flip chart), remember that you may want to modify your mind map over time. Various software packages are available to help you create and modify mind maps; specialist packages include Inspiration and MatchWare OpenMind, although general diagramming tools such as Microsoft Visio can also be used.

By using software to create your mind maps, you will find it easier to add them to your e-portfolio as evidence of the planning you have done for your project.

Go out and try!

An example of a hand drawn mind map for an 18th birthday party is illustrated on page 497. Figure 318 shows how the same mind map would appear when prepared using mind mapping software. Find out what software packages are available to you that would be suitable for creating and editing mind maps and prepare your own version.

Start a file called 'Project planning software'. Create a new bold heading called '**Mind mapping**' and describe the skills you have demonstrated in this activity.

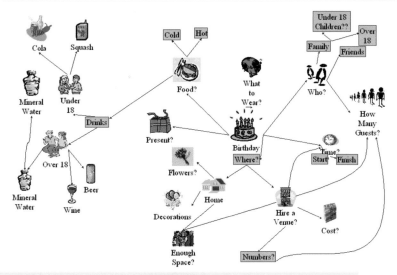

Figure 318 A simple mind map diagram created in Microsoft Visio

Project planning software

Whilst you can produce a project plan by hand or by using standard packages, the advantage of using a specialist software package such as Microsoft Project is that you can very easily modify the plan to reflect any changes you have to make during the project.

To create a project plan, you simply enter the tasks you have to complete, prioritise them, and specify the duration of each task together with the start and finish dates. The software will produce a Gantt chart that shows exactly how the project should be managed.

You can even use the built-in calendar to indicate any days that you will not be able to work on the project (Figure 319). Then the tasks will be scheduled around this time.

If you experience a hold-up in the work which means you cannot keep to the original schedule, you can amend the data you entered into the software; a modified Gantt chart will be produced to help you manage your time.

Project planning software is used extensively by organisations that run large projects. Figures 320–322 show the software in use by a construction company that had a project to build an extension to a house. The client had been given a completion date and it was important that the construction company were off the site by this date.

During the project the plasterers were held up on another job and were several days late in starting. This meant that other trades were also held up and the project had to be rescheduled. The project planning software made this task much easier and helped to ensure that the project was completed on time.

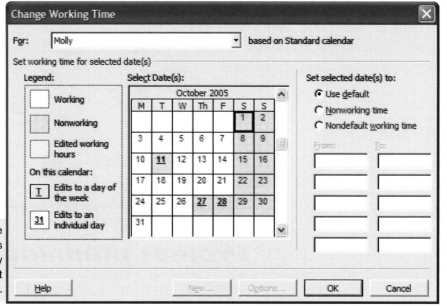

Figure 319 Molly will not be working at the weekends and has three days of holiday booked. Any plans will take this into account automaticallly.

	❶	Task Name	Duration	Start	Finish	Predecessors
1		Set site up	1 day?	Mon 11/10/04	Mon 11/10/04	
2	▦	Foundations	2 days	Mon 11/10/04	Tue 12/10/04	
3		Drainage	1 day?	Wed 13/10/04	Wed 13/10/04	2
4		Sub structure brickwork	2 days	Thu 14/10/04	Fri 15/10/04	3
5	▦	Oversite and slab	1 day?	Fri 15/10/04	Fri 15/10/04	
6		Brick/blockwork	5 days	Mon 18/10/04	Fri 22/10/04	5
7		Timber roof structure	3 days	Mon 25/10/04	Wed 27/10/04	6
8	▦	Roof covering	4 days	Mon 01/11/04	Thu 04/11/04	
9		Velux installation	1 day?	Thu 28/10/04	Thu 28/10/04	7
10	▦	Soffits and facias	3 days	Tue 02/11/04	Thu 04/11/04	
11		Windows	1 day?	Fri 05/11/04	Fri 05/11/04	10
12		Knock through	3 days	Mon 08/11/04	Wed 10/11/04	11
13	▦	Plumbing 1st fix	2 days	Tue 09/11/04	Wed 10/11/04	
14	▦	Electrical 1st fix	2 days	Wed 10/11/04	Thu 11/11/04	
15	▦	Plastering	4 days	Mon 15/11/04	Thu 18/11/04	
16		Screeding	1 day?	Fri 19/11/04	Fri 19/11/04	15
17	▦	Tiling	4 days	Mon 29/11/04	Thu 02/12/04	
18	▦	Plumbing 2nd fix	2 days	Thu 02/12/04	Fri 03/12/04	
19	▦	Electrical 2nd fix	2 days	Thu 02/12/04	Fri 03/12/04	
20		Decorating	5 days	Mon 06/12/04	Fri 10/12/04	19
21		Hoist	1 day?	Fri 03/12/04	Fri 03/12/04	17
22	▦	Move bath	2 days	Thu 02/12/04	Fri 03/12/04	

Figure 320 Details of the building project are recorded in the software

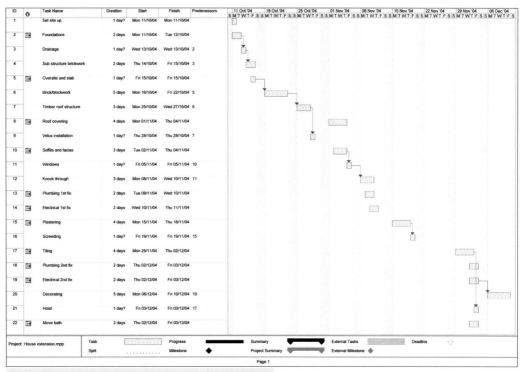

Figure 321 A Gantt chart is automatically produced

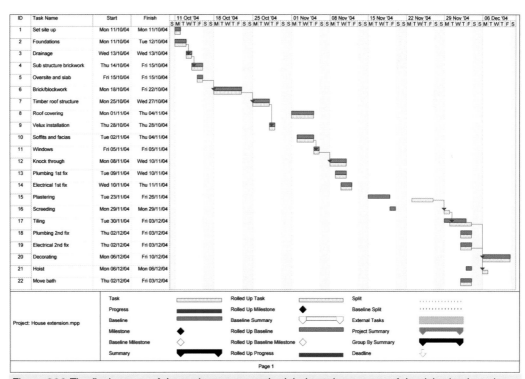

Figure 322 The final stages of the project were rescheduled to take account of the delay in plastering. The grey rectangles show the original baseline and the blue rectangles show the new schedule.

Go out and try!

1 Referring to the mind map you created earlier, use project planning software to create a list of the tasks that need to be done.

2 Go through each task and give it a duration, and set up any dependencies between tasks (for example, you can't send out the invitations until the venue is confirmed).

3 A Gantt chart should be automatically produced. See what happens to the Gantt chart if you amend the timing of some of the tasks.

Open your 'Project planning software' file. Create a new bold heading called '**Project planning software**' and describe the skills you have demonstrated in this activity.

Collaborative software

The summative project for Unit 4 will be a team effort, which you will develop with a group of other students in your school or college. For the duration of the project, you will work together to define the objectives, review progress and make decisions that will determine the final outcome. You will be working as a member of a team in a similar way to thousands of people in industry and commerce who carry out their day-to-day work as members of project teams.

Project teams use special software, known as *collaborative software* or *groupware*, to manage their work. Collaborative software enables groups of people working together to communicate effectively, to share documents, and to monitor and update the progress of a project. If your school or college hosts a virtual learning environment (VLE), such as Moodle, you may already be familiar with collaborative software.

TiP

*There are many software packages available to support collaborative working. These include **DiDAFolio, Digital Brain, Macromedia Breeze, Microsoft MSN** and **Moodle**.*

LEARNING OUTCOMES

You need to learn about

✓ using software to work as a team.

However, you do not have to use sophisticated software to work together successfully in a team. Providing you have access to a network, intranet or the Internet, there are many features built into standard software applications that can help you.

- Microsoft Outlook offers options to send email attachments as 'shared documents' and to share calendars.
- You can save a document as 'read-only' so that people can view the document but cannot make changes.
- Password protection ensures that documents remain confidential, since users without the password will be unable to open the file.
- You can use templates to ensure that all team members adopt a consistent approach when creating documents and presentations.
- You can use the reviewing tools to show proposed changes to a document.
- Document reviewers can add comments, which the rest of the team can view.

○ A document library enables team members to share a collection of files, which can be viewed through a web browser or network. Users are notified by email whenever a team member adds or changes a file, and it is easy to see whether documents are draft or final versions.

Communicating with members of a team

The telephone and email are probably the most widely used methods of communication today. However, telephone calls are usually just between two people, which means that most members of the group cannot take part in the conversation. An email, on the other hand, can be sent to any number of people so that all group members receive the same information. Features such as the ability to create mailing groups, forward messages and attach files make email an ideal method of communication for members of a team. Refer again to the Email skills chapter (page 436) to remind yourself just what email does offer.

Sharing files with other members of a team

Whilst email is usually a successful way of sharing files, some email systems will not accept attachments over a certain size, or may not accept attachments at all. Occasionally files can accidentally be forwarded to the wrong people; this could pose a security problem.

Collaborative software enables users to share files of any size and type. The files can be viewed or edited by multiple users anywhere in the world at the same time. One advantage of this is that there will only be one version of the file in use, so all members of the team have access to up-to-date and reliable information. You can set up a document library that will enable team members to share files.

If project management files, such as a Gantt chart, are available for all team members to view, this will help to ensure that everybody is working to an up-to-date project timescale.

Creating and using shared folders

How much time do you spend looking for data files because you haven't organised your folders clearly? Imagine the possible delays to a group project if the team couldn't find their files quickly! To make sure that project files and documents can be accessed quickly and stored consistently by all team members, it is essential that a suitable folder hierarchy is created from the outset of any project and that team members adopt a consistent approach when naming documents.

It can be useful to share folders with other people on the same computer (who log in with different accounts) or with other people on the same network. To do this, right-click the folder you wish to share, and select **Properties** from the menu that appears. You can use the *Sharing* tab (see Figure 323) to make the folder available to other people.

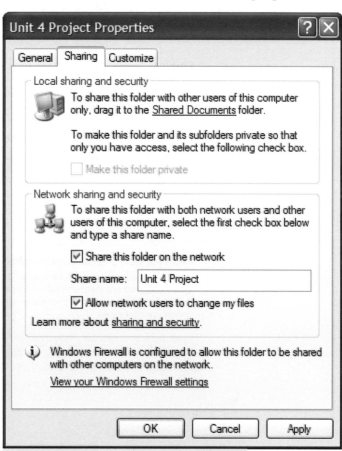

Figure 323 Sharing a folder across the network

Working collaboratively on a document

Whilst working on your project, it is highly likely that several team members will need to work on the same document. For example, it may be that individual team members each initially create part of a document, and the final work is assembled from the separate parts. Or perhaps individual team members are each researching different costs which must be incorporated in a large overall spreadsheet. By sharing documents, all team members can look at and work on the most up-to-date version of each.

You may choose to nominate just one member of your project team to make the final edits to a document. Before the document is finalised, it is possible for all team members to view the proposed changes and make their comments. The particular features of standard application software that enable you to do this are accessed through **Tools, Track Changes** and **Insert, Comment**.

Original

The first project meeting will be held on Wednesday 1 February 2006. I suggest we meet at 11.30 in Room E21. It will give provide an opportunity to discuss general project ideas.

Changed version with Track Changes

The first project meeting will be held on Thursday 2 February 2006. I suggest we meet at 09.00 in Room E21 with a second meeting at 14.00 which will provide an opportunity to discuss general project ideas.

Deleted: Wednesday	
Deleted: 1	
Deleted: 11.30	
Deleted: . It	
Deleted: give	

Comment [PDS1]: Megan – I can't make 14.00. Peter.

Final version with changes accepted

The first project meeting will be held on Thursday 2 February 2006. I suggest we meet at 09.00 in Room E21 with a second meeting at 14.00 which will provide an opportunity to discuss general project ideas.

Figure 324 You can see how changes to the original text have been tracked. The deleted text is shown in the margin and added words appear in red. A comment has been added by one of the team.

Setting up a collaborative working environment

If you have a group of people working on the same project, one of the most important requirements is that all team members are using the same version of the software. In some software applications, changes made in the most recent version are not effective in older versions.

It may also be necessary to set up permission levels that specify whether team members are allowed to edit documents or merely to read them. It may be necessary to ensure that some documents can be viewed by only certain team members. Confidential documents may require password protection.

Maintaining a team diary

The ability to set up group meetings knowing that everybody in the team is available can save a lot of time and frustration. A common diary framework, often found in collaborative software, can detect when meeting times will work for everyone and send automatic reminders beforehand to ensure that nobody forgets to attend. With large and scattered project teams, a diary can also help you to track someone down: all their day-to-day appointments will be recorded.

Microsoft Outlook has a calendar feature that can be shared with team members over a network, intranet or even the Internet.

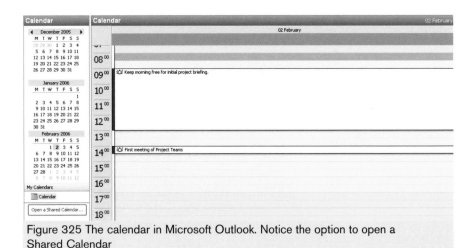

Figure 325 The calendar in Microsoft Outlook. Notice the option to open a Shared Calendar

All projects have a number of common characteristics:

- clear objectives
- a definitive outcome
- a fixed period of running time
- the possibility of being broken down into a sequence of smaller tasks.

LEARNING OUTCOMES

You need to learn about

✓ the questions you should ask yourself about your project brief

✓ how the success of your project will be judged

✓ how to create a project plan.

Most things you do, no matter how simple or complex, require careful planning and preparation in order to be successful.

Before you start it is essential to

- read the whole project brief carefully
- decide/understand what you have to do
- create appropriate directory/folder structures to organise your e-portfolio.

Even something as straightforward as baking a birthday cake needs planning to ensure you have the exact ingredients, the right size of baking tin and sufficient time for it to bake in the oven.

An example

Organising a holiday requires careful planning. Frankie and Sam would like to go on holiday together. Before they visit Travelbug to make their booking they must have a clear idea of where they would like to go, what they would like to do, and how much time they can afford to spend away from home.

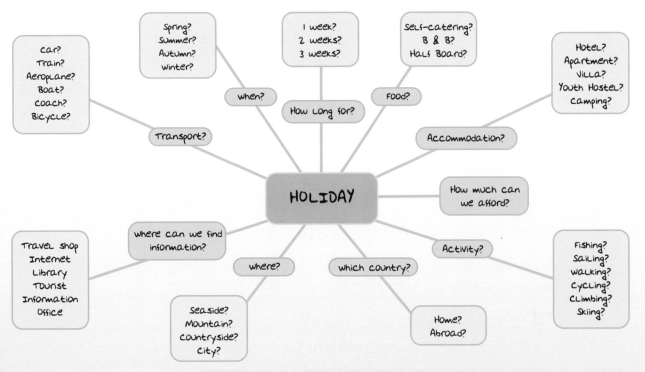

Figure 326 Frankie and Sam's spider diagram records all their suggestions and ideas

They both have so many suggestions and ideas that they decide to write them all down to be sure everything will be taken into consideration before reaching a final decision (Figure 326).

After much discussion they agree on a two-week camping and sports activity holiday in the French Alps. Now that they have a clear goal, they can really begin the preparations for their holiday. These preparations will include

- researching the holiday market and booking the holiday
- obtaining passports
- arranging travel insurance and medical insurance
- preparing for the sports activities – perhaps by getting fit and buying suitable clothing and footwear
- buying foreign currency
- arranging for their pets to be cared for
- arranging transport to the station or airport.

By the time they leave, Frankie and Sam will have put considerable effort into the planning and preparation of their holiday, so it should be a great success.

The same is true for the projects you will be completing for your Award, Certificate or Diploma in Digital Applications: if the projects are not planned carefully they are unlikely to be successful!

Your project brief

A well-written brief will enable you to identify the key features of the project. Spend time reading the project brief to familiarise yourself with its contents. After studying it, you should be able to provide answers to the following questions, which will eventually form the basis of your overall plan.

What have I been asked to do?

The answer to this question will reveal the overall purpose of the project. This may be to

- carry out research on a particular topic and present your findings
- create multimedia products
- produce images and artwork
- explore and plan for a business activity.

What do I have to produce?

When you are clear about the overall aim of the project, you should study the project brief more closely and make a list of all the separate items you must produce. These may be a combination of text, graphics, images or sound. For example, you may have to produce a letter, a web site, a presentation, a graphic image, a leaflet and a report. The items in your list will become the *objectives* of the project.

Why am I doing it?

Once you have established what you have been asked to do and what you are going to produce, you should think about *why* you are doing the work. This will ensure that your 'products' are entirely suitable for their purpose.

There will usually be a specific reason for producing the product:

- writing a report to convince people that something should change or remain the same

- producing a series of publications to educate people about a topical issue
- producing a multimedia product to convey a message to the public
- producing a graphic image to promote a product or event.

If you are unclear in your own mind as to the reason you are doing the work, it is highly likely that your audience will also have difficulties in understanding your message. To be successful you must make sure that your products convey the message in the most appropriate way.

Who are the target audience?

Another important point to consider is what type of people your product is directed at. In other words, who are the *target audience*? You would be expected to choose different methods for conveying the same information to children compared with adults.

For example, a poster aimed at children should be quite simple and straightforward, whereas you might use a more subtle approach for adults. If you were producing a written report for technical experts it would be quite acceptable to use technical language. However, you would have to reduce the level of technical jargon if the same report were to be presented to members of the general public.

It is important that you choose an appropriate style for your audience whilst ensuring that your finished product is also fit for its intended purpose.

When do I have to have it finished?

Think about your timescale and how you will fit everything in. You should expect to spend a total of about 30 hours on each project. Take into account the time you will spend on planning and preparation in addition to actually producing your products.

Include time to review your work, and allow other people time to test your products. You will almost certainly need to modify or amend your work, and this must *all* be completed within the time allocated for the project.

Allow time to locate and order multimedia components, such as video and audio recordings from film libraries or video collections, if you need to include these in your project.

TiP

Make sure you allocate some time to dealing with the unexpected. It is very unusual for everything to go smoothly, so there will almost certainly be unforeseen problems and delays along the way.

TiP

If you wish to use a photograph that somebody else has taken, you must remember the law relating to copyright and obtain written permission to use the image. This will also take time.

It is important that you do not take on something too ambitious that you will not be able to finish properly because you run out of time!

What resources can I use?

Each of the summative project briefs will include links to relevant websites or titles of textbooks that may help you. You will clearly have to use other resources too.

Some resources – such as school or college library books, the Internet, computers and printers – are probably readily available to you, but others may not be. For example, you may need to use specialist software or equipment that is available only at school or college, and you might need to share it with 20 or 30 other students. Alternatively, you might need to obtain books or other media from an outside source such as a library. This can take time to arrange.

If you know that something is going to be difficult to get hold of or restricted in use, you must keep this uppermost in your mind when planning your project. Furthermore, you must remember to record details of the sources of all the materials you use and to include these as evidence in your e-portfolio.

What else do I need to consider?

If you are working on artwork and images, you will also need to consider how the image is to be published. Consider, for example, whether it is to be published on screen or printed on paper. You can clearly see how an image will be viewed as part of a screen-based publication, but it is more difficult to visualise an image incorporated in a paper-based document. Carefully check the size of the image, the position on the page, and so on.

How will the success of your project be judged?

Your work will be presented in an e-portfolio that will be reviewed by your assessor and the moderator from the examining body, Edexcel. You will not be there to show them where to find the evidence of your work, so *your e-portfolio must be well structured and easy to use*. Follow the advice on creating e-portfolios given in the summative project briefs and in Skills Section 5 (page 510).

You will be assessed against a number of activities, including

- planning and managing your project
- reviewing your project
- presenting evidence in an e-portfolio.

The other activities differ for each project, and more information is given in the appropriate chapters. Each activity carries a range of marks, and the marks are awarded according to the complexity of each activity.

The questions the assessor or moderator will have in mind when assessing your work are

- Is the product fit for the purpose?
- Is the product fit for the intended audience?

The safest way to make sure the assessor or moderator can answer 'Yes' to these questions is to make certain your work is reviewed throughout production and that you take notice of any points your reviewers make.

Who will review my work, and when?

TiP

Remember that when you start to plan your project in detail you must ensure you allow time for other people to look at your work during production as well as at the end.

It is very easy to get sidetracked and to lose sight of the original objective when you are working under pressure. A fresh pair of eyes can sometimes help to show where you have gone adrift. So for this reason you must make sure that you ask someone to look at your work at regular intervals to ensure it is fit for both the purpose and the intended audience.

You could ask your teacher, or maybe your friends or a member of your family, to help you. You could find someone who falls into the target audience category and ask him or her for an opinion.

You should show your product to a variety of different people and welcome their opinions. Constructive feedback is very valuable and is not a criticism of your work but is offered to help you improve your work and thereby achieve better marks. Listen to what other people say and consider their ideas carefully. You may not always agree, but a second opinion is always worth thinking about.

Getting started

When you have read through the summative project brief, ask your teacher or tutor to explain anything you do not understand. In this way you will avoid wasting valuable time by starting work on something that is not required!

You might find it helpful to produce a table, similar to the one in Figure 327, where you can make notes as you work through the project brief. It will help to ensure that nothing important is overlooked. It will also form the basis for the detailed project planning that must be done before you start work.

What have I been asked to do? This is the overall aim.		
What do I have to produce? These are the objectives.	Why am I doing it? This will help you focus on the purpose.	Who are the target audience?
1	1	1
2	2	2
3	3	3
4	4	4
5	5	5
6	6	6
7	7	7
8	8	8
9	9	9
10	10	10
When do I have to have the project finished?		
What resources can I use?		
Who will review my work?		

Figure 327 A chart to help you organise your thoughts

Project ideas

You are now almost ready to embark on your project, but you are still not ready to switch the computer on! There are a few more issues to be considered.

First you need to come up with some ideas. One of the most successful ways of doing this is to hold a brainstorming session with a group of friends – just like Frankie and Sam when they were planning their holiday! Record everything you can think of so that nothing is forgotten or overlooked.

Some people find a simple hand-written list is a good method of keeping track of ideas. One of the most popular methods is to produce a *mind map*. Mind maps help you organise your thoughts on one page so that you can see the relationship between one idea and another, and your ideas can flow from one topic to the next. Simple images can help you focus your ideas in a fun way.

Record the main topic at the centre of the page. From there, branch out and add the major themes around the main topic. Add associated ideas with further branches. Once your mind map is finished you can weigh up the pros and cons of the various ideas before coming to a decision.

This mind map (Figure 328) was used to help plan an 18th birthday party.

Be SMART (see page 492) and don't get carried away by grand ideas that go off at a tangent. Always keep the target audience and project objective in mind. Some good advice is to keep things relatively simple – think 'quality' rather than 'quantity'!

Figure 328 Mind map for planning an 18th birthday party

Your project plan

After preparing a list of objectives from the summative project brief, your next job must be to rearrange the list into a logical sequence, remembering that some tasks may have to be finished before others can be started.

List the key milestones in each project, and, where possible, try to finish one thing before getting too involved in the next. Number the tasks in the order you will complete them.

Now look at each task in turn and break it down into a sequence of smaller tasks so that you know exactly what has to be done. Give each of the smaller tasks a number. Remember to include time to ask your reviewers to give you feedback on your work.

Here are some examples. If the first task of a project is to produce a poster, you might come up with a list like this:

1 Produce a poster
    1.1 Take digital photos
    1.2 Sketch out my design and show it to my teacher
    1.3 Transfer images from digital camera to computer
    1.4 Produce poster on the computer
    1.5 Proofread and print in colour
    1.6 Ask family to review poster
    1.7 Modify design if necessary

In your multimedia showcase you are going to produce some video footage with an accompanying commentary. Task 1 was designed to film the footage and Task 2 might look something like this:

2 Add commentary and music soundtrack to video footage.
    2.1 Write script to accompany video footage and show it to my teacher/tutor
    2.2 Rehearse voiceover with narrator
    2.3 Record voiceover track
    2.4 Select accompanying music
    2.5 Add voiceover and music tracks to video footage
    2.6 Ask fellow students to review the completed footage and make further edits as necessary

If the first task is to prepare a web page to advertise your school/college, you might come up with a list like this:

1 Prepare a web page to advertise school/college
    1.1 Plan the layout of your web page on paper
    1.2 Write supporting text and decide on font style and colour scheme
    1.3 Locate map of school/college
    1.4 Take the photos and/or video clips and edit as necessary
    1.5 Produce the web page
    1.6 Make any changes if necessary

Assessment Hint

Your project plans must be included in your e-portfolio as supporting evidence for each project. For this reason it is important that you record your progress as you go along.

Decide how much time to allocate to each part of the project and write down when you plan to start and finish each task. Remember that you should also include time to deal with anything that might go wrong.

You should repeat this process for each of the objectives you have identified. The flow chart in Figure 329 can be used to remind yourself of the steps to take when planning each project.

When you have planned your project in detail you must record the information in your project planning software (or you might find it helpful to record this information in table format similar to Figure 330 if you are not using project planning software).

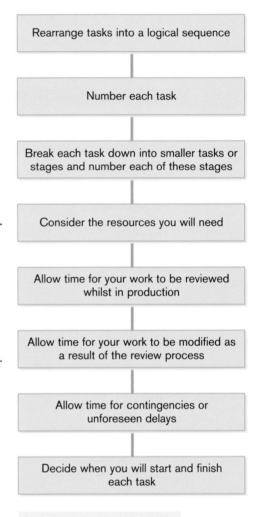

Figure 329 Planning a project

Make sure you include details of the tasks and sub-tasks. These should be in the order in which you will carry them out, and should show how much time you will spend on each and when you will ask your reviewers for feedback. You should also include

- task descriptions
- start dates
- finish dates
- times allowed
- notes to record progress and changes made to the plan.

Ask your teacher or tutor to approve your plan before you start any work on the project. As you complete each task, update your project plan. Keep a record of any changes you had to make to the plan, and say why.

Summative Project – Unit 2		Project Start Date: 9 November			Project End Date: 11 December	
What will I produce?	**How will I go about it?**	**How long will it take to complete?**	**When will I start?**	**When will I finish?**	**Done** ✓	**Record your progress and note any changes you make to the plan and why.**
Task 1 **Movie** Production of video footage to be included in multimedia showcase designed to highlight opportunities available to prospective students.	**Task 1.1** Decide which aspects to include in video.	½ hour	9 November	9 November	✓	
	Task 1.2 Arrange dates/times to take video footage.	½ hour	10 November	10 November	✓	
	Task 1.3 Produce storyboard.	3 hours	10 November	11 November	✓	
	Task 1.4 Video activities.	5 hours	12 November	~~19 November~~ 25	✓	I had flu and was ill for 5 days which delayed filming and the appointments had to be rearranged for following week.
	Task 1.5 Review/edit footage.	3 hours	~~19 November~~ 25	~~21 November~~ 27 November	✓	This delayed the edit/review process but I was able to start writing the script before I had finished editing in order to make up for lost time.
	Task 1.6 Ask other students to review footage and edit if necessary.	½ hour	~~23 November~~ 30	~~23 November~~ 30	✓	
Task 2 **Commentary** Recording of voiceover to accompany video footage and addition of music to video.	**Task 2.1** Write script.	1½ hours	~~24 November~~ 27	~~26 November~~ 28	✓	
	Task 2.2 Rehearse voiceover.	1 hour	~~26 November~~ 1 December	~~27 November~~ 1 December	✓	I had allowed 2 days to rehearse the voiceover but had to reduce this to 1 day as I was worried that I would not finish in time.
	Task 2.3 Record voiceover.	1 hour	~~30 November~~ 2 December	~~30 November~~ 2 December	✓	
	Task 2.4 Select music.	½ hour	28 November	28 November	✓	I selected the music before the video presentation was finished to save time.
	Task 2.5 Add music/voiceover to video.	1 hour	~~30 November~~ 3 December	~~2 December~~ 5	✓	
	Task 2.6 Final review/edits.	½ hour	~~3 December~~ 8	~~3 December~~ 8	✓	In spite of being away for a week I still managed to finish on time because I had allowed time for delays in my planning.

Figure 330 If you are not using project planning software you can produce your own chart to monitor progress

Use the plan to help you meet your deadlines and finish your project on time. Every time you need to modify your plan you must save it with a new filename so that you can provide evidence of the development of your project from the beginning to the end. Don't be tempted to produce the plan after you have finished your project! Keep in mind that your teachers and the moderators who will look at the plan in your e-portfolio are very experienced and can usually discover the shortcomings!

Skills check ▶▶

See also the chapter on Project Planning Software (page 480).

If you are using project planning software you will be able to produce a *Gantt chart* automatically. This style of chart helps you to see at a glance how you have spread the workload and how you can modify the plan if you run into difficulties. It is a good way of reviewing the progress of your project so you can rearrange the rest of your work if necessary.

If you are not using project planning software you can produce your own Gantt chart. Use one colour to show the time you plan to spend on each task. If necessary, you can amend it to take account of any modifications to your timescale, showing them in a different colour.

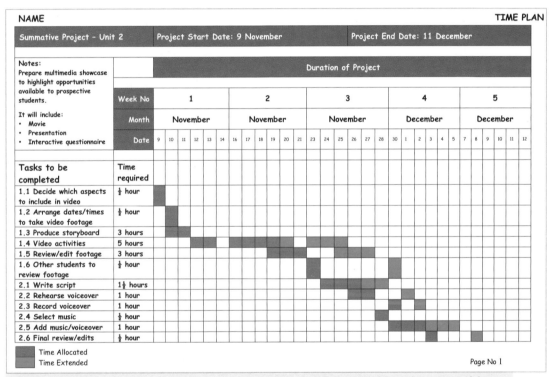

Figure 331 A Gantt chart produced using a table, but you could also consider using a spreadsheet

If you have access to Microsoft Works on your home computer, you may perhaps consider using the Project Planner to list each task of the project (Figure 332). You can also record the due date and make notes to remind you of what you have to do, or to record any reasons for modifying your project plan.

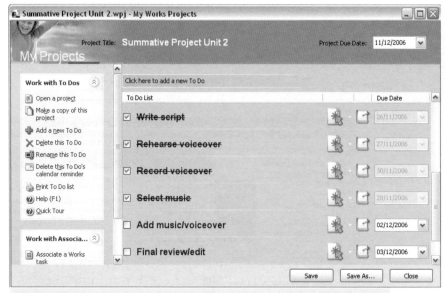

Figure 332 Microsoft Works includes this simple project planning software

Skills check ▶▶

The designers of large, commercial projects often use special project management software to help them plan and monitor the progress of their work. If you study for Unit 4 you will learn to use specialist project planning software to help you develop your plan and produce a Gantt chart. You will be able to check that the progress of the work follows the plan and, if necessary, update the plan to take account of any unforeseen delays or problems. In this way the plan will become a reliable, working document that you can refer to at any time to see what still has to be done. If you work alongside the plan and keep it up to date, it will help ensure your project is completed within the given timescale.

Hints and tips

Before embarking on your project work, you will have studied the skills chapters on word processing, spreadsheets, databases and so on. It is important that you make full use of these skills in order to create documents and on-screen publications that convey the message in the most effective way possible.

Here are some other hints to help you along the way:

- Remember to plan your e-portfolio before you start. Decide on the filenames you will use and make sure you know the appropriate format for publication in your e-portfolio. The summative project brief will specify the acceptable formats for each project. Don't waste time as you go along by converting every file into the final published format. It is a good idea to convert only the files that you will be presenting in your e-portfolio. You are less likely to get in a muddle if you do not have too many different versions of each file!

- Don't waste time in class working on things that can be done away from the classroom. Use the time you have with your teacher or tutor to get any help you need.

- Use folders and sub-folders to organise all your project work. Don't forget that you will be required to include evidence of your product from design through to implementation.

- Save updates of your work regularly with different filenames. In this way, in the unlikely event you find yourself with a corrupt file, you can revert to the previous version and you will not have too much work to repeat. This will also help you demonstrate progress in your e-portfolio.

- A USB memory stick is a good way of transferring your work between school or college and home. You will soon find the data files are too large to fit on to a floppy disk. Remember to scan your files for viruses!

- Make regular backup copies of all your data files on CD as a safety precaution. Keep the backup copies in a safe place. It is sensible to save your project work on the school or college computer system as well as at home.

When you are happy that you can put a tick against each of the following points, then you have probably done as much as you can to ensure success:

- Have you followed your plan and used it to monitor your progress?
- Have you recorded and justified any amendments you made to the plan?
- Can the history of the project be clearly seen from your plan?
- Have you kept a record of *all* the resources you used?

- Have you produced everything that you were asked to produce?
- Does your document or presentation have an appropriate layout and structure?
- Is the presentation style (font style, heading style, background colour, slide layout, and so on) consistent throughout?
- Have you used page breaks sensibly?
- Have you made effective use of space?
- Have you chosen an appropriate font size?
- Is it written in an appropriate language style to suit the target audience?
- Have you spellchecked *and* proofread your work?
- Have you used WordArt, clip art and colour in moderation?
- Are the content and images relevant and suitable for the intended audience?
- Are your images clear and a sensible size?
- Are download times acceptable for images in your web pages?
- Does your document or presentation look professional?
- Have you reviewed your work and asked somebody else to test your product?
- Have you listened to their comments and modified your product if necessary? Remember to include evidence of your modified work in your e-portfolio.
- Is the product fit for the intended purpose?
- Do all navigation routes work?
- Have you saved your work in the specified file formats?
- Does the overall size of your e-portfolio comply with the technical specification?

Keep these guidelines in mind and you should be able to produce a first-class product that will meet all the original objectives.

Good luck with all your projects!

Section 4 Review and evaluation

It is important that you undertake a thorough review of your project once it is completed. You should consider

- outcomes (the publications you have produced)
- process (how you worked)
- performance (the skills you have demonstrated).

Introduction

Think back to Frankie and Sam and their two-week camping and sports activity holiday in the French Alps (page 490). Did you imagine that when they returned from their holiday they would forget all about it? Of course not! When they came home they would have discussed every aspect of the holiday. It is quite natural to look back on the experience, reflect on the good parts and try to work out why other aspects did not go quite so well. If they decide to repeat the holiday again some time in the future they won't want to repeat the mistakes too – they will want to have an even better time.

This is exactly the same process that you will carry out when you have completed each project. The process of reviewing your work is equally as important as actually carrying out the work in the first place. A thorough and effective evaluation will consider the *outcomes* (what you produced), the *processes* (how you produced it) and *performance* (your own contribution). You will make your own judgements and will also seek the opinions and views of a variety of other people in order to provide a comprehensive evaluation with suggestions for improvement.

You will have asked several people to review your project whilst you were working on it and you should have acted on their advice. You must also ensure that your finished product is reviewed by yourself and others.

Review evidence and presentation

The evidence you collect to show that you and other people have reviewed your project should be included in your e-portfolio. It may be presented in a variety of different ways.

For example, you may have provided a questionnaire for people to complete, so you could present the results graphically, drawing your conclusions from their responses. You may have received written evaluations, which could be scanned and presented as on-screen documents. Perhaps you have spoken to several people and can include a recording of your interviews. You may decide to prepare your own written evaluation, summarising the feedback you have received from other people together with your own thoughts. You might also consider producing your evaluation as a multimedia presentation or a video or audio diary. Your evidence is likely to be a combination of two or more of these suggestions.

Most things we do show that we all have strengths and weaknesses. Sometimes things turn out well and sometimes they are not so good. For example, one day we bake a cake that turns out to be rather flat, slightly burnt and generally disappointing. We show the cake to someone who has more experience, and he or she suggests that we might have used the wrong type of flour or had the oven temperature too high. We try again and next time the cake is much better.

Perhaps it will be obvious to you that some things did not go as well as you had planned and you recognise that there are weaknesses. In this case you will usually be very receptive to suggestions for improving it. However, it is more difficult to accept criticism when you think everything is all right, but do listen to what your reviewers have to say and do not be afraid to acknowledge weaknesses and to act on their suggestions for improvement.

Three important words to keep in mind when you are evaluating your work are *explain*, *justify* and *improve*. Imagine you are looking at a poster you have produced to make people aware of a

forthcoming meeting. On reflection, you feel the font size you used was too small and not easy to read. In your evaluation don't just say 'The font size was too small' – instead *explain*, *justify* and *improve*! You might say 'The font size was too small for the poster to be read from a distance, and as a result it was not an effective publication. I should have used a font size of at least 72 point so that people passing by were aware of the date, time and place of the meeting. In addition I could have made better use of white space to make the important points stand out.'

When you were first given the summative project brief, you studied it and found answers to a series of questions:

- **What** have I been asked to do?
- **What** do I have to produce?
- **Why** am I doing it?
- **Who** are the target audience?
- **When** do I have to have it finished?
- **What** resources can I use?
- **Who** will review my work, and when?

In your evaluation you should consider whether you achieved everything you set out to do. Do not just answer 'Yes' or 'No' in each case – *explain* and *justify* your answers. What went wrong and why did it go wrong? On the other hand, what did you consider to be particularly successful and why was it a success? Were you able to make use of knowledge and skills that you already had? Alternatively, what new skills did you have to learn?

Consider the resources you used:

- Were some especially helpful and others not so useful?
- Did you have any difficulty in finding useful material?
- Were you able to use specific hardware and software successfully?
- Did you choose the most appropriate hardware and software?

Remember to *explain* and *justify* any statements you make.

- EXPLAIN who 'tested' your product during its production stages, why you asked that particular person and what their comments were. As a result of this feedback, what did you do to IMPROVE your product. Remember your 'product' might be a document, an image, a multimedia presentation or an on-screen publication. JUSTIFY your reasons for modifying your product or not modifying it.

- EXPLAIN why you asked for feedback from the people who looked at your finished project. Provide evidence that they have looked at your project, that you have considered their feedback and say whether or not you agreed with their comments. JUSTIFY your reasons for reaching your conclusions.

- How would you make sure things didn't go wrong again? What could you do better next time? Think about what you could do to IMPROVE things!

Finally, consider what you have learnt from the whole experience? Was your time plan realistic? Which areas of the project took longer than anticipated and why? Were there aspects of your own skill-base that were weak? Why? How would you rectify the weakness?

A successful evaluation will consider the project from every aspect. In particular, your assessors will be looking to see that you have reviewed the outcomes, the processes and your own performance.

Outcomes

- ✓ To what extent have the project's objectives been met?
- ✓ How effective are the final products?
- ✓ Are they fit for purpose?
- ✓ How could they be improved?
- ✓ Does the mix of components enhance the message you are trying to convey?
- ✓ Is the information organised in an appropriate manner?
- ✓ How well do your multimedia products function?
- ✓ Do you think their structure and mix of components work?
- ✓ How easy are they to use?
- ✓ Are the file formats and image resolutions suitable?
- ✓ Does your artwork convey the intended message?

Process

- ✓ How well did you plan your work?
- ✓ Did you manage your time well?
- ✓ Did you meet the deadline?
- ✓ What, if anything, went wrong?

✓ Did you choose the right or best people to review your project?

✓ Would you arrange the project differently next time?

Performance

✓ What have you learned from working on this project?

✓ Did you have appropriate ICT skills?

✓ What additional training do you feel you need?

✓ How well did you communicate your ideas to others?

✓ How could you further improve your work?

✓ What have you learned about yourself whilst working on this project?

✓ Were you able to draw on knowledge or skills you have acquired in other subjects?

✓ Are you proud of your achievements?

Section 5 · Creating an e-portfolio

You will create an e-portfolio to present evidence of your achievements. The assessor and the moderator will use your e-portfolio to judge your work, so you must make sure that it is self-explanatory and easy to use.

LEARNING OUTCOMES

You need to learn about

✓ what to include in your e-portfolio

✓ how to structure your e-portfolio

✓ how to test your e-portfolio.

What is an e-portfolio?

For most students, the idea of presenting coursework in electronic form rather than on paper is something quite new and challenging.

An e-portfolio is a multimedia stage designed to present your work. In this instance, the assessor and moderator must be able to find evidence of your achievements easily.

This is an innovative and exciting way of showing what you are able to do. Your work can come alive with graphics, animations and sound. It is environmentally friendly, saving pages and pages of paper, as well as being a very convenient way of taking your work from place to place. Ultimately your e-portfolio will contain additional information about you, your education and career and, in the longer term, is likely to be looked at by a wide range of people.

Your teacher or tutor will provide you with more detailed information on the system you will be using. However, ideally, you should be able to access your work from any PC wherever you choose: at school or college or at home.

> ### ⭐ Assessment Hint
>
> *All the work you produce as evidence towards your Award, Certificate or Diploma in Digital Applications will be presented for assessment and moderation in an e-portfolio. You will not be required to submit any documentation on paper.*

You have already looked at a wide variety of websites and are familiar with the features that make them pleasing to look at, easy to use and effective. You have evaluated their impact and appropriateness for the intended audience and looked at the combination of text and graphics, download times, and so on. Your aim is to replicate the successful features so that the assessor and moderator can easily find their way around your work. When you study each of the summative project briefs, notice how buttons and links take you from one section of the project to another, and how they also direct you to pages of hints and tips and back again to the main sections. Each one has been designed to make it easy for you to find your way around. Similarly, your e-portfolio must clearly guide users through your work.

Organisation of your e-portfolio

TiP

You will find it much easier if you plan the development of an e-portfolio alongside the planning of each project. In this way it is unlikely that important elements will be overlooked.

You must keep in mind that the people who will look at your e-portfolio will not have you at their side to help them find the evidence they will be looking for. The user interface is therefore an important element of any e-portfolio: it is essential that your e-portfolio be well organised, and structured so that anyone can find their way around it efficiently and without difficulty.

The skills you developed in Presentation Software and Website Authoring Software are equally applicable to your e-portfolio. Developing a storyboard, structure and flow charts will help ensure that suitable links are in place to make the e-portfolio easy to navigate and user-friendly.

The overall appearance of the e-portfolio is equally as important as the content. You must make sure that it is pleasing for users to look at, as well as being easy to use. Include a variety of interactive components such as buttons, hotspots, and links.

Content of your e-portfolio

The content will reflect the tasks set in the summative project briefs, so each e-portfolio will therefore be different from another. The project brief

will set out in detail what should be included, but the basic structure of each e-portfolio will be similar and will include the following

- home page
- contents page or menu
- the final work you have produced, which may include letters or reports, presentations, web pages, images, etc.
- evidence and explanations of the work you carried out, such as
  - project planning and monitoring
  - the development stages of your work – images, presentations, brochures, web pages, and so on – with comments justifying any modifications made
  - references to sources of documents or graphical components
  - evidence of data collection
  - supporting evidence of database structures or spreadsheets
  - evidence of market research or surveys
  - storyboards, structure charts and flow charts
  - review and evaluation of the project process and outcomes
  - feedback from your reviewers and suggestions for improvement
  - bibliography
  - copyright information, including acknowledgements and permissions where applicable.

Saving your work

It is quite likely that people viewing your e-portfolio may not have access to the same software that you used to produce your documents, images, presentations and so on. For this reason it is essential that you save the work in your e-portfolio in suitable formats as outlined in the summative project brief. For example, paper-based documents are most likely to be in PDF format, whereas screen presentations such as web pages will be HTML files. Images will normally be saved as JPEGs, and multimedia presentations converted to Flash SWF format.

Accessibility and testing

When your work is finished and your e-portfolio is complete you must make sure it works properly. Do not rely solely on checking it for yourself – you know the way around your work and will not be able to provide totally unbiased feedback. Let somebody else who is not familiar with the contents look at it.

As a result of this feedback, it might be necessary to modify your e-portfolio. The important thing to remember is that it must be user-friendly so that the assessor and moderator can use it without help.

In particular you should check that

- the content is complete and includes everything detailed in the summative project brief
- the e-portfolio is clearly presented, easy to use, attractive and effective
- every link goes where it should go with no dead-ends
- the e-portfolio can be displayed correctly in different browsers (e.g. Internet Explorer and Netscape)
- download speeds are acceptable
- other people can use the e-portfolio without help.

Authentication

Finally your teacher or tutor must provide authentication to confirm that the work is your own.

Go out and try!

This is an opportunity for you to produce a small e-portfolio to display evidence of the various skills you have learnt. It will also enable you to learn how to save files in suitable file formats and to check download speeds for images.

When you worked through the other skills sections you saved separate files describing the skills you had been using. You included headings for each of the activities and wrote a short description of the skills you had learnt. Can you use the headings to provide a link to the examples described?

Task

1   Design an e-portfolio that contains a home page which will direct users to three of the skills pages, and from there to two of the files that illustrate the skills described. Make sure that some of the pages include graphic images so that you can test the download speeds of the images.

For example, the flow chart in Figure 333 would result in a home page with three distinct buttons to link to the word-processing, artwork and imaging, and internet and intranet skills files. From there, links would be set up to show the worked examples of the first two activities in each.

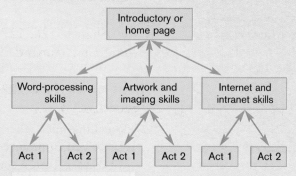

Figure 333 Flow chart

Before you create the e-portfolio, think about the file formats you should use to ensure your work can be viewed on any computer, such as using .pdf files for text pages. Ask your teacher to check that you have not forgotten anything important.

2   Ask your friends to test this e-portfolio. Consider any suggestions they make for improvement and modify your structure if necessary.

3   In turn, look at what your friends have produced and compare ideas. Think about why some e-portfolios might appear more user-friendly than others. Do you think your e-portfolio is the best possible showcase in which to display your achievements? How might you improve on your ideas when you produce the e-portfolio for your first assessment? Write a list of the improvements you might make and say why you think they are necessary – if you don't do this now you will almost certainly forget the improvements by the time you do your assessment! Save the list so that you can refer to it later.

Index

Let the web do the work!

YOUR REF. NO.
F 999 ICT 08

Why not visit our website and see what it can do for you?

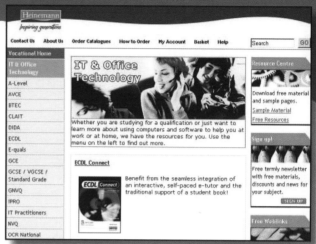

Free online support materials

You can download free support materials for many of our IT products. We even offer a special e-alert service to notify you when new content is posted.

Lists of useful weblinks

Our site includes lists of other websites, which can save you hours of research time.

Online ordering – 24 hours a day

It's quick and simple to order your resources online, and you can do it anytime – day or night!

Find your consultant

The website helps you find your nearest Heinemann consultant, who will be able to discuss your needs and help you find the most cost-effective way to buy.

It's time to save time – visit our website now!

www.heinemann.co.uk/vocational

And what's more, you can register now to receive our FREE information packed eNewsletter. Register today at www.heinemann.co.uk/vocnews.

 01865 888068  01865 314029  orders@heinemann.co.uk 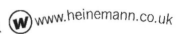 www.heinemann.co.uk

Heinemann

Inspiring generations